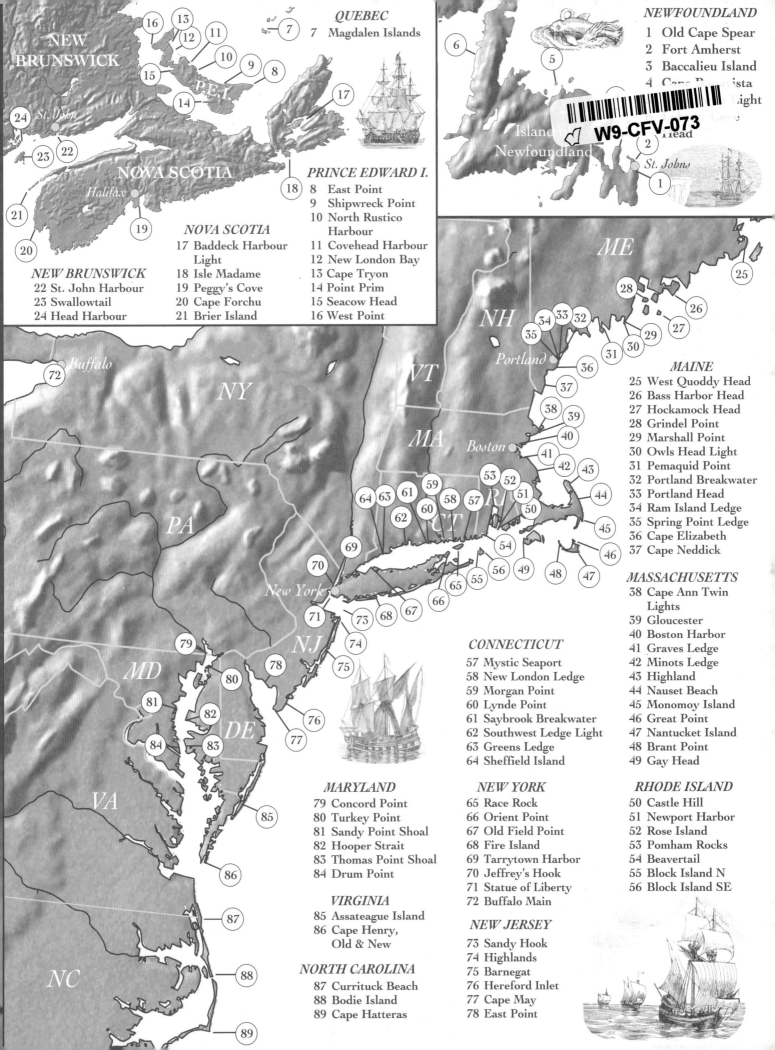

QUEBEC
7 Magdalen Islands

NEWFOUNDLAND
1 Old Cape Spear
2 Fort Amherst
3 Baccalieu Island
4 Cape Bonavista
Light
Cove

W9-CFV-073

NEW BRUNSWICK

NOVA SCOTIA

PRINCE EDWARD I.
8 East Point
9 Shipwreck Point
10 North Rustico
Harbour
11 Covehead Harbour
12 New London Bay
13 Cape Tryon
14 Point Prim
15 Seacow Head
16 West Point

NOVA SCOTIA
17 Baddeck Harbour
Light
18 Isle Madame
19 Peggy's Cove
20 Cape Forchu
21 Brier Island

NEW BRUNSWICK
22 St. John Harbour
23 Swallowtail
24 Head Harbour

MAINE
25 West Quoddy Head
26 Bass Harbor Head
27 Hockamock Head
28 Grindel Point
29 Marshall Point
30 Owls Head Light
31 Pemaquid Point
32 Portland Breakwater
33 Portland Head
34 Ram Island Ledge
35 Spring Point Ledge
36 Cape Elizabeth
37 Cape Neddick

MASSACHUSETTS
38 Cape Ann Twin
Lights
39 Gloucester
40 Boston Harbor
41 Graves Ledge
42 Minots Ledge
43 Highland
44 Nauset Beach
45 Monomoy Island
46 Great Point
47 Nantucket Island
48 Brant Point
49 Gay Head

RHODE ISLAND
50 Castle Hill
51 Newport Harbor
52 Rose Island
53 Pomham Rocks
54 Beavertail
55 Block Island N
56 Block Island SE

CONNECTICUT
57 Mystic Seaport
58 New London Ledge
59 Morgan Point
60 Lynde Point
61 Saybrook Breakwater
62 Southwest Ledge Light
63 Greens Ledge
64 Sheffield Island

NEW YORK
65 Race Rock
66 Orient Point
67 Old Field Point
68 Fire Island
69 Tarrytown Harbor
70 Jeffrey's Hook
71 Statue of Liberty
72 Buffalo Main

NEW JERSEY
73 Sandy Hook
74 Highlands
75 Barnegat
76 Hereford Inlet
77 Cape May
78 East Point

MARYLAND
79 Concord Point
80 Turkey Point
81 Sandy Point Shoal
82 Hooper Strait
83 Thomas Point Shoal
84 Drum Point

VIRGINIA
85 Assateague Island
86 Cape Henry,
Old & New

NORTH CAROLINA
87 Currituck Beach
88 Bodie Island
89 Cape Hatteras

The Ultimate Book of
LIGHTHOUSES

Introduction

Pervious pages: **Statue of Liberty, Liberty Island, New York Harbor;** *Above:* **Brant Point Light, Nantucket, Massachusetts**

"The considerations which enter into the choice of the position and character of the lights on a line of coast are either, on the one hand, so simple and self-evident as scarcely to admit of being stated in a general form, without becoming mere truisms; or are, on the other hand, so very numerous, and often so complicated, as scarcely to be susceptible of compression into any general laws."

— ALAN STEVENSON

The presence or absence of light is an enduring theme in world history. Numerous spiritual traditions present the appearance of a founder or guru as the symbol of light. Christ told his disciples that "You are the Light of the World," while the Buddha urged his followers to "Be a lamp unto yourself." Historians long called the period between the fall of the Roman Empire and the rebirth of Classical civilization in Italy the "Dark Ages." During the Renaissance, artists strove to find new ways to present light and shadow, and the eighteenth-century Enlightenment sought to cast light wherever shadows existed. The Romantic artists felt that the use of light had gone overboard, and their work demonstrated the beauty of life at the edge point, where light and darkness come together. Is it any wonder, then, that lighthouses have become a vivid symbol of the human need to cast light out into the darkness?

Today lighthouses are in danger. The advent of radar and radio beacons has obviated the need for many of the beautiful towers that grace the coasts of most of the world's seafaring countries. Will they slowly fall into ruin, or will the better angels of our natures prevail, and steps be taken to preserve the wood, stone, concrete and fiberglass towers that have provided inspiration for so many people for such a long time?

Sailors have always had a special need for light; the hazards of navigation are formidable enough on a calm day, but compounded greatly at night and in severe weather conditions and low visibility. So as sailing, exploration and trade began to increase in the world, so too did the need for navigational aids. The lighthouse provided early warning of submerged rocks, reefs and sandbars; sheer cliffs; rip tides; shallows in which ships could run aground; and other coastal hazards. They marked channels into safe harbor and served as daymarks and as landmarks by night, counteracting darkness, fog, haze, snowfall and squalls. In such conditions of low visibility, the beacon provided both a focal point and a potential source of rescue for mariners in distress, as lighthouse keepers came to play an increasingly active role in lifesaving endeavors.

The Earliest Lighthouses

The first primitive lighting systems were probably bonfires lit on beaches. The drawback of this early system was that the local areas tended to run out of wood. "Wreckers" sometimes used fires to lure ships onto rocks to be pillaged. The builders of these early lights eventually realized that the Earth's surface is curved, and that a light must be placed on high to be seen far out at sea. Statistical evidence for this premise was not available until the nineteenth century, when the tables that we take for granted today came into existence. A light placed 10 feet above sea level can be seen for 8.06 miles; one placed at an elevation of 50 feet is visible for 12.55 miles; a light that stands at 100 feet can be seen for 15.91 miles; and a tower that has its focal plane at 200 feet is visible for 20.66 miles.

The first known major beacon building project began before 270 BC, when the Pharos lighthouse was lit at Alexandria, Egypt. Alexander the Great chose this ancient Middle Eastern crossroads for his eponymous city, and during the reigns of Ptolemy I and II, the Greek architect Sostratus of Gnidus built the Pharos on a 300-square-foot base in the city harbor. The famous Library of Alexandria was built at almost the same time. One of the seven wonders of the Ancient World, the Pharos figured in both art and literature.

This massive structure, estimated to have been some 400 feet high, emitted a light that could be seen as far as 33 miles out into the Mediterranean Sea. The acme of architectural achievement during the Hellenistic Era,

it remains vivid today in the minds of those who admire Classical culture. The Pharos was in use until AD 641, when Islamic warriors conquered Alexandria and the building was damaged in the siege.

The Arab geographer Edrisi visited the Pharos in the thirteenth century and commented:

> *This lighthouse has not its equal in the world for excellence of construction and for strength, for not only is it constructed of a fine quality stone, called 'kedan,' but the various blocks are so strongly cemented together with melted lead, that the whole is imperishable....At a distance the light appeared so much like a star near the horizon that sailors were frequently deceived by it.*

Nothing, of course, is truly imperishable, and the great Pharos was finally felled by a series of earthquakes in the fourteenth century. Parts of the beacon are now being resurrected by a team of French archaeologists. Its famous name has been imparted to lights around the world: The French word for lighthouse is *"phare"* and the Spanish, *"faro."*

Pharos, Alexandria

The Mediterranean remained the center of lighthouse development for a long time. The Romans turned their hand to building lighthouses. From what we know of seacoast control during the Roman Empire, we gather that about thirty lights were established at key stations around the Mediterranean Sea and along the Atlantic coasts of France and Spain. During the reign of the Emperor Trajan, the Portus was built at the mouth of the Tiber River. One of the major engineering projects of the Imperial period, the Portus was celebrated on Roman coins bearing the image of the lighthouse. Modeled on the Pharos, the beacon was composed of three levels topped by a cylindrical apex housing the flame. Such structures as this helped to maintain the Roman concept of the Mediterranean as *Mare Nostrum* ("Our Sea").

Portus was especially important as the lighthouse illuminating the destination point for supplies of grain that were shipped from Alexandria for consumption by the people of Rome. Due to the prevailing northwesterly winds, it took the supply ships just more than a month to make their way from the Pharos of Alexandria to the light at Portus, but as little as two or three weeks to make the return trip, which was comparatively "downhill."

Other than the light at Portus, what we know about these Roman lighthouses is that they exemplified the architectural style known today as Romanesque. They were short, squat and had little window space, similar to the fortresses that were built inland throughout the Imperial period. But these lighthouses served a vital function, and many indeed were the sailors who must have been comforted by the presence of a bonfire or candles burning inside one of these crude structures. The desire for elegance in lighthouse architecture was a luxury that would have to wait.

The declining vitality of the Roman Empire after AD 300 was reflected in its architecture. Few new buildings were created, and those that existed were not repaired; thus the entire network of lighthouses and coastal connections that had made *Mare Nostrum* a reality began gradually to fade away. Not for more than 1,000 years would Europe truly recover from the fall of Rome, which is usually dated at AD 476.

One bright spot emerged to challenge what historians refer to today as the Dark Ages. During the reign of Charlemagne, King of the Franks, the old Roman lighthouse at Boulogne on the French coast was restored and made to shine. This lighthouse, built by order of the emperor Caligula, was twelve stories high, each successive story smaller than its predecessor. This intricate architecture fell prey to intervening periods of darkness, warfare, invasion and famine. Known to the French as the *Tour d'Ordre* and to English sailors as the Old Man of Bullen, the tower finally collapsed into the sea in 1644.

Sailing techniques and the use of navigational aids also fell into a long malaise. Scholars today estimate that in 1300 it took just about as long for a Venetian or Genoan galley to cross the Mediterranean as it had for a Roman craft in AD 200—more than a millennium passing without discernible progress. Thus, while lighthouses may have been needed, none (or few) were built, and only negligible advances were made in the art of

other navigational aids. Between 800 and 1100, the Norsemen (or Vikings) were the best sailors in the Western world, but to our knowledge they built no permanent coastal lights. Maritime improvements after 1300 were often due to adaptations from Arab vessels; the use of the lateen sail, for example, greatly enhanced the ability of ships to sail against the wind.

Undoubtedly, it was the ripple effect from the Mediterranean countries that made the difference in bringing lights and lighthouses closer to the world of Northern Europe, and, by extension, to North America. The advent of the High Middle Ages, and later the Age of Discovery, changed the scenario, especially for European sailors. Once again, Mediterranean sailors and architects led the way, but this time the knowledge and recognition of the need for lighthouses spread more quickly to Europe. Trade increased after 1300, and some of the new European nations began to bestir themselves and spread their canvas wings: Portugal was the first.

The European Maritime Powers

Portuguese sailors had developed the caravel by around 1400 and soon reached the waters at the Southern tip of Africa en route to the "spices of the Indies" (the Spice Islands of Indonesia). At Sagres, on the southwestern corner of Europe, Prince Henry the Navigator (who himself never went to sea) established the first school for maritime navigation about 1420.

The coastal cities of Italy continued to lead the way within the bounds of the Mediterranean Sea. The first Italian light was probably at Meloria, built in 1157. Venice, Tino and the Straits of Messina all had lighthouses, as did the port of Genoa, where Antonio Colombo, uncle of the famous Christopher Columbus, was the tower's keeper in 1449. These lights, however, were symbols of an era of Mediterranean power that was destined to end, as the Atlantic states of Portugal, Spain, France and England each took up the gauntlet of lighthouse construction.

France gained ascendancy on the seas during the sixteenth century. While navigators like Jacques Cartier and Samuel de Champlain found their way to North America and explored the St. Lawrence Gulf and River, King Henry III commissioned Louis de Foix to build a light at Cordouan, where France's wine exports from Bordeaux reached the ocean. De Foix died shortly before the completion of his work, which was ongoing from 1584 until 1611. Built to function as a light, a chapel and a royal residence, the tower stood for many years as the apogée of lighthouse development. The first Fresnel lens, with a range of 21 nautical miles, was installed in the tower in 1823. Restored several times since, the light still guides ships entering the Gironde River.

The seventeenth century brought considerable acceleration in lighthouse development. Denmark established a national lighthouse service in 1650, as did Finland in 1696. England had its Trinity House, established in 1566, but the first light was not built until 1619, and Trinity House did not assume full control over the coast of England until the 1830s. The Crown granted licenses to private enterprises that took up the challenge of confronting maritime safety issues. The first great challenge the fledgling maritime nation faced was the monster reef off its southwestern shores.

The Pilgrim ship *Mayflower* sailed from Plymouth, England, on September 6, 1620. That same day, the ship's captain noted in his log the "wicked reef of twenty-three rust-red rocks lying nine and one half miles south of Rame Head on the Devon mainland…a great danger to all ships hereabouts, for they sit astride the entrance to this harbour and are exposed to the full force of the westerly winds and must always be dreaded by mariners. Leaving Plymouth, we managed to avoid this reef." Many ships were not so lucky.

The Eddystone rocks remained unconquered even as England grew in maritime size and strength during the seventeenth century. English sailors had found their way around Chesapeake Bay, the Strait of Magellan and many other shipping hazards before a solution was found to the problem that lay so close to home. As Plymouth grew in size and importance, it became more and more imperative to find an answer to the dreaded reef. As shipping between Britain and North America

increased, so too did the need for a remedy for the problem at Eddystone. French, Dutch and Swedish sailors were also threatened by the rocks.

Henry Winstanley was a member of the English generation that saw its nation rise to maritime greatness. Referring to the War of the Spanish Succession that ended in 1713, the naval historian Alfred Thayer Mahan remarked: "Before that war England was one of the seapowers; after it she was *the* seapower, without any second." While we cannot lay all of this at the feet of Henry Winstanley or the Eddystone Light, it's safe to say that the engineering feat that culminated in its construction was one of the great leaps forward in British maritime affairs.

For a time, English sailors laboriously rowed Winstanley and his small group of workers the 14 miles to the reef, where they put in 10 hours of work per day before they were returned to Plymouth. Given the hazards of small-craft navigation, Winstanley accomplished a major feat in keeping body and soul together while he erected the light that would become one of the world's most famous.

The rocks at Eddystone are almost fully submerged at high tide, making the work even more hazardous. During the first season, all that could be accomplished was the drilling of twelve holes, to allow for building the foundation. The second season yielded greater progress: The laborers built a base that was 14 feet in diameter, and the tower rose to 12 feet. During the third year the tower rose to 80 feet, and in the fourth and final year, it reached 120 feet. On November 14, 1698, Winstanley lit eleven candles at the top of the edifice, making lighthouse history.

The great engineer did not enjoy his success for long. He perished when his light was washed away by a tremendous storm that struck the coast of England in 1703, leaving the treacherous reef unmarked. A stark reminder of its danger came when the English ship *Winchelsea* was wrecked at Eddystone soon after she returned from a voyage to Virginia.

John Rudyerd built the second light at Eddystone. Made of wood, the tower was completed in 1709 and served faithfully until it burnt in 1755. John Smeaton designed and built the third tower, completed in 1759.

Previous pages: **Boston Harbor Light, Little Brewster Island, Massachusetts;** *Above:* **Seals Point Light, Cape St. Francis, South Africa**

After standing for 120 years, it was dismantled and brought ashore to Plymouth in 1882. The fourth and current tower was completed in the same year. For many years Eddystone Light was displayed on the British penny as a symbol of the nation's maritime sovereignty.

Well before this time, the Anglican bishop George Berkeley had made the statement: "Westward the course of empire takes its way." This would hold true for the building of lighthouses as well as the development of constitutional government and democracy in North America, which includes Canada, the United States and much of Old Mexico. Upon first glance at an atlas, one is struck by the importance of river systems and the network of the Great Lakes. The St. Lawrence and Mississippi Rivers present the easiest means of finding one's way into the continent, while the Columbia and Colorado lead the traveler to the Pacific Ocean. None of this was charted in 1500, and there were no lighthouses until at least 1700. But the potential was there for exploration, adventure, colonization and exploitation.

South America and the Caribbean, colonized by the Spanish and Portuguese, narrowly jumped the gun on their neighbors to the north. To the best of our knowledge, the first lighthouse built in the New World was the Morro Light of Havana, built around 1563 on the island of Cuba. The light was later incorporated into the Castle of the Three Kings of Morro, and UNESCO declared the area a World Heritage Site in 1982.

Completed in 1698, the same year as Eddystone Light, the Santo Antonio Lighthouse was the first to be built on the mainland of either North or South America. Commissioned by the Portuguese governor of Brazil, the stone lighthouse still guards the entrance to the harbor of Salvador City. The masonry tower is 59 feet high and its focal plane is at 72 feet above sea level.

Lighthouses in the New World

France, Spain, Holland and England all built colonies in North America during the sixteenth and seventeenth centuries. Since all these colonies depended upon trade, the need for ports, harbors and lighthouses soon became apparent. The first certain example came on September 17, 1716, when the *Boston News Letter* reported:

Boston. *By virtue of an Act of assembly made in the First Year of His Majesty's [King George I] Reign, For Building and Maintaining a Light House upon the Great Brewster (called Beacon-Island) at the Entrance of the Harbour of Boston, in order to prevent the loss of the Lives and Estates of His Majesty's Subjects; The said*

*Light House has been built; and on Fryday last the four-
teenth Currant the Light was kindled, which will be very
useful for all Vessels going out and coming in to the
Harbour of Boston.*

George Worthylake was the first caretaker of this, the
first lighthouse built in North America. The light was a
material representation of the fact that the new English
colonies needed trade in order to thrive; the number of
vessels entering Boston Harbor grew apace. It was no
small feat to plan and build such a beacon: Our best estimates indicate that in 1716 there were only some seventy
lighthouses in the world. That would soon change.

French colonists erected the second light on the
mainland of North America. Located at the northern
entrance to the harbor at Louisbourg on Cape Breton
Island, the round, castlelike tower was 66 feet high
and contained a circular stairway. Finished in 1733,
the light had sixteen spermaceti whale-oil lamps. The

lighthouse burned down in 1736 and was replaced by
the first concrete, fireproof building in North America.
Ironically, the town, fortress and lighthouse were all
captured by invading militiamen from Massachusetts
in 1745; the only towns with lighthouses on the coast
of North America were fighting each other! The
lantern was shot away in the second siege of
Louisbourg, accomplished by British forces in 1758.
The tower slowly fell into ruin, and a visitor later wrote:

While on its high and rugged steep
That o'erhangs the howling deep
The sailor's beacon claims devotion —
And looks like baron's donjon keep.

As the British went on to conquer Nova Scotia and
Eastern Canada, they built the first British-Canadian
lights at places like Sambro, just outside of Halifax.
British maritime supremacy in the New World seemed
assured in the wake of the wars that brought French
Canada under her sway, but later developments would
change this. Meanwhile, the Dutch in New York's
Hudson Valley and the Swedes of the Delaware Valley
did not attempt to build any lighthouses. The Spanish
in Florida may have built one at St. Augustine during
the sixteenth century, but no positive evidence exists.

English colonists led the way in lighthouse con-
struction along the East Coast. Brant Point Light on
Nantucket Island; Tybee Island Light at Savannah;
Beavertail Light in Narragansett Bay; Connecticut's
New London Light; Sandy Hook, New Jersey, Light;
Cape Henlopen Light at the entrance to Delaware Bay;
Charles Town (later Charleston) Light; Plymouth Light;
Portsmouth Light; and Cape Ann Light were all built
prior to the American Revolution. The majority were
built north of Delaware Bay, and this would remain
the case until the 1820s.

After the American Revolution, individual states
assumed responsibility for the lights in their areas.
However, in August 1789, the seventh official act of
the newly created Congress was to take responsibility
for navigational aids throughout the new nation.
President George Washington, once a surveyor, was
involved in the process during the early years: He
appointed lighthouse keepers and negotiated with con-
tractors. Maine's Portland Head Light, and Old Cape

Opposite: **New London Harbour Light, Prince Edward Island;** *Above:* **Gloucester Light, Cape Ann, Massachusetts**

Henry Light, at the southern side of the mouth of Chesapeake Bay, were the first built under the auspices of the new U.S. government. Both still stand as vivid reminders of American initiative in maritime affairs.

Virtually no Americans had yet seen the Pacific Coast or the Great Northwest, but Russians were finding their way down from the Bering Strait and Alaska. About 1795 the Russians erected the first light on the West Coast, at Sitka, Alaska. Placed at the top of Baranoff Castle, it was reportedly 100 feet tall. Like the rest of Sitka, it was burned in an attack by the Tlingit in 1802, but was later rebuilt.

Advances in Lighting Technology

How were these towers lighted over the centuries? The answer is multifold. During Roman times, many light towers had a bonfire either on top of the structure or underneath it, whence the light was reflected upward by convex mirrors. These techniques were perfected in the ancient world, but were gradually lost during the Dark and Middle Ages. The use of candles made for positive development during the Renaissance and the centuries that followed.

Eddystone Light and the lights in colonial North America were lit by candles and rated in terms of candlepower. No major developments occurred until the mid-eighteenth century, when the Frenchman Francois-Pierre Ami Argand designed a set of lamps and parabolic reflectors. He sought to overcome the fact that light naturally diffuses both horizontally and vertically, being emitted at 360 degrees from the center. The horizontal aspect—what sailors could see as they approached the light—was positive. But the loss of a large percentage—perhaps 50 percent—of the light to the vertical dimension diminished its effectiveness.

Argand improved upon the method used for 200 years. In his catoptric system, reflectors placed behind the illuminant spread the light and magnified its strength. Invented around 1781, Argand's oil lamp with reflectors had a hollow, circular wick that allowed oxygen to pass evenly on both sides. This served to make the light brighter and smokeless.

England and France quickly adopted Argand's lamp system and their lighthouse administrations improved remarkably. It was not until 1812 that an unemployed Yankee ship captain named Winslow Lewis persuaded the U.S. government to use "his" lamp and lens system (undoubtedly copied from an example of the Argand system he had seen in Great Britain).

Lewis had installed his lamps in all of the American lighthouses by about 1816. His friendship with Stephen Pleasonton, director of U.S. lighthouses, allowed Lewis a virtual monopoly of lamps and lighting for the next forty years, thereby preventing the adoption of a revolutionary and far more efficient system.

Lens, Anacapa Island Light, Channel Island National Park, California

Augustin Jean Fresnel was born in Brittany in 1788. After studying physics, he joined the French lighthouse establishment in 1813. Fresnel turned his attention to the vexing problem of the diffusion of light, and by 1822 he had mastered the problem for the time being. He created a series of lamps, since known as Fresnel lenses. Shaped like a glass beehive, the series of concentric circles of glass refract, or bend, the light so that it shines out horizontally rather than radially. His early efforts were not perfect; perhaps 10 percent of the light still diffused vertically. But that improvement was dramatic and gave rise to a tremendous increase in lighting and lighthouse efficiency.

Fresnel tested his device at the famous Cordouan lighthouse in 1823. He died in 1827, knowing that his instrument was successful, but unaware of how soon it would transform the international lighthouse system. In Scotland, the Stevenson family took up Fresnel's lenses and experimented with them, making them even more efficient, and during the 1840s and '50s, the British lighthouses were by far the best in the world.

The Fifth Auditor of the U.S. Treasury, Stephen Pleasonton, had responsibility for all the lights between 1820 and 1852. A career bureaucrat and a conscientious bookkeeper, Pleasonton preferred economy to ingenuity. Lacking nautical expertise, he entrusted the lighting to Lewis, whose insistence on using outdated Argand lamps instead of the new Fresnel lens held the nation back for nearly forty years.

Captain Matthew Calbraith Perry, who would "open" Japan to trade with the United States in 1853, brought the first pair of Fresnel lenses to the United States in 1840; they were placed at the twin towers at Navesink. Having demonstrated their great superiority, Fresnel lenses became standard, and when the Civil War began in 1861, nearly all American lighthouses had been fitted with them.

The question of how best to illuminate the lamps remained. During the colonial period, oil had been the method of choice. Spider lamps were designed around 1790; these were pans of oil in which four or more wicks could be placed. During the first half of the nineteenth century, Americans used whale oil, which was taken from the heads of sperm whales.

Above: **Chesapeake Lightship, Baltimore, Maryland;** *Overleaf:* **Lennard Island Lighthouse, Vancouver Island, British Columbia**

The price of sperm oil rose dramatically during the 1850s, and Americans began to experiment with colza (coleseed or rapeseed oil), the standard in France. Little rapeseed grew in the U.S., however, and the search led to the use of lard oil, and then kerosene, or mineral oil. By the turn of the twentieth century, most U.S. lighthouses used incandescent oil-vapor lamps. During the 1920s and '30s, the majority were converted to electricity.

Pleasonton's personal control of the lighthouse system was replaced by the Lighthouse Board, created in 1852, which was itself superseded by the Bureau of Lighthouses, established in 1910. In 1939 administration of the lights passed to the U.S. Coast Guard.

The Golden Age of Lighthouse Construction

The most innovative and productive period for lighthouse construction in North America occurred between 1840 and 1900. Engineers faced the daunting task of finding ways to illuminate their hazardous coastlines. British Canada faced an even greater challenge on both east and west coasts due to the number of inlets, bays and zigzagging shorelines.

Henry Wadsworth Longfellow observed the importance of lighthouses. From his cottage on Nahant, north of Boston, he looked out at Minots Ledge Light, completed in 1853, and pondered:

The rocky ledge runs far into the sea,
And on its outer point, some miles away,
The Lighthouse lifts its massive masonry, —
A pillar of fire by night, of cloud by day.

Here Longfellow referred to the great accomplishment of American engineering that was to triumph over sand, shore, shoal, inlet, headland and rocky beach. Where, though, did the inspiration for that triumph come from?

The answer is Scotland. The craggy Scottish coast posed a formidable challenge to navigation. As industry and agriculture prospered during the nineteenth century, the need for improving safety along Scottish shores increased. Fortunately, one able family came to the rescue: the Stevensons. Robert Louis Stevenson, the author of *Treasure Island* and *The Master of Ballantrae*, came from a family steeped in civil engineering. His grandfather Robert Stevenson (1772–1850) became the engineer reporting to the Commissioners of the Northern (Scottish) Lighthouse Board in the 1790s. Here he undertook one of the most difficult engineering tasks ever attempted: the conquest of the reef known as Bell Rock.

The rock, or reef, stands north of the entrance to the Firth of Forth, just off the east coast of Scotland. Each high tide submerges the rock to a depth of 12 feet, and the location is at the mercy of the full blast of North Sea winds. Scottish captains reportedly skirted the rock by as much as 10 miles, but they were often driven upon it. During the storm of 1799, no fewer than seventy ships were wrecked on Bell Rock, which had earned its reputation in a medieval ballad: "And then they knew the perilous rock/And blest the Abbot of Aberbrothock."

Stevenson designed and directed the building of the Bell Rock Light between 1807 and 1811. Construction of the pillar-rock tower took enormous ingenuity. Stevenson designed a lantern for a temporary lightship whose light surrounded the mast, instead of using a number of small lanterns suspended from the yardarms. During the building of Bell Rock, he also designed the balance crane and the movable jib crane.

Alan Stevenson (1807–65) was Robert's oldest son. He planned to enter the Church, but was dissuaded, and in 1843 he succeeded his father as engineer to the

Commissioners. During his career, Alan Stevenson designed ten lighthouses, the most famous of which is the great tower at Skerryvore.

Stevenson built Skerryvore Light on a rock 14 miles from the nearest land, the Isle of Tyree, off the west coast of Scotland. Constructed between 1838 and 1843, the end product, a 138-foot tower, housed a dioptric revolving lens, the first in the world.

David Stevenson (1815–86), the third son of Robert Stevenson, succeeded his brother as engineer to the Lighthouse Board. With his younger brother, Thomas (1818–87), he designed no fewer than thirty lighthouses. His work took him to Newfoundland, India, New Zealand and the Far East. Japan, forced to open itself to trade, discovered the need for lighthouses. Prior to 1850, virtually all of its island coastlines had been lit by bonfires. The Japanese government turned to Scotland and the Stevenson family, who built the first beacon for the Japanese Islands. Responding to the need for earthquake protection along the coast, David Stevenson devised the "aseismatic arrangements" that mitigated the effect of quakes on the optical apparatus

in the towers. Soon copied and then perfected, the Stevenson model became the Far Eastern standard. China would soon follow Japan's example. In 1870 Stevenson's report on the relative advantages of paraffin and coleseed (rapeseed) oil led to the selection of the latter, called colza, for use in Scottish lighthouses.

The renowned Robert Louis Stevenson (1850–94) was a son of Thomas Stevenson. Despite the infirm health that shortened his life to forty-four years, he completed his apprenticeship in the family discipline before taking up his literary career. Certainly, the world would have been the poorer without his delightful stories, novels and poems.

While England and Scotland had mastered the art of building lights in rocky locations, the United States would improve upon that art. Not even Scotland, with its famous Skerryvore Light, would pose greater challenges than those faced by the builders of St. George's and other American lights.

It is hard for us to appreciate what a "dark and dangerous" sea the Atlantic can be, especially because of the gap between the wind and weather systems of Europe

and those of North America. Americans became aware of the Gulf Stream and its ameliorating effect upon our coastal weather during the 1770s, when Benjamin Franklin published a famous map of the stream. The fact that it brings warm air with it along the continental coast had much to do with patterns of settlement.

English, French, Dutch and Spanish navigators developed a pattern of sailing south-by-southwest from Europe to avoid the "windless" zone in the mid-Atlantic, where they risked being becalmed. Lighthouses were built to correspond with this pattern, as well as with local topography. Lights like those at Sandy Hook, New Jersey, and Cape Henlopen, Delaware, were essential for guiding in the sturdy vessels that had endured the long voyage from Europe.

North American Maritime Expansion

Americans are a "westering" people, and that influence extended to maritime affairs during the nineteenth century. Even as Brigham Young led the Mormons west from Illinois to what is now Utah, others made their way across the Isthmus of Panama; still others

Elbow Reef Light, Elbow Cay, Bahamas

rounded Cape Horn and found their way to California. There they discovered an open but lightless coast. When gold was discovered in California in 1848, there was not a single lighthouse in the area that would become Baja, California, Oregon and Washington State, not to mention British Columbia.

What did exist was tremendous potential for maritime growth and development. The natural harbors within Puget Sound, the San Francisco Bay area and San Diego represented the opportunity for Americans to become a "two-ocean" people. Merchants could foresee the ability to trade with partners on the Pacific Rim to the same extent that they already traded with Europe.

Historians who account for Great Britain's growing power during the nineteenth century often focus on the English coastline itself. They point out that wherever one stands on English soil, the sea is never more than 70 miles away, using this fact to illustrate the point that necessity is the mother of invention. The English came to rule the seas well before the days of Queen Victoria because they were bred to it.

Often overlooked is the fact that Americans enjoyed a comparable experience. Their immense coastline had now been doubled by the addition of California and the Pacific Northwest, and Americans were to gain maritime advantages that would eventually surpass those of England herself. It might be said that if the nineteenth century was the "British century" by virtue of her fleet and trade, the twentieth century belonged to the United States.

Expansion was predicted by no less astute an observer than the Frenchman Alexis de Tocqueville. In his famous *Democracy in America*, de Tocqueville commented that "No other nation in the world possesses vaster, deeper, or more secure ports for commerce than the Americans....I think that nations, like men, in their youth almost always give indications of the main features of their destiny. Seeing how energetically the Anglo-Americans trade, their natural advantages, and their success, I cannot help believing that one day they will become the leading naval power on the globe. They are born to rule the seas, as the Romans were to conquer the world."

At the time of de Tocqueville's visit, the United States was still confined, as it were, to the East Coast, the Gulf Coast and the southern rim of the Great Lakes. Another leap of expansion followed ten years later, when the U.S. war with Mexico (1846–48) brought the Southwest and California into the American fold. Suddenly, full control of the great natural harbors at Puget Sound, San Francisco Bay and San Diego showed the need to illuminate coastal areas on both the Gulf of Mexico and the Pacific.

The heyday of American maritime expansion occurred in the two decades prior to the Civil War. Between 1843 and 1855, 2,656 merchant ships of all sizes were built in the United States, validating de Tocqueville's optimistic prediction. But lights were needed on all of the coasts—East, West, Gulf and Great Lakes—to continue the process.

British Canadians faced similar challenges. Thousands of immigrants made their way to Canada along the St. Lawrence River, which presented innumerable dangers to ships. Even if a ship were fortunate enough to reach Montreal, travelers still had to make their way out to the hazardous Great Lakes.

A new era in American lighthouse building began in response to this period of increased immigration and international maritime commerce. The 1850s saw the advent of new types of construction and a special confidence that wind- and wave-swept areas could be tamed through the building of lights. Of these, Minots Ledge stands out as one of the great achievements in American engineering prior to the Civil War.

Minots Ledge lies off Cohasset, just south of Boston, Massachusetts. The reef claimed the hulls of numerous ships and the lives of hundreds of sailors before the first light was erected in 1850. It stood for only one year before it was wrecked in a storm, causing some to declare that if God had meant to have a light there, He would have placed the beacon Himself. However, intrepid engineers set about the task of rebuilding the light. They finished their work in 1860, and the light remains today. Perhaps even more than Eddystone Light, Minots Ledge stands as a remarkable triumph of man over wind and water.

Longfellow's optimistic words were vindicated:

A new Prometheus, chained upon the rock,
Still grasping in his hand the fire of Jove,
It does not hear the cry, nor heed the shock,
But hails the mariner with words of love.
"Sail on!" it says, "sail on, ye stately ships!
And with your floating bridge the ocean span;
Be mine to guard this light from all eclipse,
Be yours to bring man nearer unto man!

Race Rock Reef stands a little more than half a mile southwest of Fishers Island, New York. Eight ships were lost there between 1829 and 1837 alone, and the growth of ferry boat travel between Long Island and the Connecticut shore increased the number of people exposed to the risk. As Americans turned to pleasure boating on Long Island Sound, the danger posed by Race Rock was a growing concern. Therefore, in 1871, the engineer Francis Hopkinson Smith and Captain Thomas Albertson Scott began laying the foundations for a light. It took seven long years to build the foundations; after that, the lighthouse itself took only nine months to complete. The erection of Race Rock Light gave a tremendous boost to the morale of American mariners in the area. Francis Hopkinson Smith went on to greater fame when he laid the foundations for the Statue of Liberty, a landmark that itself served as a lighthouse from 1886 until 1902.

Northern Florida may have seen one of the first lights in North America. It is suggested, though not proven, that the Spanish had a small light at St. Augustine. We do know for certain that when the United States acquired Florida in 1821, lights were built here and on several other sites. The Cape Florida Light was actually besieged by the Seminole in 1836, making it, along with Boston, Sandy Hook and Louisbourg Lights, one of the four that have seen armed combat. In 1861 nearly all the lighthouses on the Gulf and Southeast Coasts were seized by the Confederacy and put out of action for the duration of the Civil War.

The Gulf Coast remained unlit longer than the other coastal regions. Until the 1820s, such pirates as Jean Lafitte knew the Gulf better than did the U.S. Navy. The advent of the Civil War changed this, as admirals like David Farragut staged operations in the waters off Mobile Bay and New Orleans. As a result, the waters of the Gulf became better charted, more navigated and better lit over the next thirty years.

Portland Breakwater Light, Maine

Above: Highland (Cape Cod) Light, Truro, Massachusetts; *Opposite:* Milwaukee Breakwater Light, Wisconsin

On the West Coast, mariners faced difficulties surpassing even those of the Atlantic. The most notorious "graveyard" was on the "bar" (sandbar) at Cape Disappointment, on the northern side of the mouth of the Columbia River, where Washington State and Oregon meet. The sandbar was created by the tremendous amount of silt deposited by the Columbia River on its journey to the Pacific Ocean. It was here that Meriwether Lewis and William Clark had completed their epic transcontinental journey of exploration in November 1805. By the best estimates available, we infer that more than 200 ships, large and small, came to grief at the treacherous mouth of the Columbia River. For a distance of at least 200 miles north and south of the river's mouth, dangers beset mariners in areas of the coastline that are known today for their natural beauty and splendid scenery. The federal government came forward again to assert control over the situation.

The Congressional act that established the Territory of Oregon in 1848 also provided for building lighthouses at Cape Disappointment and New Dungeness. Cape Disappointment received a first-order Fresnel lens. Even greater events began to unfold in 1852, when Congress authorized construction of sixteen lights on the West Coast: These were to be at Fort Point, Fort Bonita and Alcatraz Island in San Francisco Bay; Monterey; San Diego; Santa Barbara; the Farallon Islands off San Francisco; Humboldt Harbor; Crescent City; Smith Island; Cape Flattery (the northwest cor-

ner of the nation); Willapa Bay, Washington; and the mouth of the Umpqua River. Given the need for maritime safety, the work progressed rapidly, and all sixteen were completed by 1858.

These early West Coast lights did not appear very different from their counterparts on the East Coast. All of them were designed by the New England architect Ammi B. Young of the Treasury Department, who gave them the same Cape Cod dwelling-style design, with a tower rising through the center. The local Spanish Revival style would not emerge in lighthouse form until the end of the century.

More romantic in appearance were the Heceta Head Light in Florence, Oregon, and Cape Blanco Light in Port Orford, Oregon. Both were built in locations where navigational aids had long been needed; Spanish mariners had used the white cliffs at Cape Blanco as a landmark for centuries. But the greatest challenge that was met and overcome was that of building St. George's Light off the northwest coast of California.

Some sailors called it St. George Reef; others labeled it Dragon Rock. In either case, they referred to treacherous reefs that lay 14 miles off the coast. Many notorious sailing disasters occurred in the region; the most publicized was the loss of the sidewheeler USS *Brother Jonathan*, which came to grief there in July 1865 with the loss of 215 men. Ironically, "Brother Jonathan" was a term Victorian Britain used to describe her younger sibling, the United States.

But if St. George was to be the American equivalent of Eddystone Light, it took some time to put the pieces into place. The Lighthouse Board had the site surveyed in 1882, and between 1887 and 1892, the massive granite structure was raised at the enormous cost of $704,633 — the most expensive lighthouse built to that date in the United States.

On the Gulf of Mexico, the acquisition of Texas had brought a large new section of coastline to the United States. Much of it was not fit for navigation because of the strong tides and marshy lowlands that came right down to the shore. But some areas of Texas developed a thriving maritime commerce. One of them was Galveston, named for the Spanish governor of Louisiana during the American Revolution.

Bolivar Point Light was built on Bolivar Peninsula, just north of Galveston Island, in 1873. The sleek, brick-lined iron tower was a familiar sight to visitors to Galveston, which was known as the "Queen of the Gulf." September 8, 1900, brought an enormous hurricane that devastated the beautiful city and caused 6,000 deaths. But the 125 people who took refuge in Bolivar Point Light were safe, and the event was seen as a cause for rebuilding, rather than despair.

The navigational problems on the Great Lakes are often overlooked, yet these lakes constitute the largest body of fresh water on the planet: If they were emptied, it would take fifty years for the free-running Mississippi River to refill them to capacity. The Great Lakes could not be ignored by steamboat operators, coastal navigators and nautical engineers. Then the lumber industry developed, fueled by German and Scandinavian immigrants, and the need for navigational aids on the Great Lakes increased.

Michigan today has more lighthouses (131) than any other American state. Both Lake Michigan and Lake Superior required numerous lights to guide vessels to shore. Tides and sudden windstorms added to the maritime dangers in the region. Lighthouse engineering flourished in the Lakes area, and some specific sites, like Split Rock and Round Island, required just as much work as the coastal locations. This is also true of Canada's Cove Island Light (1855–59), which is located in Georgian Bay, at the northern end of Lake Huron.

If the Great Lakes are often overlooked, one might claim that America's inland Eastern waterway is almost forgotten. The network of rivers, lakes and canals that connect New York City, Montreal and Buffalo were once known to most Americans. In fact, for generations the Hudson and St. Lawrence Rivers, Lake Champlain, the Mohawk River and the Erie Canal were vital points of entry and connection for immigrants and tradesmen.

Isle la Motte Light stands at the northern end of the island of the same name. Crown Point Light was completed in 1859, and Colchester Reef Light went into service in 1871. In 1952 the beacon was moved carefully, piece by piece, to the grounds of the Shelburne Museum, just south of Burlington, Vermont.

In 1846 Great Britain and the U.S. had agreed to draw the boundary between Canada and the United States at the 49th parallel of north latitude. This

allowed both British and American ships to enter the Strait of Juan de Fuca and Puget Sound. The British-Canadian cities of Victoria and Vancouver grew up north of the boundary line, Seattle and Port Townsend on the American side.

Naturally, British ships tried to hug the northern side of the Strait of Juan de Fuca as they approached Victoria. Many of them ran aground, or were broken up at Race Rocks, just south of the city. This failure of maritime safety was an affront to British pride and technology. Granite blocks were cut in Scottish quarries and shipped all the way around Cape Horn to British Columbia, 16,000 miles away by sea. The work proceeded apace, and on Boxing Day (December 26) 1860, Race Rocks Light was lit. The magnificent tower remains today, one of the best examples of the famous Canadian "Imperial Lights."

Best known to mariners today is Estevan Point Light, on the west coast of Vancouver Island. Completed in 1909, the 98-foot tower has a rocketlike appearance, due to the use of reinforced concrete and a flying-buttress formation. From the time of its commissioning, Estevan Light has been a marking point for ships arriving from Hawaii and East Asia. It became known to virtually all Canadians in 1942, when the

area was shelled by a Japanese submarine. This, the first foreign attack on Canadian soil since the War of 1812, was seen as the equivalent of the attack on the U.S. naval base at Pearl Harbor.

In Eastern Canada, the first important lighthouse built on the St. Lawrence River was Il Verte, completed in 1809. It was a milestone in making the great river safer for passenger ships and was used as a model for numerous other lights. It still stands today, the second-oldest operational lighthouse in Canada.

The Republic of Mexico entered the arena of lighthouse building at a rather late date. During the Spanish Colonial era, it appears that no significant lights were attempted, but after Mexico won its independence in 1819, things began to change. What consistently thwarted development was the lack of a cohesive equivalent to the North American Lighthouse Boards. Originally, Mexico was less committed to trade than its northern neighbors, and lighthouses were not a priority.

As the twentieth century dawned, Mexico found more of a need for navigational aids. Today there are a number of prominent lighthouses, some of them often visited by tourists. Most of the Mexican lights are called simply *"El Faro."* The light at Mazatlan stands on a hill called Cerro Creston, and *El Faro Mazatlan*, at 515

Above: **Eagle Harbor Light, Michigan;** *Opposite:* **Point Pinos Light, Monterey, California**

The United States flexed its muscles and acquired thousands of miles of new coastlines during the late nineteenth century. Alaska was purchased from Czarist Russia in 1867, and the Spanish-American War of 1898 brought Puerto Rico, Guam and the Philippines into American hands. An internal uprising, fostered by the interests of Sanford P. Dole and other powerful plantation owners, had made the Hawaiian Islands a U.S. territory five years earlier.

The first American lighthouse in Alaska was built on the site of the Russian beacon of a century before. Years went by before the Lighthouse Board took any action in Alaskan waters, but the Alaskan Gold Rush of 1897–98 brought hundreds of ships into those waters, many of which were lost in the tortuous channels of the long coast. Therefore, the Lighthouse Board appropriated $100,000, and between 1902 and 1905, a total of nine lights were built, seven of which illuminated the Inside Passage between Wrangell Strait and Skagway. Two of the most famous Alaskan lights are Scotch Cap, built in 1903, and Cape Sarichef, finished in 1904. Built on the "inside" and "outside" ends of the west coast of Unimak Island, they mark Unimak Pass, the primary passage through the Aleutian Islands into the Bering Sea. Cape Sarichef Light was the only manned lighthouse on the shores of that sea.

When the United States annexed Hawaii, the island archipelago had thirty-five lights of its own, eighteen operated by the government and the others run by private corporations. In 1909 an important light was built at Makapuu Point, on the southeastern end of Oahu Island, to provide a landfall for ships bound from the United States. Kilauea Point Light, at the northern end of Kauai Island, was built in 1913 as a marker for ships bound from China and Japan.

Puerto Rico had thirteen lights, all built by the Spanish after 1853, when the U.S. took possession at the turn of the century. One of the first built was on Mona Island, marking the Mona Passage between the Dominican Republic and Puerto Rico.

The progress of France, Britain and the United States was mirrored in other countries. Spain created its lighthouse service in 1846; Italy followed suit in 1860. Chile established its service in 1867; Brazil in

feet, is the second-highest lighthouse in the world. Another beacon crowns the Santiago Peninsula in the city of Manzanillo, and still another marks the area where Baja California drops off into the ocean.

International Regulation and Standardization

The late nineteenth century was a period of standardization, especially in scientific and technical matters. Time zones were created in the 1890s, and scientific knowledge became wider in scope. Thus, lighthouse designs became more predictable after 1890, ending the era of marked individualism in tower construction. During this time, the nautical mile became an accepted unit of international measurement. Because the Earth's circumference varies between the equator and the poles, the length of a nautical mile has to vary as well. A nautical mile, which is meant to equal one minute of latitude, varies between 6,046 feet at the equator and 6,108 feet at either of the poles. Based upon latitude 48, the standard nautical mile is 6,076 feet (1,852 meters).

1876; and the recently formed Imperial Germany, in 1874. There was also a new trend toward cooperation in the construction of lighthouses: The best example occurred on the northwest coast of Africa in 1864.

Certain lighthouses stand out as "key sentinels" or "making lights," which delineate the beginning or end points of land. One of the most famous is Bishop Rock Light in the Isles of Scilly, off the southern coast of England. Bishop Rock is familiar to transatlantic passengers, who see it as the first sign of arrival in Europe. Late in 1907, the seven-masted schooner *Thomas W. Lawson*, carrying three times her own weight in cargo, came to grief on the rocks of Helewether Reef, just off Bishop Rock. So violent was the impact that all but three crew members perished at once.

Fastnet Light, located 4.5 miles off Cape Clear, the southwestern point of Ireland, is an important point of departure from European waters for vessels en route

to North America. After leaving the waters of Fastnet, on a typical transatlantic course one sees no other light until Cape Race, Newfoundland.

Cape Spartel stands at the western entrance to the Strait of Gibraltar. Through an international convention, the Jabal Kebir Lighthouse was built on the Cape between 1864 and 1867, jointly owned by the United States, Austria, Belgium, Spain, France, Italy, the Netherlands and Sweden. This was an early example of the acknowledgment that "making lights" should be the common responsibility of all countries involved.

The heyday of American lighthouses probably came about 1910. In that year, the Lighthouse Board was replaced by the Bureau of Lighthouses, with one man, George Putnam, in charge of the whole affair. Putnam soon listed the status of the U.S. lighthouse system. In 1910 there were 11,713 navigational aids of all types. These included about 1,200 lighthouses and fifty-four lightships. Putnam remained at the helm for the next twenty-five years. During that time, the number of navigational aids of all kinds more than doubled, but the number of personnel operating them fell by 20 percent. This is attributable to the new technologies that were introduced, especially electrification.

In 1939 President Franklin D. Roosevelt decided to amalgamate the Lighthouse Service with the U.S. Coast Guard. He met determined resistance in the person of William McDemeritt, keeper of the Key West Light and commander of the Seventh Lighthouse District. When the president arrived in Key West to visit the lighthouse, McDemeritt confronted him and the two exchanged angry words. A famous photograph shows Roosevelt in his car with McDemeritt leaning over him. The anger was palpable, the moment decisive. Modern technology in the form of the New Deal would soon overpower the antiquated ways of the Lighthouse Service.

The twentieth century witnessed a gradual decline in lighthouse construction in the United States, Canada and Mexico. The appearance of radio towers and consoles has obviated the need for many lights, and narrow fiberglass beacons now stand on numerous remote islands and inlets. Although many towers remain, very few of these are manned.

Opposite: Cape Byron Light, New South Wales, Australia; *Above:* Rincon Light, Puerto Rico

Trouble Spots, "Graveyards" and Notorious Shipwrecks

Numerous trouble spots around the globe have been identified as particularly hazardous for ships and sailors. The waters south of Cape Horn, Chile, are known for their fierce winds, caused by the fact that there is no other land in that southerly latitude to obstruct the winds' power. Similarly, part of the coasts of Chile and Peru are known as the "Roaring Forties" (referring to their latitude), which have been the death of many sailors. But South America has no monopoly on this type of problem: It seems as though every area of the hemisphere has its own special clusters of navigational hazards, and many "graveyards" of the Atlantic, Pacific and Caribbean have been identified.

Canadians recognize at least two specific "grave-yards" on their East Coast: the treacherous waters off Newfoundland, and Sable Island, 80 miles east of Nova Scotia. Since the days of John Cabot and the first transatlantic voyages, Cape Race, Newfoundland, has marked an important though extremely hazardous point of recognition for mariners from Europe. At least 100 ships of all sizes have been lost off Cape Race, some of them even after the first light was built there in 1856.

One of the worst disasters occurred in 1864, when the passenger liner *Anglo-Saxon* crashed on the cliffs just below the light: 290 people perished. But 130 others were rescued by the daring and fortitude of the lighthouse keepers, who risked their lives in the dark to save those who had found a ledge.

Consisting of a series of low-lying sand dunes surrounded by submerged sandbars, Sable Island lies directly in the path of merchant ships bound for Nova Scotia. Many wrecks took place on these lonely shores until a series of lights was built in the late nineteenth century. Today, the island is better known for its large number of wild horses. Where Canada and the United States meet, the tidal waves of the Bay of Fundy, between Nova Scotia and New Brunswick, are legendary for their height of up to 70 feet. The New Brunswick shore is better covered by lighthouses than the inland shore of Nova Scotia.

To the south, New England's shores have witnessed countless wrecks, many of which have occurred on the coast of Massachusetts. Reaching more than 70 miles into the turbulent waters of the Atlantic, Cape Cod presents a formidable obstacle for mariners. The combination of shifting sands and the tumultuous Atlantic makes this a deadly area. Truro's Cape Cod, or Highland, Light is one of the many beacons erected to guide vessels around the peninsula. Standing more than 150 feet above sea level, the light—the oldest on the Cape—is visible up to 20 miles at sea.

Another hazard that sailors encountered in the waters off Massachusetts was the sudden and unexpected onset of dense layers of fog. The thick fogs that settle over the waters in this area make it virtually impossible to see potential hazards at sea. Boston's Minots Ledge Light was built to safeguard ships from the dangerous submerged reef under these conditions.

Another trouble spot lies in southeastern New England, where the waters of the Atlantic Ocean, Narragansett Bay and Long Island Sound meet. This confluence has created sailing and weather conditions that shift suddenly, throwing the unsuspecting sailor into confusion and danger. This area, too, has been called the "Graveyard of the Atlantic," as have the rocky waters between Point Judith Light, on the southern tip of Narragansett Bay, and Block Island North Light.

Located at the far eastern end of Long Island, the light at Montauk Point protects vessels from becoming stranded in the shallows created by the changing tides and warns of the dangerous shoals located just off the point. Farther inland, the Twin Towers of Navesink in Highland, New Jersey, were considered one of the most important guides on the Atlantic Coast. Built on a 200-foot cliff and equipped with the nation's most powerful lenses, the twin lights helped guide mariners through the narrow channel into New York Harbor.

The Delaware and Chesapeake Bays have a less fearsome reputation. These large bodies of water contain many inlets, islands and shoals, but they are well marked by dozens of lights, and the casualty rate for shipping has not been as severe. Just south of Chesapeake Bay, however, lies one of the most formidable dangers for mariners on the East Coast: the long line of barrier islands known as the Outer Banks, off the coast of North Carolina.

It was here that the first English settlement in North America was attempted, but the foundation of Roanoke was both ill designed and ill fated. Most people know that the colonists disappeared, but legends of the "Lost Colony" do not always mention that the rescue expedition was unable to fulfill its mission because of the dangerous storms that batter the area. Delightful to modern vacationers, except in the hurricane season, the Outer Banks remain perilous to navigators.

Just south of the Outer Banks, the northbound Gulf Stream comes closer inland than usual and collides with the cold waters of the southbound Labrador Current. These diametrically opposed systems create turbulent waters that culminate in the shallow Diamond Shoals, 15 miles off the Outer Banks. The "Graveyard of the Atlantic" off Cape Hatteras has witnessed thousands of shipwrecks, and several lights were built here to combat the navigational problems. Built on shifting sandy foundations, they were particularly prone to coastal erosion. Their weight and height only aggravated the difficulties of achieving stability. As mentioned later, the majestic Cape Hatteras Light was moved in 1999 when the threat of collapse became critical.

The Mid-South Atlantic coast between the Diamond Shoals and the Florida Keys would appear to offer calm sailing. Nothing could be further from the truth, and the lighthouses necessary for safety in that region had to be much taller than their counterparts to the north, because of the lack of highlands and bluffs.

The seemingly tranquil waters of the southern Atlantic can quickly become dangerous as darkness falls. Navigating the countless shoals and shallows is always difficult, and nearly impossible when a storm flares up. Countless lives have been lost in these deceptive waters. Careful mariners were, and are, able to negotiate the Gulf Coast, although the explorer Robert Cavelier de la Salle lost his way in 1682. Trinity Shoal, which lies halfway between the Mississippi River Delta and Galveston, extends some 23 miles out into the Gulf and presents a great hazard for shipping.

In the Gulf and along the southern Atlantic coast of the Southern states, perhaps the greatest danger to ships is from hurricanes. Memorable disasters occurred in 1846 at Key West, Florida's, Sand Key Light, and in Galveston, Texas (as described on page 23), in 1900. Tornadoes posed another threat, as seen in 1812 when a tornado ripped through North Carolina's Bald Head, on Cape Fear, and toppled its lighthouse. While the

Above: **Cape Florida Light after Hurricane Andrew, 1992**

presence of a beacon can offer vessels at sea no protection from the elements in such severe weather, lighthouses in this region have compiled an impressive record of withstanding the onslaught of hurricane conditions and providing refuge. In 1992 the disastrous Hurricane Andrew wreaked devastation on parts of Florida, yet the Cape Florida Light remained standing.

Equally dangerous West Coast trouble spots for mariners include the waters that were long called the "Dragon Coast" by Spanish and, later, Mexican sailors. Southern California is known for surfing and beach parties rather than shipwrecks and disaster, but the story changes when we reach the Bay Area of central California. Sir Francis Drake was the first English mariner here, and he probably landed near what is now the site of Cape Reyes Lighthouse. This was one of the most expensive lights, due not only to the rocky cliffs and powerful surf, but to the fog that prevails here more than half the days of the year. Many Spanish ships, en route from the Philippines to Acapulco, came

to grief off the coast of northern California, but during modern times the creation of key lights like St. George's have prevented these disasters.

The Pacific Northwest and Canada's West Coast present special challenges. Some experts believe that the waters off the mouth of the Columbia River are among the most dangerous in the world because of the clash between the river and the ocean tides, which are unimpeded for thousands of miles up to that point. Even Lewis and Clark noted in 1805 that the waters in the area were "far from pacific." The rocky coastline is studded with submerged reefs, rocks and sandbars. The mouth and estuary of the Columbia River present a well-known and well-documented "graveyard"; more than 200 ships foundered there before Cape Disappointment Light began to function in 1857. Ironically, the supply bark *Oriole*, which was carrying materials for five new lighthouses, went aground on the infamous bar. The ship and its stores were lost, but the sailors were saved.

Cape Meares Light, Oregon

Less well known are the dangerous waters just off Cape Flattery, which is the extreme northwest point of the Lower 48 states. Cape Flattery remains an isolated spot today; the Coast Guard sends personnel in by helicopter to check on the station, but no one lives there on a permanent basis. The importance of the site is doubled by the fact that many of the ships passing by are oil tankers bound for Seattle and Vancouver. If one should sink, it would cause an environmental disaster at least equal to that caused by the *Exxon Valdez*. Vancouver Island, 286 miles (460 km) long, has many inlets, rocks and reefs, which were first navigated by Captain James Cook in 1778 and became part of British Canada following the treaty of 1846.

The *Kuroshio*, or Japanese Current, compounds the dangers of this coastline. Even though it warms the waters off the coast, creating what some people call the "ectopia" of the coastline of Washington State and British Columbia, the Japanese Current sweeps ships along a rocky and often desolate area on the western side of Vancouver Island. The Canadian government in Ottawa recognized the need for navigational aids

here during the 1890s, when the railroad and lumber industries boomed, increasing oceangoing traffic.

The Trans-Canadian Railroad, completed in 1883, linked St. John's, Newfoundland, with Vancouver. Soon the West Coast began to flourish as first lumberjacks, and later gold seekers, made their way over the mountains. Even today, U.S. citizens have little appreciation for the vast extent and disparate nature of Canadian topography; the creation of the Canadian railroad system was far more difficult than that of the U.S. transcontinental line, completed in 1869.

Slowly, the hazards off the coast of British Columbia were tamed by greater understanding of the conditions and the addition of many aids to navigation. One of the first major projects was the construction of Carmanah Light on the north side of the Strait of Juan de Fuca. Working in cooperation with its American counterpart, Cape Flattery Light, Carmanah reduced the number of shipping fatalities in the Strait. This became even more important in the twentieth century, as the trade between Vancouver and the Orient began to boom, creating the phenomenon known as the

"Pacific Rim" trading partners. Other important lights were built at Lennard Island and Pachena Point.

Given the variety of trouble spots that exist on the Atlantic, Gulf and Pacific Coasts and the Great Lakes, one wonders how many ships have been wrecked. There is no doubt that the answer runs into many thousands. Some historians speculate that during the golden age of sail—approximately 1650 until 1850—one vessel per day was wrecked somewhere in the world. Lacking exact figures, we may look at some individual cases and examine the importance of these wrecks.

Treasure hunters abound today. Mel Fisher and his family searched for twenty years before they uncovered the wreck of the Spanish *Atocha* and its looted riches, now held and displayed by a private museum in Key West. The wreck of the *Whydah* (sunk in 1718) has recently been discovered off the eastern shore of Cape Cod. But relatively few people known about the great unsung American treasure hunter of an earlier day: Sir William Phips of Wiscasset, Maine.

Born in 1650, and having taken the sea as his trade, Phips learned of a Spanish treasure ship which had sunk off the coast of Hispaniola (now the Dominican Republic) in 1642. After seeking consent from the English king Charles II, Phips led two treasure-hunting expeditions to the area. On his second try, in January 1687, he found the wreck of the *Nuestra Señora de la Concepción*, one of the galleons of the Spanish treasure fleet of 1642. Phips brought to England gold and silver worth 210,000 pounds sterling and became the first colonial American to be knighted. It was more loot than Henry Morgan had gained in the famous sack of Panama in 1670, and Phips's haul would not be surpassed until the twentieth century.

One of the most famous shipwrecks occurred on the Great Lakes. On Sunday, November 9, 1975, the *Edmund Fitzgerald*, also known as the Queen of the Lakes, left Superior, Michigan, bound for Detroit. Built in 1958, the *Edmund Fitzgerald* was the largest iron-ore carrier ever built on the Great Lakes; she had compiled a noteworthy career to that date. During the night, winds up to 70 miles per hour struck the ship, and on the morning of November 10 she disappeared completely from the radar screen of a vessel in her wake.

The Canadian singer Gordon Lightfoot released "The Loss of the Edmund Fitzgerald," helping to make this one of the best-known wrecks in maritime history.

The loss of the *Edmund Fitzgerald* had been foreshadowed by that of the French vessel *Griffon*, the first European-style ship built on the lakes. The explorer La Salle launched her near Niagara Falls in 1679, and she survived her first voyage to present-day Detroit, but the *Griffon* never completed her return voyage.

Pirate stories abound on the East Coast, none more infamous than that of Blackbeard, whose real name was Captain Edward Teach. In 1717 he captured a French merchant ship and renamed her the *Queen Anne's Revenge*. After having blackmailed the people of Charles Town, South Carolina, into giving him supplies, Teach turned the vessel into Topsail (now Beaufort) Inlet, North Carolina. Both of his ships were lost on the sandbar, and the marooned Teach met his end on December 3, 1718, near the site of Ocracoke Island Light, built in 1803.

Pirates roved northern waters as well. Many English and French merchant captains went "a-pirate" during the early eighteenth century, and wrecks of their vessels lie at the bottom of the ocean. The recently discovered *Whydah*, built in 1716, was commanded by the pirate Samuel Bellamy. On April 26–27, 1717, Bellamy and his men ran aground off Wellfleet while on their way to Provincetown. At that time there were no lights in the area. Today, Nauset, Highland and other Cape Cod lights overlook the waters where diver and treasure hunter Barry Clifford found the wreck in 1998.

The many oil tankers now traveling the searoads constitute an environmental hazard of great proportions. This was seen on March 16, 1978, when the tanker *Amoco Cadiz* went aground on Men Goulven Rocks, as it entered the English Channel. Thousands of French soldiers were deployed to clean up the oil spill, which nevertheless took a severe toll on the marine and coastal ecosystems of Brittany.

By 1900 both the United States and Canada had created national boards that oversaw aids to navigation. Enormous problems of distance and weather had been overcome; indeed, the whole enterprise constituted one of the great achievements in world science and engineering. But what about the human element?

Interior of Hooper Strait Light, St. Michaels, Maryland

The Lighthouse Keeper's Life

"Anything for a quiet life, as the man said when he took the situation at the lighthouse." This quotation from *The Pickwick Papers*, by Charles Dickens, exemplifies what many of us think about the life of the lighthouse keeper. In a world busy with phone, fax, e-mail and modem, not to mention television and video player, we yearn for what we no longer have: peace and quiet.

There is no way to measure the impact of all that "peace and quiet" on a human being, especially since there is only one official lighthouse keeper left in the U.S.: Scott at Boston Light. However, there were many tangible threats to the lighthouse keeper's well-being during the age of manned lighthouses, irrespective of the psychological pros and cons of extreme isolation.

Prior to the age of electricity, smoke, oils and chemicals permeated lighthouse buildings, and the keepers and their families were exposed to constant noxious, even toxic, fumes. These same substances led to a severe threat of fire, and many lighthouses burned to the ground, sometimes consuming their keepers in the flames. Every day, lenses and windows had to be cleaned to prevent oil, smoke and grime from building up and diminishing the effectiveness of the light beam.

Aside from the sheer drudgery of these onerous tasks, it entailed sustained exposure to harsh chemicals. Admired as heroes, little was known about the tedium and risks of these families' important work.

George Worthylake became America's first official keeper in 1716. The Province of Massachusetts Bay agreed to pay him 50 pounds sterling per year, which was supposed to be supplemental to the money he could earn as a harbor pilot and a tender of sheep on Little Brewster Island. But one misfortune followed another, and Mr. Worthylake soon petitioned Boston for a raise in salary. This was granted and the keeper rowed to Boston to collect the money. His small boat capsized within sight of Little Brewster Island on his return, and Worthylake and his family drowned. The incident was so distressing that the young Benjamin Franklin, still living in Boston, wrote a commemorative poem that has not survived. (Later, he assured readers that it had been less than memorable.)

Some keepers enjoyed better living quarters and easier access to the local town or port. Colonial keepers had to make the best of their situations. However, this changed with American independence—not necessarily for the better. George Washington established the Lighthouse Service as a government agency, and keepers were subjected to more guidelines than before. The worst period was the thirty years during which Stephen Pleasonton ran the Lighthouse Service. A conscientious bureaucrat, he skimped in every way he could and forced the keepers to make do. It's remarkable that anyone undertook such work under a blizzard of federal regulations and low budgets. Nor were such conditions confined to the United States.

Walter Erwin was the faithful and conscientious keeper of Point Atkinson Light, British Columbia, between 1880 and 1910. During that time he raised his family on the sum of $700 per year. The introduction of a foghorn in 1889 cut his pay in half, since he had to hire a young man at his own expense to keep the horn in operation. Erwin and his wife also experienced many health problems, largely work-related. Mrs. Erwin survived serious illness, but the couple continued to be plagued by one problem after another on their remote station. When Mr. Erwin finally stepped down from his post in 1910, he found that a meager pension of $33 per month had been allocated to him.

However, better times were in store for the keepers. After 1852 their conditions improved, and the new Lighthouse Board created both uniformity and better pay within the service. Nevertheless, the occasional American lighthouse keeper "flipped his lid." Coast Guard workers today claim that New London, Connecticut, Ledge Light is haunted by the ghost of "Ernie," one of the early keepers. When Ernie's wife eloped with the captain of the Block Island Ferry, he threw himself from the top of the light. Allegedly, his ghost still plays tricks on members of the Coast Guard.

Cape Flattery Light, located on Tatoosh Island in Washington State, stands at the extreme northwest corner of the Lower 48 states. The isolation imposed by this site apparently drove one keeper to challenge an assistant to a duel in the 1860s. No one was harmed, because another assistant loaded both of the pistols with blanks, and the men were reconciled. But later, another keeper of the same light overcome by his iso-

lation attempted suicide by throwing himself from the cliffs. He survived the attempt, was rescued, recovered and eventually returned to his duties.

So much for Charles Dickens and the popular conception of blissful solitude.

Many heroes emerged within the lighthouse systems of the United States, Canada, Mexico and elsewhere in the world. In England, Grace Horsley Darling became a figure of national pride as a result of her courage. Born in 1815, Grace Darling was the daughter of William Darling, who, like his father before him, was the keeper of a lighthouse on Longstone, one of the Farne Islands. The seventh of nine children, Grace grew up in a typically isolated environment where duty was all. Her father frowned upon playing cards and other frivolous pastimes. On September 7, 1838, the steamboat *Forfarshire* was wrecked on the rocks near the lighthouse. Through her binoculars, Grace observed that a small group of survivors had found shelter on a rock. She and her father promptly rigged a cable to their rowboat and made their way out to the rock, well aware that they would need

Above: The Lewis family inside Lime Rock Light, Newport, Rhode Island; *Overleaf:* Great Point Light, Nantucket Island, Massachusetts

the assistance of at least some of the stranded passengers to make it back to the light. On their first try, the father and daughter brought off four men and a woman. They returned with the assistance of two survivors and rescued the four who remained.

To a nation steeped in maritime glory, and embarked upon the Victorian age, Grace Darling became the ultimate heroine. Both she and her father were awarded gold medals by the British Humane Society, and a trust was created to provide an income for the family. Grace received so many requests for locks of her hair that she was in danger of going bald! However, she made few trips off the islands, and remained a distant hero to the British people until she died of consumption in 1842.

The first female light keeper in North America was a Mrs. Thomas, who was tending the Gurnet Point Light at Plymouth, Massachusetts, when the state surrendered control of its lights to the federal government in 1790. But Idawalley Zoradia Lewis was the American counterpart to Grace Darling. She grew up at Lime Rock Light, near Newport, in Narragansett Bay, Rhode Island. "Ida" was hale and

hearty. She rowed her younger siblings to the mainland so they could attend school and helped her father tend the light. Lewis made a number of daring rescues in the 1860s and '70s. Her fame spread, and she was featured on the cover of *Harper's Weekly* in 1869, the same year that President Ulysses S. Grant came to visit her at Lime Rock. She received many marriage proposals by mail, but turned them all down and eventually married a local sailor. The union was not a happy one, and the couple soon separated. Although she remained officially married for the rest of her life, there was no doubt that her true union was with the lighthouse. It is not too much to say that Ida Lewis represented a new brand of heroine and heroism for Americans. To a nation influenced by the Victorian image of what a woman should be — delicate, refined and submissive — Ida Lewis was a bold example of the pioneer spirit.

Less well known than Ida Lewis, but equally brave and competent, was Abigail Burgess of Maine. "Abbie" grew up on Mattinicus Rock, some 34 acres of land 22 miles off the coast from Rockland. Her father, Sam

Burgess, was the keeper of its light. On January 19, 1856, while her father was ashore for supplies, a vicious nor'easter enveloped the island where Abigail, her invalid mother and her sisters remained:

Early in the day, as the tide rose, the sea made a complete breach over the rock, washing every moveable thing away, and of the old dwelling not one stone was left upon another....As the tide came the sea rose higher and higher, till the only endurable places were the light towers. If they stood, we were saved, otherwise our fate was only too certain. But for some reason, I know not why, I had no misgivings, and went on with my work as usual. For four weeks, owing to the rough weather, no landing could be effected on the rock. During this time we were without the assistance of any male member of my family. Though at times greatly exhausted with my labors, not once did the lights fail. I was able to perform all my accustomed duties as well as my father's.

Marcus A. Hanna of Maine's Cape Elizabeth Light became one of the best-known lighthouse heroes of his day. On January 28, 1885, the schooner *Australia* crashed into the rocks just below the light.

Hanna made good time in reaching the ledge where the ship was wrecked, but only two of the crewmen had not been washed away. He made repeated, vigorous efforts to reach these two men, and was awarded a gold medal. Countless other examples of the legendary courage of lighthouse keepers around the world could be given.

The Lure of the Lighthouse

Lighthouses remain an enduring symbol of human courage and fidelity. Although twentieth-century improvements in navigation technology have made many of the sturdy old towers obsolete, we see growing concern for their preservation as part of our national heritage. Emma Lazarus captured this spirit in her poem on the Statue of Liberty, which concludes: "I lift my lamp beside the golden door." From the Pharos to Eddystone, and from beach bonfires to lights kindled by mineral oil and electricity, the lighthouse has served as a sign of aspiration and assurance. It remains an object of beauty in a world that is all too often purely functional.

Beach and Sandbar Towers

"The most prominent points of a line of coast, or those first made on oversea voyages, should be first lighted; and the most powerful lights should be adapted to them, so that they may be discovered by the mariner as long as possible before his reaching land."

— ALAN STEVENSON

The Scottish engineer Alan Stevenson emphasized the importance of "making lights" in his classic *Rudimentary Treatise on the History, Construction and Illumination of Lighthouses* (1850). He wrote with the confidence and authority of the leading engineer of his family, which had already designed two of the greatest lighthouses of the century: Bell Rock and Skerryvore. The Stevensons had also designed and shipped lighthouses to remote locations including Japan and India. The British Isles, however, have a greater need for reef, rock and cliff headland lights than for those designed for sandy foundations, and the family's expertise was greatest for the conditions they encountered at home.

American and Canadian engineers, who would soon be leading the way in lighthouse construction, had a wide variety of locations that required making lights, including challenging coastal sandbars and sandy lowlands like those of the Southeast region's coastline.

Today, we have a detailed understanding of the geological factors that enter into the evolution of sandbars and beaches. Sedimentary deposits brought by both oceans and rivers cause the gradual build-up of wide, shifting coastal zones. Wave erosion steadily removes and redistributes the sediment. In some areas, when erosion outweighs deposition, sandy coastlines recede over time, while in other areas the reverse is true.

Most of the East Coast has what is called a "trailing edge" coastline, which is geologically stable because it is not at or near the edge of a tectonic plate, and therefore not at risk of earthquake activity. These were the beaches and dunes that greeted some of the first Europeans who came to North America.

On the West Coast, seismic activity adds further instability to the shifting foundations of beach areas.

Previous pages: **Cape May Light, New Jersey;** *Above:* **Old (left) and New (right) Cape Romain Lights, McClellanville, South Carolina**

The engineers who built the early lighthouses did not have the advantage of knowledge of these geological features, with the consequent engineering implications, so their expertise was gained by trial and error.

A lighthouse built to guide mariners to shore from the open sea must be visible over the maximum achievable distance in order to be effective, as Alan Stevenson emphasized. This was especially crucial before the advent of other navigational aids like radar. The light source must be at a sufficient height to thwart the earth's curve for visibility at a distance. Therefore, lighthouses designed for visibility at maximum distance are placed on cliffs and headlands wherever possible, since the tower's base is already well above sea level. However, on low-lying shores lacking any cliffs or highlands, the lighthouse building itself must be tall (ideally, approximately 150 to 170 feet) in order for its light to be effective in darkness or poor visibility, or to be clearly visible from afar as a daymark.

As a result, the construction of making lights in low-lying sandbar locations poses the combined technical challenges of building tall—and therefore relatively heavy—structures on unstable foundations. They must be able to withstand exposure to the steady onslaught of the elements. In addition to height, the towers need minimal wind and wave resistance: Thus, they were usually built in cylindrical or conical forms.

The first areas of North America that were settled by European colonists included regions with long sandy coastlines. One thinks of the *Mayflower* anchored off today's Provincetown on Cape Cod, Massachusetts, where the Pilgrims signed the Mayflower Compact, and of Plymouth itself. Boston and nearby Newport, Rhode Island, as well as the sandy areas of New Jersey, follow a similar pattern of low-lying coastal shores and barrier islands with miles of beachfront. From the Pilgrim and Puritan settlements in New England and the Mid-Atlantic region to the Dutch and Swedish colonies in New York and Delaware, early mariners reached the New World on the Atlantic coastal plain. Spanish colonists came ashore as early as 1565 and founded St. Augustine in what is now Florida, where long stretches of beach and sandy soil also predominate.

Crude bonfires built along the shores probably served as the first coastal lights for these colonists. They seemed to suffice for the first eighty years, during which time the English population in North America grew to some 200,000 settlers. But as population and trade among these settlements increased, especially in the Northern colonies, the need for safe navigation grew apace. We can only guess as to how so many of the early passenger ships did manage to make it safely into port; the odds were usually against it.

Boston, Massachusetts, was the first North American town to make lighthouse construction a priority. Located on Little Brewster Island in the outer part of Boston Harbor, Boston Light was first lit in 1716, marking a milestone in maritime safety for the New World. Thirty years later, the beacon at Brant Point on Nantucket Island was put into service.

As technology improved and the population grew, many lighthouses were constructed along the shores of New Jersey and Delaware. Cape May Light, finished in 1859, at the northern entrance to Delaware Bay, is a good example of the slender, elegant towers built in the mid-nineteenth century in that region. Barnegat Light on New Jersey's Long Beach Island is a 172-foot tower that was completed in 1859 under the auspices of the Lighthouse Board.

The Mid-Atlantic and Southern shores developed less rapidly, and lighthouse construction did not occur on a similar scale until much later than in the Northeast. John Smith and the first English settlers in the Mid-Atlantic region reached the Chesapeake Bay area in 1607. "Heaven and earth never agreed better to frame a place for man's habitations," wrote Smith, the adventurer and pamphleteer of his generation. It was an agreeable location, and if there were considerable hazards for mariners to negotiate, there were also favorable harbor conditions: The current waters were so deep at Jamestown that ships could ride at anchor while tied by lines to trees. The bay consists of a series of drowned river valleys, and its tidal range varies from some 6 feet at the entrance to a level of change that is barely perceptible in the northern parts. Inside the mouth of the estuary, a series of islands, inlets, bays, coves and peninsulas demands careful navigation.

Kommetjie Light, Cape Town, South Africa

Those early colonists had to be excellent sailors, because the region did not receive its first light until 1792—Old Cape Henry Light, at the southern entrance to Chesapeake Bay. The original 90-foot tower at Cape Henry was completed in less than a year, using freshly quarried sandstone. Cracks began to appear by the 1870s, and a new cast-iron cylindrical tower was completed in 1881. The two towers stand today, vivid testimony to the engineering skill of two very different generations, almost ninety years apart.

With the development of screwpile technology in the late 1840s, several such lighthouses were constructed on Chesapeake Bay. The screwpile foundation, developed in England, consisted of up to eight long steel legs with large screws at either end. These legs were screwed deep into the ocean floor; then foundation-bearing rods were screwed into the top of the legs. This technology worked best when the legs could be drilled into solid rock or compacted sand. It was inadequate for shifting sand and unsuitable for cold climates, because the foundations proved vulnerable to floating ice. A more substantial foundation than the screwpile was achieved by adding large piles capable of supporting layers of granite upon which foundations could be laid. This method proved suitable for construction on sandbars and low-lying islands.

Chesapeake Bay marks the dividing line between the Mid-Atlantic region, which required medium-to-short towers placed on headlands as well as some taller structures, and the Southern region, where very tall towers were and are required to cast a light far enough to be useful. Many of these elegant towers are especially attractive because of the distinctive patterns and colors painted to make them effective daymarks.

The Southeast has the highest percentage of sandbar and beach lights because it has few highlands, so American architects and engineers were challenged to refine ways of rooting and anchoring lighthouses in the sand. Cape Hatteras Light, located on the Outer Banks of the North Carolina seashore, is the classic example of a beacon designed for this type of location. The light guides sailors around the treacherous reefs of the Diamond Shoals; by day, its black-and-white spiral bands are visible for miles.

Coastal erosion has threatened Cape Hatteras Light from the beginning. The second time the light was built, in 1870, it was placed more than 200 feet from the water, but constant wave erosion eventually made dangerous encroachments. In the late summer of 1999, the Cape Hatteras Light was moved farther inland.

Florida has the longest coastlines of any American state except Alaska. When the United States added Florida to the Union in 1819, there may have been one light, at Spanish St. Augustine, but that was all. This peninsular state also lagged far behind its Northern counterparts in shipbuilding and trade; one study indicates that in 1800, St. Augustine was visited by only twenty oceangoing ships while Charleston, South Carolina, received more than 800. Although explored by Europeans as early as 1542, Florida received its lighthouse system much later than the rest of the East Coast. It was the U.S. Navy that recognized the importance of improving marine safety on this coastline in the early nineteenth century, and during the 1830s and '40s numerous lights sprang up on both the east and west coasts. St. Augustine Light was put into service in 1824 and Cape Florida Light followed in 1825.

The Space Race of the 1960s made Cape Canaveral a well-known name. More than a century before, a 65-foot brick tower had been completed on the cape, in 1848. However, like St. Augustine Light to the north, it was known for the weakness of its light. In fact, many ship captains who were grounded on the shoals while searching for the light complained that they would be better off if Cape Canaveral had no light at all. The beacon was replaced in 1868 by a 145-foot tower that still stands. This second light attracted much interest both abroad and at home.

A second burst of lighthouse construction occurred in Florida during the dozen years prior to the outbreak of the Civil War. Army Lieutenant George Gordon Meade (1815–72) supervised the building of several lights, the most advanced of which was the one at Carysfort Reef, Key Largo, built in 1848 on a screwpile foundation. Meade oversaw the construction of the 110-foot iron skeleton tower, which still remains today. Its smooth, slim bars and open interior allow wind and waves to pass through with a minimum of resistance, easily surpassing the stability of the solid cylindrical and conical steel or masonry towers in this respect. Meade also designed the Jupiter Inlet Light, completed in 1860, with the future Confederate general Robert E. Lee acting as surveyor.

The size and power of the Mississippi Delta provides different conditions in the Gulf of Mexico. No fewer than three lights were placed at different exits from the delta during the nineteenth century, but all of them lost their usefulness because of the accumulation of sediment. The Louisiana coast displays one of the highest annual rises of sea level: Grand Isle, Louisiana, shows a yearly increase of 3.7 inches; Galveston, Texas, comes close with a rise of 2.4 inches; and Port Isabel, Texas, shows an increase of 1.4 inches per year.

The Gulf Coast presents a surprising variety of shores. There are beaches, rocky areas, and many bays and inlets that once served as lairs for pirates like the infamous Jean Lafitte. There are relatively few towers in this region, and most of these were constructed after 1820. Almost all of the prebellum lighthouses were disabled by Confederate troops during the Civil War, after which it took years to "relight" the Gulf.

The U.S. Navy established one of the first lights on the Gulf of Mexico in 1824 at Pensacola, on Florida's Gulf coast. This lighthouse was needed to guide the ships that were commissioned to clear the region of pirates, and Pensacola, with its excellent natural harbor, was an obvious choice. The original 45-foot tower, built on a sandy spit outside the harbor entrance, was replaced by a 160-foot brick tower in 1858. This second tower has withstood many hurricanes and even a Union bombardment during the Civil War.

The Sand Island Light at Mobile, Alabama, a mighty 150-foot brick tower, was completed in 1859 by Thomas Leadbetter, an army officer and engineer in charge of all fortifications on the Gulf Coast. A mere two years later, to prevent its use by Union forces, Confederate general Leadbetter sent a raiding party to blow up the very light he had built. The second tower on this site was completed in 1873. During the 1906 hurricane, the

Cape Hatteras Light, North Carolina

Above: **Alki Point Light, Seattle, Washington;** *Opposite:* **Assateague Island Light, Virginia**

light, its keeper, his wife and their house were swept out to sea. Still another tower was built to mark the hazardous island; this tower stands today.

Bolivar Point Light in Galveston, Texas, was first built in 1852, but it fell victim to Confederate troops during the Civil War. A second light was finished in 1872, and the 117-foot tower became a place of refuge for Galveston citizens during the hurricane of 1900. Hurricane Katrina caused devastation to a number of Gulf Coast lighthouses in August 2005, sweeping away structures and altering the coastline itself.

Spanish sailors were the first Europeans to encounter the dangers of navigating the coast of California. However, Spanish settlement was confined largely to the Franciscan Missions, and there was no parallel to the commercial growth of the East Coast during the Spanish era. Lighthouse construction on the California shores began only after the Gold Rush of 1849 and the subsequent population boom. Farther north, Russian traders and missionaries visited the shores of present-day Alaska and British Columbia, but their sailors had to navigate without lighthouses.

The Pacific shoreline is a "leading edge" coast, located where the oceanic edge of one tectonic plate converges with the continental edge of another. Therefore, it is at a high risk for earthquake activity. Erosion prevails over deposition here, creating rugged, craggy cliffs that endure waves of tremendous strength. With these highlands along the Pacific shores, the tall cylinders of the low-lying East Coast regions are rarely necessary. Few West Coast lights of the United States or Canada exceed 50 feet in height.

The Great Lakes contain a larger percentage of beach lights than any area except the Southeast. The shores of these lakes have been worn down through millennia of coastal erosion, and the action of frost and ice during the severe winters. However, conditions are no match for the ocean coasts, where the mighty surfs and tidal waves engulf and shift beaches at a much more significant rate. The lighthouses of this region are featured in chapter 5.

In spite of the diversity of lighthouse shapes and sizes, the brightly painted, soaring cylinders of those designed for sandbar locations are, for most of us, the "classic" lighthouse, as seen on the following pages.

Little Sable Point Light *Opposite*

Mears, Michigan

The tall conical light at Little Sable Point was constructed in 1874 to mark a sandy headland on this lightly populated stretch of the Lake Michigan coast. The 107-foot tower matched its counterpart 30 miles to the north, Big Sable Point Light. Although the tower at Big Sable Point has been modified over the years, Little Sable remains virtually unchanged. Its materials were transported to the site by water. Built of red brick, which was originally whitewashed, the tower retains its original third-order lens and the light is still in service. During the 1950s, the lighthouse was automated and the keeper's dwelling demolished. Its location made this beacon a reference point for ships bound for the growing port of Chicago. Other lighthouses on the shores of the Great Lakes are featured in chapter 5.

Currituck Beach Light *Above*

Corolla, North Carolina

Along with its more famous neighbors, Cape Hatteras Light and the tower at Bodie Island, the Currituck Beach Light was erected by the Lighthouse Board to illuminate the long strip of hazardous coastline along the Outer Banks. The 158-foot-tall conical tower, a classic making light for a sandy location, was completed in 1875. The masonry was left unpainted to distinguish it in daylight from the brightly painted Cape Henry Light to the north and Bodie Island Light to the south. The site also includes a picturesque Queen Anne-style keeper's house and a simple building that is used as a workshop. Now automated, the first-order Fresnel lens flashes a light every 20 seconds that can be seen up to 19 miles out to sea. Today the beacon is maintained by the Outer Banks Conservationists.

Bodie Island Light *Above*

Bodie Island, North Carolina

The distinctively painted lighthouse at Bodie Island is the third on this site. The first was built in 1848 by Francis Gibbons, who went on to design many West Coast lighthouses. The U.S. Treasury did not grant Gibbons a budget to use piles to secure the tower, and the shifting foundations caused it to lean precariously and, eventually, to topple over. Rebuilt in 1859, the second tower was blown up by Confederate troops during the Civil War. In 1872 the third beacon was erected on iron pilings in a granite foundation. Automated in 1931, the 163-foot tower is equipped with a first-order Fresnel lens that casts a light 18 miles out to sea.

Bolivar Point Light *Below*

Galveston, Texas

Discontinued in 1933, the lighthouse at Bolivar Point played an important part in the history of Galveston. Originally built in 1852, the beacon was torn down during the Civil War by Confederate troops, who reforged the cast iron for weapons. A second light was completed on the site in 1872. Standing 117 feet tall, the brick-lined conical, cast-iron structure was equipped with a second-order Fresnel lens. During the hurricane of September 8, 1900, the tower provided refuge for 125 of the town's residents who were able to climb to safety.

Dry Tortugas Light *Above*

Loggerhead Key, Florida

In 1836 the vessel *America* ran aground on the shoals surrounding Florida's Loggerhead Key. The wreck was attributed to the poor quality of the nearby Bush Key (now Garden Key) Light and the lack of a light on Loggerhead Key itself. Completed in 1858 at a cost of $35,000, the 157-foot tower, with its distinctive black and white painted markings, has withstood countless tropical storms and hurricanes to provide a strategic aid to safe navigation ever since. Now automated, its second-order Fresnel lens was replaced with a modern optic in 1986. The flashing white light can be seen at a distance of up to 25 miles at sea.

Cape Henry Old and New Lights *Below*

Virginia Beach, Virginia

The decision to build a lighthouse to mark the entrance to Chesapeake Bay was made as early as 1774. Its construction, however, was interrupted by the outbreak of the Revolutionary War. In 1791 Secretary of the Treasury Alexander Hamilton appropriated $24,077 toward its completion and appointed John McComb contractor. Less than a year later, the 90-foot sandstone pyramidal tower (shown at right, below) was finished. Confederate forces successfully extinguished the light at the beginning of the Civil War, but Union forces restored it by 1862. During the 1870s, cracks began to compromise the structure, and plans were made to construct a new tower. The new building was placed on steadier foundations approximately 350 feet from the original light. Built of cast iron and painted in panels of black and white to make it an effective daymark, New Cape Henry stands 160 feet tall.

Fire Island Light *Left*
Fire Island, New York

The first tower on this site, which is close to the busy port of New York City, was built in 1826. Only 74 feet tall, it was widely believed to provide inadequate warning of the dangerous shoals that lie along the ocean coast of Fire Island. When the freighter *Elizabeth* ran aground in 1850, losing most of her crew, Congress was prompted to organize the Lighthouse Board to monitor all lighthouses in the United States. Shortly after its creation, the Lighthouse Board authorized the construction of a new tower on this site. Standing 180 feet tall, the black-and-white striped beacon at Fire Island is equipped with a first-order Fresnel lens whose light is visible up to 25 miles out to sea. The flashing light earned the lighthouse the affectionate nickname "Winking Woman." Decommissioned in 1974, the tower has since been restored and relighted by a local preservation society.

Isla Contoy Light *Opposite*
Quintana Roo, Mexico

A national wildlife park and bird sanctuary, Isla Contoy lies near the larger Isla Mujeres off the busy resort of Cancún, on the eastern coast of the Yucatán Peninsula. This island of sand dunes is fringed by treacherous coral reefs, and its location in the Caribbean Sea makes it vulnerable to hurricane-force storms each year. Cancún is Mexico's most popular tourist destination and a frequent stop for cruise ships.

Mijas Costa Light *Page 52*
Andalusia, Spain

This handsome tower of local stone, attached to a tile-roofed keeper's dwelling, overlooks the coast near the entrance to the Mediterranean Sea, a route plied by ships since Phoenician times.

Cousins Shore Light *Page 53*
Prince Edward Island

Originally part of the Cape Tryon Light, the beacon at Cousins Shore was moved to its current location during the 1950s. It is now used as a cottage.

Point Prim Light

Prince Edward Island

The lighthouse at Point Prim is located on the south shore of Prince Edward Island and marks the long peninsula that juts into the Northumberland Strait. Completed in 1846, the 60-foot tower's focal plane is 69 feet above sea level. The whitewashed conical tower—the oldest of this shape on the island—was designed by Sir Isaac Smith in 1845. Automated in 1969, the tower emits a flashing white light that can be seen up to 20 miles at sea.

Barnegat Light *Opposite*

Barnegat, New Jersey

Winslow Lewis built the first lighthouse on Long Beach Island, the low-lying barrier island off the coast of central New Jersey, in 1835. Almost twenty years later, lighthouse expert George Meade declared the tower structurally inadequate for this exposed site. His criticism fell on deaf ears though, and the light remained unaltered. Less than a year later, a storm destroyed Lewis's tower. The 172-foot beacon that stands on the site today was constructed in 1859 under the supervision of the Lighthouse Board at a cost of $45,000. The first-order Fresnel lens, visible up to 30 miles at sea, cost an additional $15,000. To avoid destruction by future storms, the tower has two concentric walls, the outer of which is 4 feet thick. Called "Old Barney," Barnegat Light was decommissioned in 1944.

Sandy Hook Light *Above*

Sandy Hook, New Jersey

Sandy Hook Light has the honor of being the oldest continuously operating lighthouse in the United States. First lit on June 11, 1764, with a system of 48 wicks, the beacon was later equipped by its creator, Winslow Lewis, with an Argand lamp. In 1857 a third-order Fresnel lens was installed. Strategically located on a narrow point projecting 5 miles into New York's Lower Bay, the lighthouse was built to encourage trade via New York Harbor and was known originally as the New York lighthouse. After years of conflict between New York and New Jersey as to who should control the light, it was taken over in 1790 by the federal government. Today, Sandy Hook remains an important navigational aid and displays a fixed white light that can be seen 20 miles out to sea.

Lynde Point Light *Opposite*

Old Saybrook, Connecticut

When the first tower on this site at the western entrance to the Connecticut River was built in 1803, it was lit with whale-oil lamps. Because it was often obscured by low coastal fog and mist and was not tall enough to be visible at a distance, the original 35-foot-tall octagonal wooden tower was replaced in 1838 with a sturdy 65-foot pyramidal stone tower. Now automated, the fifth-order Fresnel lens displays a fixed white light that can be seen up to 14 miles at sea. A fog bell was added to the complex in 1854.

West Point Light *Above*

Seattle, Washington

Since it was put into operation in November 1881, the 23-foot square-shaped lighthouse at West Point has marked the promontory at the northern entrance to Seattle's Elliot Bay. Located at the foot of Magnolia Bluff in what is now Discovery Park, the beacon guides vessels through this heavily trafficked part of Puget Sound. The stucco-covered West Point Light is equipped with a complex fourth-order Fresnel lens that displays an alternating red and white light, which can be seen from more than 15 miles away.

Nauset Beach Lighthouse

Eastham, Massachusetts

This site on the Atlantic Coast of Cape Cod was first lighted by three wooden towers known as the Three Sisters. Originally the north tower of the twin lights at nearby Chatham, the Bureau of Lighthouses had the Nauset Beach Light building moved from Chatham in 1923 to replace the remaining wooden tower at Nauset. Standing 48 feet tall, the conical cast-iron tower has its focal plane 114 feet above sea level. The light was relocated again in 1996, when coastal erosion threatened the site. Now automated, the red-and-white tower makes an effective daymark.

Monomoy Island Light *Below*

Monomoy Island, Massachusetts

Monomoy Point is located on the southern end of Monomoy Island, which is a long, narrow island south of the coast of Cape Cod at Chatham, projecting into Nantucket Sound. The first lighthouse on this exposed site was built in 1823. It was rebuilt in 1855 and again during the 1870s. No longer an active aid to navigation, the light at Monomoy Island is now part of the Monomoy National Wildlife Refuge, and is the property of the U.S. Fish and Wildlife Service.

Old Field Point Light *Opposite*

Stony Brook, New York

Deactivated in 1933, Old Field Point Light marked the entrance to the natural harbor of Port Jefferson on Long Island's north shore. Mainly frequented by pleasure boaters, this harbor is also used as a terminus for the passenger ferry to Bridgeport, Connecticut. This beacon is the second lighthouse on the site, one of many navigational aids on a stretch of coastline characterized by numerous inlets, bays, rocks and reefs. The first light, built in 1823, was replaced with the current tower, which is similar in design to several contemporaneous lights in the area, in 1868.

West Point Light *Page 64*

Prince Edward Island

The black-and-white striped, square pyramidal tower at West Point was the first light built on Prince Edward Island by the Department of the Marine. Completed in 1875, scenic West Point Light stands on the southwestern tip of the island and was manned until 1963 by just two successive keepers: William MacDonald guarded the light from 1875 to 1925, and Benny MacIsaac served from 1925 until 1963. Standing 58 feet tall, its focal plane is 67 feet above sea level, making it the tallest square-shaped lighthouse on Prince Edward Island. Its flashing white light is visible from up to 12 miles at sea. Originally red-and-white striped, the tower's colors were changed to black and white by the Canadian government in 1915.

Great Point Light *Page 65*

Nantucket Island, Massachusetts

Every 5 seconds the third-order Fresnel lens of the Great Point Light flashes alternate white and red lights that warn sailors away from the dangerous waters surrounding Nantucket Island. Located on the southern end of the island, the first tower was built on this site in 1785. After burning to the ground in 1816, it was rebuilt two years later as the existing 60-foot rubblestone beacon at a cost of $7,400. A third-order Fresnel lens was installed in the lighthouse in 1857. A storm destroyed the 1818 light in 1894, and in 1986 this white-painted landmark was reconstructed farther inland. The Great Point Light is now a part of the Coatue Wildlife Refuge.

Sheffield Island Light *Above*

Norwalk, Connecticut

Restored and maintained since 1986 by the Norwalk Seaport Association, the Sheffield Island (once called Smith Island) Light is now part of a wildlife refuge. The two-story stone tower, one of a series built on the shores of Long Island Sound to a similar design, was built in 1868, the second lighthouse on the 53-acre site; the first was completed in 1826. After marking the entrance to the channel into the Norwalk River for almost two-thirds of a century, Sheffield Island Light was decommissioned in 1902, when the nearby Greens Ledge Light was constructed.

Block Island North Light *Opposite*

Block Island, Rhode Island

The 50-foot-tall Block Island North Light is the third lighthouse to mark Sandy Point, a dangerous sandbar that extends several miles north of the island. The first tower was built in 1829 and was 40 feet tall. In 1837 it was moved one-quarter of a mile inland. In 1857 a new tower was built on the site; it was replaced in 1867 with the existing building. The gray granite building is two stories high and served sailors approaching both Long Island Sound and Narragansett Bay. Automated in 1955, the light was decommissioned in 1973 and purchased by the U.S. Fish and Wildlife Service. In 1984 the town of New Shoreham bought the lighthouse and restored and relit the light with a federal grant five years later.

Cliff Lights

"The elevation of the lantern above the sea should not, if possible, for sea-lights, exceed 200 feet; and about 150 feet is sufficient, under almost any circumstances, to give the range which is required. Lights placed on high headlands are subject to be frequently wrapped in fog, and are often thereby rendered useless, at times when lights on a lower level might be perfectly efficient. But this rule must not, and indeed cannot, be strictly followed, especially on the British coast, where there are so many projecting cliffs, which, while they subject the lights placed on them to occasional obscuration by fog, would also entirely and permanently hide from view lights placed on the lower land adjoining them. In all such cases, all that can be done is carefully to weigh all the circumstances of the locality, and choose that site for the lighthouse which seems to afford the greatest balance of advantage to navigation."

—ALAN STEVENSON

Cliffs and rocky coasts have long posed challenges to lighthouse builders and engineers, yet their prominence and height above sea level make some cliffs ideal locations for navigation lights. Many hazardous areas in Europe remained unlit for generations because engineers could not find a way to properly site and mount a lighthouse. On level or gently sloping headlands, access to cliff-edge lighthouse sites was simple. But on rocky, inaccessible cliffs with steep approaches from all angles, construction was necessarily problematic. With rare exceptions, these latter locations had to manage without lighthouses until the middle and second half of the nineteenth century, when technical advances in the design and materials used, including pulleys, screws and cables, allowed for easier hauling of masonry, wood and steel—and laborers—to the sites.

Previous pages: **Cape Disappointment Light, Fort Canby State Park, Washington;** *Above:* **Cape Forchu (Yarmouth) Light, Nova Scotia**

Roughly three-quarters of the world's continental and island margin areas are made up of rocky coastlines, often with concomitant strong tides, huge waves and high cliffs. In polar and subarctic regions, floating ice impedes waves and disperses some of their strength. Coral reefs have a similar effect. The characteristics of a coastline depend on a combination of the surf's strength and the type of rock involved, whether igneous, sedimentary, or metamorphic: Each type erodes in different patterns.

The West Coast of North America has high cliffs that are continuously eroded by the force of wave action traveling virtually unimpeded across the Pacific Ocean. Earthquake activity also destabilizes the coastline, where rock slides are common, especially along the mountainous coast of California. The shores of northern New England, where the Appalachian range approaches the ocean, are also characterized by rocky cliffs, notably in Maine. Newfoundland's coastline is similarly rugged.

The earliest cliff lighthouses on the continent were built on sites located on headlands and promontories with ready access for building. Several of these were constructed on the Maine coast. Portland Head Light, finished in 1791, is an 80-foot tower built on a 20-foot elevation, placing its light at 100 feet above sea level. It provides a welcome beacon for sailors entering Casco Bay. Pemaquid Point Light, built in 1827, warns sailors away from the dangerous rock formations of this site. Although it is only 38 feet tall, the light's focal plane is 80 feet above sea level, allowing for ample range.

The Twin Lights of Navesink, New Jersey, on the Atlantic Highlands, are another example of early cliff lights. Maritime traffic has entered New York Harbor for centuries, some vessels docking in Manhattan and others making their way up the Hudson River, as shown in Henry Hudson's log of exploration in 1609. U.S. lighthouse administrators recognized the need for a clear, strong signal in this region. Although New Jersey's Sandy Hook Light, finished in 1764, was already in place, its lantern was not sufficiently high above sea level to serve the purpose.

Two rubblestone towers were constructed on the Highlands at Navesink in 1828 to mark the western

Above: **West Quoddy Head Light, Lubec, Maine**

entrance to New York Harbor. Despite their height— 246 feet above sea level—ship captains complained that the lights were inadequate. It was not until 1840, when Commodore Matthew C. Perry brought the first two Fresnel lenses from France to Navesink, that a major improvement occurred. From then on, the entrance to New York Harbor became known as one of the best-lit in the world (later, the Statue of Liberty would serve for a time as another harbor light for Manhattan Island).

Alan Stevenson's 1850 treatise on lighthouse construction included the advice that: "Views of economy…should never be permitted to interfere with placing [a lighthouse] in the best possible position; and, when funds are deficient, it will generally be found that the wisest course is to delay the work until a sum shall have been obtained sufficient for the erection of the lighthouse on the best site." During the thirty years prior to 1850, considerations of economy had prevailed in the American lighthouse establishment, largely because of the influence of Stephen Pleasonton, the Fifth Auditor of the U.S. Treasury. Pleasonton had prevented the introduction of Fresnel lenses for as long as possible, always finding ways to skimp on building materials for new lighthouses. His decisions often resulted in false economies, as seen at the "Leaning Light" of Bodie Island (discussed in chapter 1). The funding situation changed, however, when the new Lighthouse Board was created in 1852.

Composed of nine unpaid but well-qualified members, the Lighthouse Board began by dividing the nation into twelve districts, the first of which started at the border between Maine and New Brunswick, Canada, and the last encompassing the entire West Coast, where new research and surveying were needed urgently.

The acquisition of the western coastal states of California, Oregon and Washington in the second half of the nineteenth century presented engineers with a new and significantly different topography and geology. With the sole exception of the light in the old Russian fortress at Sitka, Alaska, the West Coast of the United States and Canada was as yet unlit: There were no existing navigational aids—and no major population centers—along this vast shoreline. The waters of the Pacific build tremendous strength in transit, and the surf slams into the coast with great force, carving high cliffs from mountainous and plateau areas from California up to British Columbia. What vacationers view as wonderful scenery was anything but for nineteenth-century mariners, and countless ships were lost along these shores. Navigational aids were imperative, and planners had to find suitable locations, disallowing sites that were undercut by wave action, or particularly subject to rock slides and erosion.

Two men played important roles in shaping the American lighthouse system on the West Coast. Ammi B. Young, an architect and engineer for the Lighthouse Board, designed compact lighthouse buildings that combined the keepers' quarters with the light itself, in the form of a Cape Cod-style dwelling with a short tower rising through the roof of the house. These structures were relatively simple, but there was often a problem in siting them and securing foundations adequate for stability and wind resistance.

Major Hartman Bache, who built the nation's first screwpile lighthouse in Delaware Bay in 1852, went west to pave the way for the new construction commissioned by the Lighthouse Board. A man of rare energy and foresight, he surveyed and sketched many areas where the first lights on the West Coast would be built, often at considerable elevations. Old Point Loma Light, built in San Diego in 1855, is only 40 feet tall, but it stands 460 feet above sea level. One of the region's first lights, Old Point Loma was deactivated in 1891 and replaced with an iron skeleton tower. Construction began in 1899 on the Point Sur Light, at Big Sur—a formidable challenge. By 1891 the builders had completed a 40-foot granite tower atop the cliffs with a focal plane 250 feet above sea level.

Point Reyes, 20 miles north of San Francisco, stands precariously on a 250-foot cliff and still displays its first-order Fresnel lens. The area is shrouded in fog for up to 110 days a year (a problem common to many cliff locations), and several keepers voiced their dissatisfaction with the site. "Solitude, where are your charms?…Better dwell in the midst of alarms than in this horrible place," wrote one of them in 1885.

Point Arena Light stands on a rugged cliff created by movement of the San Andreas Fault line. The first tower was built here in 1870, but the earthquake of 1906—which devastated San Francisco farther south—destroyed the station. A new 115-foot tower was finished the same year, this one buttressed against seismic activity by walls of reinforced concrete.

Point Cabrillo Light at Mendocino, California, was built in 1909. Only 47 feet high, it stands on a site 422 feet above sea level, making this the highest light in the United States. Both the light and its fog signal were vital for ships carrying lumber from Mendocino to San Francisco in the early part of the twentieth century.

As one travels north from Mendocino, the terrain becomes even more rugged. Trinidad Head Light occupies a jagged cliff face some 200 feet above the Pacific, and Battery Point (or Crescent City) Light, Oregon, illuminates some of the most beautiful scenery—and the most dangerous waters—along the West Coast. Cape Blanco Light is on the westernmost site in the Lower 48 states. Named by Spanish sailors

for its white cliffs, Cape Blanco received its light in 1870. The 59-foot conical tower has a focal plane 245 feet above sea level. Perhaps even more commanding is Heceta Head Light, in Florence, Oregon. It took two years and $180,000 to build the station, which houses a first-order Fresnel lens. Popular with photographers and tourists, Heceta Head is one of the most-admired scenes on the West Coast.

Tillamook, Oregon, is the site of a major achievement in American engineering. Tillamook Rock, rough and sheer, overlooks the most dangerous part of the Oregon coast. Here Pacific waters meet the powerful currents of the Columbia River estuary, creating a turbulent sea with record-breaking waves. It took weeks for surveyors to get a single man ashore to take measurements with a pocket tape measure. The builders then installed a derrick with a long boom, so that materials could be hoisted to the summit. Even so, it took from October 1879 until January 1881 to construct the tower, which is only 48 feet high. Every year it is assaulted by massive storms. In 1886 an official document reported that "the sea from the south-west broke over the rock, throwing large quantities of water above and on the building [a height of 150 feet]. The roofs on the south and west sides of the fog-signal room, and on the west side of the building, were crushed in."

Opposite: **Gay Head Light, Martha's Vineyard, Massachusetts;** *Above:* Nantucket Island Light, Massachusetts

The mouth of the Columbia, the West's greatest river, is roughly four miles wide. Lewis and Clark arrived here in December 1805, but it was not until 1856 that Cape Disappointment received its lighthouse. The nearby North Head Lighthouse was completed in 1898, making this one of the best-lit estuaries in the world. Even so, the Cape Disappointment Coast Guard Station performs many life-saving missions each year, because sailors underestimate the power of this mighty confluence.

Countless vessels have foundered in the waters off the treacherous coast of the Pacific Northwest. The rugged terrain here made it almost impossible for nineteenth-century engineers to build lighthouses using existing methods, and lack of settlement made their construction less of a priority. Public outcry over the tragic wreck of the passenger steamer *Valencia* in 1906 was the catalyst needed for the U.S. and Canadian governments to begin work on beacons here.

Although there were some towers in British Columbia, including Vancouver's Cape Beale Light (1874) and Queen Charlotte's Egg Island Light (1874), large stretches of this irregular coastline were shrouded in darkness. Plans to build a light station on Vancouver Island's Pachena Point—the site of the fatal wreck of 1906—were quickly drawn up, and construction began within months. The combination of the treacherous cliff location and violent storms made construction a difficult—at times, an impossible—task. After more than a year of work, the nearly completed light was swept out to sea in one such storm. The construction team remained determined to emplace a light here.

Equipped with a first-order Fresnel lens, the lighthouse at Pachena Point went into service on May 21, 1908. Standing 188 feet above sea level, the tower emits a light that can be seen up to 35 miles at sea. The first keeper of the beacon at Pachena Point was John Richardson, who was joined by his sister and assistant, Gertrude. The remote location and isolation bred severe depression, and in the fall of that same year, Gertrude threw herself from the cliff to her death.

Although the volcano-born Hawaiian Islands were acquired by the United States in 1898, the Lighthouse Board did not assume responsibility for Hawaii's navigational aids until January 1, 1904. At this time,

Hawaii, which had nineteen primitive lighthouses, became a sub-district of the Twelfth Lighthouse District. Many of the existing towers were fitted with Fresnel lenses; others were rebuilt. More were constructed, including a number of notable cliff lights.

The isolated beacon at Kilauea Point was built on the island of Kauai in 1913 to service ships voyaging between the United States and the Orient. The 53-foot conical tower is located on a 180-foot-high promontory—the most northerly point of the principal islands. On the island of Oahu stands Makapu'u Point Light, built in 1909 to guide eastbound maritime traffic. Not only is the site 420 feet above sea level, but the 46-foot tower was equipped with a 12-foot-high Fresnel hyperradiant lens with an inside diameter of 8.5 feet, which is among the largest in use today. Automated in 1974, the light is visible for up to 28 miles at sea.

While large stretches of America's East Coast are low-lying, some crucial lights were built at well-known sites on cliffs and headlands. One example is Block Island Southeast Light, erected in 1875. Built in the Victorian Gothic style, Block Island Southeast was moved farther inland when the Mohegan Bluffs became eroded by the Atlantic. The lighthouse itself is only 67 feet high, but the cliffs give the first-order Fresnel lens an elevation of some 260 feet above sea level—the highest on the East Coast. Its location in Long Island Sound, at the entrance to busy Block Island Sound, makes it extremely important to mariners. During the notorious hurricane of 1938, the dedicated lighthouse keepers turned the lens by hand for several days to alert seamen to the dangers here. The Mohegan Bluffs continued to erode throughout the twentieth century, and in 1994 the lighthouse building was moved 200 feet west to its present location.

Newport, Rhode Island, remains one of America's prime attractions for yachtsmen and other pleasure boaters. Castle Hill Light marks the entrance to this busy harbor. Built into the side of the cliff on the southeastern entrance to the harbor, it has a long and interesting history. The prominent naturalist Alexander Agassiz (1835–1910) refused to allow a light station on his strategically located property. In response, steamboat captains painted the rugged cliffs white in order to

Magdalen Islands Light, Quebec

provide a point of reference visible by night. A light was finally built on this site in 1890. A working navigational aid today, its fifth-order Fresnel lens flashes a red light at 42 feet above sea level.

Maine's Bass Harbor Head Light, on the southwest side of Mount Desert Island, is justly considered one of the handsomest lighthouses in North America. The compact brick tower guards the entrance to Bass Harbor and is perched on a cliff that lifts the lantern's focal plane 56 feet above the water. Located near beautiful Acadia National Park, Bass Harbor Light is still equipped with its original fourth-order Fresnel lens.

Atlantic Canada displays a highly variable coast, ranging from the sands along the Bay of Fundy and Prince Edward Island to the glacier-molded rock of Cape Breton Island and Newfoundland. One of the most famous Canadian lighthouses is Peggy's Cove, located at the entrance to St. Margaret's Bay, just south of Halifax, Nova Scotia. While the cliff height here is not remarkable, immense Devonian granite ledges and boulders distinguish the site. Legacies of the last Ice Age, these formations are some 400 million years old. A massive monument to the generations who have made their living from the sea depicts thirty-two fishermen, their wives and children, a guardian angel and the legendary Peggy, for whom the village was named.

The changing coast of Atlantic Canada features sandy shores and rolling pastures alongside steep cliffs, as seen in the province of Prince Edward Island. Located on the northeastern tip of the island, the East Point Light was built in 1867 to overlook the dangerous confluence of the Gulf of St. Lawrence and the Northumberland Strait. The 65-foot wooden tower is perched on a steep cliff that places its focal point more than 100 feet above sea level. Three years after a British warship was wrecked in these treacherous waters in 1882, the octagonal light was moved farther west to provide greater visibility at sea. In 1908, threatened by severe erosion, the lighthouse was moved farther inland. A fog-alarm building was also added at this time. One of Prince Edward Island's last lights to be automated, the beacon at East Point continues to guide ships safely through these waters.

Lighthouses were constructed on steep cliffs and craggy outcroppings across the continent during the late nineteenth and early twentieth centuries, as trade and populations grew. Although these towers were often deceptively simple in design, the isolated and dangerous locations of many made it particularly hazardous to build them. Determined engineers and builders braved the elements to construct the beacons, many of which still signal mariners today.

Pemaquid Point Light *Previous pages*
Damariscotta, Maine
Constructed in 1827 to mark the entrance to St. Johns Bay, Pemaquid Point Light is easily recognized by the unusual striated rock formations that surround it. Carved from glacial ice, the rock is a dangerous hazard to mariners. The first lighthouse on the site was built during John Quincy Adams's presidency at a cost of $4,000. Rebuilt in 1857, the tower was equipped with a fourth-order Fresnel lens. The 38-foot tower has its focal point 79 feet above sea level.

Battery Point (Crescent City) Light *Left*
Crescent City, California
Congress designated Crescent City as a lighthouse site in 1856 because it was one of the most important lumber centers on the West Coast. Outfitted with a fourth-order Fresnel lens, the simple Cape Cod-style dwelling guided ships safely through the treacherous waters that characterize this area. In fact, much of the redwood that passed through this harbor was used to build San Francisco. The light—isolated on its rocky site—was kept by Captain John Jeffrey and his family from 1875 until 1914. Automated in 1953, the tower was discontinued in 1965. Maintained by the Del Norte County Historical Society, the beacon was relit in 1982 as a private aid to navigation. Today the station houses the Battery Point Light Museum, which can be reached by visitors at low tide.

Amphitrite Point Light *Overleaf*
Vancouver Island, British Columbia
Located on the west-central shore of Vancouver Island, the light station at Amphitrite Point was established in 1915. The unusual tiered tower overlooks the entrance to Barkley Sound. Poised on a craggy outcropping 51 feet above sea level, the tower emits a light that can be seen 16 miles at sea.

Owls Head Light *Left*
Rockland, Maine

Perched on a steep cliff, 30-foot-tall Owls Head Light stands more than 100 feet above sea level. Built in 1825–26 to guide freighters carrying limestone into Rockland Harbor, the squat tower—which gained its name from the owl-like formation visible in the cliff face—remains largely unchanged. The cylindrical beacon is equipped with a fourth-order Fresnel lens that casts a fixed white light visible up to 16 miles at sea. During the 1930s, the keeper owned a spaniel named Spot. The dog learned to sound the fog bell by pulling on the rope when he heard a boat approaching.

Beavertail Light *Page 84*
Jamestown, Rhode Island

The tower on Rhode Island's Conanicut Island is the third on this site. The first was built in 1749, but it was burned by the British during the Revolutionary War. The lighthouse was restored to service in 1790. The present tower dates from 1856. Originally equipped with a fourth-order Fresnel lens, the 52-foot square granite tower marks the entrance to Newport Harbor and Narragansett Bay. In 1991 Beavertail Light was outfitted with a modern optic that emits a flashing white light.

Portland Head Light *Page 85*
Portland, Maine

On January 10, 1791, George Washington appointed Captain Joseph Greenleaf the first keeper of the Portland Head Lighthouse—Maine's first light and the first to be built under the auspices of the U.S. government. Construction on this historic tower had begun in 1787; in 1791 the light was equipped with a second-order bivalve lens and put into service. As technology advanced, the bivalve was replaced with a fourth-order Fresnel lens that was automated in 1989. Two years later, Portland Head received a new optic with a modern revolving beacon. This emits a flashing white light that is visible up to 25 miles at sea. Standing 80 feet tall, the graceful masonry lighthouse stands 101 feet above the entrance to Casco Bay.

Seacow Head Light *Previous pages*

Prince Edward Island

Built in 1863, Seacow Head Light is located on the south shore of Prince Edward Island. The white octagonal tower is 61 feet tall, but its location places the focal plane 90 feet above sea level. Its flashing white light can be seen up to 12 miles at sea. Overlooking Northumberland Strait, the beacon at Seacow Head was eventually moved farther inland to protect it from erosion of the cliff face.

Covehead Harbour Light *Opposite*

Cape Stanhope, Prince Edward Island

The Covehead Harbour Light overlooks the beach at Cape Stanhope in Prince Edward Island National Park. The 27-foot wooden tower stands 34 feet above sea level and guides traffic on the Gulf of St. Lawrence. The red-and-white pepper-shaker-style lighthouse emits a flashing white signal that can be seen for up to 7 miles. The building also serves as a program center of the national park.

Cape Byron Light *Overleaf*

Byron Bay, New South Wales, Australia

Constructed of prefabricated concrete by Charles Harding, successor to James Barnet as the colonial architect of New South Wales, the lighthouse at Cape Byron was completed in 1901. The 59-foot tower is 387 feet above sea level and has the distinction of being Australia's most powerful lighthouse. Henry Lepaute, of the Parisian *Société des Establishment*, equipped the beacon with a first-order optical lens comprising some 760 pieces of prism glass. Visible up to 27 miles at sea, Australia's easternmost light emits a flashing white signal every 15 seconds.

Ponta da Piedade Light *Below*

Lagos, Algarve, Portugal

Located on the southern coast of Portugal, the town of Lagos overlooks the Gulf of Cádiz. The area is renowned for its picturesque beaches, many of which are surrounded by eroded cliffs. The Ponta da Piedade Light stands on the outermost point of the rugged Ponta da Piedade promontory.

Split Rock Light *Opposite*

Two Harbors, Minnesota

This majestic light overlooks Lake Superior in Split Rock Lighthouse State Park. Materials for its construction had to be hoisted up the towering 120-foot cliffs. Completed in 1910, Split Rock Light is equipped with a third-order bivalve-type Fresnel lens that emits a fixed light visible up to 22 miles away. The lens comprises 252 different panels and weighs more than 4 tons. No longer an active aid to navigation, the light shines every year on November 10 to commemorate those who were lost in 1975 on the *Edmund Fitzgerald*.

Point Cabrillo Light *Above*

Mendocino, California

Point Cabrillo Light was built in 1909 to mark the entrance to California's Big River. Equipped with a third-order Fresnel lens, the 47-foot tower stands 422 feet above sea level, making it the highest lighthouse in the United States. Automated during the 1970s, the light was later replaced with an airport-style beacon, after which it slowly fell into disrepair. Developers had chosen the site for construction of fifty-five houses when the California Coast Conservancy rescued the light and restored it to its former beauty.

Head Harbour (East Quoddy) Light *Below*
Campobello Island, New Brunswick

Easily identified by its huge red cross, what Americans refer to as East Quoddy Light and Canadians call Head Harbor Light stands on the northern end of rugged Campobello Island, which is perhaps better known as the location of the summer residence of Franklin Delano Roosevelt and his family. The light station was built on the rocky outcropping in 1829 and marks the international boundary between Canada and the United States. Now automated, the 45-foot octagonal tower emits a fixed red signal. The lighthouse is accessible only for two hours at low tide; visitors can easily become stranded at the light when high tide returns at the alarming rate of five feet per hour. Like many of Canada's lights, East Quoddy is marked with a red cross.

Cape Neddick Light *Opposite*
York, Maine

Rutherford B. Hayes signed the order establishing the Cape Neddick Light in 1879. The 40-foot-tall cast-iron tower is on a rocky island affectionately referred to by locals as "the Nubble." Standing 88 feet above sea level, the tower is connected to the keeper's dwelling by a covered walkway. The picturesque cottage was designed in the Victorian style and built in the shape of a cross. Local pilots overflying the site check their directions on the north-south axis of the house. On January 12, 1923, the *Robert W.* was wrecked on the dangerous submerged rocks here. Keeper Fairfield Moore sprang into action and rescued Captain Mitchell and his son Stanley. Automated in 1987, the beacon emits a flashing red light.

East Point Light *Previous pages*
Prince Edward Island

Originally located on the easternmost point of Prince Edward Island, this light overlooks the confluence of the Gulf of St. Lawrence and Northumberland Strait. Built in 1867, the 65-foot white tower was moved in 1885 to provide better visibility. The erosion of the cliffs threatened the lighthouse, and in 1908 the octagonal wooden structure was moved farther inland. A fog-alarm building was added that same year. Today the light stands some 100 feet above sea level. One of the last on the island to be automated, East Point flashes a white signal visible up to 20 miles.

Bass Harbor Head Light *Above*
Mount Desert Island, Maine

Located in what is now Acadia National Park, the Bass Harbor Head Light was built to guide traffic entering Blue Hill Bay and Bass Harbor. The original tower and attached keeper's dwelling, built in 1858, still stand. Clinging precariously to the cliff face, the beacon displays a flashing red light every 4 seconds.

Point Conception Light *Opposite*
Lompoc, California

The original lighthouse at Point Conception (1855) was one of the first sixteen lights built on the West Coast of the United States. Located high on a headland, its tower rose through the roof of the keeper's dwelling. When cracks began to appear in the structure, a new light was built on a lower site. Now 133 feet above sea level, its beacon is visible for 26 miles. For some years, Point Conception and Pigeon Point were the only lights along this dangerous part of the Pacific Coast.

Cape Blanco Light *Opposite*

Port Orford, Oregon

Oregon's oldest continuously operating and southern-most lighthouse was first lighted on December 20, 1870. The conical brick tower at Cape Blanco is 59 feet high, but its steep vantage point places it 245 feet above sea level. The white cliffs here—named for their color by the Spanish—give the beacon its name. Originally equipped with a first-order Fresnel lens handmade in Paris by the renowned Henry Lepaute, Cape Blanco was equipped with a second-order rotating lens whose light is visible up to 22 miles at sea. The U.S. Coast Guard assumed control of the light in 1939.

Fisgard Light *Above*

Victoria, British Columbia

Located on the west side of Esquimalt Harbour on Vancouver Island, the Fisgard Light was built in 1860 with brick shipped from Great Britain. This was British Columbia's first official lighthouse, funded by the British Empire's Board of Trade like other Canadian "Imperial Lights." Standing 72 feet above sea level, the 56-foot cylindrical tower is attached to a Victorian-style dwelling, both of which were designed by John Wright. Constructed upon a granite foundation 2 feet thick, the station has 4-foot-thick brick walls. Named for the British frigate *Fisgard*, the light went into service on November 16, 1860, under the supervision of George Davies. The flashing red, white and green signal was automated in 1929. Still operational, Fisgard now has an aero-marine beacon and is located in the Fisgard Lighthouse National Historic Site.

Block Island Southeast Light *Above*

Block Island, Rhode Island

The Block Island Southeast Light was built in 1875 at a cost of $75,000. The 67-foot octagonal brick tower stands on the Mohegan Bluffs, placing its focal plane more than 200 feet above sea level. Equipped with a $10,000 first-order Fresnel lens made by the Parisian Henry Lapaute Company, the beacon emits a flashing green signal. In 1993 the Victorian lighthouse and attached dwelling were moved 300 feet inland to protect them from erosion.

Highlands (Navesink) Lights *Opposite*

Highlands, New Jersey

Overlooking the Lower Bay, the Twin Lights of Navesink were built of brownstone in 1841 to guide ships into New York Harbor. The first lighthouses in the United States to employ Fresnel lenses, the beacons made Sandy Hook Light obsolete. One of the 200-foot-tall octagonal towers exhibited a flashing light and the other, a fixed light. The north tower was discontinued in 1894, when authorities began to phase out paired lights. The south tower was extinguished in 1953, but it has a small sixth-order light to commemorate the importance of this historic site.

Point Bonita Light *Opposite*

San Francisco, California

The Point Bonita Light was built to guide ships entering San Francisco Bay through the narrow Golden
Gate Straits. The first lighthouse was erected on a ledge
more than 300 feet above water level in 1855. Mariners
complained that it was often obscured by fog and low-
lying clouds, so in 1877 this second tower was constructed on a dangerously narrow ledge 124 feet above
sea level. The 33-foot tower is accessible only by a
wooden suspension bridge.

Cape Arago Light *Above*

Charleston, Oregon

Two miles southwest of Coos Bay, the Cape Arago light
is the third to stand on this site. The first, built in 1866,
was an iron tower designed to guide ships entering
Oregon's thriving lumber port of Charleston. When
erosion threatened, the tower was replaced with a
wooden light. In 1934, when erosion encroached again,
the present lighthouse was constructed. Made of concrete, the 44-foot octagonal tower was equipped with a
fourth-order Fresnel lens. Standing some 100 feet above
sea level, the light is visible up to 16 miles at sea. The
lighthouse is reached by an iron footbridge.

Old Cape Spear Light

St. John's, Newfoundland

Located 20 miles east of Newfoundland's capital, St. John's, the Old Cape Spear Light was built on the easternmost point in North America and marks the entrance to St. John's Harbour. The picturesque station was the second in the province and the first built under the direction of the Newfoundland Lighthouse Board. The light stands in the center of the dwelling, 300 feet above sea level on a sandstone cliff. In 1955 the Old Cape Spear Light was moved farther inland and replaced with the New Cape Spear Light, an octagonal concrete structure. Old Cape Spear Light is now the centerpiece of the National Historic Park that was opened in 1983 by Great Britain's Prince Charles and Diana, the late Princess of Wales.

Shipwreck (Naufrage) Point Light *Above*

Naufrage, Prince Edward Island

The 48-foot pyramidal tower at Shipwreck Point stands
99 feet above sea level in an open field on the north
side of Prince Edward Island. The picturesque white
lighthouse is one of two concrete towers on the island.
Built in 1913 to guide ships through Naufrage Harbor,
the tower was repaired and moved west in 1968. Its
flashing white light can be seen 18 miles at sea.

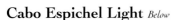

Cabo Espichel Light *Below*

Lisbon, Portugal

The picturesque Cabo Espichel Light is located in Lisbon, the capital city of Portugal and the country's most important port. Lisbon's magnificent natural harbor made the area a strategic trading center from Phoenician times; legend tells that the city itself was found by Ulysses. Carefully maintained, the pyramidal light tower overlooking the Mar de Palha is surrounded by a cluster of whitewashed buildings.

Cape Tryon Light *Overleaf*

Prince Edward Island

Built in 1865, the original Cape Tryon tower and keeper's house were relocated because of erosion. The present lighthouse was built in 1905. Automated in 1965, the 39-foot square wooden tower overlooks the Gulf of St. Lawrence, where it provides a welcome beacon to traffic passing along the north side of Prince Edward Island. The Cape Tryon Light stands 117 above sea level; its flashing white light can be seen 18 miles at sea.

Trinidad Head Light *Above*
Trinidad, California

Fred Harrington was the keeper of the Trinidad Light in 1940 when a giant tidal wave swept over the tower, which is located on a 200-foot cliff. Inside the lighthouse, Harrington hung on for dear life as water rushed in through the broken windows. Despite the force of the wave, the tower survived the onslaught. Built in 1871 to guide traffic into and out of Trinidad Harbor, Trinidad Light is now automated.

Heceta Head Light *Previous pages*
Florence, Oregon

Named for the Spanish explorer Don Bruno de Heceta, who charted this area in 1755, the jagged cliffs at Heceta Head posed a tremendous challenge to nineteenth-century engineers. Materials had to be transported to the site by boat and hoisted up the 200-foot cliffs. The 56-foot tower was completed in 1894 at an exorbitant cost of $180,000. Equipped with its original first-order Fresnel lens, which casts a light visible for 21 miles at sea, the Heceta Head Light continues to guide traffic along the Pacific Coast.

Point Sur Light *Opposite*
Big Sur, California

Point Sur Light stands on a near-vertical sandstone cliff. Engineers constructed a special railway to transport materials to the site for construction of the lighthouse, which took two years and $100,000 to build. Completed in 1889, the beacon at Point Sur warns mariners of the Big Sur coastline, a treacherous outcropping that extends south for 100 miles. The granite light clings to a precarious site more than 250 feet above sea level. Its original first-order Fresnel lens is now on display at the Monterey Station Center. Weighing 3 tons, the lens is 10 feet tall and 6 feet in diameter, comprising more than 1,000 prisms. Point Sur is now equipped with an automated aerobeacon that flashes every 15 seconds and is visible 25 miles at sea.

Lobster Cove Head Light *Above*

Gros Morne National Park, Newfoundland

The picturesque lighthouse at Lobster Cove Head was built in 1892 to guide ships entering Newfoundland's rugged Rocky Harbour. Located in what is now Gros Morne National Park, the cylindrical white-painted beacon, which is attached to a two-story keeper's residence, has served generations of the island's fishermen. It was automated in 1970.

Fort Amherst Light *Opposite*

St. John's, Newfoundland

Built on top of the Fort Amherst Harbour battery in 1813, the Fort Amherst Light was Newfoundland's first navigational aid, built and maintained by voluntary contributions. It was constructed to mark the entrance to the Narrows—the channel that connects the Atlantic Ocean to St. John's Harbour. The original wooden tower was replaced in 1852 and again in 1951.

Admiralty Head Light *Below*

Whidbey Island, Washington

The first lighthouse above the Straits of Juan de Fuca on Whidbey Island was completed on Red Bluff in January 1861, just weeks before the outbreak of the Civil War. Equipped with a fourth-order Fresnel lens, it guided vessels through Admiralty Inlet into Washington's Puget Sound. Its fixed white light was visible up to 16 miles away. The tower was demolished during the Spanish-American War for construction of Fort Casey. In 1903 the present Spanish Colonial-style complex was built 127 feet above water on Admiralty Head, near Coupeville. During World War I, it was used as an officers' residence for U.S. Army personnel. After shipping routes changed, the light became obsolete, and in 1927 the tower was darkened and its lantern placed in the New Dungeness Light. Today the Admiralty Head Light, acquired by Washington State, has been restored to its former beauty with the help of the Island County Historical Society.

Cape Elizabeth Light *Opposite*

Portland, Maine

Two rubblestone towers were built on Cape Elizabeth in 1828 to mark the entrance to Portland Harbor from Casco Bay. They were replaced in 1874 with a pair of cast-iron towers separated from each other by 300 yards. During the 1920s the west tower was decommissioned. The east tower's second-order Fresnel lens continues to serve as a navigational aid, with a focal point 129 feet above the water. The picture opposite shows the light (which was immortalized by Edward Hopper) before it was totally remodeled in 1999.

Rua Reidh Light *Overleaf*

North West Highlands, Scotland

Built in 1910 by David Stevenson, a cousin of Robert Louis Stevenson, Rua Reidh Light is located on a remote peninsula in Scotland's North West Highlands. Now automated, the tower overlooks the Minch, the channel separating the Outer Hebrides from the mainland.

Long Point Light *Above*
Twillingate, Newfoundland

Newfoundland's Long Point Light is attached to a fog-horn building by a covered walkway. Perched on a rocky ledge some 280 feet above the entrance to Notre Dame Bay, the red-and-white lighthouse is located off the northeast corner of Twillingate. The site extends into the "iceberg corridor," where the Titanic met with disaster. It provides visitors with a stunning view of gigantic icebergs floating by. They are seen most frequently during the months of June and July.

Cape Bonavista Light *Opposite*
Bonavista, Newfoundland

Cape Bonavista Light was built in 1843 to mark the entrance to Trinity and Bonavista Bays. John Cabot first sighted the headland known as Cape Bonavista from H.M.S. *Matthew* on June 24, 1497. The massive red-and-white striped lighthouse was deactivated in 1966, when it was replaced by a nearby steel tower. The brightly painted original Cape Bonavista Light is now a Newfoundland Provincial Historic Museum.

Swallowtail Light *Overleaf*
Grand Manan Island, New Brunswick

The octagonal white Swallowtail Light was built on New Brunswick's Grand Manan Island in 1860 to mark the entrance to the Bay of Fundy. Now automated, the sturdy tower is still an active aid to navigation. The nearby former keeper's house is now a picturesque bed-and-breakfast inn.

Inlet and Harbor
Channel Guides

Previous pages: **Marshall Point Light, St. George, Maine;** *Above:* **Grindel Point Light, Isleboro, Maine**

"Being thus arrived in a good harbor, and brought safe to land, they fell upon their knees and blessed the God of Heaven who had brought them over the vast and furious ocean, and delivered them from all the perils and miseries thereof, again to set their feet on firm and stable earth, their proper element."

—WILLIAM BRADFORD

Thus the future governor of the Pilgrim settlement at Plymouth, Massachusetts, recorded the historic landing of the Mayflower. His journal *Of Plimoth Plantation* (1620–47) gives some idea of the hardships involved in seventeenth-century sea travel and the relief experienced in finding safe harbor. Such havens have been important since travel and commerce by sea became a part of human history. Many people are familiar with the stories of Greek and Phoenician sailors who found their way around the Mediterranean Sea in ancient times by dead reckoning. They became expert at gauging the wind and waves, and they found accessible harbors in southern Europe, the Middle East and on numerous islands. Since these ports were unmarked, it took a combination of luck and skill to deliver cargo and passengers safely. The Phoenicians kept their routes a secret in order to maintain a monopoly on trade in the Mediterranean.

Lighthouses built for in-harbor locations are sometimes overlooked, even by lighthouse aficionados, because they are usually less exposed than clifftop lights, and do not dominate their surroundings as a tall beach light does. Given a choice among New England's Minots Ledge, Portland Head and Derby Wharf Lights, all within the radius of a day's drive, the lighthouse fancier will often choose the most dramatic or remote—in this case, Minots Ledge. But should one travel to Salem's Derby Wharf, he or she will be rewarded with a site that can be seen and explored at close range.

Harbor lights became important during the Middle Ages, when Italian city-states like Venice, Genoa and Pisa built beacons of dense, nonporous stone to guard the entrances to, and guide vessels into, their enviable harbors, the primary source of their wealth. In fact, some historians assert that without the stimulus provided by those city-states and their Mediterranean trade, the Italian Renaissance would not have occurred.

Antonio Columbo, the uncle of Christopher Columbus, kept Genoa's Lanterna, the most celebrated Italian lighthouse, in 1449. Perhaps he told his nephew seafaring tales that helped inspire the historic voyage of 1492.

One of the most long-lived harbor-entrance towers was the one at Boulogne, northern France. First built by order of the notorious Emperor Caligula, and rebuilt during the time of Charlemagne, the Tour d'Ordre (English sailors called it "the Old Man of Bullen") was an octagonal stone shaft twelve stories high and 124 feet above sea level. Its upper levels grew progressively smaller, like those of a ziggurat. This lighthouse served off and on until 1644, when it collapsed.

Both of the first lighthouses built in the Americas marked entrances to harbors. The famous Morro of Havana, Cuba, was constructed around 1563, and rebuilt in 1763 and 1845. Today it is a UNESCO World Heritage Site. The Santo Antonio Light in Salvador, Brazil, was built by the Portuguese government in 1698, as part of the colony's first fortress. Now painted in bold black and white bands that make it an effective daymark, and fitted with a powerful halogen light, it remains a major South Atlantic landmark.

Among the vital requirements for a functional harbor are: sufficient water depth at low tide to accommodate vessels; shelter from storms and heavy surf; and a navigable route to ensure safe passage between the harbor and open water. In sandy areas, regular dredging may be required to maintain harbor channels. Rocky locations may have numerous submerged rocks and reefs that must be marked with warning lights and buoys. Few harbors have ideal navigating conditions, and each poses its own set of challenges for maintenance and safety.

The world's most successful port cities have developed along the banks of easily navigable rivers, like London, or on exceptional natural harbors. The sheltering islands surrounding the Hong Kong Harbor make its conditions for ready access and secure shelter for a large number of ships almost ideal. Lisbon, Portugal's capital city, is built on hills overlooking a protected bay several miles long. Antwerp, Belgium's largest port—one of the world's busiest—is located on a long, protected inlet. New York City's harbor has the dual advantage of shelter from the New Jersey coast and the western side of Long Island. French colonists chose Louisbourg Harbour on Nova Scotia's Cape Breton Island because it was one of the few inlets in that area that did not freeze in the winter.

Considering the diversity of natural conditions at these and countless other harbors and inlets along our shores, it should come as no surprise that the lighthouses stationed there display so much variety in their styles and sizes. From the monumental making lights at harbor or inlet entrances, like Boston Harbor and Ponce de Leon Inlet Lights, to breakwater markers, as at Spring Point Ledge, Portland, Maine, to unique monuments including the Statue of Liberty, navigational aids of all descriptions can be found at or near harbors and along their entrance channels.

Boston Light, on Little Brewster Island in Boston Harbor, was the first lighthouse built in North America. Blown up by the British during the Revolutionary War, Boston Light was rebuilt in 1783 and is now the only manned lighthouse in the United States. Boston Harbor and Massachusetts Bay itself are littered with islands and reefs and subject to heavy storms. The light was provided with walling more than 7 feet thick at the base during the reconstruction of 1783.

Old Yaquina Bay Light, Newport, Oregon

Fort Point Light, San Francisco, California

The second North American light of which we have certain knowledge was built by the French to guard the entrance to the harbor at Fortress Louisbourg on Cape Breton Island, off Nova Scotia. Completed in 1733, it succumbed to fire in 1736 and was rebuilt as a concrete, fireproof structure. This tower overlooks the historic fortress—recently restored to its original condition, when this was one of the Eastern Seaboard's three largest ports. In 1745 New England farmers and fishermen joined a British fleet to besiege and capture Louisbourg. Its light was destroyed in 1758, but it was rebuilt in 1833 and remains an important symbol of the opening of Eastern Canada, much as Boston light is symbolic of early New England.

British-American colonists built eleven other lights prior to the American Revolution. Nearly all of them were at or near harbors, indicating the importance of commerce to the early colonists. Brant Point Light guarded the south side of Nantucket Harbor; Tybee Island Light guided sailors into Savannah; Beavertail Light stood at the entrance to Narragansett Bay. Connecticut's New London Light was built in 1760; New Jersey's Sandy Hook Light guarded busy New York Harbor (as it does today); South Carolina's Morris Island Light marked the entrance to Charles Town (later Charleston) Harbor; and Plymouth and Portsmouth Lights illuminated their respective harbors in Massachusetts and New Hampshire. Meanwhile, British Canada built a light on Sambro Island, at the entrance to the harbor of Halifax, Nova Scotia. The red-and-white octagonal tower still stands.

New England continued to build harbor lights as its post-Revolutionary commerce flourished. The first New Haven Harbor Light was established in 1805. The island light at Scituate, Massachusetts (1811), indicated the coastal harbor there, and the 1820s saw construction of important new markers for the ports of Newport, Rhode Island, and Stonington, Connecticut. In busier ports, additional lights and markers were installed gradually to improve navigation along the heavily used or most hazardous channels. Portland, Maine's largest port, had four lighthouses when Ram Island Ledge Light was activated in 1905.

The acquisition of new areas of coastline in the nineteenth century created the need for additional harbor lights. From Florida to Texas, the Gulf Coast presented numerous challenges to architects and builders. The Gulf Coast is more irregular than that of the Atlantic, with countless inlets, both estuarial and tidal. Even the great Gulf ports of Pensacola and Mobile result from a whole series of inlets rather than comprising natural harbors. This holds true all the way to the Mississippi Delta.

Alabama's Mobile Point Light has been built three times: in 1822, 1873 and 1966. A series of barrier islands and reefs force ships to enter Mobile Bay through the narrow channel that runs past Mobile Point. The original 55-foot brick tower here served its purpose until 1864, when Union gunners blasted it and Fort Morgan to bits at Admiral David Farragut's famous command: "Damn the torpedoes; full speed ahead!" After the Civil War, an iron skeleton tower was erected on a bastion of the fort (1873). This structure, now lying on its side, was replaced in 1966 with a tall skeleton tower.

On the Pacific Coast, harbor lights to guide vessels into the increasingly busy San Francisco Bay area were the first priority of the Lighthouse Board in 1852. Fort Point Light was completed in 1853, and Alcatraz Island Light went into service the following year. The Bay Area also acquired Point Bonita light (see chapter 2), on the Golden Gate Strait, in 1855.

Meanwhile, construction of lighthouses at harbors and inlets continued on the East Coast. Derby Wharf Light in Salem, Massachusetts, one of three lights to guide traffic into Salem's inner harbor, was finished in 1871. Placed at the end of the famous Derby Wharf (self-named for the nation's first millionaire), the short square tower resembles a brick box. Ironically, it was built after the heyday of Salem shipping; it stands today (relighted in 1983) as part of the Salem Maritime National Historic Site.

By contrast, the new light that rose in New York Harbor in 1886 was celebrated for its beauty as a monument. The Statue of Liberty served as a lighthouse for more than twenty years. Steamboats, tugboats, ocean liners, fishing trawlers—all vessels making port in New York City were greeted by this regal gift from France.

The need for harbor and channel lights on the Great Lakes increased as inland waterways multiplied. The first lighthouse of record at Buffalo, New York, was built in 1818. Just seven years later, completion of the Erie Canal made Buffalo a major port, and construction of a new beacon was planned. Finished in 1833, the octagonal limestone lighthouse stands at the end of a 1,400-foot pier. Other growing ports on the Great Lakes that were illuminated during this period include Toronto (Gibraltar Point, 1808) and Chicago (1832). As the century progressed, lighthouses were built to mark harbors all along the Great Lakes' shores.

The mid-nineteenth and early twentieth centuries saw the addition of many lighthouses in Canada. Halifax, Nova Scotia, was the greatest Canadian harbor and port of the time. Comparable to New York City in terms of immigration, Halifax received 96,000 newcomers from abroad in 1913, the same year that immigration to the United States was at its peak. Halifax itself had a population of only 46,000 at the time. Marking the entrance to Halifax Harbour, the Chebucto Head Light was built in 1872. On a breakwater nearby stands Maugher Beach Light, built in 1828 and also known as Halifax Harbour Middle Range. In the middle of the harbor itself is Georges Island Light, an octagonal white tower that illuminated this site from 1876.

Vancouver, British Columbia's most flourishing port city, had several lighthouses to mark its major hazards and shipping routes by the early twentieth century. Atkinson Point Light, built in 1875 and rebuilt in 1910, stands at the harbor entrance. Prospect Point Light lies 3 miles farther along the channel, and the inner-harbor lighthouses include Brockton Point (1890) and Capilano Point (1908). This deep, sheltered harbor is one of the best natural havens on the continent, but its dangerous rocky approaches had to be identified clearly before it could reach its full potential for maritime commerce and, more recently, leisure boating.

In addition to the wide variety of lighthouses featured on the following pages, North America's harbors and inlets are made safer by the myriad buoys, daymarks, range lights, sound signals and other navigational aids (see chapter 8) that guide ships in and out to open water. Radar, radio and digital satellite systems have greatly reduced the importance of lighthouses for commercial vessels. Today, both merchant ships and passenger vessels use them to make their way to harbor and inlet entrances. However, when navigating through narrow channels and preparing to dock by night, lights remain vital. And for the thousands of pleasure boaters whose craft lack sophisticated equipment, safe passage still relies upon lighthouses, as it did for the sailors of earlier times.

Boston Harbor Light *Previous pages*

Little Brewster Island, Massachusetts

The first lighthouse built on the mainland of North America, Boston Light stands on Little Brewster Island, at the outer extremity of Boston Harbor. First built in 1716 by order of the Massachusetts legislature, it stood until the Revolutionary War, when it was blown up by retreating British soldiers. Rebuilt soon after, this was one of the nation's key beacons until Boston's importance as a port of entry was superseded by that of New York City. Standing 75 feet above sea level, Boston Harbor Light has withstood more than two centuries of winds and weather. Its historic significance was recognized in 1989, when Congress voted to keep the lighthouse manned: Today it is the only one in the United States that has a permanent keeper.

Morgan Point Light *Above*

Noank, Connecticut

The U.S. government built the first lighthouse on this peninsula that marks the mouth of the Mystic River in 1832. The native Mohegan called the land "Naiag," which means "a point." Because of increased commerce, this granite tower was replaced in 1868 by a second granite beacon, outfitted with a light imported from Germany. The three-story structure combines the keeper's dwelling with the lighthouse and reflects Noank's transition from a simple fishing community to a modest seaside resort, as seen in the decorative Eastlake decoration that adorns the light's gable. Discontinued in 1922, the light was replaced with an automatic electric beacon. Today, the Morgan Point Light, listed on the National Registry of Historic Places, is privately owned.

East Point (Maurice River) Light *Below*

Delaware Bay, New Jersey

Built in 1849 to mark the entrance to the Maurice River from Delaware Bay, the East Point Light was called the Maurice River Light until 1913. The two-story lighthouse, one of New Jersey's oldest, guided oyster schooners traveling to Port Norris and Port Elizabeth. During World War II, the simple Cape Cod-style structure was used as an aircraft spotter post. After almost a century of service, the light was deactivated in 1941; it was later restored and eventually reactivated, in 1980. The building's exterior was further restored in 1998, and work on the interior is still ongoing. There are plans to open a maritime museum and wildlife center at the site.

Elbow Reef (Hope Town) Lighthouse *Overleaf*

Elbow Cay Harbour, Abaco, Bahamas

As England's maritime trade increased, it became necessary to construct lighthouses along the shores of her colonies, including the islands of the Bahamas. Some native Bahamians objected to this decision because they had come to depend on salvaging the cargo of wrecked ships. The British identified the need for a lighthouse at Hope Town—the site of countless wrecks—to guide sailors around the dangerous Elbow Reef. The candy-cane-striped tower was completed in 1864 and equipped with a standing wick-type light. In 1936 London's Imperial Lighthouse Service moved the first-order Fresnel lens from the Gun Cay Light to the Elbow Reef Light. The fixed light can be seen up to 17 miles at sea. Maintained today by the Bahamas Lighthouse Preservation Society, the mechanically operated light is one of three kerosene-powered lighthouses in the world.

Spring Point Ledge Light *Below*

Portland, Maine

One of four lighthouses along the rocky passage to the harbor at Maine's largest city, Spring Point Ledge Light was completed in 1897 to warn navigators away from a dangerous submerged ledge. The prefabricated cast-iron structure was originally anchored on an isolated caisson that took two years to complete. The light was connected to the mainland by a 900-foot granite breakwater in 1950. Its fifth-order Fresnel lens emits both white and red flashes at an interval of 5 seconds.

Castle Hill Light *Opposite*

Newport, Rhode Island

Castle Hill Light was built in 1890 on the property of the famous naturalist Alexander Agassiz (1835–1910). Believed to have been designed by influential architect Henry Hobson Richardson, this handsome granite structure built into a cliff face is one of many navigational aids for ships making their way into Newport and Providence. Castle Hill Light remains important, especially since Newport became a center for American yacht racing. Countless races have begun there or ended as the lead vessel sails past the lighthouse. Automated by the Coast Guard in 1957, its fifth-order Fresnel lens continues to guide traffic into the main shipping channel of Narragansett Bay.

Newport Harbor Light *Left*

Goat Island, Rhode Island

While Castle Hill and Beavertail Lights guide the mariner into Narragansett Bay, this beacon on the northern end of Goat Island directs traffic into Newport's harbor. Constructed in 1842, the 35-foot octagonal lighthouse is made of granite blocks painted white. It stands on a pier just below Newport Bridge and is one of the first landmarks seen as visitors approach the city. Equipped with a 250mm optic, the tower emits a fixed green light.

Saint John Harbour Light *Page 142*

Market Square, Saint John, New Brunswick

Founded in 1785 by the Loyalists after the American Revolution, Saint John is the oldest incorporated city in Canada. Saint John Harbour is located where the 450-mile-long Saint John River reaches the Bay of Fundy. This confluence causes an extraordinary natural phenomenon called the Reversing Falls. Twice a day, the incoming Fundy tide pushes the river's waters upstream—an impressive sight, as the Saint John River has been referred to as the Rhine of North America. Still one of Atlantic Canada's most important harbors, Saint John embraces a multiethnic heritage including American Loyalists, French Acadians and Irish immigrants. This replica of Canada's many simple clapboard lighthouses commemorates the seafaring heritage of this historic port.

Brant Point Light *Page 143*

Nantucket Island, Massachusetts

Located in Nantucket's sheltered harbor, Brant Point Light has its focal plane only 26 feet above sea level, but its light can be seen from 10 miles at sea. The first light at this spot was built in 1746, to protect Nantucket's whaling ships as they entered the harbor. This was the third light (after Boston and Nova Scotia's Louisbourg) built in British North America. Brant Point was rebuilt in 1759, and the present picturesque salt-shaker-style lighthouse dates from 1901; it stands near its immediate predecessor.

Peggy's Cove Light

St. Margaret's Bay, Nova Scotia

Canada has many remarkable lighthouses, but none as well known or loved as Peggy's Cove, southwest of Halifax, Nova Scotia. The 37-foot octagonal tower was finished in 1868, one year after the Confederation of Canada was formed. The tower is surrounded by large granite ledges that are estimated to be 400 million years old. A monumental stone carving on one of the boulders commemorates the nautical emphasis of life in the Canadian Maritimes. It depicts thirty-two fishermen, their wives and children, and the legendary Peggy. The lighthouse doubles as a post office, and letters sent from here bear a special lighthouse stamp.

Hillsboro Inlet Light *Opposite*

Pompano Beach, Florida

The iron-skeleton tower of this 132-foot lighthouse rises 136 feet above sea level, marking an inlet between Boca Raton and Fort Lauderdale that leads to the Intracoastal Waterway. Prefabricated in a Chicago foundry, the beacon was originally exhibited at the St. Louis Exposition of 1904. Reassembled on Hillsboro Inlet, the black-and-white metal cylinder houses the stairwell to the now automated lantern, which is equipped with a second-order bivalve Fresnel lens. Its flashing white light can be seen 28 miles at sea.

Ponce de Leon Inlet Light *Below*

Ponce de Leon, Florida

This is the second-tallest of all American lighthouses; at 175 feet, it is surpassed only by Cape Hatteras Light at 196 feet. The need for a light here was recorded by the Lighthouse Board during the 1870s, and the work was accomplished between 1884 and 1887. Originally known as Mosquito Inlet, and since 1927 as Ponce de Leon Inlet, this strip of land lies just south of busy Daytona Beach. Prior to construction of this impressive tower, there was no light on the 60-mile stretch of coast between St. Augustine and Cape Canaveral. Discontinued 1970–82, the light was restored and relit in 2004 with a third-order Fresnel lens.

Mystic Seaport Light
Mystic, Connecticut

The Connecticut coast is dotted with narrow inlets, and many famous ships sailed from the small sheltered ports on the eastern shore at Mystic, New London, Groton and Stonington. Today Mystic is foremost among the old whaling towns in maintaining its historic maritime connections. The restored Mystic Seaport welcomes Tall Ships and thousands of visitors and hosts seminars on the age of sail. Its lighthouse, a copy of Nantucket's Brant Point Light, lies 2 miles upriver from Noank at Mystic's whaling harbor.

Mukilteo Light *Left*

Mukilteo, Washington

Built in 1906, Mukilteo Light was designed to guide ships through Possession Sound en route to Everett, Washington, which was then a thriving lumber and railroad center. Located just south of Everett, this 30-foot octagonal wooden tower is one of Puget Sound's many "street lights." Equipped with a fourth-order Fresnel lens, the Victorian-style beacon was also outfitted with a Daboll trumpet, which was used to warn ships during severe weather. Today it is a landmark seen by the many commuters and tourists who take the nearby ferry to scenic Whidbey Island. Everett is one of several harbor towns in the vicinity that never realized their full potential due to the tough competition posed by Seattle's deep-water harbor.

St. David's Light *Overleaf*

Lighthouse Hill, St. David's Island, Bermuda

First lighted on November 3, 1879, St. David's Light was the second and final beacon to be built in Bermuda, the oldest British colony. Only 22 square miles in total area, Bermuda is made up of seven main islands that are located in the middle of the Atlantic Ocean. Cape Hatteras, North Carolina, is the closest land, 600 miles to the west. Constructed of local limestone, the 55-foot red-and-white striped lighthouse was built at the easternmost end of Bermuda. Standing 285 feet above sea level, the tower guides vessels entering Castle Harbour from the Atlantic Ocean. The picturesque lighthouse was recently refurbished.

Hereford Inlet Light *Opposite*

North Wildwood, New Jersey

This unusual Victorian stick-style lighthouse rises 50 feet above sea level in North Wildwood, which was once known as the fishing village of Anglesea. Completed in 1874, the light overlooks a wide inlet leading from the Atlantic Ocean to the Intra-Coastal Waterway. The light was moved from its original location after a severe storm in 1913 damaged the foundation. Hereford Inlet Light was decommissioned in 1964, when an automatic light tower was built nearby. The former station has been restored as a private aid to navigation.

North Rustico Harbour Light *Below*

Prince Edward Island

This picturesque light guards the western entrance to North Rustico Harbour, which serves a small fishing community of Acadian heritage on the northern side of Prince Edward Island. Because of erosion, the 33-foot tower has been moved several times since its completion in 1899. Like the island itself, the area around Rustico Bay is known for its scenic beauty and unhurried way of life. The white light station with bright red trim and its adjoining keeper's dwelling are typical of the lighthouses in the small harbor towns of the island.

Baddeck Harbour Light *Right*

Cape Breton Island, Nova Scotia

Baddeck Harbour Light stands on low ground overlooking the Bras d'Or, the largest salt-water lake on the east coast of North America. The low structure tapers gracefully from base to lantern and marks the resort town of Baddeck, located in the scenic Cape Breton Highlands. Alexander Graham Bell had a summer home here, and Baddeck is a popular point of departure for one of the world's best-known scenic marine drives—the Cabot Trail.

Wave-swept,
Reef and
Island Lights

Previous pages: **Ram Island Ledge Light, Portland, Maine;** *Above:* **Thomas Point Shoal Light, Maryland**

"Lights intended to guard vessels from reefs, shoals and other dangers, should, in every case where it is practicable, be placed seaward of the danger itself, as it is desirable that seamen be enabled to make the light with confidence."
—ALAN STEVENSON

Reefs present one of the greatest hazards to even the most experienced mariners. Only in the nineteenth century was significant progress made in marking these dangerous rock formations, which are often wholly or partly submerged. Early lighthouse engineers could not find a way to emplace structures on wave-swept reefs as they had on coastal headlands.

Alan Stevenson was among the few engineers of his time who knew a great deal about lighthouse construction on reefs and wave-swept islands: His family had specialized in tackling such challenges for more than half a century. But although England, Scotland and France had led the way, architects and engineers from other nations were exploring new paths based on their own terrain and requirements. In North America, these pioneers of the mid-1800s included Captain Barton Stone Alexander and Thomas Albertson Scott, who were instrumental in creating the lights at Minots Ledge, Spectacle Reef, St. George's Reef, Race Rock and others. Lieutenant George G. Meade and Major Hartman Bache were pioneers in developing the screwpile lighthouse. The first protected screwpile light in North America was built in the Delaware Bay at Brandywine Shoals in 1850. It was supported on eight screw-tipped iron stilts, cross-braced and anchored deeply in the sand below water level. Several more lighthouses of this type were built in the Chesapeake region, including at Thomas Point Shoal (1875) and Drum Point (1883). The technology was refined for exposed locations in the Florida coral reefs, including at Carysfort Reef (1852) and Fowey Rocks (1873), by securing large foot plates of iron above the screw tips to provide extra stability.

Wave-swept lighthouses were uncommon until the eighteenth century, but one notable early exception was at Cordouan, off the mouth of the Gironde River in France's Bay of Biscay, where a wooden tower was first erected on a cliff in a group of treacherous rocks and islets during the thirteenth century. It was replaced by a 53-foot stone tower in 1360. More than two hundred years later, renowned architect Louis de Foix began work on a new, elaborate lighthouse that would become one of the world's best known. Construction of this graceful tower, which served as a light, a chapel and a royal residence, was ongoing from 1584 until 1611, and the result was enduring. De Foix's 227-foot tower of ashlar (cut stone) on a wide circular base still stands majestically on its exposed site. The light was registered as a historic landmark in 1862, and it is staffed to this day.

At Eddystone Rocks, off the English port of Plymouth, a wave-swept lighthouse was built in the late seventeenth century. Engineer Henry Winstanley and his workers were rowed daily to the reef, 14 miles from Plymouth, for almost two years to construct the 80-foot tower on this dangerous site. Eddystone Light first displayed its candles in 1698. The tower was destroyed by waves in 1703, and a second, built of wood, was completed in 1709. The second lighthouse burned down in 1755 and was replaced four years later by an interlocking masonry-block tower built by John Smeaton. It is an interesting coincidence that this light was completed in England's *annus mirabilis* — the year when she gained access to an over-seas empire in Canada and India through command of

the seas. This third light at Eddystone stood for more than 120 years before it was dismantled and brought ashore to Plymouth in 1882. The fourth tower was built on an adjacent rock in 1882 and still stands today. Perhaps the best-known of all lighthouses, Eddystone reminds us of the Herculean efforts made by eighteenth-century builders who lacked machine power of any kind.

Scotland came next in the fame of its lighthouses, especially those built on islands and reefs. Robert Stevenson built the historic Bell Rock Light on the east coast between 1807 and 1811. He must have been gratified by the fact that for the rest of his life, no ship was wrecked on the treacherous reef that had claimed some seventy vessels in a single year, 1799. His son Alan Stevenson built Skerryvore on a challenging reef off the west coast of Scotland between 1838 and 1842. This remarkable achievement bolstered the Stevensons' reputation as the world's preeminent lighthouse builders and established Scottish engineering as perhaps the best of its day.

North America's convoluted coastlines, thousands of miles in extent, are dotted with rocks and reefs that can dash a vessel to pieces. The mouth of the St. Lawrence River, gateway to Canada, is filled with such dangers — as is the whole coastline of the Maritime Provinces, and that of Maine. The Pacific Coast and, to a lesser extent, the Great Lakes, present similar hazards to navigation, but the combination of lighthouses and other navigational aids has made maritime disasters like the loss of the *Edmund Fitzgerald* in 1975 comparatively rare. Several factors are responsible for this increase in safety along our coasts.

From colonial times through about 1840, American and Canadian sailors had to rely mainly on skill, luck and good weather. But discoveries in engineering and more accurate charting from the mid-nineteenth century onward fostered the growth of shipping, whaling and allied industries. It was a period of expansion on many fronts, and improved lighthouses and other navigational aids were one sign of the times.

Two towers of the 1850s exemplify the skill and determination of the lighthouse engineers of the age: Bishop's Rock and Minots Ledge Lights. The former is a granite peak 7 miles southwest of the Scilly Isles, off the southwestern coast of England, once the first "making" light seen by most eastbound transatlantic passengers (until Ireland's Fastnet Light was built). Bishop's Rock, some 155 feet long and 52 feet wide, took a heavy toll on passenger ships. British engineers built a 94-foot iron tower between 1847 and 1850, but this was swept away soon after completion. Nicholas Douglass, the engineer in charge, then built a stone coffer dam around the only feasible building site and had the area pumped dry and filled. It took seven years to erect the new 120-foot tower that was lit in 1858, but the result was safer passage for ships bound for the English Channel ports.

At almost the same time, American engineers tackled one of their worst navigational hazards: Minots Ledge, off the southeast side of Massachusetts Bay. A contemporary observer noted that: "These rocks or ledges, with others in their immediate vicinity, are also known as the 'Cohasset Rocks,' and have been the terror of mariners for a long period of years; they have been, probably, the cause of a greater number of wrecks than any other ledges or reefs upon the coast. The Minots are bare only at three-quarters ebb, and vessels bound in with the wind heavy at north-east, are liable, if they fall to the leeward of Boston light, to be driven upon these reefs."

It was decided to build on Outer Minot, the most seaward of the group of ledges. Between 1847 and 1850, Captain William Henry Swift, who had traveled in Europe and become familiar with iron lighthouses, built an octagonal tower 25 feet wide at the base anchored to the ledge by pilings. The bottom half of the structure was open to provide less resistance to the fierce storms called "Nor'easters" that batter the area. Despite all this, a three-day gale in 1851 swept away the tower and two keepers.

The disaster prompted renewed action, because Bostonians had seen a sharp decrease in the loss of ships and lives while the tower stood. Between 1855 and 1860, Captain Barton Stone Alexander supervised the work that resulted in the second Minots Ledge Light. The new structure stood 102 feet high and was built of interlocking iron-braced granite blocks that bonded even more tightly under wave pressure—the same principle used successfully by Smeaton at Eddystone. This lighthouse, which weighs more than 2,300 tons, was automated in 1947.

Other engineers were at work in Florida and on the Gulf Coast. Here, unmarked wholly or partially submerged sandbars, reefs and shoals caused ships to run aground. Lieutenant George G. Meade undertook to build an exposed iron-pile lighthouse on Carysfort Reef, Key Largo, in the northern Florida Keys. A lightship had been on duty there since 1825. Meade's workers drove iron piles 10 feet into the ocean floor. The eight piles were connected by braced cross members and anchored by massive iron discs for stability and resilience. The 110-foot iron skeleton, built in open water directly over the reef, represented a new era in American lighthouse construction. When the light was finished in 1852, its two platforms supported a keeper's dwelling 24 feet in diameter and the lantern, accessed by an enclosed central stairwell. The light has been unmanned since 1960, when battery-charged solar panels were installed.

The American Civil War (1861–65) provided a new impetus for lighthouse development. Existing lights on the Southeastern and Gulf Coasts had been "blacked out" by Confederate forces during the conflict, but nearly all had been restored to operation by 1868. At the same time, thousands of civil engineers became available at war's end, some of whom turned to the construction of navigational aids on locations once thought impossible. The decades between 1870 and 1890 saw major progress in building lighthouses on wave-swept locations. This period also saw a rapid increase in the nation's population and industry, and many navigational aids were needed as a result.

Foremost among the new generation of builders was Major Orlando Metcalfe Poe, who had been the chief U.S. Army engineer on General Sherman's Civil War march through Georgia to the coast. On Michigan's Cheboygan Island, in Lake Huron, Poe set out to create a tower that would protect mariners from the submerged limestone shoals at Spectacle Reef. Blocks of limestone were shipped in from Marblehead, Ohio, and a crib, or wooden case, was towed to the rock, securely bolted by long metal rods and filled with stone to support the lighthouse foundation. Accessible only by boat, Spectacle Reef Light has a base 32 feet in diameter and 11 feet below water level. The tower's focal plane is 97 feet above the lake. Built between 1870 and 1874, the monolithic beacon still stands, 12 miles northeast of Cordwood Point. Automated in 1972, the lighthouse is now solar-powered.

Race Rock Light, near Fishers Island, New York, was also under construction during the 1870s. Francis Hopkinson Smith (1838–1915) was given the challenge of building a light on the underwater reef. He had made a name for himself constructing harbor breakwaters, and he worked at Race Rock with foreman Captain

Thomas Albertson Scott. It took seven years to lay the masonry foundation on the reef—an artificial island of stone and concrete—and build the lighthouse, which comprises a granite dwelling with a square tower attached. Visible for up to 14 miles, the 67-foot tower was equipped with a fourth-order Fresnel lens and went into service on February 21, 1879.

Another new technology that came into use on American shores during the 1870s was the caisson foundation, as seen at Duxbury Pier Light, Massachusetts (1871). First developed in England in 1845, this method of building an underwater foundation involved sinking a shell of plate iron into the sea bed, pumping in air to expel the water, then filling the caisson with concrete, sand or rocks. The process was much quicker and

Above: **Sandy Point Shoal Light, Skidmore, Maryland;** *Overleaf:* **Alcatraz Island Light, San Francisco, California**

cheaper than laying underwater foundations piecemeal and more suitable for northern locations than the screw-pile lighthouses, which could not withstand the ice.

Island lighthouses have played an important role on the East Coast since about 1800. Only two of the original thirteen Colonial lights (Little Brewster's Boston Harbor and Nantucket's Brant Point) were built on small islands, because of the difficulty involved in construction and maintenance. One of the first areas in the U.S. to receive a section, or number, of island lights was the coastal waters off Connecticut and Long Island. Falkner's, Little Gull and Sands Point Islands were lit in 1802, 1806 and 1809 respectively.

Additional lights were erected on small islands between 1815 and the Civil War, when maritime commerce continued to prosper in the northeast. In 1827 Matinicus Rock, some 25 miles off the coast of Maine, received two wooden towers. Rebuilt with stone in 1848, they became the venue for one of the nation's early lighthouse heroines—Abigail Burgess—who, at the age of seventeen, first tended the lights in her father's absence when a storm raged for weeks along this isolated stretch of coast.

Mount Desert Rock Light, 26 miles from Maine's coast, was first lit in 1830. Mount Desert Rock was considered one of the most exposed (and loneliest) assignments in the Lighthouse Service. An important "making" light for sailors coming from Europe or Atlantic Canada, the first beacon here was an octagonal wooden tower adjacent to the keeper's house. In 1847 Boston architect and engineer Alexander Parris designed a new conical granite tower for the site. Automated in 1977, it remains active today under the auspices of the U.S. Coast Guard.

British Canada planned to overcome one of the most formidable obstacles on its West Coast late in the 1850s. The granite blocks for Race Rocks Light were cut in Scottish quarries and shipped 16,000 sea miles to Victoria, British Columbia. Located in the Strait of Juan de Fuca, just south of Victoria, Race Rocks had claimed many ships and the lives of hundreds of sailors. When the rusticated-granite tower went into service on Boxing Day (December 26), 1860, migration to British Columbia became considerably safer.

American engineers, too, were addressing the dangers of the Pacific Northwest coastline. This area had been frequented by many ships well before 1850—Spanish and English explorers, Russian fur traders and others. One site that was identified as needing a light during the West Coast Survey of the early 1850s was Cape Flattery, the extreme northwestern point of present-day Washington State. The point marks the entrance to the Strait of Juan de Fuca, an important shipping route for the growing lumber trade of what was then Oregon Territory. Cape Flattery Light stands on Tatoosh Island, an area sacred to the local Neah tribe. The 65-foot stone tower, rising from the keeper's dwelling, was finished in 1857. The site is subject to strong gales and the powerful surf crashing constantly at the steep cliffs of the island. Although the light is on level ground well above sea level, construction was problematic because of the difficulty gaining access to the island. Several keepers succumbed to the isolation of this site. One threw himself off the cliff, but failed in his suicide attempt, while another pair nearly fought a duel with pistols.

Island lights on the West Coast are not numerous, but some notable examples include East Brother Island and Alcatraz Island Lights, in California's Bay Area, and Anacapa Island Light, off Ventura County, California. The remote Farallon Islands Light, 26 miles west of San Francisco, was constructed in 1856 on South Farallon Island. Like Maine's Mount Desert Rock, keepers were reluctant to man this lonely outpost, especially when the so-called "Egg War" broke out. Poachers came to the islands regularly to retrieve eggs from the millions of seabirds that nested on South Farallon and its neighbors. Disputes over "gathering rights" escalated from fist fights to gunfights before California lawmen finally intervened to end the fracas.

Construction of lighthouses on reefs, underwater hazards and previously inaccessible islands came to the fore during the nineteenth century. Taking the lessons learned by European engineers—and sometimes improving upon them—American and Canadian engineers erected marvels of architectural and engineering accomplishment in these most challenging, remote locations.

Saybrook Breakwater Light *Above*

Old Saybrook, Connecticut

Known to locals as the "Outer Light," this breakwater light is a veritable fortress—50 feet of cast iron. Its strength was proved when it withstood the ferocious hurricane of 1938. First lighted in 1886, the lighthouse is a Connecticut landmark and appears on many of the state's license plates. Prior to its construction, Lynde Point Light, known as the "Inner Light," had been the sole guardian of the Connecticut River's point of entry into the Atlantic. Automated in 1959, Saybrook Breakwater Light is an active aid to navigation.

Greens Ledge Light *Opposite*

Norwalk, Connecticut

This sturdy cast-iron tower, painted red-brown and white as a daymark, was completed in 1902 at the outer end of a mile-long ledge jutting into Long Island Sound across the entrance to the channel into Norwalk Harbor. Located slightly west of historic Sheffield Island Light (1826 and 1868, deactivated in 1902), Greens Ledge still flashes its alternating red-and-white signal for commercial lobster boats and leisure crafts. Now equipped with a modern 190mm optic, the 52-foot beacon was automated in 1972.

Minots Ledge Light *Opposite*

Cohasset, Massachusetts

Many ships were wrecked on this ledge before 1850, when the first lighthouse was constructed on the shoal. Built on pilings in the open-leg style, the iron skeleton tower was swept away in a fierce gale less than a year later. Engineers pored over plans for a new light and resolved upon this 97-foot tower of 1,079 interlocking granite blocks, completed in 1860. The result is one of the most remarkable wave-swept lighthouses in North America—its massive walls are actually strengthened by the pressure of storm-driven waves. Minots Ledge Light's unique flashing sequence earned it the nickname "Lover's Light," from locals who read the 1–4–3 light sequence as "I Love You."

Race Rock Light *Above*

Fishers Island, New York

Race Rock Light is one of the continent's best known. Located just off Fishers Island, New York, Race Rock Light guards sailors from a reef that claimed at least 100 ships during the nineteenth century. Built between 1871 and 1878, it was designed by Francis Hopkinson Smith, who later engineered the foundation for the Statue of Liberty. Construction was particularly challenging because of the powerful currents around this part of the Long Island shore. A manmade island of stone and concrete was created on the submerged shoal to accommodate the granite tower/dwelling. Its flashing red signal, 67 feet above sea level, still warns fishing vessels and pleasure boaters of this dangerous shoal today.

Graves Ledge Light *Previous pages*

Boston Harbor, Massachusetts

Boston Harbor Light was first built in 1716, and the short-lived skeleton tower at Minots Ledge was completed in 1850. Even after its replacement in 1860, this rocky coast remained a dangerous area, and in 1905, Graves Ledge Light was lit for the first time to guide ships entering the Broad Sound Channel. Named for Thomas Graves, an important merchant of colonial Massachusetts, the 113-foot tower of granite housed a first-order Fresnel lens. The station was automated in the Bicentennial Year 1976, which saw the Tall Ships sail majestically into Boston Harbor. Its original 12-foot Fresnel lens is now at the Smithsonian Institution.

New London Ledge Light *Below*

New London, Connecticut

New London Ledge Light rises midway through the channel where the Thames River enters the Long Island Sound. Built in the Second French Empire style on a monumental concrete platform secured on underwater foundations like at Race Rock, this lighthouse was designed to augment nearby New London Harbor Light. New London Ledge is rich in lore: Reportedly, one its keepers, nicknamed "Ernie," committed suicide here after his wife ran away with the captain of the Block Island Ferry. Legend has it that his ghost still haunts the station where he leaped to his death. Completed in 1909, the beacon was automated in 1987.

Fowey Rocks Light *Above*

Key Biscayne, Florida

This screwpile reef light, first lighted on June 15, 1878, was a model for many later beacons along the Florida coast. It superseded the state's first lighthouse, Cape Florida, which commanded the south end of scenic Key Biscayne from 1825. Fowey Rocks Light was named for the British frigate H.M.S. *Fowey*, which was wrecked on the shoal in 1748. The 110-foot tower was constructed on the northernmost offshore reef at a cost of $163,000, using recently developed exposed screwpile technology to anchor the steel legs into the ocean floor. Now automated, the light's first-order Fresnel lens is on permanent display at the U.S. Coast Guard's National Aids to Navigation School in Yorktown, Virginia.

Rose Island Light *Below*

Newport, Rhode Island

Built in 1869, this 35-foot tower rises from a mansard-roofed keeper's dwelling in the Second French Empire style of the day. Equipped with a sixth-order Fresnel lens, it helped to guide vessels through the east passage of Narragansett Bay and those entering Newport Harbor until 1971, when the Coast Guard closed the station upon completion of the Newport Bridge. The Rose Island Lighthouse Foundation assumed control of the light in 1985 and restored the old station in conjunction with the City of Newport. The light station is now a private aid to navigation. Across the bay from the 16-acre island is the Ida Lewis Yacht Club, built on the site of Lime Rock Lighthouse, which was tended by America's lighthouse heroine Ida Lewis.

Pomham Rocks Light *Above*

East Providence, Rhode Island

First lighted on December 1, 1871, this picturesque French Empire dwelling with frontal tower, fencing and outbuildings marked the main shipping channel for the busy port of Providence. Named for the Narragansett chief Pomham, it housed a sixth-order Fresnel lens until 1939, when it was replaced with a fourth-order lens. The station was deactivated in 1974.

Orient Point Light *Above*

Long Island, New York

An example of the "coffeepot" style or sparkplug light-house, Orient Point is a cast-iron cylinder only 21 feet in diameter at the base and 64 feet high. It was built on the end of the North Fork in 1899 to warn sailors away from Oyster Pond Reef, one the most feared obstacles off the coast of Long Island. Buttressed by hundreds of tons of broken rock, it was manned by Norwegian immigrant N.A. Anderson for twenty years. Automated in 1966, the station emits a white flash every 5 seconds that can be seen 17 miles at sea.

Southwest Ledge Light *Below*

New Haven, Connecticut

Also referred to as New Haven Breakwater Light, Southwest Ledge Light was constructed in Baltimore and exhibited at the 1876 Centennial Exposition in Philadelphia before being shipped to New Haven, where it was emplaced in 1877. Marking the tip of New Haven's eastern breakwater, the 45-foot cast-iron cylinder was automated in 1973. Visitors can contrast its modest appearance with that of the elegant tower of nearby Five Mile Point Lighthouse, built in 1845 and decommissioned in 1877.

Amelia Island Light *Above*

Fernandina Beach, Florida

Florida's most northerly lighthouse, this 64-foot white tower stands 107 feet above sea level on Amelia Island, near the mouth of the St. Marys River, the peninsular state's border with Georgia. It was built in 1838 from the discontinued Cumberland Island Light at a cost of $17,000. During the Civil War the light was extinguished. It was renovated in Victorian style in 1885. Automated in 1956, the tower is equipped with a third-order Fresnel lens, whose white light, visible for 19 miles at sea, still guides ships through Nassau Sound. The former keeper's dwelling now houses U.S. Coast Guard personnel.

Old Charleston (Morris Island) Light *Opposite*

Charleston, South Carolina

The present Old Charleston lighthouse was built in 1876, but two others, dating from 1767 and 1837, occupied this site before it. The first lighthouse was one of two south of Delaware Bay after the Revolutionary War (the other was on Tybee Island, Georgia). Erosion claimed first the keeper's dwelling and then the entire island: Old Charleston Light is now surrounded by water. It survived a massive earthquake in 1885, probably because it rests on piles sunk up to 50 feet to support a timber and concrete foundation. Deactivated in 1962, the light is now in private hands.

Isle Madame Lighthouse *Right*

Cape Breton Island, Nova Scotia

Located off the southern tip of Cape Breton Island, Isle Madame is surrounded by Lennox Passage to the north, Chedabucto Bay to the southwest, the Strait of Canso—separating Cape Breton Island from the rest of Nova Scotia—to the west, and the Atlantic Ocean to the east. The simple light station consists of a white-painted two-story keeper's dwelling with the lens system protruding from its roof. Before the lighthouse was automated, keepers lived a lonely existence on this rugged outcropping, which was named for Madame de Maintenon, the second wife of France's King Louis XIV.

Cape Ann Twin Lights *Left*

Thacher Island, Rockport, Massachusetts

Gloucester and Rockport, Massachusetts, were already important fishing centers in 1771, when the first set of twin lights was built on Thacher Island. The 124-foot towers that stand today were erected in 1861, the year the Civil War began. In 1919 they may have saved the life of American president Woodrow Wilson and fellow passengers, whose fog-blinded ship, the *George Washington*, was returning from Europe after the Versailles peace conference that ended World War I. Cape Ann's nautical tradition was enhanced by the British writer Rudyard Kipling, who wrote *Captains Courageous* about the region's fishermen. The Cape Ann lights are now the United States' last operating twin lights. The north tower is open to the public, and Thacher Island is a National Historic Landmark. Visitors can stay in the keeper's quarters, renovated in 2002.

Hockamock Head (Burnt Coat) Light *Right*

Swans Island, Maine

Built in 1872 to mark the entrance to Maine's Burnt Coat Harbor, the Hockamock Head Lighthouse stands 75 feet above sea level on the southern tip of Swans Island. When the island was purchased by its namesake, Colonel James Swan, in 1784, lumbering was the main industry. Today the picturesque site is home to a thriving fishing community. The 32-foot light, a simple square-shaped structure, was originally connected to the keeper's house by a covered walkway. Automated in 1975, the beacon is equipped with a 250mm lens.

Race Rocks Light *Overleaf*

Victoria, British Columbia

One of the famous "Imperial Towers" built by the British-Canadian government during the nineteenth century, Race Rocks Light stands in the Strait of Juan de Fuca, just south of the entrance to Victoria Harbour, on Vancouver Island. The lighthouse was designed in Britain, and its granite blocks were quarried and cut to size in Scotland and shipped 16,000 sea miles to Victoria. When the 105-foot light went into operation on December 26, 1860, it curtailed the many shipwrecks that had occurred on these reefs, which lie directly in the path of ships approaching Victoria. The treacherous, rocky strait is also prone to impenetrable fog, and a series of fog horns were mounted on a nearby tower to further improve safety in the area.

Baccalieu Island Light *Above*

Newfoundland

Typical of Newfoundland's coastline, the terrain on Baccalieu Island is rugged and includes precipitous cliffs rising more than 450 feet above sea level. Two lightkeepers, along with their dog, maintain the lonely beacon on this otherwise uninhabited island, which is now an ecological reserve. Located just north of the Avalon Peninsula, Baccalieu Island boasts the most numerous and diverse colony of seabirds in eastern North America. More than 3 million breeding pairs of Leach's Storm-Petrel and 45,000 pairs of Atlantic Puffins nest on the four-square-mile island.

Anacapa Island Light *Opposite*

Channel Islands National Park, California

Anacapa Island is one of three islets—the peaks of a mountain range that sank beneath the sea thousands of years ago. Located 11 miles off the coast of Ventura County on the southernmost of the three islands, the light was first built in 1912 as a steel tower, which was replaced in 1932 by this cylindrical masonry tower 277 feet above the sea. At that time, a fog horn was added. No keepers live on the island today: It was once populated mainly by rabbits introduced by the U.S. Navy during World War II to ensure a reserve food supply. The light was recently renovated at a cost of $350,000.

East Brother Island Light *Above*

Richmond, California

Built in 1874, East Brother Island Light marks the channel through the narrow, often fog-bound, San Pablo Straits connecting the Sacramento River estuary with San Francisco Bay. Construction here was difficult: Laborers had to dynamite most of the island to level the site. The square light tower is attached to a Stick-style dwelling, which has been modernized over the years. The lighthouse was automated in 1969, and the station and its outbuildings were restored to their original condition for use as a bed-and-breakfast inn.

Lime Point Light *Right*

San Francisco, California

Lime Point Light is situated below the Golden Gate Bridge on the north side of the strait. It began as a fog-signal station in 1883; the present light tower was built seventeen years later. Automated in 1961, the 20-foot concrete tower is still an active aid to navigation. Most travelers are more familiar with the discontinued Fort Point Light, which stands under the bridge on the San Francisco side, and with the still-operational lighthouse on nearby Alcatraz Island.

Lake and River Beacons

Previous pages: **Boularderie Island Light, Bras d'Or Lake, Nova Scotia;** *Above:* **Kenosha North Pier Light, Kenosha, Wisconsin**

avigation on North America's inland waterways has been important since the seventeenth century, when colonial settlers transported passengers and cargo along the Hudson and St. Lawrence Rivers, building thriving new towns along their banks.

As early as 1797, navigational improvements were made along the Hudson River, because of the volume of commercial traffic, which was steadily increasing with population growth. Whaling vessels, lumber, grain and all manner of cargo was transported by barge between the growing Hudson Valley towns. During the nineteenth century, traffic burgeoned with the opening of the Erie, Delaware and Hudson, and Champlain Canals, which linked the river with the Great Lakes. The canals were upgraded under the New York State Barge Canal project, completed in 1918, to accommodate container barges up to 300 feet long and 43 feet wide with a draft of up to 12 feet. Ocean-going vessels were constantly plying the waterway, and they required the protection of navigational aids at trouble spots.

The first lighthouse on the Hudson was the Stony Point Lighthouse, built in 1826. Another five were in service by the end of the 1830s, including those at Saugerties and Upper Kinderhook, south of Albany. By century's end there were eleven (perhaps the most famous of which, Jeffrey's Hook, was illuminated for only eleven years, but still serves as a daymark).

Burlington, Vermont, on the shores of Lake Champlain, became a busy port after the opening of the new canals: It was now within easy reach of the Great Lakes ports and New York City. Traffic entering Burlington's harbor was threatened by a reef off nearby Colchester Point, and in 1871 a lighthouse with keeper's dwelling was constructed on a massive granite pier over the reef. The four-bedroom dwelling eventually served eleven successive lighthouse keepers and their families. The light remained in use until 1933.

The St. Lawrence Seaway connects the Atlantic Ocean with the Great Lakes ports and has a total length of over 2,500 miles, from the Gulf of St. Lawrence to the St. Louis River, west of Duluth, Minnesota, the westernmost point of the Great Lakes. Only 740 miles of this route is the St. Lawrence River proper, between the eastern end of Lake Ontario and the Gulf. The Seaway is navigable for ten months of the year: In winter, parts of it are icebound. Around 60 percent of the Seaway's traffic carries goods between North America and overseas ports, via seven locks, and with the aid of many lighthouses and other aids to navigation.

For several centuries before the 1959 improvements in locks and maintenance were completed for the Seaway, this was one of the world's busiest inland waterways. Traders used the river soon after its earliest explorations by Jacques Cartier in the 1530s. Over time, westward population migration into the Great Lakes region increased the prominence of the river as a trading route. Traffic from the Canadian provinces of Quebec and Ontario and the American states of Illinois, Michigan, Minnesota, Indiana, Wisconsin, Ohio, New York and Pennsylvania are all connected to the Atlantic Ocean via this waterway—hence its enormous volume of commercial activity.

Lighthouses on the St. Lawrence River include Tibbett's Point Lighthouse (first built in 1854) at Cape Vincent, New York, the entrance to Lake Ontario; and Rock Island and Sunken Rock Lights, both built in the 1880s. Many more lighthouses line the shores of the Great Lakes themselves.

By about 1800, Americans had crossed the Allegheny and Appalachian Mountains and were making their way into the broad lowland expanse of the Ohio and Mississippi River Valleys. In 1807 Robert Fulton demonstrated the possibility of steamboat travel with his famous Hudson River trip on the *Clermont* from New York City to Albany and back. The question was, could that feat be duplicated on the many transmontane waterways drained by the Mississippi?

One answer came in the form of the steamboat *New Orleans*, financed by Fulton and Robert Livingston and built in Pittsburgh, Pennsylvania. The 371-ton vessel made her maiden voyage in November 1811 and reached New Orleans in January 1812, having survived the worst earthquake in recorded North American history—at New Madrid, Missouri, on December 16, 1811.

By the 1820s, steamboats were replacing flat-bottomed boats and keelboats on the inland waterways, from Louisville, Kentucky, and Cairo, Illinois, to St. Louis and New Orleans. However, as the pressure to meet timetables and delivery schedules increased, steamboats began to travel by night, leading to a rash of accidents. Between 1825 and 1850, 1,400 people were killed on the Western rivers in steamboat explosions. The Civil War increased steamboat traffic, and on April 27, 1865, the *Sultana* exploded just above Memphis, Tennessee, killing 1,647 persons, most of them Union soldiers returning home from Confederate prisons at war's end. It was the nation's worst maritime disaster to date.

On June 23, 1874, the U.S. Congress authorized expanding the jurisdiction of the Lighthouse Board to the Western rivers. Two new lighthouse districts were created: the Fourteenth, which encompassed the Ohio and Mississippi Rivers between Pittsburgh and New Orleans; and the Fifteenth, comprising both the Mississippi from St. Paul, Minnesota, to Cairo, Illinois, and the Missouri River from Kansas City to its mouth. The act provided for "establishment of such beacon-lights, day-beacons and buoys as may be necessary for the use of vessels navigating these streams."

From the start, it was clear that these would not be lighthouses on the scale of open-water beacons, but sporadic warning lights emplaced at riverbends, sandbars and snags that had proved hazardous to steamboats. Known to local people as post lights, they consisted of a 14-inch hand lantern enclosed in a square or triangular tin case with plain glazed sides. These lamps burned kerosene and usually emitted a fixed white light, although some had red globes or shades. The more sophisticated post lights had braces and steps to the lantern. In some areas, they were attached to trees.

The first river lights designed and maintained by the U.S. Lighthouse Board, as opposed to private enterprise, were those at Jefferson Barracks, near St. Louis, and at Twin Hollows, Missouri, both placed in 1874. The Mississippi River was also lit at the dike below

The Lighthouse Board continued its work into the twentieth century, and by 1915 there were 1,798 lights and 861 buoys marking 4,226 miles of the Mississippi and Ohio Rivers and their tributaries. Many new post lights indicated crossings and bends in the river channels. These simple lights consisted of either a flat wick lamp in a small pressed-glass lens, or an ordinary hand lantern enclosed in a triangular tin case with glass sides. Set on posts along the river banks, they had large painted wings to make them daymarks as well.

This ingenious system had a rather makeshift appearance, and so did the arrangements with its keepers. Since the lights required minimal maintenance, people living in the vicinity were paid a small wage to keep them supplied with oil. The system resembled that used by the Dutch to maintain their dikes. Later in the twentieth century, battery-powered blinkers 20 feet tall were installed. They are serviced by a number of Coast Guard tenders, including seven in the area between Cairo and New Orleans. One of them, the *Chena,* tends to 175 channel buoys and 101 lights.

The rapid lighting of these major rivers came too late for the steamboat, whose day had largely passed by the turn of the century. Steamboat pilots had their heyday between 1820 and 1880, when there were few aids to navigation. By the time they were in place, the railroads had become paramount in transportation.

Late in life, Mark Twain looked back on his experience as a pilot and reflected: "No, there's nothing known to man like piloting on the Mississippi River....I was not much better than a half-baked amateur at it, but the memory of its raptures [has] never left my finger ends. To this day, I had rather take a good steamboat through Coon Slough than hold any other job I ever heard of. By comparison, to be king of England must be like washing dishes."

River lights increased rapidly, too, in other parts of the country, and by the start of World War I, the Klamath, Platte, Rio Grande, Brazos, St. Johns and Columbia Rivers had numerous navigational aids. Lights were also erected along the 2,000-mile Intracoastal Waterway, a navigable route consisting of a series of canals, rivers, bays, lagoons and sounds connecting ports between Boston and Key West, and Gulf Coast ports.

Des Peres, completed at the end of that year. Between St. Louis and Cairo, the lanterns were fueled by mineral oil. Riverboat pilots considered this 180-mile stretch the worst on the river: Sunken rocks and submerged islands wrecked so many vessels that the area around Cairo was known (inevitably) as the Graveyard. In *Life on the Mississippi,* Mark Twain (Samuel Clemens) reported that one Illinois farmer claimed: "Twenty-nine steamboats had left their bones strung along within sight from his house." The great American humorist had worked on the river as a pilot himself, and derived his pen name from a phrase used in depth soundings. "Mark Twain" indicated a depth of two fathoms.

Congress changed the boundaries of the river districts in 1876, and in 1887 it created a Sixteenth Lighthouse district because of the growing number of light stations. By 1890 there were 359 Mississippi beacon lights, or buoys, between St. Paul, Minnesota, and Cairo, Illinois, and another 320 from Cairo to New Orleans. More than 450 lights marked the Ohio River, the best-lit waterway in the nation. Other tributaries of the Mississippi included: the Missouri River, 27; Illinois River, 37; Tennessee River, 37; Kanawha River, 27; and the Red River, 7. In short, 1,276 lights had been installed along the Western rivers within six years.

The long-standing problem of navigating the mouth of the Mississippi River became acute as ship traffic increased. The river's current carried logs, sand, debris and silt to pile up at or near the mouth of the river, which was known as the Great Muddy for its quantity of alluvial soil. To complicate matters, there were four passes through the river delta to the Gulf (Northeast, Pass à l'Outre, Southwest and South Passes), all of which reconfigured themselves from year to year, making navigation not only hazardous, but sometimes impossible.

The first efforts to light the area came after the United States acquired Louisiana from the French in 1803. Benjamin Latrobe, architect of the U.S. Capitol, designed Franks Island Light, built by Winslow Lewis in 1818. It succumbed to the pressure of mud almost at once, but its replacement, finished in 1823, still stands, although its foundation has sunk 20 feet into the subsoil. The river's ever-changing flow began to favor the Pass à l'Outre, and a lighthouse was built there in 1856. The 82-foot iron tower guided shipping until 1930, when the channel became nearly impassable due to sedimentation. Other lighthouses at the river mouth marked the South Pass

(1832, 1881), the Southwest Pass (1836, 1962) and the Head of Passes (1836). All these towers remain.

In 1874 Congress debated the relative merits of building a cutoff pass or jetties at the mouth of the Mississippi. The latter solution was favored, and between 1875 and 1879, James Buchanan Eads (1820–87), who had designed Eads Bridge over the Mississippi at St. Louis, built a series of jetties to contain the silt and sandbars that had wrecked so many ships. The acid test of his system came in 1883, when the British cable ship *Silvertown* left New Orleans with the heaviest cargo ever loaded there. Totaling 5,020 tons, and drawing 25 feet and 4 inches, the *Silvertown* made her way safely through the delta into the Gulf.

Both Americans and Canadians in the Great Lakes region needed protection for vessels carrying passengers and goods between ports. After the United States and British Canada negotiated the Rush-Bagot Agreement in 1817, many new lighthouses were built. Among the first on Lake Erie were those at Presque Isle (later Erie, Pennsylvania), and Buffalo, both built in 1818. Buffalo's original light was replaced in 1833, and a third was built at the end of a 1,000-foot-long

Opposite: Keweenaw Waterway Upper Entrance Light, Keweenaw Waterway, Michigan; *Above:* Umpqua River Light, Winchester Bay, Oregon

Buffalo Main Light, Buffalo, New York

breakwater in 1872. The oldest lighthouse still in operation on the Lakes is Marblehead Light, at Sandusky, Ohio, built in 1821. The 65-foot stone tower still flashes its green light over Lake Erie.

Ship captains on the five Great Lakes had to be their own aerologists, as these freshwater "seas" at the heart of the continent lie in the path of cyclonic storm systems. Thousands of miles of flat prairies and plains border the Great Lakes, and polar-chilled fronts from the north often collide with warmer, moister winds from the south. The result: unpredictable gales, blizzards, fog banks and thunderstorms. Winter temperatures on the eastern side of Lake Michigan can be 20 to 30 degrees higher than those on the western (Wisconsin) shore. A ship leaving Buffalo, New York, on a clear summer day may have to put in at Erie a few hours later to evade a storm or fog system.

During the last 150 years, records have been kept of the major storms that buffet the Lakes region. A four-day hurricane in 1869 caused the destruction of

7 steamships, 1 tugboat, 8 barks, 4 brigs, 56 schooners, 18 scows and 3 barges—a total of 97 vessels. U.S. government records show that 5,999 vessels were wrecked between 1878 and 1898, and of these, as many as 1,093 were deemed unsalvageable.

Of necessity, shipping declines during the winter months, when the Lakes are often icebound. Keepers of the lights were once removed from their stations by December 15, leaving behind enough kerosene to light the lamps for two more weeks. The problems faced by lighthouse engineers here differed from those of coastal builders in American waters because of the danger posed by ice. Most major Great Lakes lighthouses were built after the 1850s, when the crib and caisson styles of lighthouse building had been perfected.

As mentioned earlier, several feats of construction had enabled greater mobility on the Lakes. Irish-Americans newly arrived from their homeland were instrumental in building the great Erie Canal between 1817 and 1825, and British Canadians finished the Welland-Niagara Canal, between Lakes Ontario and Erie, in 1829. Together, these manmade waterways connected New York City, Montreal and several other ports to the Lakes and were crucial to the land and timber booms that followed.

Some of the most important port city lights were built before the Civil War. Chicago's first light, known as the "old light tower in the town," was built on the south bend of the Chicago River in 1832. Located on Lake Michigan, Chicago would become one of the great inland ports and harbors before the turn of the twentieth century. The great fire of 1871 devastated the port facilities, but reconstruction was rapid and efficient. The present active lighthouse here, built in 1893, is a 48-foot brick-and-steel tower that was moved to the end of the harbor breakwater. The tower houses a fine third-order Fresnel lens that had been displayed at Chicago's World's Columbian Exposition in 1893.

An enormous volume of ship traffic passes through the Detroit River, Lake St. Clair and the St. Clair River, which comprise one of the major waterways in North America, linking Lakes Erie and Huron. Detroit received its first light in 1837 at the outlet of Lake St. Clair; a second was placed at the mouth of the Detroit

River a year later. The Detroit River Lighthouse rises from 22 feet of water near the channel in the mouth of the river. Completed in 1885, it has a wooden crib foundation filled with concrete.

Ohio's Toledo Harbor Light (1904), on Lake Erie, is one of the most remarkable of its type. Architecturally, it is a unique blend of Romanesque arches and Russian-Orthodox-style rooflines. Structurally, the light is anchored solidly to its stone-and-concrete foundation.

The first Canadian lighthouse on the Lakes was at the mouth of the Niagara River on Lake Ontario, built in 1804. Next came Gibraltar Point Light, built on the island that forms the harbor of Toronto. Canadian beacons on other Lakes include Long Point tower, on Lake Erie, 1830; Goderich Light, on Lake Huron, 1847; and Thunder Bay Light, on Lake Superior, 1939. Canada also built six "Imperial Lights" on the northern Lakes (1855–59), including Chantry Island Light, Cove Island, Griffith Island, Nottawasaga Island and Point Clark, all on Lake Huron and Georgian Bay.

Two lights stand out as examples of construction on the Great Lakes. The first is Spectacle Reef Light, built by the Lighthouse Board between 1870 and 1874. Located at the eastern end of the Straits of Mackinac, where Lake Huron meets Lake Superior, Spectacle Reef was described by a contemporary observer as "probably more dreaded by navigators than any other danger now unmarked throughout the entire chain of lakes." When two ships were wrecked upon the rock simultaneously in 1867, the need for a beacon here could no longer be ignored.

Spectacle Reef Light (begun 1870) was built in much the same way that Minots Ledge, in Massachusetts, had been: A crib dam was placed around the site, the water was pumped out and the building crew went to work. Once the foundation was leveled, the men bolted preshaped stones to the rock with three-foot bolts. The tower is a solid mass of limestone rising five stories (95 feet) to the lens. Work stopped for the winter in mid-December 1873, and when the engineers returned in the spring, they had to hack their way through ice that had piled up to a height of 30 feet to finish their job. First lit in 1874, the tower still guides ships past this bottleneck near the Straits of Mackinac.

Rock of Ages Light guards the western tip of Isle Royale on Lake Superior. This was an especially dangerous spot for ships bound for the iron-ore port of Duluth, Minnesota. The five-level, 130-foot steel tower is one of the most isolated stations in North America: Keepers had to cross 50 miles of turbulent water to see a doctor, or pick up supplies. It was the Great Lakes equivalent of the light at Tillamook Rock, Oregon. In 1933 the freighter *George M. Cox* ran onto a nearby reef shrouded by fog. Rescued by the keeper and his assistant, 125 survivors huddled in the lighthouse until emergency vessels arrived to transport them to the mainland.

The renowned "Big Storm" on the Lakes occurred on November 9–11, 1913. Forty vessels were wrecked and 235 lives lost, but all of the lighthouses remained intact, confirming the engineering skill and determination of the Great Lakes builders. By 1945 there were 698 lights on the American side and almost one-third as many significant beacons on the Canadian. After World War II, increasing use of automation and radar began to reduce both the number of functioning lighthouses and their importance.

Two Harbors East Breakwater Light, Two Harbors, Minnesota

Racine North Breakwater Light *Above*

Racine, Wisconsin

With a population of 84,000, the port of Racine lies 20 miles southeast of Milwaukee on Lake Michigan. The town improved its harbor after the first lighthouse here was constructed in 1839; it was replaced after the Civil War, when the railroad increased local prosperity. The present lighthouse, now inactive, is a pyramidal steel tower on a skeletal base that has survived winter's ice and storms since 1912.

Manistique East Breakwater Light *Left*

Manistique, Michigan

Completed in 1917, this pyramidal cast-iron lighthouse stands on a concrete pier at the end of the eastern breakwater marking the entrance to the Manistique River, on northern Lake Michigan. The 35-foot-tall tower is sheathed with steel plating. Automated in 1969, its original fourth-order Fresnel lens was replaced with a lighter 300mm plastic lens as its optic.

Manistee North Pierhead Light
Manistee, Michigan

This Lake Michigan station was established at Manistee in 1875; the present cylindrical tower was built in 1927 at the end of the North Pierhead to mark the entrance to the Manistee River. The old wooden catwalk by which the keepers entered the light was often damaged by storms, so it was replaced by a sturdy steel-and-wire walkway. The 39-foot lighthouse stands 55 feet above Lake Michigan. Now equipped with a 300mm lens, the light is still an active aid to navigation.

Point Betsie Light *Below*

Frankfort, Michigan

In 1858 Point Betsie Light was built to mark a key point for ships entering or leaving the Manitou Passage. The 37-foot brick tower, painted white, is attached to the two-story dwelling. Until 1996, when the rotating mechanisms for the lens failed, the lantern (automated in 1983 and still active) retained its original third-order Fresnel lens. The lens has now been removed for display at the Sleeping Bear Dunes Maritime Museum.

Lake Dora Light *Opposite*

Mount Dora, Florida

Lake Dora Light is the only lighthouse on a freshwater lake in Florida. Civic groups in the region raised the funds to construct this lighthouse in Mount Dora's Gilbert Park. The 35-foot brick-and-stucco tower was dedicated on March 25, 1988. Equipped with a 750-watt photocell, the beacon guides boaters back to the Mount Dora dock. From the nearby boardwalk, visitors can see alligators, otter, herons and other wildlife.

Grosse Point Light *Opposite*

Evanston, Illinois

Located on Lake Michigan just north of Chicago, Grosse Point Light, with its imposing Tudor Revival-style dwelling, was built in 1873 at a cost of $50,000. The 113-foot tower, made of brick encased in concrete, was equipped with a second-order lens; the fixed white light emitted a red flash every 3 minutes. The Bureau of Lighthouses automated the light in 1935, and it was decommissioned by the Coast Guard in 1941. Evanston citizens restored and relit the lighthouse after World War II, when the property reverted to the city.

Turkey Point Light *Above*

Elk Neck, Maryland

Turkey Point Light stands at the end of Elk Neck, a 12-mile-long peninsula that juts into the head of Chesapeake Bay. Built in 1833, the 38-foot masonry tower, on a 100-foot elevation, was designed as a marker for ships coming up the bay or down the Susquehanna River via the Chesapeake and Delaware Canal. The last civilian woman in the lighthouse service kept the station until she retired in 1947. Elk Neck Light was automated at that time and now stands in a state park and game preserve.

Round Island Light *Above*

St. Ignace, Michigan

Round Island lies in the Straits of Mackinac, which separate Lakes Michigan and Huron. The light was built in 1895 near St. Ignace, Michigan, to mark the dangerous shoals in the heavily traveled channel between Round and Mackinac Islands. The square tower is integral with the Gothic Revival dwelling, which fell into disrepair after the light was automated in 1924. Decommissioned in 1947, the site was saved by a consortium of preservation groups working with the U.S. Forest Service. Today it is the most-photographed lighthouse on the Great Lakes, viewed by countless passengers on hydroplane ferries to Mackinac Island.

Holland Harbor ("Big Red") Light *Opposite*

Holland, Michigan

Located at the end of Holland's south inner pier, Holland Harbor Light is a massive square building with an integral cast-iron tower. The steel-plated structure (the fourth on this site) marks the narrow channel that connects Lakes Michigan and Macatawa. It was built in 1936 and owes its size and design to the need to house the huge boilers that powered the station's steam fog signal. Painted red, like many Lake Michigan lighthouses, Holland Harbor Light is a familiar landmark known affectionately as "Big Red."

Algoma North Pierhead Light *Left*

Sturgeon Bay, Wisconsin

The station at Algoma, Wisconsin, was established in 1893, and the tower was rebuilt in 1908 as a conical cast-iron-and-steel structure. Located at the end of the city's north pier, the present light was installed in 1932 by placing the older 26-foot tower on a new steel base and raising the lantern's height to 42 feet. Automated in 1973, it is still in service.

South Haven South Pier Light *Below*

South Haven, Michigan

This is the second light at the South Haven station, which was established in 1872. Built in 1903, the conical cast-iron tower is accessed by a steel catwalk and overlooks summertime art festivals on the resort town's south pier. Once a commercial crossroads on Lake Michigan, South Haven is now frequented mainly by pleasure boaters. Its light is still active.

Mendota (Bete Grise) Light *Right*

Bete Grise, Michigan

Built in 1895 to mark the Mendota Ship Channel near Bete Grise, Michigan, this station was deactivated in 1960 and is now a private residence. The square brick tower is integral with the brick dwelling, with its steeply sloping gabled roof. This Lake Superior station was established in 1870, when maritime activity on the Great Lakes was already flourishing.

Copper Harbor Light *Below*

Copper Harbor, Michigan

Lake Superior's original Copper Harbor Lighthouse, on Michigan's Upper Peninsula, was established in 1849 after a rich vein of copper was discovered nearby. This sturdy yellow-brick keeper's dwelling with its square frontal tower was built in 1867. In 1933 its light was moved to an adjacent skeleton tower, and the well-kept old building is now a maritime museum in Fort Wilkins State Park.

Coquille River Light *Above*

Bandon, Oregon

This handsomely restored fog-signal station with attached tower was built in the classical style in 1895 to mark the entrance to Oregon's Coquille River. The 40-foot conical brick tower, covered with stucco, was reclaimed from vandalism along with the fog-signal station by the U.S. Army Corps of Engineers and the State of Oregon after the light was deactivated in 1939.

Cheboygan Crib Light *Right*

Cheboygan, Michigan

This crib-foundation structure was established in 1852 on a strong concrete base designed to resist the region's destructive ice floes. First lit in 1910, the 25-foot tower marked the entrance to the Cheboygan River on the Michigan shore of Lake Huron. In 1988 the deactivated octagonal cast-iron tower was moved to the base of the west pier in what is now a Cheboygan city park.

Hooper Strait Light *Below*

St. Michaels, Maryland

Today the Hooper Strait Light stands on Navy Point, beside the Chesapeake Bay Maritime Museum on Maryland's eastern shore. It is the second of two screwpile lighthouses built to mark the difficult channel of Hooper Strait. The first, built in 1867, was swept away by a massive ice floe; the second, completed in 1879 with platform dwelling, served faithfully until 1954, when the 44-foot-wide hexagonal lighthouse was discontinued and purchased by the museum.

Drum Point Light *Opposite*

Solomons, Maryland

Typical of the "cottage-style" screwpile lighthouse, Drum Point Light was built in 1883 to mark a sandy spit. Originally located at the entrance to Maryland's Patuxent River, it was equipped with a fourth-order Fresnel lens and anchored in 10 feet of water some 100 yards off the point. Tidal patterns changed, and by the 1960s, the lighthouse stood completely above water at low tide. The Coast Guard decommissioned the light in 1962, and it was moved two miles upriver to the Calvert Marine Museum in 1975.

Michigan City East Pier Light *Previous pages*

Michigan City, Indiana

Built in 1904 on Michigan City's outer pierhead, this massive structure replaced the original lighthouse, called Old Michigan City, which is now a museum on the mainland. Constructed on a concrete platform, the 49-foot octagonal tower rises from the boiler-powered fog-signal building, reached by an elevated catwalk. Automated in 1960, the station is still an active Coast Guard facility.

Port Sanilac Light *Below*

Port Sanilac, Michigan

The Michigan city of Port Sanilac established this lakeside lighthouse in 1886, and it is still an active aid to navigation, although the Tudor-style keeper's dwelling is now a private residence. The octagonal brick tower stands 69 feet above lake level, and its beam can be seen for 16 miles.

Lake Buchanan Light *Above*

Lake Buchanan, Texas

This privately owned lighthouse overlooks Lake Buchanan, the largest of the first four Highland Lakes in central Texas. Located near the Buchanan Dam, this pyramidal tower has been carefully maintained.

Tarrytown Harbor Light *Left*

North Tarrytown, New York

This sturdy steel caisson lighthouse was built in 1883 to warn Hudson River navigators of the Tarrytown Shoals. Rising from a stone pier, the five-story conical tower was staffed until 1957, when the light was automated. Now inactive, it is part of Kingsland Point Park.

Sturgeon Bay Ship Canal Lights *Below and overleaf*

Sturgeon Bay, Wisconsin

This 98-foot skeletal tower (below) on Lake Michigan was built in 1903 as a marker for the Sturgeon Bay Ship Canal entrance. Still an active Coast Guard facility, its companion light (overleaf) is on the North Pierhead of the canal entrance. Constructed in 1882, the North Pierhead Light is a cast-iron-and-concrete tower integral to the massive fog-signal building.

Concord Point Light *Above*

Havre de Grace, Maryland

Built in 1827 at a cost of $3,500, this 32-foot stone tower now displays a fixed green light. It is located near the U.S. Naval Academy at Annapolis and shares this institution's distinction in naval history. Until is was automated in the 1920s, Concord Point Light was tended entirely by members of the family of John O'Neil, a hero of the War of 1812, who was the first keeper.

Ludington North Breakwater Light *Below*

Ludington, Michigan

Constructed in 1924, the U.S. Coast Guard renovated this lighthouse in 1993. The 57-foot, square pyramidal tower is constructed of steel and reinforced concrete. It is painted white, and is topped by a black lantern. The light originally used a fourth-order Fresnel lens, which was loaned to the Mason County Historical Society for display at the White Pine Village Maritime Museum. It was automated in 1972, and it has a height of focal plane of 55 feet above sea level. There is now a radiobeacon on the site, which is owned by the U.S. Coast Guard.

Tawas Point Light *Below*

Tawas City, Michigan

The original Tawas Point Light on the Michigan shore of Lake Huron was built in 1853 to mark the entrance to Saginaw Bay. Only twenty years later, the lake's boundaries had shifted to the point where the beacon was more than a mile from the water. The present 67-foot conical brick tower was built in 1876 and equipped with a rotating fourth-order Fresnel lens. The site remains an active Coast Guard facility.

Wind Point Light *Opposite*

Racine, Wisconsin

It took three years to build Lake Michigan's Wind Point Light with attached dwelling 3.5 miles north of Racine Harbor. Completed in 1880, the 108-foot conical brick tower displayed two Fresnel lenses: a third-order, with a flashing white light, and a fifth-order, which marked Racine Reef with a red light. Automated in 1964, the station is now owned by the village of Wind Point and is still an active aid to navigation.

Jeffrey's Hook Light *Overleaf*

Fort Washington Park, New York City

Since the 1930s, children have delighted in the story of *The Little Red Lighthouse and the Great Grey Bridge*, written by Hildegarde Hoyt Swift. It celebrates Jeffrey's Hook Light, a steel-plated tower built in 1921 to replace a pair of stake lights on the Hudson River. Only eleven years later, the conical 40-foot light was rendered obsolete by completion of the George Washington Bridge. Discontinued by the Coast Guard in 1947, the site was for sale until Swift wrote her classic and popular protest demanded that the diminutive light remain. Jeffrey's Hook Light was acquired by New York City, incorporated into Fort Washington Park, and relighted in 2001.

Eagle Bluff Light *Below*

Ephraim, Wisconsin

Established in 1868 to mark the entrance to the East Channel into Green Bay, the 43-foot Eagle Bluff Light stands 75 feet above Lake Michigan. One of the first beacons in the U.S. to be automated, its original third-order Fresnel lens was replaced with a 300mm solar-powered lens. The brick tower is still an active aid to navigation.

St. Joseph Inner and Outer Pier Lights *Opposite*

St. Joseph, Michigan

This unusual site has a pair of lights on the same pier at the mouth of the St. Joseph River. The cylindrical tower stands in front of an octagonal tower rising from the fog-signal station on Lake Michigan. Both lights were constructed in 1907, to function as front and rear range lights to guide mariners into the channel.

Anatomy of a Signal

Previous pages: Lightship *Nantucket,* Bridgeport, Connecticut; *Above:* Big Sable Point Light, Ludington, Michigan

As we have seen briefly in the previous chapters, many different types of navigational aids have been used in conjunction with, or in addition to, the lighthouse itself. These include daymarks; sound signals such as fog horns, bells, whistles and sirens; range lights; several major types of lenses housed in lighthouse and lighted marker lanterns; and lightships, widely used as mobile navigation aids for more than a century. Different types of buoys, both lighted and unlighted, have also played a major role in maritime safety.

Visible Aids to Piloting

Landmarks used to negotiate waters close to shore include daymarks: boldly striped or patterned structures, including lighthouses, readily seen from a distance—and buoys, both of which are identified on nautical charts for the mariner's guidance. Buoys are floating objects anchored in harbors, lakes, rivers and other waterways as markers. They were first employed in North America on the Delaware River in 1767. The

first lighted buoy, which burned oil gas, was put into service outside New York Harbor in 1881, and bell buoys were introduced four years later.

Over time, a color-code system was developed in the United States whereby red buoys marked the right side of a channel, as viewed by a vessel entering a harbor, and black ones, the left. Buoys with black-and-white vertical stripes marked the middle of a channel, and those with horizontal red and black stripes indicated danger spots. The color-coding system was eventually altered to conform to international convention, and the black buoy indicating the left side of a channel was changed to green.

Spar buoys are wooden or metal poles that are tall and tapered. The can buoy is a metal flat-topped cylinder, while the nun buoy is cone-shaped. Buoys sometimes have lights for night piloting: The color of their lights and the length of their flashes, in conjunction with a chart, tell the navigator what their signals identify. By the mid-twentieth century, these lights were operated by compressed gas or electric batteries.

Pairs of fixed lights called range lights in some harbor, port and estuarial areas give directional signals in which two lights must be lined up to indicate a safe channel. These may consist of a pair or set of three buoy lights or a small light used in tandem with a local lighthouse. Another range system in major channels consists of two lighthouses at different elevations standing a short distance, perhaps a half-mile, apart. The mariner steers to keep the two lights in line, one above the other, to find passage through the channel. Many of these two-house range lights have been built on Canadian waterways, including the St. Lawrence and Ontario's Wilson Channel. In the United States, a number are found on Great Lakes harbor channels, including those at Presque Isle, Michigan. Such two-house systems usually incorporate the phrases "Front Range" and "Rear Range" in the name of the lighthouse.

Sound Signals

Most lighthouses were equipped with fog signals, and some stations had such signals before the lighthouse itself was erected. Sound signals can be confusing because, to the human ear, sound seems to travel unpredictably over water. The strength of a sound signal varies considerably, too, with changes in wind direction. However, in thick fog, the presence of a sound signal can provide the only practical warning of a hazard, so their use remains vital, especially to vessels not equipped with radar or global positioning systems.

For almost thirty years, San Francisco's Point Montara had only a fog signal house to warn sailors of the jagged rocks below its clifftop site. A wooden tower, built in 1900, was replaced by the present cast-iron beacon in 1928, and the fog signal now sounds from a buoy anchored offshore.

Puget Sound's Point Robinson Light, on Maury Island, was originally a fog-signal station, established in 1885 to guard a busy "intersection" between Tacoma and Seattle, Washington. Two years later, a red light was placed on top of a 25-foot scaffold, and the station was rebuilt in 1915 to include a keeper's dwelling with a frontal tower housing a fifth-order Fresnel lens.

Steam whistles, bells, cannon fire, horns and sirens have all been used as fog-signals that can be identified in heavy weather or darkness at particular spots on the navigator's chart. The haunting quality of the fog horn has been memorialized in sea chanteys and folklore, like the lonely sound of a train whistle on the night air, vanishing into the unknown. Many types of sounding buoys are activated by the motion of the waves to signal their message by bells, gongs, or whistles. In still waters, they are now automated to signal at regular intervals when fog obscures the lighted buoys. In the United States, the government publication *Notices to Mariners* regularly advises navigators of changes to these and other aids to navigation.

Lightships

The captain of the *Sandy Hook* lightship described the challenges faced by his crew in an 1851 report to the Lighthouse Service: "If you will but look at the model of this ship, you will at once perceive that her broad bluff bow is not at all calculated to resist the fury of the sea, which, in some of the gales we experience in the winter season, break against and over us with almost impending fury....The model of the present ship and her bottom is similar to a barrel; she is constantly in motion, and when it is any ways rough she rolls and labors to such a degree as to heave the glass out of the lanterns, the beds out of the berths, tearing out the chain-plates, &, rendering her unsafe and uncomfortable." In fact, lightship service at this time was both dangerous and monotonous, but it was essential in high-traffic areas where a lighthouse was not feasible: over sandbars that might shift after a storm and before offshore foundation techniques were developed; at the infamous Diamond Shoals off Cape Hatteras; at complex harbor entrances like the one to New York City; and in estuaries including that of the Columbia River.

Great Britain was the first country to use lightships. In 1731 a British entrepreneur secured a patent that allowed him to station a lightship at the Nore Sandbank, in the mouth of the Thames River. This single-masted sloop had two ship's lanterns placed 12 feet apart on a cross-arm attached to the mast. The vessel proved so effective that Britain soon had five lightships in use, and more would follow.

Rear Range Light, Bailey's Harbor, Wisconsin

The first American lightship went into service in 1821, anchored off Craney Island at the entrance to the Elizabeth River, near Norfolk, Virginia. Four other lightships were placed in Chesapeake Bay in 1822, and the first "outside," or oceanic, lightship was stationed in the Atlantic 7 miles off Sandy Hook, New Jersey, in 1823. At 230 tons, this was the largest of the early lightships. Only two others were placed at outside stations: at Five-Fathom Bank and Carysfort Reef, Florida.

Lightships multiplied along American shores during the tenure of Stephen Pleasonton, Fifth Auditor of the Treasury Department. There were twenty-six in operation by 1837 and forty-two when Pleasonton yielded control of the service to the Lighthouse Board in 1852. During this period of growth, lightship duty was especially trying. A conscientious bureaucrat, with no experience at sea, Pleasonton economized rigorously to keep lighthouse expenditures below the Congressional budget. Thus for a long period, no tender (relief) ship was provided. In 1852 there was only one such ship to serve the needs of forty-two lightships. When something went wrong aboard a lightship, whether due to a crew member's illness, or the loss of

critical equipment, the ship simply returned to port, leaving its station without a light. The tragicomic aspect of Pleasonton's thrift was manifested in 1826, when the Diamond Shoals lightship off Cape Hatteras snapped her moorings and had to make harbor at Norfolk, Virginia. Rather than purchase a new anchor and cable, Pleasonton ordered a search for the missing equipment, with the incentive of a $500 reward. Only when this approach failed did he replace the anchor and cable, having left the treacherous Diamond Shoals without a lightship from May through November.

Improvements came soon after the Lighthouse Board assumed control in 1852. All of its members had some type of maritime experience, and responded to complaints like those from the *Sandy Hook's* captain. One of the first new lightships was stationed at Minots Ledge, off Cohasset, Massachusetts, in 1854. It remained until the famous lighthouse on the reef was finished in 1860. The Lighthouse Board began the practice of numbering the ships, beginning on the Northeast coast and ascending to the Southeast. From that time, lightships retained their original numbers even when they changed their stations.

To millions of immigrants who arrived before 1914, the *Fire Island* lightship was their first glimpse of the New World. The red hull of the flush-deck, schooner-rigged ship, with her dual masts, rode in 96 feet of water, 10 miles south of the Fire Island Lighthouse. From there, they were guided into the New York Harbor channel by the *Ambrose* lightship, which served until 1967 and is now on display as part of New York City's South Street Seaport Museum.

On the West Coast, the *Blunts Reef* lightship was stationed off Cape Mendocino, and another was anchored at San Francisco. Canada found the need for a lightship where the Fraser River runs into the Strait of Georgia, just outside Vancouver, when British Columbia's population exploded with the discovery of gold in 1858. The government purchased the *South Sands Head* and anchored her off the river's mouth. Despite severe gales and low morale, the *South Sands Head* remained on station for fourteen years, until 1879, when she was no longer serviceable. She ended her career as a fishing barge. The lightship was replaced by the North Sands Lighthouse, which stood guard until 1905, when shifting sands rendered it obsolete. The lightship *Mermaid*, which was once rammed by a steamship, served at the confluence until 1911. Two years later, the *Thomas F. Bayard*, an American ship, was rechristened *Sands Head Number 16* and anchored in the channel. She remained on station until 1957, and the Canadians built a new lighthouse in 1960.

Marine architects made significant improvements to lightships late in the nineteenth century. They installed bilge keels, to reduce the amount of roll, and flattened the hulls, while considering new types of building material. The original lightships were, of course, made of wood, and in 1851, Pleasonton noted that the lifetime of the average ship was only five to ten years. In 1852 the Lighthouse Board found that a marine worm was the culprit: "A whole plank is completely riddled with wormholes before the least indication is visible on the skin of the ship inside. A small leak is a sure warning that the vessel must be docked right away." Even then, it was not until 1886 that the Board recommended replacing wooden-hulled ships with iron-hulled vessels. The first "iron boat," weighing 400 tons, was placed at Merrills Shell Bank, Louisiana, in 1847. From 1882 onward, new lightships were built of either iron or steel.

A number of lightship tenders were either purchased or built after 1852. At first, all were sailing vessels; the steam tender *Shubrick* was introduced in 1858, on the West Coast. After the Civil War, steam-powered tenders became the norm. It was customary to name them for flowers, trees and other plants, for example, the *Iris*, *Cactus*, *Geranium* and *Heliotrope*. The tenders displayed the Lighthouse service flag, which was adopted in 1869. Triangular in shape, with a red border, it bore a blue lighthouse on a white field.

Even as these developments improved safety and increased the longevity of lightships, their use was declining as offshore lighthouse building techniques enabled permanent beacons to mark many of the hazards formerly patrolled by ships. Lightships were expensive, requiring large crews perhaps fifteen to twenty strong, and hazardous, often endangering crew members' lives. A fixed structure would prove far more economical by comparison with a lightship within just a few years of

its construction date. In addition to the various types of lighthouses described in chapter 4, by the twentieth century lighthouses could be built far offshore, like the "Texas Towers." These openwork steel structures are based largely on the design of offshore oil and gas wells and have upper decks housing the light, power plant, equipment and, in some cases, personnel accommodations. In 1967 the last lightship anchored at Ambrose Channel, the entrance to New York Harbor, was replaced by a platform light, which was automated in 1988. Some fifteen towers of this type have replaced the old lightships in American waters in the past few decades.

Lamps and Lenses

Early light sources for lighthouses, as we have seen, included wood fires, coal grates and candelabra, as used at Eddystone. The next refinement was the introduction of lamps with up to ten wicks, which needed careful trimming and frequent replacement. Soot for the glass chimneys housing the wicks, as well as the reflectors and lenses, required relentless cleaning. Anything that impaired visibility through the thick panes of storm glass that protected the lens from the elements had to be removed. Fuel oil was carried daily from a separate oil house into the tower. Whale oil was used until the

Port Washington Breakwater Light, Port Washington, Wisconsin

Light mechanism, Point Reyes Light, Point Reyes, California

The study of double refraction was Fresnel's last major contribution to optics. Thereafter, his responsibilities on the Lighthouse Commission absorbed most of his time. He brought the same concentration and inventiveness to the design, construction and location of lighthouses that he had demonstrated in his work on scientific and mathematical theories. His *Complete Works* were published in three volumes in the 1860s, thirty-five years after he died of tuberculosis at the age of thirty-nine. They contained almost everything that was known about optics up to the time of his death in 1827.

The first lighthouse lens Fresnel developed was a "dioptric" system, which combined the use of lenses and prisms. He devised a concentric series of thin lenses in a ring, centered around a bulls-eye lens. Prisms placed in conjunction with these lenses captured light that would otherwise have diffused outward and refracted it into the main light beam. In this way, the available light was concentrated, creating a powerful beam from a much less heavy system than from a similar-strength solid lens. The parabolic reflector, pioneered in the seventeenth century and refined during the 1760s by Antoine Lavoisier, was an enormous improvement over previous light sources because it concentrated the light beam. Fresnel improved his system by adding reflectors, to create a lamp known as "catadioptric" system when combined with the lenses and prisms. This new compound system of reflection and refraction dramatically increased the range of light beam: In a first-order lens, the signal could be seen more than 20 miles away—much farther than a comparable weight of structure using a solid lens, or a system without prisms and reflectors.

Fresnel's lenses were rapidly adopted throughout Europe and, some decades later, in North America. Although few Fresnel lenses remain in service today, a great many have been preserved in nautical and naval museums. However, Fresnel's principle of lenses made from a series of glass rings to concentrate light beams is still used in the production of automobile headlights, spotlights, traffic signals and projectors.

Fresnel lenses were made in seven different sizes called "orders." The largest, first-order lenses, were employed in seacoast towers: Their beams of light were visible for

1850s, when it became too expensive; it was replaced first by lard oil and later by kerosene.

The Argand Lamp, introduced in 1781, had a hollow circular wick and produced an intense smokeless light. In 1789 it was paired with a parabolic reflector and served long and usefully, being adopted and modified later by the French physicist Fresnel.

Jean-Augustin Fresnel was born on May 10, 1788, in Broglie, Normandy. At the age of sixteen, he began studies in engineering. After completing his training, he entered government service as a civil engineer. Fresnel became interested in optics, and his scientific investigations included light interference, diffraction and polarization. He was particularly influenced by the ground-breaking optical research of mathematician Antoine de Condorcet, who pioneered the development of compound lenses built up of concentric lens rings with prismatic cross-sections. Fresnel's most brilliant writings, relating light-polarization phenomena to Thomas Young's hypothesis of transverse waves, were published between 1818 and 1821. They won him unanimous election to the *Academie des Sciences* in 1823 and to the Royal Society of London four years later.

more than 20 miles. Some 6 feet in diameter and 10 to 12 feet high, they weighed more than 4 tons. Fourth- and fifth-order lenses were used mainly for harbor-entrance lights and were about 3 feet high by 20 inches in diameter, a little smaller in fifth-order systems. Each lens was made in brass-framed sections, with numbers inscribed into the frames. They were shipped in sections from their factory of origin in several European locations and were reassembled at their destinations.

Lighthouse lenses were designed to allow adjacent lights to display a characteristic signal that distinguished it from its neighbors. Some lights cast a constant beam, while flashing lanterns varied in time sequences and/or colors. Sequencing was determined by the varying combinations of lighted and blank panels. Rotation systems were also devised for these heavy lenses, supported on ball bearings or, later, mercury baths. Initially, lens rotation was done by a hand-wound clockwork mechanism; later, the process was automated. These advances meant that paired lights, once built routinely to enable the pair to be distinguished from nearby markers, soon became obsolete.

While the lens systems were undergoing these radical changes, so, too, were the light sources themselves and the fuel used to power them. Early fuels, from whale oil to paraffin (a coal by-product introduced in the nineteenth century), were highly flammable. Various gases also came into use for lighthouse lamps in the nineteenth century, and these, usually amplified by an incandescent mantle, were easier to maintain than oil lamps. By the turn of the twentieth century, acetylene was becoming the norm.

In 1901 Arthur Kitson invented the pressurized vapor burner, in which an inflammable gas burned under pressure in an incandescent mantle. Burner technology was advanced by Sweden's Nils Gustav Dalén, who produced his Dissolved Acetylene Gas Burner in 1906. In the absence of electricity, this burner is still the normal method of illuminating unmanned lights. Dalén also invented a solar-activated light-valve that increased the intensity of light as night approached and decreased it before dawn, thereby conserving fuel by almost half.

The early twentieth century witnessed tremendous increases in candlepower, far beyond anything the early pioneers of illumination had imagined. In the two decades following 1909, a maximum candlepower of 25,500 grew to 930,000. Great advances in safety and maintenance costs were also accomplished, paving the way for the automation of lighthouses. Eventually, most gas-powered lamps were replaced by electrical systems, some incorporating modern solar cells, and their beam was concentrated with lightweight, low-maintenance plastic optical systems.

Through all the vicissitudes of technology, navigational techniques and patterns of traffic on the world's waterways, the lighthouse has maintained its hold on the popular imagination as a symbol of safety and security. It is heartening to see the growing concern about lighthouse preservation and history at a time when many landmarks have been obliterated by the march of "progress," or allowed to fall into ruin through disuse and neglect. These proud features of the manmade landscape have fascinating stories to tell generations to come, and they are eminently worth our efforts to maintain them as monuments to architecture, engineering and our maritime heritage.

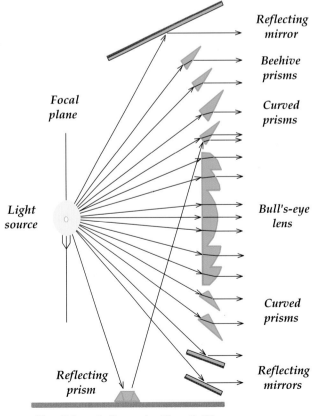

Fresnel lens light-path diagram by Glenn O. Myers

Brier Island Light
Brier Island, Nova Scotia

Just 4 miles long and 2 miles wide, Brier Island is located at the southern end of Digby Neck, on the southwestern side of Nova Scotia. Standing at the entrance to St. Mary's from the Bay of Fundy, which is famous for its high tides, the boldly striped 60-foot lighthouse is the first marker seen by most navigators as they approach the entrance to the bay on the Canadian side. Built in 1944, the red-and-white tower, painted to stand out against the snow, is the second lighthouse on the site: The first was constructed in 1807.

Holland Channel Marker *Below*

Holland, Michigan

Located on the eastern side of Lake Michigan, Holland Channel Marker is a tall cylindrical tower supported on four sturdy posts at the outer end of the northern pier. The marker is red-and-white striped to make it an effective daymark. The channel to the port of Holland flows between converging breakwaters and eventually reaches Lake Macatawa.

Nauset Beach Light *Opposite*

North Eastham, Massachusetts

This was once the site of the "Three Sisters of Nauset," the only set of triple lights built in the United States. The first set rose on Cape Cod in 1838 and was replaced in 1892. Eventually, the triple lights were replaced by the existing 48-foot conical cast-iron tower, painted a bright red and white. Erosion often threatens the Nauset tower, and in 1996 it was moved inland, where it continues to flash its automated red-and-white signal.

Split Rock Light *Opposite*

Two Harbors, Minnesota

Split Rock (see chapter 2) is one of the most impressive and frequently photographed of American lighthouses. The area it lights, along Lake Superior, was especially hazardous to mariners because local iron-ore deposits confounded compasses. After a disastrous 1905 storm, the Lighthouse Board had this octagonal brick tower built on a promontory 130 feet above the lake, complete with a separate building that housed diaphone fog horns, an oil house and two storage barns. Finished in 1910, the 54-foot tower was in use until 1969, when the Coast Guard decommissioned it. Restored by the Minnesota Historical Society, the station is now the centerpiece of 100-acre Split Rock State Park.

Baccalieu Island Light *Below*

Baccalieu Island, Newfoundland

Newfoundland's coastline, where frigid continental air meets the warmer North Atlantic air masses, is often enveloped by fog, and its rock- and reef-studded areas become even more hazardous to mariners. This modest frame station is equipped with powerful automated sound signals that augment the light tower under conditions of low visibility. Supplies must be hoisted up the jagged cliff face to this inaccessible light station, which is guarded today by two keepers and their dog.

Lightship Ambrose *Opposite and below*
South Street Seaport Museum, New York
The 488-ton *Ambrose* took up its station at the entrance to the eponymous channel into New York Harbor on December 1, 1908. Built to mark the hazardous shoals and sandbars of this deep bay, the 112-foot-long lightship was a breakthrough in safe passage for the busy harbor's many passenger and commercial vessels. After 1933, the *Ambrose* was moved closer to Sandy Hook, New Jersey, where she served as the *Scotland* lightship until 1963. Each of its two steel masts supported gimbal-mounted oil lamps that were replaced in 1936 with 1,000-watt lamps with 375mm lenses (opposite, top). The main fog horn is mounted on a cylindrical tower amidships (detail, opposite below). In 1968 the Coast Guard transferred the *Ambrose* to New York City's maritime museum.

Lightship Columbia *Below*

Astoria, Oregon

The *Columbia* was the last lightship to serve on the U.S. West Coast. It kept its station at the entrance to the Columbia River on the Pacific Ocean, southwest of Washington State's Cape Disappointment, from 1951 until 1974, when the Columbia River Maritime Museum acquired it from the Coast Guard and moved it to Astoria's waterfront. Built at the Rice Brothers Shipyard in East Boothbay, Maine, the steel-hulled vessel is 128 feet long, with steel light towers and twin diaphone fog signals. Still in operating condition, it has a 7,000-pound mushroom anchor.

Lightship Huron *Above*

Port Huron, Michigan

Designated "No. 103" (the order in which it took up its station), Lightship *Huron* first went into service on May 1, 1920, as a relief vessel on Lake Michigan. Built between 1918 and 1920 by the Consolidated Ship-building Corporation, the lightship is 97 feet long and weighs approximately 340 tons. From 1936 until 1970, it was stationed at Corsica Shoals on Lake Huron. The only surviving lightship from the Great Lakes and the smallest surviving lightship in the United States, the *Huron* was decommissioned in 1970. The City of Port Huron acquired the light in 1971 and docked it on the St. Clair River near Pine Grove Park.

Lens detail, Cape Blanco Light *Below*

Port Orford, Oregon

The oldest and southernmost of Oregon's major lights, Cape Blanco went into service on December 20, 1870. The 59-foot conical tower stands 245 feet above sea level, and its original first-order Fresnel lens is rated at one million candlepower, visible up to 22 miles. Unfortunately, vandals damaged several prisms in the classical lens in 1992, but it has been painstakingly restored by master optician Larry Hardin of nearby Bandon, Oregon.

Heceta Head Light *Above*

Florence, Oregon

First lighted on March 30, 1894, the lantern at Heceta Head Light still has its original first-order Fresnel lens, with a focal plane 205 feet above sea level. An important making light, it now focuses an automated light visible at 21 miles. Perched on a jagged cliff, the 56-foot conical masonry tower here was built on a scenic headland bearing the name of a Spanish explorer, Don Bruno de Heceta, who first charted the area in 1755.

Lens detail, Anacapa Island Light *Above*

Channel Islands National Park, California

The original third-order Fresnel lens on this inaccessible clifftop site went into service in 1912, focusing an automated acetylene lamp. The Channel Islands had posed a danger to shipping here for centuries. The steamer *Winfield Scott* was wrecked on Anacapa's rocks in 1853, stranding its 250 passengers for several weeks, but it would be sixty more years before a skeleton tower was engineered with materials brought from the mainland. A new 39-foot masonry tower replaced it in 1932, when resident keepers were appointed for the first time. Automated in 1969, the station's Fresnel lens was replaced with a modern lens, as shown here, in 1991.

Point Sur Light *Below*

Big Sur, California

A powerful first-order Fresnel lens was installed in the 1889 lighthouse at Big Sur, a 50-foot granite tower on a sandstone cliff south of Monterey. Keepers had to climb almost 400 steps twice a day to service the light, which emitted red and white flashes. The station was automated in 1972, when a rotating aerobeacon replaced the original Fresnel lens.

I n compiling this gazetteer we have tried to cover extant U.S. light stations as comprehensively as possible, but opinion varies as to the precise definition of a lighthouse. By and large, we have based our criteria for inclusion as an historic lighthouse on the standards set by the National Maritime Initiative, a program within the History Division of the National Park Service, which is charged with surveying and evaluating U.S. light stations. The National Maritime Initiative's lighthouse inventory currently lists nearly 600 historic light stations. The Initiative defines an historic light station as one that required a resident keeper and often, therefore, consisted of a tower and a complex of outbuildings (such as a keeper's dwelling, an oil house, a cistern, and a boathouse or garage). At the bare minimum, a station would have a light tower with an internal keeper's quarters (and this is the case for many of the lighthouses we have included). With a few exceptions, most stations listed are at least 50 years old, and the majority of them have been included in the National Register of Historic Places. We have limited our descriptions to the light stations as they appear today, with only brief historical details, because space prohibits a full history of the structures that preceded the current ones at each lighthouse site. Historic lighthouses that are no longer standing, unless very recently destroyed, have mostly been omitted from this gazetteer. The location given for each light is usually the nearest town: in the case of island lights, this is generally the nearest town on the mainland. Occasionally, sources differ as to dates of construction, lens details, etc.: we have mostly favored the National Park Service or Lighthouse Depot database information, but we welcome comments and corrections from readers who believe they find an error.

NEW ENGLAND

Connecticut

Avery Point Light
University of Connecticut Avery Point campus, near Groton
Constructed in 1944 on the grounds of the former U.S. Coast Guard training station at Avery Point, this lighthouse is meant as a memorial to the Coast Guard's lightkeeping duties. The last lighthouse built in Connecticut, it consists of an unpainted, 55-foot octagonal-cylindrical concrete block tower. The light was extinguished in 1967, when the Coast Guard moved its training facility, and it was placed on *Lighthouse Digest* magazine's "Doomsday List" in 1997. After an extensive fundraising campaign to save and restore the tower, its lantern was relit as an active aid to navigation on October 15, 2006.

Black Rock Harbor (Fayerweather Island) Light
Bridgeport, Fairfield County
In 1933, this 1823 lighthouse was replaced with an offshore beacon. The historic light was renovated in 1998 and its lantern relit in 2000, although it no longer serves as an active aid to navigation. The 47-foot octagonal granite rubble tower is painted white and is topped with a black lantern. It uses a fifth-order Fresnel lens (originally, eight lamps with 14-inch reflectors) and has a height of focal plane of 44 feet above sea level. The keeper's house burned down in 1977. This site, which is open to the public, now serves as a nature preserve.

Faulkners Island Light
Guilford, New Haven County
Located off of Guilford Harbor, on Long Island Sound, this lighthouse was constructed in 1802 and is still active today. The white octagonal tower stands at 46 feet and is constructed of brownstone, with a brick lining. It originally used nine lamps with 16-inch reflectors. Today, the light is fitted with a 190 mm solar-powered optic, and it has a height of focal plane of 94 feet above sea level. Also on site is a brick/masonry sound signal building, constructed in 1922; two cisterns; a wooden boathouse, dating from 1940; a jetty; an observation shelter; and a wharf and breakwater. The keeper's house burned down in 1976. This light station also serves as a national wildlife refuge, and it is not open to the public.

Five Mile Point (Old New Haven) Light
New Haven, New Haven County
First lit in 1845, this historic lighthouse was deactivated in 1877. The octagonal sandstone tower, standing at 70 feet, is painted white and topped with a black lantern. It used 12 lamps, with 21-inch reflectors and, later, a fourth-order Fresnel, and had a height of focal plane of 97 feet above sea level. The keeper's dwelling is an 1835 brick farmhouse, standing at 2.5 stories high. (The tower and the dwelling were previously attached by a covered walkway.) The city took over this light station in 1949, and the site currently functions as a city park.

Great Captain Island Light
Greenwich, Fairfield County
This lighthouse was operational from 1868 until 1970, when it was replaced with a modern skeletal tower. The historic granite and wood tower stands at 51 feet and is octagonal in shape. It used a fourth-order Fresnel lens and had a height of focal plane of 74 feet above sea level. The 2.5-story keeper's quarters are integral to the tower. Other structures on site include an oil house and a storage building.

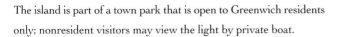

The island is part of a town park that is open to Greenwich residents only; nonresident visitors may view the light by private boat.

Greens Ledge Light
See page 166

Lynde Point (Saybrook) Light
See page 59

Morgan Point Light
See page 134

Mystic Seaport Light
See pages 148–49

New Haven Long Wharf Light
New Haven, New Haven County

First established in 1854 in the inner harbor, the original iron post light was replaced with an iron tower in 1900 and then later with a modern skeletal tower, whose automatic light is operational today.

New London Harbor Light
New London, New London County

This active lighthouse is a white, octagonal pyramidal tower, standing at 89 feet, with a height of focal plane of 90 feet above sea level. The tower is constructed of brownstone and is painted white, with a black lantern. It was first lit in 1801, when it used 11 lamps with 13-inch reflectors. The light was automated in 1912 and still uses its original fourth-order Fresnel lens. Visible for 15 miles, the light is located on the west side of the entrance to New London Harbor. The keeper's house, dating from 1863, is a 2.5-story brick (gable-style) structure. The tower is owned by the New London Maritime Society, though the keeper's house has been a private residence since 1912. This site is not open to the public.

New London Ledge Light
See page 172

Peck Ledge Light
Norwalk, Fairfield County

This cast-iron tower, standing at 54 feet and conical ("spark plug" style) in shape, is painted white, with a brown band, and stands upon a black pier. It was constructed in 1906, was automated in 1933, and is still in use today. Today, the tower uses a 250 mm optic

(it originally had a fourth-order Fresnel), and it has a height of focal plane of 61 feet above sea level. The keeper's quarters are located within the tower. This light station is owned and managed by the U.S. Coast Guard, and it is not open to the public.

Penfield Reef Light
Fairfield, Fairfield County

Situated at the entrance to Black Harbor, on Long Island Sound, the octagonal wood tower of this lighthouse is painted white and topped with a black lantern. Standing at 35 feet, it was constructed in 1874, automated in 1971, and it is still in use today as an aid to navigation. It is fitted with a DCB-24 optic (originally, a fourth-order Fresnel) and has a height of focal plane of 51 feet above sea level. The granite and wood keeper's quarters are integral with the tower. This light, restored in 2001, is owned and managed by the U.S. Coast Guard, and it is not open to the public.

Saybrook Breakwater Light
See page 166

Sheffield Island (Norwalk) Light
See page 66

Southwest Ledge (Newhaven Breakwater) Light
See page 177

Stamford Harbor (Chatham Rocks) Light
Stamford, Fairfield County

This 1882 lighthouse was deactivated in 1953 and was renovated circa 1984. Today, it functions as a private aid to navigation, and it is not open to the public. The cast-iron tower stands at 60 feet. It has a conical ("spark plug") shape and is painted white, and it sits upon a cylindrical red pier. The light has a height of focal plane of 80 feet above sea level and it originally used a fourth-order Fresnel lens. Today, the tower is fitted with a 200 mm optic. The keeper's quarters are contained within the tower.

Stonington Harbor Light
Stonington, New London County

First erected at Windmill Point, this beacon was moved to the east side of Stonington Harbor in 1840. It was in use until 1889, when it was replaced by the Stonington West Breakwater Light, which was destroyed by a hurricane in 1938. The old lighthouse has functioned as a museum since 1925. It consists of an octagonal granite tower, standing at 35 feet. It used a sixth-order Fresnel lens (which is now on display in the lighthouse museum) and had a height of focal plane of 62 feet above sea level. The keeper's house, which is attached to the tower, is a 1.5-story granite house dating from 1840. The museum is owned and managed by the Stonington Historical Society.

Stratford Point Light

Stratford, Fairfield County

This historic lighthouse has an interesting history: its original lantern was removed to accommodate a DCB-224 optic in 1969, and then was replaced in 1990. The 35-foot conical cast-iron tower—first lit in 1881 and automated in 1970—is painted white, with a red band midway, and a black lantern. Today, it uses a 190 mm optic (originally, a third-order Fresnel), and it has a height of focal plane of 52 feet above sea level. Also on site is a brick sound signal building, dating from 1911; a 1.5-story wooden (carpenter gothic–style) keeper's house, from 1881; and a radiobeacon. Owned by the U.S. Coast Guard, this light station serves as an active aid to navigation and as Coast Guard housing. It is not open to the public.

Stratford Shoal (Middle Ground) Light

Bridgeport, Fairfield County

First lit in 1877, this granite block structure consists of an octagonal tower atop a square dwelling. The lighthouse, topped with a white lantern, was automated in 1970 and is still in use today. The tower stands at 35 feet and has a height of focal plane of 60 feet above sea level. Its original, fourth-order Fresnel lens has now been replaced with a 190 mm solar-powered optic. The keeper's quarters are located within the tower. Also on site is a radiobeacon. This light station is owned and managed by the U.S. Coast Guard, and it is not open to the public.

Tongue Point (Bridgeport Breakwater) Light

West side of Bridgeport Harbor entrance, Bridgeport

Dating from 1895, this active lighthouse consists of a 31-foot cast-iron tower with a 155 mm lens. The entire tower is painted black, and there are no keeper's quarters (the light was originally tended by the keepers at the nearby Bridgeport Harbor Light and its signal was automated in 1954). The tower was relocated in 1919, when the breakwater was shortened. The light is managed by the U.S. Coast Guard, and the site and tower are closed to the public (but may be viewed from Sound View Park and from the Bridgeport–Port Jefferson, NY, ferry).

Maine

Baker Island Light

Islesford, Hancock County

This cylindrical masonry tower is white with a black lantern and stands at 43 feet. It was first lit in 1855 and was automated in 1966. With a height of focal plane of 105 feet above sea level, the Baker Island Light has a 300 mm solar-powered lens (which replaced the original lens, a fourth-order Fresnel). The tower stands next to the keeper's quarters, also dating from 1855, a 1.5-story wooden Cape Cod–style dwelling. (The tower was once connected to the keeper's quarters via a passageway.) Other structures include an 1895 brick oil house, a 1905 shingled fuel house, two storage buildings. An offshore lighted buoy replaced this lighthouse as an active aid to navigation in 2002. This site is open to the public during the summer.

Bass Harbor Head Light

See page 98

Bear Island Light

Northeast Harbor, Hancock County

First lit in 1889, this light was inactive from 1981 until 1989, and it now serves as a private aid to navigation. The cylindrical, exposed brick tower (with a black lantern) stands at 31 feet and is attached to a workroom. It originally used a fifth-order Fresnel lens (this optic has now been removed) and had a height of focal plane of 100 feet above sea level. Other structures include a 1.5-story wooden (gambrel roof–style) keeper's quarters; a stone oil house, dating from 1905; a boathouse; and a barn, dating from 1889. This lighthouse is owned by the National Park Service, on lease to a private owner, and is not open to the public.

Blue Hill Bay Light

Brooklin, Hancock County

Set on Green Island, Blue Hill Bay Light was operational from 1857 until 1933. The cylindrical masonry tower is painted white, with a black lantern, and stands at 22 feet. It used a fifth-order Fresnel lens and had a height of focal plane of 26 feet above sea level. The keeper's quarters—a 1.5-story wooden colonial cape-style house—dates from 1856. The lighthouse was sold in 1995, and it currently serves as a private summer home. In 1935, an automated skeletal tower was constructed nearby. The modern tower uses a solar-powered optic and has a height of focal plane of 25 feet above sea level.

Boon Island Light

Island off York Beach,
York County

This 1855 cylindrical granite tower was the third lighthouse constructed on this site—one of the most isolated and dangerous stations off of the Maine coast. Standing at 133 feet on a relatively flat island, the tower often appears to be rising up out of the sea (especially when the clouds are par-

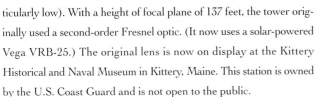

Above: **Engineer's plan of Boon Island Light, Maine**

ticularly low). With a height of focal plane of 137 feet, the tower originally used a second-order Fresnel optic. (It now uses a solar-powered Vega VRB-25.) The original lens is now on display at the Kittery Historical and Naval Museum in Kittery, Maine. This station is owned by the U.S. Coast Guard and is not open to the public.

Browns Head Light

Vinalhaven Island, Knox County

Standing at 20 feet, this cylindrical brick tower (white, with a black lantern) uses a fourth-order Fresnel lens (it originally used a fifth-order Fresnel) and has a height of focal plane of 39 feet above sea level. This lighthouse was constructed in 1857 (it replaced an earlier tower, dating from 1832), was automated in 1987, and is still active today. The keeper's quarters, dating from 1857, is a 1.5-story wooden cottage. There is also an oil house, dating from 1903. The sound signal building has been destroyed, and the original fog bell is now on display in the Vinalhaven Historical Society Museum. The light station is currently the residence of the Vinalhaven town manager, and only the grounds are open to the public.

Burnt Coat Harbor Light

Swans Island, Hancock County

A square masonry tower standing at 32 feet, the Burnt Coat Harbor lighthouse was first lit in 1872 and was automated in 1975. The tower is white with a black lantern, uses a 250 mm optic (which replaced the original, fourth-order Fresnel), and has a height of focal plane of 75 feet above sea level. Other structures include a 1911 wooden, trapezoidal sound signal building (though the bell is now inactive); an 1872 L-shaped Cape Cod–style keeper's quarters (which was originally connected to the tower by a covered passageway); and an 1895 brick oil house. This light is owned and managed by the Town of Swans Island and the U.S. Coast Guard, and its grounds are open to the public.

Burnt Island Light

Southport, Lincoln County

Erected in 1821 at the entrance to Boothbay Harbor, this conical, rubble-stone lighthouse stands at 30 feet. It has a height of focal plane of 61 feet above sea level, uses a 300 mm optic (it originally used Lewis Patent reflectors), and is painted white with a black lantern. The light is attached to the 1857 keeper's quarters (a 1.5-story wood cottage). Other structures include an 1889 oil house, an 1857 covered walkway (between the tower and the keeper's quarters), an 1880 boathouse, the original fuel house, an 1877 barn, and a 1907 hen house. This site was automated in 1989. It is owned by the Department of Marine Resources and the grounds are open to the public.

Cape Elizabeth Light

See pages 118 and 119

Cape Neddick "The Nubble" Light

See pages 94 and 95

The Cuckolds Light

Cape Newagen/Booth Bay Approach, near Southport

This station began as a fog signal station in 1892, and the light tower was placed on the roof of the fog signal building in 1907. This light was automated in 1975 and is still operational. The octagonal wooden tower stands at 48 feet (with a height of focal plane of 59 feet above sea level) and uses a Vega 25 optic. (The original, fourth-order Fresnel lens is on display at the Shore Village Museum in Rockland, ME.) The tower is painted white, with red trim. There is also a radiobeacon on the site. The 1892 keeper's quarters have been destroyed. This light is owned and operated by the U.S. Coast Guard and is not open to the public.

Curtis Island Light

Camden, Knox County

Located at the entrance to Camden Harbor, on Penobscot Bay, this 1896 cylindrical masonry tower (painted white, with a black lantern) stands at 25 feet and has a height of focal plane of 52 feet above sea level. In 1994, the original, fourth-order Fresnel lens was replaced with a 300 mm solar-powered optic. (The Fresnel is now on display at the Camden Public Library.) The nearby keeper's quarters, dating from 1889, is a 1.5-story wooden farmhouse. Also on site are a barn and a boathouse, both dating from 1889, and an oil house from 1895. This lighthouse, known for years as Negro Island Light, is owned by the Town of Camden and the grounds are open to the public.

Deer Island Thorofare Light
Mark Island/Deer Island Thorofare,
near Stonington, Hancock County

This lighthouse is known locally as Mark Island Light. Standing at 25 feet, the 1858 square brick tower (white, with a black lantern) was automated in 1958. It uses a 250 mm solar-powered lens (it originally used a fourth-order optic) and has a height of focal plane of 52 feet above sea level. The tower is attached to a square workroom. Other structures (including the sound signal building, boathouse, and oil house) were demolished in the 1970s. The original keeper's quarters were destroyed by fire in 1959. Today, the lighthouse is owned and operated by the Island Heritage Trust, and it serves as an active aid to navigation and as a bird sanctuary.

Dice Head Light (Old)
Castine, Hancock County

Located at the mouth of the Penobscot River, this 1829 lighthouse was deactivated in 1937 (when its light was removed to a new, skeletal tower on the north side of the entrance to Castine Harbor). It is a conical granite rubble-stone tower, painted white with a black lantern. It originally used a Lewis Patent apparatus and had a height of focal plane of 130 feet above sea level. The tower was attached to the 1.5-story colonial cape-style keeper's quarters, which burned down in 1999. Other structures include an 1888 barn and an 1895 oil house. The lighthouse now functions as a private residence but it is open to the public.

Doubling Point (Kennebec River) Range Lights
Arrowsic Island, Sagadahoc County

These relatively small towers—standing at 13 and 21 feet—were first lit in 1898 and were automated in 1980. They are octagonal in shape, are constructed of wood, and are painted white with red roofs. Originally equipped with fifth-order reflectors, each tower now uses a 250 mm optic, projected through a small, square window. Also on site are an 1898 sound signal building, a 1902 oil house, a 1901 boathouse, an 1897 fuel house, and a walkway that runs between the structures. This site is owned and operated by the Range Light Keepers and the grounds are open to the public.

Doubling Point Light
Arrowsic Island, Sagadahoc County

This light station was established in 1898, was automated in 1988, and is still operational today. The white, octagonal wooden tower is located at the end of a footbridge. It uses a 300 mm lens (the original, fourth-order Fresnel is on display at the Shore Village Museum in Rockland, Maine). Other structures include a sound building (which is no longer active) and an L-shaped, 1.5-story keeper's quarters (both dating from 1898), as well as an oil house, and a storage building. The Friends of Doubling Point own the tower, but the dwelling is privately owned. The grounds are open to the public.

Eagle Island Light
Town of Deer Island, Hancock County

This 1838 light is situated on east Penobscot Bay. The white, conical tower (constructed of granite rubble stone) stands at 30 feet and has a black lantern. It was automated in 1959, uses a 300 mm solar-powered lens (originally, a fourth-order Fresnel), and has a height of focal plane of 106 feet above sea level. The bell tower–style sound signal building was built in 1939. All other structures, including the keeper's quarters and an oil house, have been razed. The Eagle Light Caretakers own the lighthouse tower, and the bell tower is privately owned. This site is not open to the public.

Egg Rock Light
Winter Harbor, Hancock County

Signaling the entrance to Frenchmans Bay, near Winter Harbor, Egg Rock Light was first lit in 1875 and was automated in 1976. The square masonry tower stands at 40 feet and has a height of focal plane of 64 feet above sea level. The original lantern room (containing a fifth-order Fresnel) was removed to accommodate an airport-type beacon, but was restored with an aluminum replica in 1986. Today, the tower uses a 250 mm rotating optic, which was installed in 1980. The brick sound signal building dates from 1904, and the 1.5-story (wood-constructed) keepers quarters date from 1875 are integral to the tower. This site is managed by the Maine Coastal Islands National Wildlife Refuge and is not open to the public. A number of sightseeing cruises depart from Bar Harbor.

Fort Point Light
Entrance to Penobscot River, near Stockton Springs,
Waldo County

Standing adjacent to Fort Point State Park, this lighthouse is now being developed as a museum. The 31-foot, square brick tower (painted cream, with black trim) was first lit in 1857. It was automated in 1988 and remains operational today. The lighthouse retains its original, fourth-order Fresnel lens and has a height of focal plane of 88 feet above sea level. The tower is attached to the keeper's quarters, a 1.5-story, L-shaped colonial cape-style dwelling. Also of interest is the sound signal building, a pyramidal wooden bell tower dating from 1890. (The original bell is displayed outside the tower.) Other structures include a barn and a brick oil house, both dating from the 1890s. This site is owned by the State of Maine and is open to the public.

Fort Popham Light
Phippsburg, Sagadahoc County

Established in 1899 on a spindle next to the 1861 fort, the light was moved to the top of the fort walls in the 1940s. Now automated, it is still maintained by the Coast Guard. The grounds are open to the public.

Franklin Island Light
Friendship, Lincoln County

Established in 1805, this is the third-oldest lighthouse site in Maine. The current tower dates from 1855. Rising at 45 feet, this cylindrical brick tower (painted white, with gray and red trim) uses a 250 mm solar-powered lens (which replaced the original, fourth-order Fresnel) and has a height of focal plane of 57 feet above sea level. The Franklin Island Light was automated in 1967 and is still in use today. (It is operated by the U.S. Coast Guard and is not open to the public). The keeper's quarters (once attached to the tower) was dismantled in 1967, though the 1895 oil house still remains on site. Franklin Island is uninhabited.

Goat Island Light
Kennebunkport, York County

This light station, on Cape Porpoise Harbor, was first established in 1834 and the current lighthouse dates from 1859. The cylindrical masonry tower, white with a black lantern, stands at 25 feet and has a height of focal plane of 38 feet above sea level. In 1990, when the tower was automated, its fifth-order lens was replaced with a 300 mm optic. The original sound signal building has been destroyed, though the 1860 keepers quarters—a 1.5-story, L-shaped colonial cape-style dwelling—still remain. The site also contains a 1907 brick oil house, a 1905 wooden boathouse, and a launchway. This light is owned by the Kennebunkport Conservation Trust and the grounds are open to the public.

Goose Rocks Light
North Haven, Knox County

This light, located at the east entrance to Fox Islands Thorofare, was first lit in 1890. The cast-iron, "spark plug" style tower (painted white, with black base and trim) stands at 51 feet tall, upon a concrete and cast-iron caisson, and has a height of focal plane of 51 feet above sea level. The light was automated in 1963, and the original, fourth-order lens has been replaced with a 250 mm solar-powered optic. The keeper's quarters are contained within the tower. This lighthouse is owned and operated by the U.S. Coast Guard and is not open to the public.

Great Duck Island Light
Frenchboro, Hancock County

Located on this isolated island at the Blue Hill Bay approach, the Great Duck Island lighthouse was first lit in 1890 and was automated in 1986. The cylindrical, white brick and granite tower (with a black lantern) stands at 42 feet. It uses a VRB-25 solar-powered optic (which replaced the original, fifth-order Fresnel) and has a height of focal plane of 67 feet above sea level. The square brick fog signal building, also dating from 1890, retains its original, bell type foghorn. Also on site are the original keeper's quarters (a 1.5-story wood-framed cottage), a stone oil house, a storage building, and a boathouse. This light station is owned and managed by the College of the Atlantic and is not open to the public.

Grindel Point Light
Islesboro, Waldo County

First lit in 1874, this square masonry tower stands at 39 feet and is painted white, with black trim. In 1934, this light was functionally replaced by a new skeleton tower that was built nearby. In 1987, at the request of local citizens, the Coast Guard moved the light back into the old tower and removed the modern tower. The tower now uses a 250 mm optic (it originally had a fifth-order Fresnel), and it has a height of focal plane is 39 feet above sea level. Also on site are the original keeper's quarters (attached to the tower), an oil house, and a boathouse. This light is owned by the Town of Islesboro and is open to the public.

Halfway Rock Light
South Harpswell, Cumberland County

This conical, white granite tower (located on Casco Bay, off Bailey Island) stands at 76 feet, has a black lantern, uses a Vega VRB-25 solar-powered optic (the original, third-order Fresnel was removed in 1994), and has a height of focal plane of 77 feet above sea level. The light was automated in 1975 and is still in use today (it was licensed to the American Lighthouse Foundation in 2000 and is not open to the public). Except for the tower, most of the original structures (including the keeper's quarters) were washed away during a particularly bad storm in 1991.

Hendricks Head Light

West Southport, Lincoln County

The square masonry tower of Hendricks Head Light stands at 39 feet tall and has a height of focal plane of 43 feet above sea level. Established in 1829, the present tower was built in 1875 and held a fifth-order Fresnel lens, but it is now fitted with a 250 mm optic. The tower is painted with a plain whitewash and has a black lantern. It was deactivated from 1933 until 1951, automated in 1975, and remains in operation today (though it is privately owned and is not open the public). Other structures on the site include a pyramidal bell tower (dating from 1890), a two-story Victorian keeper's dwelling (dating from 1875), two cisterns, a brick oil house, and a barn (dating from 1880).

Heron Neck Light

Vinalhaven, Knox County

Situated on Green's Island, this cylindrical masonry tower (painted white, with red and black trim) stands at 30 feet, on a granite block foundation, with a height of focal plane of 92 feet above sea level. This lighthouse was first lit in 1854 and was automated in 1982 (when its fifth-order Fresnel was replaced with a 300 mm optic). The masonry sound signal building dates from 1944 and retains its original foghorn. The 1895 keeper's dwelling, which is attached to the lighthouse and was damaged in a fire in 1989, is a 1.5-story L-shaped structure made from wood. This working lighthouse is owned by the Island Institute and also functions as a research and education facility. It is not open to the public.

Indian Island Light

Rockport, Knox County

The Indian Island light station (located on Rockport Harbor) was first established in 1850, and the historic lighthouse was built in 1875. The square brick tower used a fourth-order Fresnel lens and was in use until 1934 (when it was replaced by the Lowell Rock Pole Beacon). The original keeper's quarters is still on site—a 1.5-story, T-shaped brick/frame house. Also on site is an oil house (dating from 1904), a fuel house (from 1888), and two storage buildings. This inactive lighthouse is privately owned and is not open to the public.

Isle Au Haut (Robinson Point) Light

Isle Au Haut, Knox County

First lit in 1907, this granite and brick lighthouse stands at 40 feet and has a height of focal plane of 48 feet above sea level. Its upper section is painted white, with a black lantern. The tower was automated in 1934 and it now uses a 250 mm solar-powered lens (the original, fourth-order Fresnel is now on display at the Shore Village Museum in Rockland). The 2.5-story Victorian keeper's house dates from 1907 and is now a bed and breakfast inn. Also on site are an oil house, a boathouse, a catwalk, a wood shed, and an outhouse. The tower is owned by the Town of Isle Au Haut, was completely restored in 1999, and is open to the public.

Ladies Delight Light

Lake Cobbosseecontee, one mile south of Island Park, Manchester, Kennebec County

This 16-foot stone tower, with a frame lantern, was built in 1908 and is seasonally lit. The light is leaning and is in need of restoration, though some repairs were made in 2001. Accessible only by boat, the site and tower are owned by the Cobbosseecontee Yacht Club and are not open to the public.

Libby Island Light

Machiasport, Washington County

This 1822 lighthouse was automated in 1974 and is still in use today. It is located at the entrance to Machias Bay. Standing at 42 feet, the conical, granite block tower has a black lantern, uses a DCB-224 optic (originally, it used a fourth-order Fresnel), and has a height of focal plane of 91 feet above sea level. Also on site are a brick sound signal building (dating from 1884), an oil house (1883), and a generator building. The keeper's quarters has been dismantled and a boat launch is deteriorating. This site is owned by the Fish & Wildlife Service and is open to the public.

Little Mark Island Monument

Little Mark Island, one mile southwest of Bailey Island

Built in 1827, this square pyramidal, unpainted granite monument has a modern beacon mounted at the top, with a height of focal plane of 74 feet above the sea. The tower has a room at the base, which is now used for storage. The structure was never intended to be used as a lighthouse, and it is uncertain when it came in use as an aid to navigation. The site is open (and accessible only by boat), but the tower is closed. The lighthouse is visible from the end of ME 24 on Bailey Island.

Little River Light

Little River Island (Cutler Harbor), Washington County

This cylindrical cast-iron and brick tower was operational from 1876 until 1980 (when it was replaced by a skeletal tower) but was relit in 2001 with its VRB-25 optic serving as an active aid to navigation. It is painted white, with a black lantern, and stands at 41 feet. The tower originally housed a fifth-order Fresnel lens and has a height of focal plane of 56 feet above sea level. The L-shaped Victorian keeper's house, currently under restoration, stands at 1.5 stories and dates from 1888. Also on site are a brick oil house and a boathouse. This site is now owned by the American Lighthouse Foundation and is not open to the public.

Lubec Channel Light

Lubec, Washington County

A conical, "spark plug" style tower, the Lubec Channel lighthouse consists of a 40-foot white cast-iron tower on a black (concrete and cast-iron caisson) cylindrical pier. It was automated in 1939 and, in 1985, its fourth-order Fresnel lens was replaced with a 155 mm solar-powered optic. The tower's height of focal plane is 53 feet above sea level. The keeper's quarters are contained within the tower, and there are cisterns located in the basement. This light is owned and operated by the U.S. Coast Guard and is not open to the public. It was substantially restored in 1993–1994, and the original fog bell is in the local museum in Lubec.

Marshall Point Light

Port Clyde, Knox County

Standing at 31 feet, this cylindrical white granite and brick tower has a black lantern. The tower was first lit in 1857, and it was automated in 1980. In 1981, its original, fourth-order Fresnel was removed (to the Shore Village Museum in Rockland) and replaced with a 300 mm optic. The 1895 keeper's house—a 1.5-story colonial revival dwelling—is still on site and houses a museum which is open to the public. Other structures include an oil house and a wooden catwalk (attaching the tower to the land).

Matinicus Rock Light (Twin Towers)

Rockland, Knox County

First lit in 1857, this operational lighthouse was automated in 1983 and uses a Vega VRB-25 solar-powered lens. The North light was discontinued in 1924; its original, third-order Fresnel lens is now on display at the Shore Village Museum in Rockland.) The cylindrical, granite block South tower stands at 48 feet. Other struc-

Above: **A U.S. Coast Guard period photograph of Matinicus Rock Light**

tures include the keeper's quarters (a rectangular, two-story granite and wood structure dating from 1846), a storage building, a boathouse (dating from 1890), the assistant keeper's quarters, and a brick generator building. This site is owned by the U.S. Fish & Wildlife Service and is open to the public.

Monhegan Island Light

Monhegan, Lincoln County

This cylindrical granite block lighthouse was first lit in 1850 (it was automated in 1959) and is still in use today. The tower stands at 47 feet and has a height of focal plane of 178 feet above sea level. In 1995, its second-order Fresnel optic was replaced with a Vega VRB-25 solar-powered lens. The keeper's house, dating from 1874, is a 1.5-story Gothic revival structure. Other structures on the site include a cistern, an oil house (circa 1893), a garage, a storage building, a chicken coup, a catwalk, and 1998 replicas of the assistant keeper's quarters and the adjacent storage shed (the originals were razed in 1922). This light station is owned by the Monhegan Historical & Cultural Museum and is open to the public.

Moose Peak Light

Mistake Island/Eastern Bay (near Jonesport), Washington County

The light station was first established on Mistake Island in 1827, and the current tower (also known as the "Mistake Island Light") was first lit in 1851. Standing at 57 feet (with a height of focal plane of 72 feet above sea level), it is conical in shape and painted white (with black trim). The lighthouse was automated in 1972 and, in 1993, its second-order Fresnel was replaced with a DCB-24 rotating optic. The 1902 keeper's house was dismantled in 1982, but the 1912 brick foghorn building remains on site. This station is owned by the U.S. Coast Guard, on lease to the Nature Conservancy, and is not open to the public.

Mount Desert Rock Light
Frenchboro, Hancock County

Situated in the south of Mount Desert Island, this lighthouse was designed by the noted architect and engineer Alexander Parris (it replaced a previous wooden lighthouse, built in 1830). The conical granite block tower stands at 58 feet and has a height of focal plane of 75 feet above sea level. It was first lit in 1847, was automated in 1977, and remains in use today. The tower's black lantern originally held a third-order Fresnel lens, which was replaced with a Vega VRB-25 solar-powered optic in 1993. Other structures include the keeper's quarters (a wooden colonial duplex structure dating from 1892), a cistern, a storage building, and a boathouse (from 1895). This site is owned by the College of the Atlantic (used for marine mammal research) and is not open to the public.

Narraguagus (Pond Island) Light
Millbridge, Washington County

Dating from 1853, this white cylindrical lighthouse was constructed of granite blocks upon a stone foundation. The tower stands at 31 feet and had a height of focal plane of 54 feet above sea level. It was in use until 1934. Also on site are the keeper's quarters (dating from 1875), two storage buildings, and an oil house (from 1905), and a brick workroom (from 1885), which attaches the tower to the keeper's quarters. The tower is now privately owned and is not open to the public.

Nash Island Light
South Addison, Washington County

Standing at the southeast mouth of Pleasant Bay, the Nash Island Light was in use from 1874 until 1982. (This lighthouse—which replaced a previous, round stone tower of 1838—was itself replaced by a buoy.) The square white brick tower is 36 feet tall. It used a fourth-order Fresnel lens and had a height of focal plane of 51 feet above sea level. All of the other original buildings have been dismantled: the keeper's quarters and sound signal, a workroom, a storage shed, a boathouse, an oil house, and a bell tower. The site is owned by the Friends of Nash Island, Inc., who are working to restore the tower, and is not open to the public.

Owls Head Light
See pages 82 and 83

Pemaquid Point Light
See pages 76-77 and 79

Perkins Island Light
Perkins Island/Kennebec River (near Georgetown), Sagadahoc County

This operational lighthouse was first lit in 1898 and was automated in 1959. The octagonal white tower is constructed of wood and is topped with a red lantern. It stands at 23 feet, uses a 250 mm optic (which replaced a fifth-order lens), and has a height of focal plane of 41 feet above sea level. The pyramidal wooden sound signal tower was constructed in 1902, and the two-story Late Victorian keeper's house was constructed in 1898, is owned by the state of Maine, and is in a state of severe disrepair. Other structures include a brick oil house (from 1906), a barn (from 1897-8), and a boathouse (from 1901). The tower was licensed by the U.S. Coast Guard to the American Lighthouse Foundation in 2000, and is not open to the public.

Petit Manan Light
Millbridge, Washington County

Located off of Petit Manan Point, this conical granite block lighthouse has been in use since 1855. It was automated in 1972 when its second-order Fresnel lens was replaced with a DCB-224 optic, which has since been replaced with a VRB-25 optic. The original lens is on display at the Shore Village Museum in Rockland. The tower stands at 119 feet and has a height of focal plane of 123 feet above sea level. Other structures include a brick sound signal building (from 1887), the wood-framed keeper's quarters (from 1875), and engine house (from 1876), a boathouse, an outhouse, and an oil house. The U.S. Coast Guard owns the tower, and the U.S. Fish & Wildlife Service owns the grounds and the remaining structures. This site is not open to the public.

Pond Island Light
Popham Beach, Sagadahoc County

Standing at 20 feet, this cylindrical white brick tower (with black trim) uses a 250 mm (previously, a fifth-order) lens and has a height of focal plane of 52 feet above sea level. The original sound signal building and keeper's quarters have both been removed. The site, owned by the U.S. Coast Guard, serves as an active aid to navigation and as a bird refuge. It is not open to the public.

Portland Breakwater Light ("Bug Light")
South Portland, Cumberland County

Standing at 26 feet, this conical iron plate tower resembles a fourth-century Greek monument. It was first lit in 1875, was automated in 1934, deactivated in 1942, and relit in 2002. The tower's focal plane is 30 feet above sea level. In 1993, its original, sixth-order Fresnel lens was removed and later replaced with a 250 mm optic. The sound signal building and the keeper's quarters have both been removed, and the site (which is owned by the City of South Portland) now serves as a town park.

Portland Head Light
See pages 83 and 85

Prospect Harbor Point Light
Prospect Harbor, Hancock County

First lit in 1891, this lighthouse was de-activated in 1859, reactivated in 1870, automated in 1934, and remains in use today. The 38-foot conical wood-framed tower (white, with a black lantern) uses a 250 mm lens (originally, a fifth-order Fresnel) and has a height of focal plane of 43 feet above sea level. The 1.5-story keeper's house is in the classical revival style (dating from 1891) and is now used as a Navy guest house. Also on site are a stone oil house (circa 1905) and a wooden boat shed. This light station is located on an active military base and is not open to the public.

Pumpkin Island Light
Little Deer Isle, Hancock County

Built on Eggemoggin Reach (on Penobscot Bay), this 1854 light-house was in use until 1933. The cylindrical white brick tower (with a black lantern) stands at 28 feet. It used a fifth-order Fresnel lens and had a height of focal plane of 43 feet above sea level. The 1854 keeper's house (which has been modified) is a colonial cape structure standing at 1.5 stories. Other structures include a boat-house and a brick oil house. This site is privately owned.

Ram Island Ledge Light
Cape Elizabeth, Cumberland County

Located on Casco Bay, the Ram Island Ledge Light is a conical granite block structure standing at 72 feet tall and with a black lantern. The tower was first lit in 1905, was automated in 1959, and is still operational today. It uses a 300 mm lens (originally, a third-order lens) and has a height of focal plane of 77 feet above sea

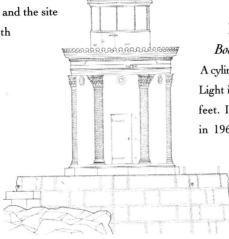

Above: **The Greek ornamentation on Portland Breakwater Light**

level. The keeper's quarters are contained within the tower. This light was licensed to the American Lighthouse Foundation in 2005 and is not open to the public.

Ram Island Light
Boothbay Harbor, Lincoln County

A cylindrical brick (on granite) tower, the Ram Island Light is white with a black lantern and stands at 35 feet. It was first lit in 1883 and was automated in 1965. Its fourth-order Fresnel lens has now been replaced with a 250 mm optic. The keeper's house, dating from 1883, is still present on site. It is a Victorian dwelling, standing at 1.5 stories. This operational lighthouse is owned by the Grand Banks Schooner Trust and its grounds are open to the public.

Rockland Harbor Breakwater Light
Rockland, Knox County

Rising 25 feet above Jameson Point, this 1902 lighthouse consists of a square, stone and brick tower built above its brick fog signal build-ing. The light originally used a fourth order Fresnel and now uses a 250 mm rotating lens (automated 1964). The attached (gambrel-style) keeper's quarters are constructed of wood. This site is owned by the City of Rockland and only the grounds are open to the public.

Rockland Harbor Southwest Light
Rockland, Knox County

Maine's newest lighthouse, built between 1981 and 1987, is a wood tower with a fifth-order Fresnel lens atop a private residence. It is the only privately built lighthouse in New England to serve as an official aid to navigation.

Saddleback Ledge Light
Vinalhaven, Knox County

First lit in 1839, the Saddleback Ledge Light station is one of the loneliest on the coast of Maine. The conical granite tower stands at 42 feet and has a height of focal plane of 52 feet above sea level. It was automated in 1954, and its fifth-order lens has now been replaced by a 300 mm optic. The keeper's dwelling was dismantled after

Above: **Saddleback Ledge Light in 1960**

1960, and there are no other structures on the site. This light station was the site of a curious event in 1927, when (according to the then keeper, W.W. Wells) the tower received a "bombardment" of at least 124 sea birds who were blown in on a storm, breaking windows and even putting out the lantern light. The station is owned and managed by the U.S. Coast Guard and is not open to the public.

Seguin Island Light
Bath, Sagadahoc County

The Seguin Island lighthouse is located on the Kennebec River, south of Georgetown. It was first lit in 1857, automated in 1985, and is still operational today (and still using its original first-order Fresnel optic—the only light station north of Rhode Island to do so). The cylindrical, granite block and brick tower (white, with a black lantern) stands at 53 feet and has a height of focal plane of 180 feet. Also on site is a brick sound signal building (dating from 1889) and the keeper's quarters (dating from 1857). Other structures include a cistern, a brick oil house (from 1892) a wooden boathouse (with a ramp and an electric winch), a wharf, and a wooden donkey house. This light station, which is owned by the Friends of Sequin Island, Inc., houses a free museum in the keeper's house with pictures and exhibits on its history. It is open to the public.

Spring Point Ledge Light
See page 158

Squirrel Point Light
Arrowsic Island, Sagadahoc County

This octagonal, wooden lighthouse was first lit in 1898 and stands at 25 feet (with a height of focal plane of 33 feet above sea level). The tower is white, with a black lantern. It was automated in 1979, and its fifth-order Fresnel has been replaced by a 250 mm lens. The tower is attached to its sound signal building, also made of brick. The keeper's house is a 1.5-story Victorian dwelling. Other structures include a brick oil house, a boathouse, a garage, and a frame barn. This station is owned by the Squirrel Point Association, Inc., and its grounds are open to the public.

Tenants Harbor Light
Tenants Harbor, Lincoln County

This lighthouse, on Southern Island, was in use from 1857 until 1933. The cylindrical, brick tower (painted white, with a black lantern) stands at 27 feet on a stone foundation. It used a fourth-order Fresnel lens and had a height of focal plane of 25 feet above

sea level. The tower is attached to a replica of its original, pyramidal sound signal building. The colonial cape (wood-framed) keeper's house stands at 1.5 stories and dates from 1857. Other structures include an oil house, a storage building, a brick covered passageway connecting the tower to the keeper's house. This site is privately owned and is not open to the public.

Two Bush Island Light
Two Bush Channel/Penobscot Bay Approach, near Sprucehead

First lit in 1897, this square, brick tower stands at 42 feet and has a height of focal plane of 65 feet above sea level. It was automated in 1964 and is still in use today, now using a DCB-224 in place of its original fifth-order lens. The brick sound signal building, attached to the tower, also dates from 1897. The original keeper's dwelling has been destroyed. This station is owned by the U.S. Fish & Wildlife Service and is not open to the public.

West Quoddy Head Light
Lubec, Washington County

This brick, red-and-white-striped tower stands at 49 feet and is topped with a black lantern. It was automated in 1988, has a height of focal plane of 83 feet above sea level, and still uses its original, third-order Fresnel lens. Also on site are a brick sound signal building (dating from 1887), a 1.5-story Victorian keeper's dwelling (from 1858), and an oil house (from 1892). This lighthouse is owned by the Maine Division of Natural Resources and is open to the public.

Whaleback Ledge Light
Kittery Point, York County

Located on Portsmouth Harbor, the Whaleback Ledge Light is a conical, granite block structure standing at 50 feet (with a height of focal plane of 59 feet above sea level). The light is still in use today (it was automated in 1963) and now uses a VRB-25 (originally, a fourth-order Fresnel) optic. The keeper's quarters are located within the tower, and the sound signal building is no longer present. This station is owned by the U.S. Coast Guard and is not open to the public.

Whitehead Island Light
Tenants Harbor, Knox County

With its conical, granite and asphalt tower, the Whitehead Island lighthouse stands at 41 feet and has a height of focal plane of 75 feet above sea level. It was first lit in 1852, automated in 1982, and is still operational today (using a 300 mm optic). The original, third-order fixed Fresnel lens is on display at the Shore Village Museum in Rockland. Also on site are a sound signal building (a one-story brick building dating from 1888) and the keeper's quarters (a 1.5-story, T-shaped duplex dating from 1891). Other structures include an oil house (from 1891), a boathouse, a school house (from 1891), and a granite wharf (from 1871). The keeper's house is currently under restoration. Only the grounds are open to the public.

Whitlock's Mill Light

Calais, Washington County

This lighthouse was built in 1910 on the south bank of the St. Croix River. It was automated in 1969 (when its fourth-order Fresnel lens was replaced by a 250 mm optic with a flashing green signal) and is still in use today. The cylindrical, brick tower stands at 25 feet, with a height of focal plane of 32 feet above sea level. It is painted white, with a black lantern. Also on site are a wooden, pyramidal bell tower (dating from 1910), and a wood/stucco Dutch colonial keeper's cottage (from 1909), an oil house (from 1910), and a storage building. The tower is owned by the St. Croix Historical Society and the dwelling is privately owned. This site is not open to the public, but it may be viewed from nearby on U.S. Highway 1.

Winter Harbor Light

Winter Harbor, Hancock County

This diminutive light on Mark Island was first lit in 1856 and de-activated in 1934, when it was sold into private hands and replaced by a lighted buoy. Also known as the "Mark Island Light," it consists of a white, cylindrical, brick-and-asphalt tower (standing at 19 feet) with a black, cast-iron lantern, which is attached to the other structures. Also on site are the red-roofed keeper's house (a two-story Victorian dwelling dating from 1876), a boathouse (from 1878), a stone oil house (from 1905), and a brick workroom. The original fifth-order Fresnel lens has been removed. When active, the signal's focal-plane height was 37 feet above sea level. This light is still privately owned and is not open to the public, but can be seen from Schoodic Point in Acadia National Park.

Wood Island Light

Biddleford Pool, York County

This conical, granite rubble tower stands at 47 feet (with a height of focal plane of 71 feet). It was first lit in 1858 and is still operational today. The lantern was removed from the tower in 1976 (when its fourth-order Fresnel lens was replaced with a VRB-25), and it was restored when the light was automated, in 1986. The tower is white, with a black lantern. The keeper's house, which dates from 1857

but was modified in 1906, is a two-story Dutch colonial structure. Other structures include an oil house (from 1903), a storage building, and a wooden walkway. The buildings are owned by the U.S. Coast Guard, and the Maine Audubon Society owns the island. This site is not open to the public unless by special arrangement.

Massachusetts

Annisquam Harbor Light

Annisquam, Essex County

This light station was first established in 1801, and Rudyard Kipling lived in the original keeper's house (which is still standing) while writing "Captain Courageous." Located at Wigwam Point, on Ipswich Bay, the current lighthouse was first lit in 1897. It was automated in 1974 and is still operational today. The white cylindrical tower stands at 41 feet and is topped with a black lantern. The original fifth-order Fresnel lens was replaced with a 190 mm optic. Other structures on the site include an oil house, a garage, and a walkway (which was replaced in 1978). The light station is owned by the U.S. Coast Guard and only the grounds are open to the public.

Bakers Island Light

Salem, Essex County

First lit in 1820, this operational lighthouse was automated in 1972 and now uses a 190 mm optic, with a height of focal plane of 111 feet above sea level. The original, fourth-order Fresnel lens is on display at the Shore Village Museum in Rockland. The white, conical granite tower stands at 59 feet. The brick sound signal building was constructed in 1907, and the keeper's house (a Victorian, wooden structure) dates from 1878. Also on site are an oil house, and a second keeper's dwelling. This site is owned by the U.S. Coast Guards (on lease to the Bakers Island Association) and is not open to the public.

Bass River Light

West Dennis, Barnstable County

Established in 1855 on Bass River Harbor, this light was deactivated in 1914. It was automated and reactivated in 1989, and has since been in use as a private aid to navigation. The conical iron tower rises at 44 feet above the wooden house. It is painted white with red trim. Also in 1989, the original, fourth-order Fresnel was replaced with a 300 mm optic. The wooden keeper's house stands at 2.5 stories and is in the (modified) Gothic revival style. This light is now an inn and restaurant, open to the public.

Bird Island Light

Marion, Plymouth County

This station was established on Sippican Harbor, off Buzzards Bay, in 1819. The light was deactivated from 1933 until 1997 (when it was automated) and it now serves as a private aid to navigation. The 31-foot conical rubble-stone tower is white with a black lantern. It originally used 10 lamps (with 14-inch reflectors) and, later, a fourth-order Fresnel. Since 1997, the light has been equipped with a Tidelands ML-300-TF optic. It has a height of focal plane of 37 feet above sea level. None of the other original structures remain. This site is owned by the Town of Marion and the island serves as a nesting ground for endangered roseate terns. It is not open to the public.

Borden Flats Light

Mount Hope Bay/Taunton River,
Fall River

This active lighthouse was first lit in 1881 and was automated in 1963. The conical, "spark plug" style tower (with a white top and a black bottom) stands at 50 feet. In 1997, its original, fourth-order Fresnel was replaced with a 250 mm lens. It has a height of focal plane of 47 feet above sea level. The keeper's quarters are contained within the tower, and a cistern is located within the foundation. This light is owned and managed by the U.S. Coast Guard and is not open to the public.

Boston Harbor Light

See page 134

Brant Point Light

See page 141

Butler Flats Light

New Bedford, Bristol County

First lit in 1898, this light was automated in 1978 and now serves as a private aid to navigation. The white conical tower (at 53 feet, the same as its height of focal plane) stands upon a black cylindrical base and has a black lantern. In 1998, the tower's fifth-order Fresnel lens was replaced with a RB-300 Maxlumina rotating beacon. The keeper's quarters are contained within the tower. This light is owned by the U.S. Coast Guard (on lease to the City of New Bedford) and is not open to the public.

Above: **Cape Cod (Highland) Light**

Buzzards Bay Entrance Light (Site)

Buzzards Bay Main Channel

This "Texas Tower" style lighthouse was demolished in 1996 (and replaced with a 75-foot high tower resting on three legs). The historic, 66-foot tower was first lit in 1961. The four-sided skeletal steel superstructure was painted red and had "Buzzards" written on it. The keeper's quarters were contained within the tower, and there was also a helicopter landing deck. This site is not open to the public.

Cape Ann Light (Twin Lights)

See page 181

Cape Cod (Highland) Light

North Truro, Barnstable County

This light station was first established in 1797, and the current lighthouse dates from 1857. The conical brick tower is painted white, with a black lantern, and it stands at 66 feet. It was automated in 1987 and is still in use today, using a VRB-25 optic (in place of its original Fresnel) and having a height of focal plane of 183 feet above sea level. The tower has been moved once, in 1996. Also on site is the 1.5-story keeper's house, a wooden Queen Anne–style dwelling dating from 1857. Other structures include a new keeper's house (constructed in 1961 and relocated in 1996), and a walkway attaching the tower to the dwelling. This site is owned by the National Park Service and is open to the public.

Cape Poge (Pogue) Light

Edgartown, Dukes County

Located on Chappaquiddick Island, this conical wood shingle tower (dating from 1893) rises at 35 feet. It is painted white, with a black lantern that holds a 300 mm solar-powered lens (with a height of focal plane of 65 feet above sea level). The tower's original, fourth-order Fresnel lens is on display at the Martha's Vineyard Historical Society Museum in Edgartown. The light was automated in 1943, and it has been moved four times (in 1907, 1922, 1960, and 1987). All of the other original structures on site have either deteriorated or have been destroyed. The light is owned and operated by the U.S. Coast Guard, on lease to the Trustees of Reservations, and only the grounds are open to the public. The tower may be toured by special arrangement.

Chatham Light

Chatham, Barnstable County

This 1877 lighthouse was built as a twin to what is now Nauset (Beach) Light (which moved from Chatham to Eastham in 1923). Automated in 1982, it is still in use today. The conical, white cast-iron (plate) tower stands at 48 feet, and its black lantern holds a DCB-224 optic (with a height of focal plane of 80 feet above sea level. The original, fourth-order Fresnel is on display in the Old Atwood House & Museum in Chatham. Other structures on site include the original keeper's house (a 1.5-story wooden duplex), a radiobeacon, a lookout tower, an oil house, and a garage. This light is owned and operated by the U.S. Coast Guard and it is not open to the public.

Clark's Point Light

West shore of New Bedford Harbor, New Bedford

The previous light—a 42-foot, octagonal stone tower—was erected in 1804. In 1860, construction began on a seven-sided fort, adjacent to the lighthouse. The walls of Fort Taber (now called Fort Rodman) eventually blocked the view of the light, and the lantern room and keeper's quarters were relocated to the top of the fort in 1869. The old stone tower was finally demolished in 1906. The fort is now host to a popular public park (with foot and bike trails, a boathouse, a bath house, and a community center), and the city completely restored the tower in 2001, when it was relit as an active aid to navigation.

Cleveland East Ledge Light

Pocasset, Barnstable County

On Buzzards Bay, this lighthouse was first lit in 1943 and is still in use today. The 70-foot tower is white, with a black lantern, and is cylindrical in shape. Constructed of reinforced concrete, it sits atop the square, two-story art deco keeper's dwelling on a caisson foundation. When the tower was automated, in 1978, its fourth-order Fresnel lens was replaced with 190 mm optic. The tower has a height of focal plane of 74 feet above sea level. There is also a radiobeacon on site. This light is owned and managed by the U.S. Coast Guard and it is not open to the public.

Deer Island Light

Winthrop, Suffolk County

This brown, flaring cylindrical fibreglass tower was erected in 1983 on the foundations of a cast-iron tower of 1890. Its modern optic emits alternating flashes every 10 seconds (red and white, with red sector) at a focal plane height of 51 feet above sea level.

Derby Wharf Light

Salem Harbor, Salem

This beacon was constructed in 1871, during the decline of the Salem fishing trade. Because it is so close to the town, the lighthouse was maintained by keepers until its automation in 1970. The light was deactivated in 1977 and then relit, in 1983 as a private aid to navigation. The 23-foot, white, square brick tower is topped with a black cast-iron lantern. It now uses a 155 mm, solar-powered lens.

Dumpling Rock Light

Dartmouth , Bristol County

This light station was established in 1828. The current steel skeleton tower was erected after its predecessor (an 1890 square wooden tower with attached keeper's house) was damaged in the hurricane of 1938. An active aid to navigation, the skeleton tower is best seen by boat.

Duxbury Pier Light ("Bug Light")

Duxbury, Plymouth County

This is a conical, "spark plug" style tower, rising at 47 feet with a height of focal plane of 35 feet above sea level. The tower is white, with a red base, and is constructed of cast iron. It was first lit in 1871, was automated in 1964, was refurbished in 1984, and today uses a 250 mm solar-powered optic (in place of its original, fourth-order Fresnel). The keeper's quarters are contained within the tower. The light is owned by the U.S. Coast Guard, on lease to Project Bug Light, and it is not open to the public.

East Chop (Telegraph Hill) Light

Oak Bluffs, Dukes County

Marking the Vineyard Haven entrance to Martha's Vineyard, the East Chop lighthouse has been in use since 1878. The conical, cast-iron tower is white, with a black lantern, and stands at 40 feet. The tower was automated in 1933 and it uses a 300 mm optic (and has a height of focal plane of 79 feet above sea level). The original keeper's dwelling has been demolished, and there are no other structures on the site. The site is owned by the U.S. Coast Guard, on lease to the Martha's Vineyard Historical Society, and is open to the public.

Eastern Point Light

Gloucester, Essex County

This light station was first established in 1832, and the current light was completed in 1890. It consists of a white brick tower (with a black lantern and a red roof) that stands at 36 feet and having a height of focal plane of 57 feet above sea level. The tower was automated in 1985 and, in 1994, the original, fourth-order Fresnel lens was replaced with a DCB-224 optic. The original lens is on display at the Cape Ann Historical Association Museum in Gloucester. The keeper's house, dating from 1879, is a two-story Gothic revival duplex constructed of wood. Also on site is a bell tower (dating from 1951), a radiobeacon (from 1931), a covered passageway, a "dog bar" breakwater (from 1905), an oil house (from 1894), a shed, and an assistant keeper's dwelling (from 1908). This site is owned and operated by the U.S. Coast Guard and is not open to the public.

Edgartown Harbor Light
Edgartown, Dukes County

Located at the eastern end of Martha's Vineyard, this 1873 lighthouse was relocated from Ipswich in 1939 after a previous tower was destroyed during a storm, in 1938. It consists of a conical, cast-iron tower (painted white, with a black lantern) standing at 45 feet (the same as its height of focal plane). The tower was automated in 1939 and, in 1988, its fourth-order Fresnel was replaced with a 250 mm solar-powered optic. Still in use today, this lighthouse is owned by the U.S. Coast Guard and is on lease to the Martha's Vineyard Historical Society. It is open to the public.

Fort Pickering (Winter Island) Light
Salem, Essex County

First lit in 1871, this light station was inactive from 1969 until 1983, and is in use today as a private aid to navigation and a public park. The 32-foot, cylindrical cast-iron (and brick) tower is painted white, with a black lantern, and has a height of focal plane of 28 feet above sea level. It uses a ML-300 solar-powered lens. Other structures on the site include a U.S. Coast Guard Air & Sea Rescue Station (which was active from 1934 until 1969).

Gay Head Light
Aquinnah, Dukes County

This light station was established at Martha's Vineyard in 1799. The current, 51-foot, conical, redbrick and sandstone tower was first lit in 1856 and is still in use today. Its black lantern holds a DCB-224 lens (which replaced the original, fourth-order Fresnel in 1953) and has a height of focal plane of 170 feet above sea level. (The Fresnel was given to the Duke County Historical Society/Vineyard Museum.) This lighthouse was automated in 1960. All other structures on site, including the keeper's quarters, have been demolished. This light is owned by the U.S. Coast Guard, on license to the Martha's Vineyard Historical Society, and it is occasionally open to the public.

Gloucester (Dog Bar) Breakwater Light
Dog Bar Breakwater, Gloucester

Constructed in 1902, this rather unlikely-looking lighthouse consists of a 37-foot, chimneylike, square cylindrical tower, attached to an oil shed and mounted atop a skeletal foundation. The tower and oil shed are painted red and white. Managed by the U.S. Coast Guard, the site is open but the tower is closed to the public.

Graves (Ledge) Light
See page 172

Great Point (Nantucket) Light (Replica)
See page 63

Hospital Point (Range Front) Light
Beverly, Essex County

This 1872 light marks the channel to Salem Harbor. The square pyramidal tower is white, with a black lantern, stands at 45 feet, and is constructed of brick. It was automated in 1947, uses a third-order Fresnel lens, and has a height of focal plane of 70 feet above sea level. It is attached to the keeper's house (which was modified in 1968), a two-story Queen Anne revival structure. Also on site is a brick oil house (from 1871), a wood garage (from 1942), and an equipment building (from 1875). This site is in use as an active aid to navigation and as housing for the U.S. Coast Guard. It is not open to the public.

Hospital Point (Range Rear) Light
Beverly, Essex County

Discarded lightship equipment was installed in the steeple of Beverly's First Baptist Church in 1927; its fixed white signal is the only functioning harbor light positioned in such a location in the United States. The site is open to the public.

Hyannis (Range Rear) Light
Hyannis, Barnstable County

This lighthouse was active from 1849 until 1929. The conical brick tower is painted white (with a replica black lantern) and stands at 19 feet. The tower used an oil lamp, with a reflector, and had a height of focal plane of 42 feet above sea level. It is attached to the keeper's house, a 1.5-story wooden Cape Cod structure that was modified in 1929 (and has since received three later additions). There is also a brick oil house, dating from 1902. This light is privately owned and is not open the public.

Long Island Head Light

Quincy, Suffolk County

Established at the northeast end of Long Island, on Boston Harbor, this lighthouse was first lit in 1901. It was automated in 1918, was inactive from 1982 until 1985, and is still in use today. The cylindrical brick tower is white, with a black lantern, and it stands at 52 feet. The original, fourth-order Fresnel lens was replaced with a 250 mm solar-powered optic (focal-plane height of 120 feet above sea level). The original keeper's quarters have been removed. The light is now operated by the U.S. Coast Guard and is not open to the public.

Long Point Light

See page 122

Marblehead Light

Marblehead, Essex County

First lit in 1896, the Marblehead Light was automated in 1960 and is still in use today. The square skeletal tower (with a cylinder) stands at 105 feet and has a height of focal plane of 130 feet above sea level (using a 300 mm optic). It is brown, with a black lantern, and is constructed of cast iron. There is also a brick oil house on the site. The keeper's house was demolished in the 1960s. The U.S. Coast Guard owns the tower, and the Town of Marblehead owns the grounds, which are open to the public.

Minots Ledge Light

See page 169

Monomoy Island (Monomoy Point) Light

See page 62

Nantucket Cliff Range Lights

Nantucket, Nantucket County

Established in 1838 and rebuilt several times, these small white wooden conical towers were sold after deactivation in 1912 and now stand on private property on Bathing Beach Road.

Nauset (Beach) Light

See page 61

Ned's Point Light

Mattapoisett, Plymouth County

This lighthouse was constructed at the entrance to the Mattapoisett Harbor in 1838. The conical stone tower is white, with a black lantern, and rises at 39 feet. Automated in 1923, it remains in use today (although it was inactive from 1952 until 1961). Its original fifth-order Fresnel lens has since been replaced with a modern 250 mm optic with a focal plane height of 41 feet above sea level. The keeper's dwelling, which dated from 1888, was relocated to the Wing's Neck Light in 1923, and the only other structure on site is an oil house. The tower is owned by the U.S. Coast Guard, and the grounds are owned by the Town of Mattapoisett. This site is open to the public.

Newburyport Harbor (Plum Island) Light

Newburyport, Essex County

In 1788, this light station was established at the north end of Plum Island. In 1830 the *Lady Howard* was wrecked in the vicinity, and during a notorious storm in 1839, the *Pocahontas* and *Richmond Packet* were both lost here. The current lighthouse was first lit in 1898, and it was automated in 1951 and is still in use today. The 45-foot tower is conical in shape and is constructed of wood. It is painted white, with a black lantern that retains its original fourth-order Fresnel lens. The tower has a height of focal plane of 50 feet above sea level. Also on site is the keeper's house, a two-story Victorian structure dating from 1872. This light station also serves as a National Wildlife Refuge, and it is open to the public.

Newburyport Harbor Range Lights

Newburyport, Essex County

These two towers were first lit in 1873, and they remained in use until 1961. The privately-owned, four-sided, 53-foot Rear Range tower is constructed of brick, cast iron, and wood. It had a height of focal plane of 58 feet above sea level. The 15-foot Front Range tower is conical in shape, is constructed of steel (with a brick lining), and is painted white, with an orange and white lantern. The Front Tower is owned by the U.S. Coast Guard. This site is not open to the public.

Nobska Point Light

Woods Hole, Barnstable County

First lit in 1876, this light was automated in 1985 and is still operational today. The cylindrical tower is white, with a black lantern, stands at 40 feet, and is constructed of iron. It retains its original, fourth-order Fresnel lens and has a height of focal plane of 87 feet above sea level. The wooden Victorian keeper's house is 1.5 stories tall and dates from 1876. Other structures on site include a brick oil house and paint lockers (from 1876), a garage (from 1931), and a radiobeacon building (from 1937). This light station also serves as housing for the U.S. Coast Guard. The grounds are open daily and the tower, occasionally.

Palmer Island Light

New Bedford, Bristol County

This conical rubble-stone tower, standing at 24 feet, was first lit in 1849. It was automated in 1941, was deactivated in 1962, and is in use today as a private aid to navigation. The lighthouse is white, with a black lantern. In 1999, its original, fifth-order Fresnel lens was replaced with the current, 250 mm solar-powered lens (focal plane 34 feet). The tower has been moved once, and it suffered some fire damage in 1966. The sound signal building has been dismantled, and the keeper's dwelling was destroyed in 1938. This light is owned by the City of New Bedford, and the grounds are open to the public.

Plymouth (Gurnet) Light

Duxbury, Plymouth County

Standing at 34 feet, this octagonal pyramidal tower is constructed of cedar shingles and is painted white, with a black lantern and a red roof. The tower was constructed in 1843 and is still operational today. It was automated in 1986, when its fourth-order Fresnel was replaced with a 190 mm lens. (The original lens is on display at the Hull Lifesaving Museum in Hull, Mass.) The tower has been moved once, in 1998. Also remaining on site is the keeper's house, a modern ranch house constructed in 1963. This site is not open to the public.

Point Gammon Light

Great Island, Hyannis

This 1816 fieldstone tower, of a very unusual design, was in use until 1858. It stands at 70 feet, with a stone lantern. The keeper's quarters were dismantled in 1935. The site and tower are now privately owned, and are not open to the public. However, the tower can be viewed from the Hyannis-Nantucket ferries.

Race Point Light

Provincetown, Barnstable County

Standing at the northern tip of Cape Cod, the Race Point lighthouse rises at 45 feet and has a height of focal plane of 67 feet above sea level. The conical tower is white, with a black lantern, and is constructed of iron plates with a brick interior. The tower, which is still active today, dates from 1876. It was automated in 1978 and, in 1998, its fourth-order lens was replaced with a Vega VRB-25 solar-powered optic. There is also a sound signal building, a two-story Victorian keeper's quarters, and an oil house (all dating from 1876). This site is open to the public.

Sandy Neck Light

West Barnstable, Barnstable County

This conical brick lighthouse (without a lantern) is painted white with black trim. It was in use from 1857 until 1931, when the shoreline changed and an automated acetylene lamp was installed nearby. The tower rises at 40 feet. It used a fifth-order Fresnel lens and had a height of focal plane of 47 feet above sea level. Also on site is the keeper's house, a 1.5-story carpenter gothic-style wooden structure dating from 1880. This light is privately owned and is not open to the public.

Sankaty Head Light

Siasconset, Nantucket County

First lit in 1850, this light was automated in 1965 and is still in use today. The cylindrical brick and granite tower is white, with a red band midway and a black lantern, and it stands at 70 feet. (Only the lower parts of the tower are original. It has a reproduction lantern and stairs.) In 1987, the tower's second-order Fresnel lens was replaced with a DCB-224 and the Fresnel was moved to the Nantucket Whaling Museum. The original keeper's house has been destroyed. This site is owned by the U.S. Coast Guard, on lease to Sconset Trust, and is open to the public.

Scituate Light

Scituate, Plymouth County

Marking Cedar Point, this 1811 lighthouse was inactive from 1850 until 1852 and then again from 1860 until 1994, and is in use today as a private aid to navigation. The 50-foot, white, octagonal granite and brick tower is topped with a green lantern room and roof. The tower is attached to the keeper's quarters (a Cape Cod structure also dating from 1811) by a covered walkway. It uses a FA-250 optic (which replaced the original, Pan Lamp, in 1991). This light station is owned by the Scituate Historical Society and the Town of Scituate, and it is open to the public.

Above: **The East elevation of Scituate Light**

Stage Harbor Light

West Chatham, Barnstable County

This cast-iron tower is conical in shape and no longer has its lantern. It is painted white with red trim and it stands at 36 feet. The light was active from 1880 to 1933, when it used a fifth-order Fresnel lens and had a height of focal plane of 40 feet above sea level. The keeper's house is attached to the tower. This lighthouse is privately owned and is not open to the public.

Straitsmouth Island Light

Rockport, Essex County

This station was established in 1835, and the current light dates from 1896. The 37-foot cylindrical tower is constructed of brick and asphalt, and is painted white (with a black lantern). It was automated in 1967 and is still operational today. It uses a 250 mm solar-powered lens, and has a height of focal plane of 46 feet above sea level. The keeper's house, a 1.5-story Gothic (wood framed) structure, dates from 1878. The U.S. Coast Guard owns the tower, and Massachusetts Audubon Society owns the keeper's dwelling. This light station also serves as a bird refuge. It is not open to the public.

Tarpaulin Cove Light

Gosnold, Dukes County

On Naushon Island, the Tarpaulin Cove Light dates from 1891 (it was automated in 1941) and is still in use today. The 38-foot, white brick tower is cylindrical in shape and is attached to a work room. It uses a 300 mm optic and has a height of focal plane of 78 feet above sea level. The original keeper's house was demolished in 1962, and there are no other structures remaining on the site. This light station is owned and managed by the U.S. Coast Guard and it is not open to the public.

Ten Pound Island Light

Gloucester, Essex County

This 1881 lighthouse was inactive from 1956 until 1989, and it is in use today as an active aid to navigation. The conical cast-iron tower (painted white, with a black lantern) stands at 30 feet and has a height of focal plane of 57 feet above sea level. In 1989, its fifth-order lens was replaced with a 250 mm optic. Also on site is a granite oil house, which was built in 1821 and restored in 1995. The original keeper's house has been destroyed. The City of Gloucester owns the tower, and the U.S. Coast Guard owns the optic. This light station is not open to the public.

Three Sisters Lights (Three Towers)

Eastham, Barnstable County

Two of the three towers were active from 1892 until 1911, while the third remained in use until 1923. After several moves they were relocated near Nauset Beach Light, where they have been restored and arranged in their original configuration and serve as an interpretive museum (owned and operated by the National Park Service). Two of the towers do not have lanterns. They are constructed of wood and they used fourth-order Fresnel lenses. The keeper's house, a Gothic revival structure dating from 1875, remains at the original site.

Above: **The Three Sisters at their original location**

West Chop Light

Tisbury, Dukes County

Located on West Chop Road in Martha's Vineyard, this cylindrical brick lighthouse dates from 1891. It stands at 52 feet (with a height of focal plane of 84 feet above sea level) and is painted white, with a black lantern. The tower was automated in 1976, though it retains its original, fourth-order Fresnel lens. Also on site is a Cape Cod sound signal building (dating from 1891), and a Victorian keeper's house (which dates from 1847 and was remodeled in 1881). There is also a garage (from 1835), a storage building, and an oil house (from 1895). This site is owned by the U.S. Coast Guard, on lease to the Vineyard Environmental Research Institute, and it is not open to the public.

Wings Neck Light

Pocassett, Barnstable County

This 1889 light is located on Buzzards Bay and it was in use until 1945. The hexagonal pyramidal tower is constructed of wood and stands at 32 feet. It is painted white, with a black lantern. The tower used a fifth-order Fresnel lens, and it had a height of focal plane of 50 feet above sea level. The keeper's house is attached to the tower by a covered walkway. Other structures on the site include an oil house (from 1849), and an 1870s keeper's house (relocated from the Ned's Point Light). This is now a private residence and is not open to the public.

Wood End Light

Provincetown, Barnstable County

First lit in 1872, the Wood End lighthouse marks the entrance to Provincetown Harbor (it was automated in 1960 and is still in use today). The square brick tower is painted white, with a black lantern, and stands at 39 feet (with a height of focal plane of 45 feet above sea level). In 1998, its fifth-order Fresnel was replaced with a Vega VRB-25 solar-powered lens. The sound signal building and the keeper's dwelling have both been demolished. A brick oil house (dating from 1896) remains on site. This light station is owned by the U.S. Coast Guard, on lease to the American Lighthouse Foundation, and is not open to the public.

On construction in 1936, the *Nantucket* was the largest lightship ever to be made. Decommissioned in 1975, she was sold in 1986, and is currently under repair at New Bedford's State Pier. The *Nantucket II* lightship was built in 1952 and was stationed in Nantucket from 1979 until its deactivation in 1983. She is currently under restoration in Wareham. The lightship *New Bedford* (1930) served in several locations before "retiring" to the New Bedford waterfront.

New Hampshire

Burkehaven Light
Lake Sunapee, Burkehaven

Still active as an aid to navigation, this is a 1994 restoration of the 1936 replica of an 1893 tower that was destroyed by ice. The beacon is mounted atop a white hexagonal tower. The site and tower are closed but may be viewed from tourist cruises of the lake.

Herrick Cove Light
Lake Sunapee, southern entrance to Herrick Cove

The beacon of the Herrick Cove Light (1893) is mounted atop a white, hexagonal frame tower. The lighthouse is situated on the northwestern shore of the lake, near Georges Mills. It is accessible only by boat, and is visible from the tourist cruises of the lake. Both the site and the tower are closed to the public.

Isles of Shoals (White Island) Light
Portsmouth, Rockingham County

Marking the entrance to the Piscataqua River, this 1859 lighthouse was automated in 1987 and is still operational today. The 58-foot conical, granite and brick tower uses a VRB-25 optic (originally, a second-order Fresnel lens was installed) and has a height of focal plane of 82 feet above sea level. Other surviving structures include the 1.5-story keeper's quarters and an oil house. This site is owned by the State of New Hampshire and is on lease to a diving school. The grounds are open to the public.

Loon Island Light
Lake Sunapee

This was the first of the three lights built in the 1890s on Lake Sunapee and now managed by the New Hampshire Marine Patrol

Bureau. It was destroyed by fire after a lightning strike in 1960, but rebuilt the same year. All three of these lake lights had new solar-powered optics fitted during the 1980s.

Portsmouth Harbor (Newcastle) Light
Newcastle, Rockingham County

This conical, cast-iron tower stands at 48 feet and is painted white with a black lantern. A fog signal building is attached. The light was constructed on Fort Point in 1877, was automated in 1960, and is still in use today. It retains its original fourth-order Fresnel optic (focal plane 52 feet). The keeper's house, a wood-framed structure standing at 1.5 stories, dates from 1872. The light is owned by the U.S. Coast Guard (on lease to the American Lighthouse Foundation). It is not open to the public.

Rhode Island

Beavertail Light
Jamestown, Newport County

This 1856 lighthouse is located on Conanicut Island, at the entrance to Narragansett Bay. The square granite tower stands at 45 feet and is topped with a black lantern. The tower was automated in 1972, and it now uses a DCB-24 (it was originally equipped with a third-order, and later a fourth-order, Fresnel). It has a height of focal plane is 68 feet above sea level. The sound signal building has now been moved to the main shore. Attached to the tower is the keeper's house, a two-story brick/stucco structure. Other structures on the site include an assistant keeper's dwelling (constructed in 1898). The light station is open to the public.

Block Island (North) Light
See page 66

Block Island (Southeast) Light
See page 102

Bristol Ferry Light
Bristol, Bristol County

Located on the strait between Mount Hope and Narragansett bays, this light consists of a brick house and an attached 28-foot square brick tower (painted white) topped with a wooden deck and lantern. It was first established in 1855, using a sixth-order classical lens and a whale oil lamp. In 1902, this optic was replaced with an electrified fifth-order Fresnel. In 1916, the tower was raised six feet (to its present height) to accommodate a cast-iron lantern that was removed from the old Roundout Lighthouse on the Hudson River. The Bristol Ferry Light was discontinued in 1927 (after it was made obsolete with the building of Mount Hope Bridge) and, in 1928, the government removed the lantern room and sold the property. In 1996, the owners installed a new, faux lantern room containing and automatic light that comes on for two hours each evening. This light now serves as a private residence and is not open to the public.

Castle Hill Light
See page 138

Conanicut Island Light (Old)
Jamestown, Newport County

This light was active from 1886 until 1933, when it was replaced with a skeletal steel tower. The historic lighthouse consists of a square wooden tower, without a lantern, and is painted red, with white trim. It used a fifth-order Fresnel lens and had a height of focal plane of 47 feet above sea level. The brick sound signal building was constructed in 1907, and the two-story keeper's house (a red, wooden structure in the Gothic revival style) dates from 1886. Also on site are a barn (dating from 1897) and a brick oil house (from 1901). This lighthouse now serves as a private residence, and it is not open to the public.

Conimicut Shoal Light
Warwick, Kent County

Situated at the mouth of the Providence River, this light was first lit in 1883 (it was automated in 1966) and it is still operational today. The conical cast-iron ("spark plug" style) tower is painted white, with a black lantern, and stands at 58 feet. It originally used a fourth-order Fresnel lens, but now uses a 250 mm optic, and it has a height of focal plane of 55 feet above sea level. The keeper's quarters occupy three floors within the tower. Under the National Historic Lighthouse Preservation Act of 2000, ownership of this lighthouse was transferred to the City of Warwick in September 2004. The light is still maintained by the Coast Guard, and it is not open to the public.

Dutch Island Light
Jamestown, Newport County

First lit in 1857, this lighthouse was automated in 1947 and remained in use until 1979. The square brick tower (painted white, with a black lantern) stands at 42 feet and was once attached to the keeper's dwelling (which was destroyed in 1960). It used a fourth-order Fresnel lens (focal plane 56 feet). Dutch Island is owned by the Rhode Island Department of Environmental Management, and the tower is owned by the U.S. Coast Guard. In 2000, the lighthouse was licensed to the American Lighthouse Foundation. The Dutch Island Lighthouse Society was formed as a chapter of the foundation and it is currently working to restore the tower, which is listed on the Lighthouse Digest Doomsday List of endangered lighthouses. The grounds are open to the public.

Hog Island Shoal Light
Portsmouth, Bristol County

This lighthouse was first lit in 1901, was automated in 1964, and it is still active today. It consists of a conical ("spark plug" style) cast-iron tower (painted white, on a black base). The tower stands at 60 feet, uses a 250 mm optic (originally, a fifth-order Fresnel), and has a height of focal plane of 54 feet above sea level. The keeper's quarters are located within the tower. This lighthouse is owned and operated by the U.S. Coast Guard, and it is not open to the public.

Ida Lewis Rock Light (Formerly "Lime Rock")
Newport, Newport County

This square, white brick tower stands at 13 feet and is topped with a black lantern. It was first lit in 1854, was automated in 1927, and functions today as a yacht club and as a private aid to navigation. It originally used a sixth-order Fresnel lens, which is now on display at the Museum of Newport History, and it has a height of focal plane of 30 feet above sea level. Attached to the tower is the keeper's house, a two-story granite/brick Greek Revival structure built in 1856. This lighthouse is not open to the public.

Nayatt Point Light
Barrington, Bristol County

This lighthouse was only in use from 1856 until 1868. It consists of a 25-foot square brick tower (painted white, with black trim) attached to the two-story brick keeper's house (which was constructed along with an earlier tower, in 1828). It used a fourth-order Fresnel lens, which was eventually removed to the Conimicut Light, and it had a height of focal plane of 31 feet above sea level. This lighthouse now serves as a private residence, and it is not open to the public.

Newport Harbor (Goat Island) Light
See page 141

Plum Beach Light

North Kingstown, Washington County

A conical ("spark plug" style) cast-iron tower, the Plum Beach Lighthouse is painted white (on a black base) and stands at 53 feet. This light was in use from 1899 until 1941. It used a fourth-order Fresnel lens and had a height of focal plane of 54 feet above sea level. The keeper's quarters are located within the tower, along with the assistant keeper's quarters and a cistern (in the basement). This lighthouse is owned by the State of Rhode Island, on lease to the Friends of Plum Beach Lighthouse, Inc. The group received funding for restoration under the Transportation Act for the 21st Century, and work on the exterior of the tower was completed in December, 2003. The lighthouse has also been relit as a private aid to navigation. It is not open to the public.

Point Judith Light

Narragansett, Washington County

This lighthouse was first lit in 1857. It was automated in 1954 and is still in use today. The octagonal conical tower is constructed of brownstone and stands at 51 feet. Its lower parts are painted white, its upper parts are brown, and the lantern is black. The tower still retains its original, fourth-order Fresnel lens, and it has a height of focal plane of 65 feet above sea level. The sound signal building, which dates from 1923, is constructed of dressed stone. Other structures on site include a brick oil house and a radiobeacon building. The keeper's dwelling was demolished in 1954. This light station is owned by the U.S. Coast Guard, on lease to the Point Judith Lighthouse Society, and is grounds are open to the public.

Pomham Rocks Light (Old)

See page 175

Poplar Point Light

North Kingstown, Washington County

First lit in 1831, this octagonal wooden lighthouse is painted white, with black trim. The Poplar Point Light was in use until 1880. (It was replaced by the Wickford Harbor Light.) It used eight lamps, with 14.5 inch reflectors (replaced with a fifth-order Fresnel lens in 1855), and it had a height of focal plane of 48 feet above sea level. The keeper's house is a 1.5-story modified cape structure, constructed of wood. This lighthouse now serves as a private residence, and it is not open to the public. It is Rhode Island's oldest lighthouse tower in its original location, and one of the oldest wooden lighthouses in the United States.

Prudence Island (Sandy Point) Light

Portsmouth, Newport County

This 1823 structure is Rhode Island's oldest lighthouse. It was moved here, from Goat Island in Newport Harbor, in 1851. During a hurricane in September of 1938, five persons—including the wife of the lighthouse keeper—were carried out to sea and drowned when the dwelling house was swept away. The white, octagonal granite block tower stands at 30 feet and is topped with a black, birdcage-style lantern. The light was automated in 1961 and it is still operational today. Originally equipped with a fifth-order Fresnel lens, it now uses a 250 mm optic with a flashing green signal (which replaced a fourth-order Fresnel that was installed in the 1930s) and has a height of focal plane of 28 feet above sea level. This light station is owned and operated by the U.S. Coast Guard (it is leased to the American Lighthouse Foundation), and was restored in 2001.

Rose Island Light

See page 174

Sakonnet Light

Little Compton, Newport County

This conical, 66-foot cast-iron tower is white, on a black base, with a red band at the top. It was in use from 1884 until 1955, and it was automated and relit in 1997 (and it now serves as a private aid to navigation). The tower originally used a fourth-order Fresnel lens, which is on display at the Shore Village Museum in Rockland, Maine. It now uses a solar-powered optic, and it has a height of focal plane of 70 feet above sea level. The keeper's quarters are located within the tower. This light is owned and managed by the Friends of Sakonnet Lighthouse, Inc., and it is not open to the public.

Warwick Light

Warwick, Kent County

This 1932 lighthouse is still operational today. The white cast-iron tower stands at 51 feet and is topped with a black lantern. It is cylindrical in shape, with an octagonal base and lantern. The tower was moved in 1939. When the light was automated, in 1985, its fourth-order Fresnel lens was replaced with a 250 mm optic. It has a height of focal plane of 66 feet above sea level. The keeper's dwelling, which dates from 1889, is a 1.5-story Victorian home. There is also a garage and a storage building on site. This lighthouse is owned and managed by the U.S. Coast Guard, and it is not open to the public.

Watch Hill Light

Watch Hill, Washington County

Situated on the east approach to Fishers Island Sound, the Watch Hill Light was first lit in 1857. It was automated in 1986 and is still operational today. Colonists used this beautiful resort are during the French and Indian War, giving the town, and the light (then a rudimentary beacon), their names. Watch Hill's first tourists were paying guests at the lighthouse during the tenure of keeper Jonathan Nash, around 1900. Today, the resort attracts many wealthy New Yorkers, who make this their summer retreat. The lighthouse is a square, unpainted granite tower with a red-roofed, white cast-iron lantern that rises to 45 feet. Its original, fourth-order Fresnel lens has been replaced with a VRB-25 optic with an alternating red-and-white signal, and the tower's height of focal plane is 61 feet above sea level. There is also a one-story brick sound signal building, constructed in 1986, and a two-story keeper's house, painted white with a red roof, dating from 1857. Other structures on the site include an oil house, a garage, and a radiobeacon. The lighthouse grounds and the Watch Hill Lighthouse Museum (in the oil house) are open to the public.

Vermont

Burlington Breakwater Lights

Burlington, Chittenden County

Two replica wooden lights were lit on the breakwater at Burlington Harbor in 2003, reconstructing the originals that were first lit there in 1857. These small, white, pyramidal lights are operational, serving as an active aid to navigation. The original lights were rebuilt and moved on several occasions, and, at times, there was only one in service. A third, middle light was added in 1890, and the north and middle lights were replaced with skeleton towers in 1925 (the south light was replaced in 1950). The site is not open to the public.

Colchester Reef Light

Shelburne, Chittenden County

This light was replaced with a buoy and relocated from Lake Champlain to the Shelburne Museum in 1952. Operational from 1871 to 1933, this lighthouse consists of a square wood tower (situated on top of the dwelling) that stands at 35 feet. It is painted white, with dark trim. It used a sixth-order lens. The fog bell is located on the dwelling, which is constructed of wood (in the second empire style).

Isle La Motte Light (Old)

Isle La Motte, Grand Isle County

This lighthouse on Lake Champlain was active from 1881 until 1933 (it was relit in 2001 for use as a private aid to navigation). The conical, faded red tower is constructed of cast-iron plates and stands at 25 feet. It originally used a sixth-order Fresnel, but on its reactivation it was installed with a 300 mm optic which flashes its white signal every six seconds at a focal-plane height of 46 feet above sea level. In 1933, this light was replaced with a black steel skeletal tower (which stands nearby to a height of 46 feet). The old lighthouse now functions as a private residence, and it is not open to the public, but it can be glimpsed through the trees from Lighthouse Point (at the end of Shrine Road), from points along the shore in Chazy, New York, or by boat. The light station was originally established in 1829 with a privately operated lantern. A stone pyramid with lantern replaced this from 1857 until the present structure was erected in 1881.

Juniper Island Light (Old)

Burlington, Chittenden County

This Lake Champlain light station was first established in 1826, and the existing historic lighthouse dates from 1846. This light is no longer operational today, having been replaced, in 1954, by a skeleton tower. The conical, cast-iron plate tower is painted white, with a red lantern, and stands at 25 feet. When active, it used a fourth-order Fresnel lens, and it had a height of focal plane of 93 feet above sea level. The tower is attached to the keeper's quarters, a recenty reconstructed two-story brick/stucco home. This lighthouse is now privately owned, and it is not open to the public, but it can be viewed from the water.

Windmill Point Light

Alburg, Grand Isle County

Situated on Lake Champlain, this light was first lit in 1858. It was eventually replaced with a modern, black steel skeletal tower, but the original structure was relit (in 2002) for use as a private aid to navigation. The octagonal, unpainted, blue-limestone tower stands at a height of 40 feet and is topped with an orange lantern. In 2002, the tower's sixth-order Fresnel was replaced with a 300 mm lens (flashing white every four seconds). It has a height of focal plane of 52 feet above sea level. The keeper's house, a 1.5-story granite structure, is attached to the tower via a passageway. This lighthouse now serves as a private residence, and it is not open to the public, but it can be viewed from Windmill Point Road.

THE MID-ATLANTIC

Delaware

Baker Shoal Range Lights

Port Penn, New Castle County

Originally established 100 years earlier, the present range front light is a skeleton tower constructed in 2002 on wooden pilings, offshore from Reedy Island, with a fixed green signal at a focal-plane height of 35 feet. The 57-foot skeleton tower of the current range rear light originally served as the Port Penn-Reedy Island (Old) Range Rear Light in Port Penn. It served there from 1896 until 1904 when the opening of a new channel caused the old range to be discontinued. The site is not open to the public.

Bellevue Range Rear Light

Wilmington, New Castle County

This lighthouse is situated on the Christina River, where it meets the Delaware River. It was first lit in 1909 and has been in use ever since. The pyramidal skeletal tower is constructed of black cast iron and stands at 104 feet. It sits upon a concrete foundation. Today, the light is fitted with an RL 24 optic. It has a height of focal plane of 100 feet above sea level. The Bellevue Range Rear Light is owned and managed by the U.S. Coast Guard. The former front range light was deactivated in the 1980s and has since been destroyed.

Cape Henlopen Light

Lewes, Sussex County

First established in 1765—one of the earliest in colonial America—this light station was so significant as to merit brief inclusion here, despite the fact that the lighthouse, a 69-foot whitewashed granite tower, collapsed into the sea during a 1926 storm. The light had been decommissioned some 18 months previously due to serious undermining by beach erosion, clearly visible in the photograph here. The lighthouse was originally financed by Philadelphia residents to mark the entrance to Delaware Bay and the hazardous shoals around the cape. A supplementary beacon was added nearby. Proposals to reconstruct the lighthouse are under preliminary discussion.

Above: Cape Henlopen Light

Cherry Island Range Lights

Edgemoor, New Castle County

These range lights were established in 1880, with the construction of a small tower with red lantern on the pier (range front) and a square wooden tower attached to a keeper's dwelling (range rear). Both have since been replaced with modern skeleton towers.

Delaware Breakwater Light

Lewes, Sussex County

Located on Lewes Harbor, at the entrance to the Delaware Bay, this lighthouse (along with some lightships) took over the duties of the Cape Henlopen Light after it was demolished during a storm in 1926. The Delaware Breakwater Light was in use from 1885 until 1996. It consists of a 49-foot conical ("spark plug" style) brick tower (with cast-iron plates), on a white pier. It originally used a fourth-order Fresnel lens (later, a 375 mm optic), and it had a height of focal plane of 61 feet above sea level. The keeper's quarters are integral to the tower. This light is owned by the General Services Administration. It is not open to the public.

Fenwick Island Light

Fenwick Island, Sussex County

First lit in 1859, this light is located on the Delaware/Maryland border. (Behind the storehouse of the light station is a stone monument with the arms of William Penn carved on the north side and the arms of Lord Baltimore on the south side. This is the first stone erected in association with the Mason and Dixon line.) The total cost of the tower was $23,748.96. It consists of a conical brick tower, standing at 84 feet and painted white with a black lantern. The tower retains its original third-order Fresnel lens, and it has a height of focal plane of 83 feet above sea level. The original keeper's house is a two-story gothic home, built to accommodate two families. Also on site are a second keeper's house (built in 1881), a garage, a barn, a cistern (under the first keeper's house), and a generator house (from the 1940s). Today, this station serves as a museum and as a private aid to navigation. It is open to the public, though the two keeper's houses are privately owned.

Fourteen Foot Bank Light

Bowers Beach, Kent County

This operational lighthouse was built in 1888 to replace a lightship. It was the nation's first caisson lighthouse structure (of the submarine type). The Fourteen Foot Bank Light consists of a 40-foot square cast-iron tower, painted white, on a black sub cast-iron/concrete caisson foundation. The tower originally held a fourth-order Fresnel lens. It was automated in 1972 and, since 1997, has used a solar-powered optic (focal plane 59 feet). The keeper's quarters are integral to the tower. This lighthouse is owned and managed by the U.S. Coast Guard. It is not open to the public.

Harbor of Refuge (South) Breakwater Light

Lewes, Sussex County

On Lewes Harbor, at the entrance to the Delaware Bay, this lighthouse has been operational since 1926. The conical cast-iron tower stands at 76 feet. It is painted white and brown, with a black lantern. Automated in 1973, it originally held a fourth-order Fresnel lens, but today uses a DCB-36 solar-powered optic. The keeper's quarters are integral to the tower. There are occasional public tours.

Liston Range Lights

Taylor's Bridge, New Castle County

Situated on the Delaware River, the historic Liston Rear Range Light was first lit in 1877, automated in 1976, and is still in use today. (This tower formerly served as the Port Penn Range Rear Light. It was relocated in 1905.) The 120-foot, pyramidal skeletal tower (with a central cylinder) is constructed of black wrought iron and retains its original second-order Fresnel lens. The front range tower was constructed in 1906 and stands at 45 feet. The keeper's house, built in 1907, is a two-story Greek Revival (frame) structure. This station is not open to the public.

Mahon River Light

Port Mahon, Kent County

This steel skeleton tower was first lit in the 1950s and is still in use today. The station was established in 1831, and an octagonal tower atop a two-story wooden keeper's dwelling stood here from 1903 until its destruction by fire in 1984.

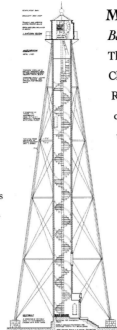

Above: **Liston Range Rear Light**

Marcus Hook Range Lights

Bellefonte, New Castle County

These historic towers are located on the Delaware River Channel, where they are still in use today. The Marcus Hook Rear Range Light was first lit in 1918. Its square reinforced concrete tower stands at 100 feet (focal plane 250 feet). The tower originally held a fourth-order range Fresnel lens. Today, it uses an RL 24 optic. The Front Range tower, located 1.5 miles to the northeast of the Rear Range, dates from 1925. It has a skeletal structure and is constructed of steel, on a concrete foundation. The 2.5-story brick keeper's house, in the colonial revival style, dates from 1918. These lights are owned and managed by the U.S. Coast Guard, and are not open to the public.

Mispillion Light (Old)

Milford, Sussex County

This lighthouse was operational from 1873 until 1929 (when it was replaced by a 60-foot steel skeletal tower that was active until 1984). The square wood-frame tower rose to 65 feet atop a two-story carpenter gothic keeper's house. In 2002, the tower was severely damaged by a lightning strike, and dismantled, but a campaign to build a replica has been launched.

New Castle Range Lights

New Castle, New Castle County

Two steel, skeleton towers have been active on this site (which was established in 1876) since the mid-twentieth century. The original square, wooden towers (the rear of which was attached to the corner of a wooden keeper's dwelling) are no longer standing.

Above: **Reedy Island Range Rear Light**

Reedy Island Range Rear Light

Taylor's Bridge, New Castle County

Located at the mouth of the Delaware River, this light was first lit in 1910 and remains in use today. The black skeletal tower is constructed of cast iron and stands at 110 feet upon a foundation of nine concrete piers. It originally used a fifth-order range lens, but is now fitted with a DCB-224. The keeper's house, a 1.5-story colonial revival structure dating from 1906, burned down in 2002. This station is not open to the public. The range front light, an integrated cottage-style building and lantern, was replaced by a post light in 1951 and subsequently destroyed.

Ship John Shoal Light

Greenwich, Cumberland County

This light was first lit in 1874, and it was automated in 1973 (and remains in use today). It consists of an octagonal cast-iron tower (with a mansard roof). The keeper's quarters are integral to the tower, and the entire structure is painted brown. The tower originally held a fourth-order Fresnel lens, which was replaced, in 1997, with a solar-powered optic. It has a height of focal plane of 50 feet above sea level. (The fourth-order lens is now located at the Coast Guard Air Station in Ponoma, NJ.) This light station is owned and managed by the U.S. Coast Guard. It is not open to the public.

Located in the Overfalls Maritime Museum, Lewes, the *Overfalls* was the last lightship to be built by the United States Lighthouse Service (1938). Considered "state of the art" at the time of its construction, it served a distinguished career before its decommission in 1972.

Maryland

Baltimore Light

Gibson Island, Anne Arundel County

Located at the south entrance to Craighill Channel, off the mouth of the Magothy River, this was one of the last lighthouses built on the Chesapeake Bay. The octagonal brick tower stands at 38 feet. At the time of its completion, in 1908, it was the tallest caisson light in the world. It is painted white, with a black lantern. It originally held a fourth-order Fresnel lens. Today, the light uses a 300 mm solar-powered lens, and it has a height of focal plane of 52 feet above sea level. The keeper's quarters are integral to the tower. In 1964, the light was converted to run off power supplied by a small atomic reactor, thereby making it the first nuclear-powered lighthouse in the world (although this experiment only lasted for one year). Owned and managed by the U.S. Coast Guard, this lighthouse is not open to the public.

Above: **The derelict Cedar Point Light in 1981**

Bethel Bridge Light (Replica)

Chesapeake City

This is a 1996 reconstruction of one of a number of lights that were situated on the Chesapeake and Delaware Canal before it was discontinued in 1927. The inactive, 30-foot, square frame tower, was sponsored by the Chesapeake City Lions Club. It stands a short walk from the C&D Canal Museum in Chesapeake City.

Bloody Point Bar Light

Claiborne, Queen Anne's County

First lit in 1882, this brown cast-iron lighthouse is located on the south of Kent Island. The conical ("spark plug" style) tower stands at 40 feet. In the winter of 1882–83, severe storms caused the light to tilt noticeably. Riprap stone was set around the base, to help stabilize the tower and to protect it from the sea. In 1884, sand was dredged from one side to bring it to a more upright position, and an apron of more than 750 tons of stone was laid at the caisson base. Today, the tower still has a slight list. In 1960, the light was rapidly engulfed by a fire that began in the equipment room. The two Coast Guard attendants fought the blaze and barely escaped alive. The tower was completely gutted and, though still in use today, it is just an iron shell with an internal ladder to access the lantern. The light originally used a fourth-order Fresnel lens. It now has a 300 mm solar-powered optic (focal plane 54 feet). It is not open to the public.

Cedar Point Light

Solomons, St. Mary's County

This 1896 cottage-style lighthouse stood on a partially submerged island that subsequently suffered serious erosion. The station was shut down in 1954 and the building was abandoned to dereliction. Its lantern was removed to the Patuxent River Naval Air Museum in 1981, and is reportedly under reconstruction so that it can be displayed inside the new museum building. In 1996 the wooden portion of the keeper's quarters was delivered to the Calvert Marine Museum in Solomons. The remaining brick walls of the first two floors were knocked into the water.

Concord Point Light (Havre de Grace Light)

See page 224

Cove Point Light

Lusby, Calvert County

Dating from 1828, the Cove Point Light is a conical brick tower (with a cement coating that was added in 1953), standing at 51 feet (focal plane 45 feet). It is painted white, has three small windows, and is topped by a black cast-iron lantern. The tower contains a wooden spiral staircase, and a counterweight shaft that runs from the lantern to the ground. Its light originally consisted of a number of parabolic reflector lamps. In 1928, the lantern was refitted with a fourth-order Fresnel lens, which it still uses. The keeper's house, dating from 1828, is a two-story vernacular duplex, constructed of brick. Automated in 1986, The light was given to the Calvert Marine Museum in Solomons in 2000, and trips to the light depart from the museum. (Note: the surrounding area is a private community and visitors are not permitted to drive directly to the light.

Craighill Channel Lower Range Lights

Sparrows Point, Baltimore County

The front range light is an offshore, 35-foot, red, spark-plug lighthouse (1873), with white trim and a black lantern, standing on a black caisson. After Duxbury Pier Light in Massachusetts, this is the second-oldest spark-plug lighthouse in the United States, and the only such light with single-story keeper's quarters, making its design unique. It has two solar-powered lights, one of which works in tandem with a rear range light (1873), a 105-foot, square pyramidal skeletal tower with a central cylinder. The upper part of this tower is faded red and the lower part, white. Both lights remain active today. They are not open to the public and best seen by boat.

Craighill Channel Upper ("Cutoff Channel") Range Lights

Entrance to the Patapsco River, Chesapeake Bay

These lights were commissioned in 1886 and are still active today. The 64-foot rear light consists of a simple pyramidal iron skeleton supporting a square wood-encased stairway that is covered with corrugated iron and leads to the lantern room. A keeper's dwelling was built nearby. The 15-foot front light is an octagonal brick tower that was constructed upon the foundation of the old North Point Rear Light. Initially, a small bridge connected the light to the shore, where a keeper's dwelling was built, but this was destroyed by a storm in 1893. The keeper's quarters were subsequently moved into the less than 12-square-foot lighthouse. The lantern was moved to outside of the tower, and a skiff was employed for traveling to and from the shore. Both the Rear and Front lights were fully automated in 1929.

Drum Point Light

See page 214

Fishing Battery Light

Fishing Battery Island, south of Havre de Grace (northern Chesapeake Bay)

Fishing Battery is a man-made island in the northern Chesapeake Bay. First lighted in 1853, the Fishing Battery Light consists of a one-story, 13-by-16-foot brick dwelling with a lantern mounted on the roof. It originally stood at 32 feet and it was outfitted with a system of five lamps and reflectors, which was replaced by a sixth-order Fresnel lens in the mid-1850s. The lantern has been replaced twice, in 1864 and in 1867. In 1899, a fifth-order Fresnel lens was installed. As a result of the grade of the island being raised, the lighthouse had to be removed and relaid in 1887. At that time, the dwelling was enlarged. In 1921, the light was moved to a 38-foot steel tower, next to the original lighthouse, and it was converted to acetylene gas. (This light was automated in 1939, and it now runs off solar cells and batteries.) The island is now under the jurisdiction of the Blackwater Wildlife Refuge and the lighthouse has been severely endangered by neglect.

Fort Carroll Light

Patapsco River, just before the Frances Scot Key Bridge

In 1854, a small wooden lighthouse was built on the man-made island of Fort Carroll, to mark the turn from the Brewerton Channel to the Fort McHenry Channel going into the Baltimore Harbor. The keeper lived in a separate dwelling on the Fort's grounds. The light was moved several times during the fort's construction, and it was completely rebuilt in 1898. This light was discontinued in 1931 and, following World War II, both the fort and the beacon were abandoned. Today, the light is in a state of extreme decay.

Fort Washington Light

Fort Washington National Park, across from Mount Vernon

Standing at 28 feet, this beacon is a converted wooden fog bell tower, dating from 1882. (A keeper's dwelling was added in 1885.) A pole light tower had been erected on this site in the 1850s, but, by 1900, other construction at the fort had partially obscured the light. Because Congress would not fund a new tower, the light was "temporarily" moved to the fog bell tower in 1901. It is still there today, and its flashing red light can be seen for seven miles. Renovated as recently as 1999, this is the only fog bell tower of this (once common) type still standing on the Chesapeake Bay.

Hooper Island Light

Hoopersville, Dorchester County

This 35-foot, conical ("spark plug" style) cast-iron tower was first lit in 1902. It is painted white, with a brown cylinder, and a black lantern. The tower originally held a fourth-order Fresnel lens, which was stolen in 1976, and it now uses a 300 mm optic. It has a height of focal plane of 63 feet above sea level. The keeper's quarters are integral to the tower. This light is still in use today. It is owned and managed by the U.S. Coast Guard, and it is not open to the public.

Hooper Strait Light

See page 214

Lazaretto Point Light

Baltimore, Chesapeake Bay

This 1985 structure is a replica of the 1831 white, conical lighthouse that was replaced by a skeleton tower in 1926.

Love Point Light

Kent Island, Chesapeake Bay

A small automated beacon stands on the site of this former lighthouse, which was a hexagonal screwpile structure built in 1872, automated in 1953, and destroyed in 1964.

Piney Point Light

Piney Point, St. Mary's County

Built in 1836, this is the oldest lighthouse on the Potomac River. It is known as the "Lighthouse of Presidents" because several heads of state have spent their summers here—beginning with James Madison and continuing through Teddy Roosevelt. The 30-foot conical brick tower is painted white with red trim. It had a height of focal plane of 34 feet above sea level. In 1855, the old 10 lamp/10 reflector Argand-style lighting system was replaced with a fifth-order Fresnel lens. The light was automated in 1939. In 1884, the keeper's dwelling was expanded with a second story, a porch, and new windows. In 1964, the lighthouse was decommissioned but the Coast Guard continued to use the dwelling over the next 15 years. The station is now managed by the St. Clement's Island Potomac River Museum. A chief petty officer's cottage (constructed in the 1950s) now serves as a gift shop and museum.

Above: **Love Point Light, ice-bound in this 1902 view**

Point Lookout Light (Old)

Scotland, St. Mary's County

Operational from 1830 until 1965, this lighthouse was witness to much action during the Civil War. First, the Point was host to a large military hospital and, after 1863, to a Union prisoner of war camp (notorious for its squalid conditions and the thousands of Confederate soldiers who died there—and the site is now said to be haunted). The light consists of a 36-foot octagonal iron tower that rises up from its 2.5-story, square brick keeper's house. It is painted white, with red trim. A fourth-order Fresnel lens was installed in the 1850s, and the lamp was also upgraded in 1860 and, again, in 1899. The tower had a height of focal plane of 41 feet above sea level. This site is currently under restoration and is used as a Naval Air Test Center. The lighthouse is open to the public once a year, in November, though the site adjoins a small park, from which visitors can view and photograph the tower.

Point No Point Light

Dameron, St. Mary's County

This light was first lit in 1905 and it is still operational today. It was fully automated in 1938, but it remained manned until 1962. The octagonal brick tower stands at 35 feet (focal plane 52 feet) and is painted white, with a red base and a black lantern. It originally used a fourth-order Fresnel lens (it currently holds a 375 mm solar-powered optic). The keeper's quarters are integral to the tower. This light station is owned by the U.S. Coast Guard, and it is not open to the public.

Pooles Island Light

Aberdeen, Harford County

The Pooles Island Light, the oldest lighthouse still standing in Maryland, was operational from 1825 until 1939. The conical brick tower stands at 40 feet. It was originally painted white, though it is now natural, and it is topped with a black iron lantern. In 1857, the original system of seven Argand lamps and reflectors was replaced with a fourth-order Fresnel lens. In 1917, the island was purchased by the U.S. Army and it was made part of Aberdeen Proving Ground. It was automated the following year. The keeper's dwelling and other structures were torn down after the light was decommissioned. In the 1990s, the Army took major steps to renovate the tower, in hopes that it can be turned back over to the Coast Guard and relighted. This light is not open to the public.

Sandy Point Shoal Light

Skidmore, Anne Arundel County

Consisting of a 37-foot octagonal brick tower, this lighthouse dates from 1883 and is still operational today. It originally held a fourth-order Fresnel lens. The light was electrified in 1929, and it was automated in 1963. The keeper's dwelling, which is red with a white roof, is integral to the tower (which is topped with a black lantern). In 1979, the Coast Guard found that the light had been badly vandalized and someone had smashed the nearly 100-year-old handmade crystal Fresnel lens. The tower is now fitted with a 300 mm solar-powered lens, and it has a focal plane 51 feet above sea level. This light is not open to the public, but it is visible from the Chesapeake Bay Bridge.

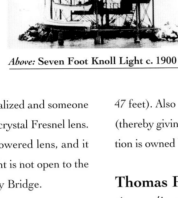

Above: **Seven Foot Knoll Light c. 1900**

Seven Foot Knoll Light

Baltimore, Baltimore City (relocated from the Patapsco River)

Seven Foot Knoll Light was first lit in 1856, when it was situated at the mouth of the Patapsco River. It consists of a cylindrical wrought iron tower that stands at 40 feet. It is painted barn red. The tower originally held a fourth-order Fresnel lens. The original octagonal keeper's cottage, built in 1855, was replaced in the 1870s with the current cylindrical house. The light was fully automated in 1948. It was deactivated in 1987 and, by October of 1988, it had been replaced by a steel tower and the title to the historic tower was obtained by the City of Baltimore. The 220-ton tower was cut from its pilings and shipped to Pier 5 in Baltimore's Inner Harbor. It is now open to the public, along with the lightship *Chesapeake* (1930–70) and the World War II submarine, *Torsk*.

Sharps Island Light

Fairbank, Talbot County

Since suffering ice damage in 1976 and 1977, this operational 1882 tower has leaned. The brown conical tower stands at 35 feet and is constructed of cast iron. Its height of focal plane is 54 feet above sea level. The light was automated in 1938. Around 1940, Sharps Island was completely covered by the waters of the Chesapeake Bay. Because of the ice damage received in the 1970s, the original fourth-order Fresnel lens was removed and replaced with a plastic lens. The keeper's quarters are integral to the tower. This light is owned and managed by the U.S. Coast Guard, and it is not open to the public.

Solomons Lump Light

Crisfield, Somerset County

This 35-foot square brick tower (on a cylindrical pier) was first lit in 1895 and it is still operational today. The tower is painted white, with a brown base and a black lantern. It originally held a fifth-order Fresnel lens, which was replaced by a fourth-order Fresnel in 1919. Since 1950, when the light was automated, it has used a 200 mm optic (focal plane 47 feet). Also in 1950, the wooden keeper's dwelling was torn down (thereby giving the lighthouse a lopsided appearance). This light station is owned by the U.S. Coast Guard and is not open to the public.

Thomas Point Shoal Light

Annapolis, Anne Arundel County

The only screwpile light on the Chesapeake Bay still in its original location, this is possibly the most widely recognized lighthouse in Maryland. The square wood tower rises at 25 feet atop its 1.5-story hexagonal keeper's dwelling. It is painted white, with a red roof, and topped with a black lantern. It uses a 250 mm solar-powered lens. (The original fourth-order Fresnel lens is now located in the Commandants Office, in Baltimore's Curtis Bay Yard.) This light is not open to the public. Manned until 1986, this was the last lighthouse on the Chesapeake Bay to be fully automated.

Turkey Point Light

See page 205

New Jersey

Absecon Lighthouse

Atlantic City, Atlantic County

First lit in 1857, this light remained in use until 1933 — when the lights from the fast-growing Atlantic City made it useless. In 1966, it was relit and was opened to the public during the summer months. The conical brick and iron tower stands at 169 feet and was attached to the keeper's quarters. It is painted yellow with a red band midway. The tower retains its original, first-order Fresnel lens (in combination with an oil lamp). The original keeper's house was destroyed, but has been reconstructed and now houses a visitor center.

Above: **Absecon Lighthouse, c. 1900**

Barnegat Light
See page 57

Brandywine Shoal Light
Cape May, Cape May County

This light station was established on the Delaware Bay in 1823, though the current light dates from 1914. It was preceded by a lightship and an 1850 tower that was demolished later. The 1850 tower was the first screwpile lighthouse in the United States. The current tower was automated in 1974 and is still in use. It is cylindrical in shape (in the "spark plug" style) and constructed of cast iron. Standing at 45 feet, it is painted white, with a red top. The tower originally held a third-order Fresnel lens (which is now on loan to Tuckerton Seaport), though today it uses a solar-powered optic (focal plane 60 feet). The keeper's quarters are integral to the tower. This light is owned by the U.S. Coast Guard and is not open to the public.

Cape May Point Light
Cape May, Cape May County

Located at the entrance to the Delaware Bay, this 1859 lighthouse is still in use today. The 157-foot tower is conical in shape and is constructed of brick. It is painted beige, with a red lantern, and it has a height of focal plane of 165 feet above sea level. In 1946, when the light was automated, its first-order Fresnel lens was replaced with a DCB-36 optic. The original first-order lens is on display at the Cape May County Courthouse. The two-story wooden keeper's house was constructed in 1860, in the Cape Cod style. Other structures include a storage building, and a brick oil house (from 1893). This light station is owned by the State of New Jersey, on lease to the Mid-Atlantic Center for the Arts. It is now part of a state park.

Chapel Hill Range Rear Light
Leonardo, Monmouth County

First lit in 1856, this now inactive light is situated on New York Harbor's Sandy Hook Bay. The square wooden tower stands at 31 feet. It is beige in color. It originally held a second-order lens, and it had a height of focal plane of 224 feet above sea level. A subsequent lens, of the fourth-order, is now on display at the Navesink Twin Lights Museum. The keeper's quarters were integral to the tower. This lighthouse now functions as a private residence, and it is not open to the public. Together with the Conover Beacon (see

Above: **Cape May Point Light seen through the ruins of the previous tower, which was demolished in 1859 (*see also* pages 36–37)**

below), this is the best-preserved example of three sets of identical 1856 range towers. It has since been replaced with a modern skeletal tower.

Conover Beacon (Chapel Hill Front Range)
Leonardo, Monmouth County

This inactive lighthouse was first lit in 1941, when it held a 375 mm optic. The red and white skeletal tower, rising at 40 feet, is conical in shape and is constructed of metal. It sits upon a concrete foundation. This lighthouse is owned by the U.S. Coast Guard, and it is not open to the public. (It replaced an earlier, six-sided wooden tower, which was constructed in 1856.)

East Point (Maurice River) Light
See page 135

Elbow of Cross Ledge Light
Delaware Bay, three miles northwest of Miah Maull Shoal

A relatively new lighthouse (dating from 1954), the Elbow of Cross Ledge Light was built on the round iron caisson of the first lighthouse constructed at this station, in 1910. It consists of a square skeletal tower mounted on a square workroom. The tower is painted red, the workroom is white, and the caisson is black. The beacon has a height of focal plane of 61 feet above sea level. The light is operational and can only be viewed by boat.

Finns Point Range Rear Light
Pennsville, Salem County

Situated on the Delaware River, this light was first lit in 1877. The solid black skeletal tower (with an internal cylinder) stands at a height of 115 feet and is constructed of wrought iron. It originally held a Fresnel lens, and it had a height of focal plane of 105 feet above sea level. During the 1930s, the front range light that was paired with it was destroyed (to be later restored, in 1983). The Range Rear Light was also automated in the 1930s. In the 1950s, however, the channel the lighthouse marked was altered, and the lighthouse became obsolete. The keeper's quarters were destroyed in 1977, after a series of vandalism damaged the property. The light station is now part of a national wildlife refuge. In September 2006, it was announced that the lighthouse is closed to the public until further notice.

Great Beds Light
Raritan Bay, off Staten Island

This lighthouse was first lit in 1880, and it was automated in 1945. Standing at 60 feet, the conical cast-iron tower is painted white, with a black lantern. Originally fitted with a fourth-order Fresnel lens, the lantern now holds a 155 mm optic, and it has a height of focal plane of 61 feet above sea level. At four stories, the keeper's quarters are integral to the tower. The site is owned and managed by the U.S. Coast Guard and is not open to the public.

Hereford Inlet Light (Old)
See page 155

Ludlam (Ludlum) Beach Light
Ludlum Beach, Sea Isle City

Built in 1885, this lighthouse once consisted of a square wooden tower on the roof of a one-story keeper's dwelling. After fire damage, it was replaced in 1924 by a light on a steel tower. The tower has since been removed, and the keeper's house is now a private residence. In 2006, the owner announced plans to destroy it, or to donate the building if someone can move it. The Friends of the Ludlum Beach Lighthouse are working to find a new site.

Miah Maull Shoal Light
Downe, Cumberland County

First lit in 1913 and automated in the 1970s, the Miah Maull Shoal Light still functions as an active aid to navigation (using a 500 mm optic). The conical cast-iron tower (with a brick lining) stands at 45 feet (focal plane 59 feet). The tower is painted red, with a red watch room and a black lantern. It originally held a fourth-order Fresnel lens. The keeper's quarters are integral to the tower (occupying three stories). This lighthouse is owned and managed by the U.S. Coast Guard, and it is not open to the public.

Navesink Twin Lights
Highlands, Monmouth County

Navesink Light was first established in 1828. It consisted of a pair of rubble towers. In 1862, these were replaced with two brownstone towers — the south tower being square and the north tower octagonal. They stand at 73 feet and are connected by a keeper's dwelling. Today, only the south tower is operational (the north tower was discontinued in

Above: **Miah Maull Shoal Light**

1898). In 1841, the first Fresnel lens to be used in the United States was imported from France and installed in the original south tower. In 1898, the oil lamps in the south tower were replaced with an electric arc lamp — making this the first primary lighthouse in the country to use an electric light. It was also the most powerful coast light in the country, with an estimated candlepower of 25,000,000. In 1949, the Coast Guard automated the lights. The north tower is now open for climbing, and the keeper's house functions as a museum and gift shop.

Robbins Reef Light
See New York listings

Romer Shoal Light
Staten Island (officially, New Jersey waters)

First lit in 1898, the Romer Shoal Light was automated in 1966 and is still operational today. The 54-foot conical tower is constructed of cast iron and is painted white, with a red band midway. It was originally equipped with a fourth-order Fresnel lens — later, a 190 mm optic — with a height of focal plane of 54 feet above sea level. The keeper's quarters are integral to the "spark plug" style tower. This lighthouse is owned and managed by the U.S. Coast Guard, and it is not open to the public.

Sandy Hook Light
See page 57

Sandy Hook Point Light
North entrance to Sandy Hook Bay, Highlands

This steel, pyramidal skeletal tower replaced an 1880 cast-iron lighthouse, which was relocated to Jeffrey's Hook, upper Manhattan, in 1921 (where it became famous as "The Little Red Lighthouse"). Still active today, the Sandy Hook Point Light stands at 35 feet, with a small enclosure at the base. The grounds are open to the public.

Sea Girt Light
Sea Girt, Monmouth County
(relocated from Sea Girt Inlet)

Constructed in 1896, this light consists of a square redbrick tower with a black and white lantern. It stands at 44 feet, with a height of focal plane of 60 feet above sea level. The lantern originally held a fourth-order Fresnel lens. It was electrified in 1924.

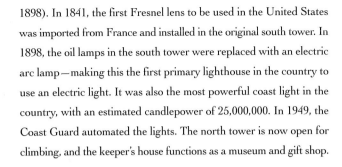

In 1941, the light was shut down and the Fresnel was removed. At the end of World War II, a new light was installed at the top of the lantern room, and the light was automated in 1945. In 1955, the lighthouse was discontinued and the light was moved to another tower on the lighthouse property. In 1980, the Sea Girt Lighthouse Citizens Committee was formed to restore the lighthouse and, in 1982, the light was relit. It is now open to the public, and tours are available.

Ship John Shoal Light

Delaware Bay, off Cohansey Point

This lighthouse was named after a vessel, the *Ship John*, which was grounded on a shoal near the mouth of the Cohansey Creek in 1797. Constructed in 1877, the lighthouse sits on a caisson. (A steel cylinder was sunk 30 feet below the surface of the water and filled with rock, and the foundation was then surrounded by riprap, to protect the structure from ice and sea.) A Victorian-style cottage sits atop the caisson foundation, with a copper roof and paned windows, and topped with a lantern room. The entire structure is painted red.

Tinicum Island Range Rear Light

Paulsboro, Gloucester County

Located on the Delaware River, this 1880 lighthouse was automated in 1967 and is still operational today. It consists of an 86-foot, black-painted, skeletal iron tower (with a central cylinder), on a stone masonry foundation. It was originally installed with a parabolic reflector lens, but currently holds a DCB-24 optic (focal plane 83 feet). The keeper's house is no longer present. This light station is occasionally open to the public.

Tucker Island Light (Replica)

Tuckerton Seaport (originally Little Egg Inlet), Tuckerton

This is a replica of the original lighthouse, dating from 1868, which was swept out to sea in 1927. The replica—a 45-foot, square tower, atop a two-story keeper's dwelling—is part of a museum complex in Tuckerton, and it serves as an interpretive center. The museum is open from 10 A.M. until 5 P.M. daily.

Now located at Pyne Poynt Marina in Camden, the *Barnegat* lightship served from 1904 until 1967. The *Liberty (Winter Quarter)* lightship was built in Bath, Maine, in 1923 at a contract price of $200,000. Retired from duty in 1968, she now functions as the Lightship Bar and Grill, located at Liberty Landing Marina.

New York

Barber's Point Light (Old)

Westport, Essex County

Located on Lake Champlain, this light was operational from 1873 until 1935 (when it was replaced with a steel skeletal tower). The octagonal, blue limestone tower is painted white, with black trim. It stands at 36 feet atop the keeper's dwelling. This light used a fifth-order Fresnel lens and had a height of focal plane of 83 feet above sea level. The keeper's dwelling is a two-story stone cottage, to which an addition was added in the 1950s. This lighthouse now serves as a private residence, and it is not open to the public.

Barcelona (Portland Harbor) Light

Westfield, Chautauqua County

Originally called the Portland Harbor Light, this was significant as the first public building to be lit by natural gas. Operational from 1829 until 1859, this conical fieldstone tower stands at 40 feet. It originally used 11 lamps, with 14-inch reflectors. In 1962, the tower was refitted with a gas "street lamp." The keeper's house is a 1.5-story fieldstone cottage, constructed in 1829 and modified in the 1890s. This lighthouse now functions as a private residence, and it is not open to the public.

Blackwell Island Light

Roosevelt Island (formerly known as Blackwell Island), New York

Built in 1872, by convicts from New York's former Blackwell Island Prison, this 50-foot lighthouse can be seen from the city's FDR Drive, as well as from the John Finley Walk (near Gracie Mansion) and from 1st Street in Astoria, Queens. It is a Gothic-style, octagon shaped tower made from gray gneiss stone, which is found on the island. The site is open to the public.

Bluff Point (Valcour Island) Light

Plattsburgh, Clinton County (Lake Champlain)

Operational from 1874 until 1930 (when it was replaced with a skeletal tower), this historic light consists of an octagonal, blue limestone and wood tower, which is painted red and white and stands at 35 feet atop a square keeper's house. The tower used a fifth-order Fresnel lens and had a height of focal plane of 95 feet above sea level. The 1.5-story keeper's house is constructed of blue limestone and dates from 1871. Owned and managed by New York State and the Clinton County Historical Association, this site now serves as a state park.

Braddock Point Light

Hilton, Monroe County

Situated on Lake Ontario, the Braddock Point Light was first lit in 1896 and remained in use until 1954. It consists of an octagonal redbrick tower, which stands at 40 feet and is topped with a faux lantern. (The original upper two-thirds of the tower was removed in 1954 because of structural damage.) The tower originally used a third-and-a-half-order Fresnel lens. The keeper's house is a 2.5-story Victorian brick dwelling, constructed in 1896. Also on site is a carriage house. This site is now privately owned, and it is not open to the public.

Brewerton Range Rear Light

Oneida River, Brewerton

This unpainted concrete tower, with no lantern, stands at 85 feet (with a height of focal plane of 92 feet above sea level). Located on the north bank of the Oneida River, close to county road 37, just west of US 11 in Brewerton, the light was constructed in 1917. The site and tower are closed to the public, but the lighthouse can be viewed from outside the gate.

Buffalo Harbor South Entrance Light

South Buffalo, Erie County

This tower was first lit in 1903. The 27-foot, conical, steel structure with white markings rests on a foundation of dressed stone and timber. It is believed that the original optic was the fourth-order Fresnel that is now in the 1833 Buffalo Main Light. A new 300 mm optic on a nearby modern post has replaced it (focal plane 40 feet). A utilitarian concrete sound-signal building stands adjacent to the tower. This light station, located on Stony Point Breakwater, is owned and managed by the U.S. Coast Guard and is not open to the public.

Buffalo Harbor has had as many as nine lighthouses and a lightship marking its entrance. Buffalo Intake Crib Light (1920) is an active optic (flashing white) atop a circular stone water-intake crib. The original Buffalo Breakwater Light of 1872 was rammed several times by ships; it became known as the "leaning lighthouse," and has since been demolished.

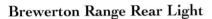

Above: **Buffalo North Breakwater South End Light, left, and Buffalo (Main) Light, right**

Buffalo (Main) Light

Buffalo, Erie County

This lighthouse is known locally as "Chinaman's Light," because it welcomed immigrants to the mouth of the Buffalo River. Active from 1833 until 1914, the octagonal limestone and cast-iron tower stands at 61 feet. It was originally fitted with a third-order Fresnel lens (which was given to the Buffalo & Erie County Historical Society in 1961), and had a height of focal plane of 76 feet above sea level. This lighthouse has been carefully preserved (and a new fourth-order Fresnel lens fitted), and is now part of an outdoor museum located on the grounds of the U.S. Coast Guard Station.

Buffalo North Breakwater South End Light

Buffalo Waterfront (relocated from the North Harbor entrance)

First lit in 1903, with a sixth-order Fresnel, this beacon was automated in 1960 and remained in use until 1985. It is a white, bottle-shaped boiler plate/cast-iron tower, standing at 29 feet. The light is now managed by the Buffalo Lighthouse Association, Inc., and it is open to the public.

Cape Vincent Breakwater Light

Relocated from the eastern entrance to Cape Vincent, Cape Vincent

Built in 1900 and inactive since 1934, the Cape Vincent Breakwater Light consists of a short, square concrete block tower (now covered in aluminum siding) with a black lantern. It was formerly located at the end of a breakwater, but was relocated to the grounds of the Cape Vincent town hall in 1951.

Cayuga Inlet and Cayuga Inlet Breakwater Lights

Lighthouse Point, Ithaca

The 1917 Cayuga Inlet Lighthouse was relocated from the west bank to the east bank of the creek, at Lighthouse Point, when the nearby Cayuga Inlet Breakwater Light was constructed in 1927. Both towers stand at 25 feet, and both have wood framing and are covered in sheet metal plates. The Cayuga Inlet Light is white and the Breakwater Light is red. Both are lit with rotating, solar-powered beacons. The site, which is open to the public, is accessible by a 3/4-mile hike from the western end of Pier Road.

Cedar Island Light (Old)

Sag Harbor, Suffolk County

This historic lighthouse was first lit in 1868 and it was deactivated in 1934. The square tower stands at 40 feet and is constructed of unpainted granite. It used a sixth-order Fresnel optic (which was later moved to the more modern Breakwater Light) and had a height of focal plane of 44 feet above sea level. The two-story keeper's house, an L-shaped granite structure, is integral to the tower. This light station is owned by the Suffolk County Department of Parks, and it is currently planned to undergo preservation work.

Cold Spring Harbor Light

Relocated to Long Island

This lighthouse was built in 1890 on Cold Spring Harbor at the Point of Shoal. In 1965, the lighthouse was deactivated. At that time, a local resident saved the light from destruction by purchasing it for $1 and moving it to her property, where the light still resides. The square pyramidal tower is constructed of wood and stands at 35 feet. It originally used a fourth-order Fresnel lens (later, a 300 mm lens), and it had a height of focal plane of 37 feet above sea level. This lighthouse was refurbished in 1994. It is not open to the public.

Coney Island (Nortons Point) Light

Brooklyn, Kings County

This 70-foot steel skeletal lighthouse was constructed in 1920 and is still active today (it was automated in 1989). It is painted white, with black trim. The tower's original, fourth-order Fresnel lens is now on display at New York City's South Street Seaport Museum. Today, the tower is fitted with a 190 mm optic. It has a height of focal plane of 75 feet above sea level. The keeper's house is a two-story wood cottage constructed in 1896. This light station is currently used as an active aid to navigation and as housing for the U.S. Coast Guard. It is not open to the public.

Cooperstown Marina Light

Fair Street, south end of Ostego Lake, Cooperstown

Built circa 1955, this is a (approximately) 40-foot cylindrical tower, painted white, with a horizontal red band, and topped with a black lantern. (However, the beacon is actually on a short mast at the top of the lantern, not inside the lantern.) The light is still active, with a quick-flashing white light and a focal plane of about 45 feet above sea level. The site is open to the public.

Above: **Crossover Island Light**

Crossover Island Light

Hammond, St. Lawrence County

This 1882 tower was replaced by an offshore skeletal buoy in 1941. The historic lighthouse consisted of a conical cast-iron tower (with a brick and wood lining), painted white and topped with a red lantern. It used a sixth-order Fresnel lens. The keeper's dwelling, dating from 1882, is a 1.5-story wood-framed (Queen Anne) house. This light station is now privately owned, and it currently serves as a summer cottage. It is not open to the public.

Crown Point Light

Crown Point, on Lake Champlain

This lighthouse was established in 1858 near the historic Grenadier Battery fortification ruins. The base of the tower stood at 57 feet above sea level. By 1894, the tower had been fitted with a fixed fifth-order lens. In 1926, the lighthouse was deactivated. As part of the commemoration of the 300th anniversary of the discovery of the lake by Samuel de Champlain, the states of New York and Vermont removed the old tower and replaced it with an ornamental cylindrical tower made of cut granite blocks and surrounded by eight Doric-style columns. On the pedestal is a grouping of bronze figures with Champlain himself at the center, designed by the famous French sculptor Rodin and presented by the Republic of France.

Cumberland Head Light (Old)

Plattsburgh, Clinton County (Lake Champlain)

Established in 1868, this light station consists of a 50-foot, unpainted, conical limestone tower attached to a two-story granite keeper's dwelling. It originally held a fourth-order Fresnel lens, but was deactivated in 1934 after the construction of a red steel skeletal tower on a concrete crib nearby. Relit as an active aid to navigation in 2003, the old lighthouse currently serves as a private residence, and it is not open to the public.

Dunkirk (Point Gratiot) Light

Dunkirk, Chautauqua County

With many of its historic structures still standing, this light station serves as an active aid to navigation and as a museum. Dating from 1875, the square tower stands at 61 feet and is constructed of rubble stone, encased in brick. The upper two-thirds is painted white, the lower two-thirds is natural, and the lantern is red. The light retains its original third-order Fresnel lens, with a height of focal plane of 82 feet above sea level. The two-story redbrick keeper's house is in the high Victorian Gothic style. Other structures include a cistern, garage, storage building, barn, an oil house, and a bandstand. In addition, the following structures have been relocated to the museum: a steel lifesaving boat (dating from 1926), a 45-foot lighthouse buoy tender, a 50-foot tower from the Dunkirk Harbor (dating from 1939), and a 21-foot tower from Grand Island, NY (dating from 1929).

Dunkirk Pierhead Light

End of the west pier in Dunkirk, Lake Erie

This lighthouse replaced a skeletal tower, built in 1939, which is now on display at the Dunkirk (Point Gratiot) Light. It is a cylindrical "D9" type tower, painted white, with a narrow red band. The beacon gives off a red flash every six seconds, and it has a height of focal plane of 36 feet above sea level. Managed by the U.S. Coast Guard, the tower is closed to the public (though there is a parking and picnic area adjacent to the tower, off NY 5).

East Charity Shoals Light

Brownsville, Jefferson County

This light, located off of Cape Vincent, on Lake Ontario, was constructed in 1877 and is still operational today. The octagonal cast-iron tower originally served at Vermilion Station, from 1877 until 1929, when it was relocated after being damaged in an ice storm. It is painted white, with a black lantern, and it stands at 16 feet. It originally had a fifth-order Fresnel lens, and it has a height of focal plane of 52 feet above sea level. This light station is owned and managed by the U.S. Coast Guard, and it is not open to the public.

Eatons Neck Light

Huntington, Suffolk County

First lit in 1799, an 1837 inspection found this light to be defective, because its light was not visible at 10 miles. The following year, 12 lamps with 13-inch reflectors were installed to improve the visibility of the light. The octagonal pyramidal tower, painted white, with a red roof, stands at 73 feet and is constructed of fieldstone with a brick lin-

ing. It has a height of focal plane of 144 feet above sea level. Following a series of renovations and lamp changes, the light now uses third-order Fresnel lens. The keeper's house is constructed of wood. Also on site is a lifesaving station. One of only six lighthouses in the United States to survive from the 1700s, Eatons Neck Light was designed by John J. McComb, a prominent architect who was also responsible for New York's City Hall (1803–12). This active light station is owned and managed by the U.S. Coast Guard. It is open to the public.

Elm Tree (Swash Channel Range Front) Light

Miller Field, Staten Island

The Elm Tree Light was so named because Dutch mariners used to use an elm tree located on the site as a marker when they entered the Swash Channel. The first tower was constructed in 1856 and the light worked as a front range to the New Dorp (rear range) Light. The present concrete aviation tower replaced the first Elm Tree Light in 1939. In use until 1964, it showed a green light for aviators and a white light for mariners.

Esopus Meadows (Middle Hudson River) Light

Esopus, Ulster County

This lighthouse was active from 1872 until 1965 (when it was replaced with a modern pole tower). The octagonal wood tower stands at 25 feet, atop the square keeper's house, on a granite pier foundation. It used a fifth-order Fresnel lens, and had a height of focal plane of 58 feet above sea level. This site is owned and managed by Esopus Meadows Lighthouse, Inc., and it is not open to the public. As of 2002, restoration and preservation work on the lighthouse continued. In 2003, it was relit as a private light after almost forty years of darkness.

Execution Rocks Light

New Rochelle, Nassau County

Designed by Alexander Parris, this 1850 lighthouse is located on the west end of Long Island Sound. The conical granite tower stands at 60 feet, with a height of focal plane of 62 feet above sea level, and is painted white, with a brown band midway. The keeper's house was added in 1868, so that the keeper no longer had to live in the cramped quarters inside the tower. In 1918, a fire caused $13,500 in damage to the lighthouse. The engine house and machinery were destroyed, and the tower, oil house, windows, woodwork, gutters, and eaves were all damaged. In 1979, the lighthouse was automated and a Vega lantern replaced the fourth-order Fresnel lens. Today, it uses a APRB-251 solar-powered optic. Owned by the U.S. Coast Guard, the light station is not open to the public.

Fire Island Light
See page 50

Fort Niagara Light
Youngstown, Niagara County

Located on the south shore of Lake Ontario, this lighthouse was operational from 1872 until 1993 (when the tower was replaced by a modern beacon in order to save some trees that were obstructing the historic lantern). The 61-foot, octagonal limestone tower is topped with a black lantern. It retains its original, fourth-order Fresnel optic, and it has a height of focal plane of 91 feet above sea level. The wooden keeper's house, dating from 1897, is a two-story Queen Anne structure. Also on site is an iron plate oil house (from circa 1900–1905). The lighthouse now functions as a museum.

Fort Wadsworth Light
Staten Island, Richmond County

The Fort Wadsworth Light was operational from 1903 until 1965 (when it was replaced with a modern pole tower). Located on the East Verrazano Narrows, the cylindrical redbrick tower stands at 15 feet. It was originally fitted with a fourth-order Fresnel lens and had a height of focal plane of 75 feet above sea level. The historic tower is owned by the National Park Service, and the site now serves as a national park.

Frenchman's Island Light
Frenchman's Island (about 5 miles east southeast of Brewerton)

This is an unmanned, 20-foot steel skeletal tower mounted atop an 85-foot unpainted concrete tower. It has a height of focal plane of 123 feet above sea level, and no lantern. The beacon was completed in 1918 and is still operational. It was built by the state as part of the Erie Canal System.

Galloo Island Light
Sackets Harbor, Jefferson County

This lighthouse was constructed in 1867 at the southwest end of Galloo Island, on Lake Ontario. It was automated in 1963 and is still in use today. The conical gray limestone tower stands at 55 feet and contains a 190 mm optic. It originally used a fourth-order Fresnel lens, and it had a height of focal plane of 58 feet above sea level. The sound signal building is a one-story redbrick structure dating from 1897. The 1.5-story keeper's house is constructed of gray limestone and dates from 1867. This site is not open to the public.

Above: **Fire Island's old and new lighthouses**

Grand Island Range Front Light
Tonawanda Channel, near the southern tip of Grand Island

Constructed in 1917, this inactive, white octagonal frame tower stands at 36 feet and is topped with a blue frame lantern. The site is private and the tower is closed.

Great Beds Light
See New Jersey listings

Horse Island (Sacketts Harbor) Light
Sacketts Harbor, Jefferson County

On Lake Ontario, Horse Island was used as a staging area for the British Attack in the War of 1812. The Horse Island Light was operational from 1870 until 1957, when it was replaced with a nearby skeletal tower. The white, square tower with black lantern holds a fifth-order Fresnel lens and is attached to a Queen Anne Italianate keeper's house built of brick on a limestone foundation. Other structures on site include a barn, a privy, and an oil house. The historic tower is privately owned, and it is not open to the public.

Horton Point Light
Southold, Suffolk County

Dating from 1857, this light was deactivated in 1933, when a skeleton tower was lit on the shore. In 1990, following a major restoration effort, the historic tower was relit and the skeleton tower was removed. Today, the lighthouse serves as an active aid to navigation and as a museum. Visitors are allowed to climb the square stucco, brick, and granite tower, which stands at 58 feet and is attached to the rectangular keeper's house. Originally, the tower was equipped with a third-order Fresnel lens. Since 1990, it uses an FA 251 optic. It has a height of focal plane of 103 feet above sea level. The keeper's house is a two-story duplex dating from 1857. Other structures include a barn, the foundation from an oil house, and cisterns beneath the dwelling.

Hudson-Athens (Hudson City) Light
Hudson City, Columbia County

This lighthouse was active from 1874, was automated in 1949, and is still active today. The 30-foot square tower is constructed of dressed stone, with a redbrick pattern and a black lantern. Today, it uses a 300 mm optic and has a height of focal plane of 46 feet above sea level. The tower's original fifth-order Fresnel lens is on display at the Mystic Seaport Museum. The keeper's house, a 1.5-story Second Empire–style structure, is constructed of dressed stone and brick and dates from 1874. This site is owned and managed by the U.S. Coast Guard and the Hudson-Athens Lighthouse Preservation Committee, Inc. It is occasionally open to the public.

Huntington Harbor Light (Formerly Lloyd Harbor)

Huntington Village, Suffolk County

This operational lighthouse is currently under restoration (having been gutted by a fire in 1947). The tower was first lit in 1912 and it was automated in 1949. The square Beaux Arts (castle-style) tower is constructed of cast reinforced concrete and stands at 42 feet (with a height of focal plane of 41 feet above sea level). In 1967, the original fifth-order Fresnel lens was replaced with a 300 mm optic. The light station is only open to the public on tours managed by the Huntington Lighthouse Preservation Society, who are also developing a maritime museum in the keeper's quarters.

Irondequoit Bay Light

Irondequoit, Monroe County

This is a modern post light, and is white with a red band. It flashes a red signal every four seconds at a focal-plane height of 16 feet.

Jeffrey's Hook Light ("Little Red Lighthouse")

See page 227

Latimer Reef Light

Fishers Island Sound, Suffolk County

This conical ("spark plug"style) tower was first lit in 1884, was automated in 1974, and is still operational today. It is constructed of cast iron and brick, stands at 49 feet, and is painted white, with a brown band midway, and has a brown base. In 1983, the original fifth-order Fresnel lens was replaced with a 300 mm optic. The tower has a height of focal plane of 55 feet above sea level. The keeper's quarters are contained within the tower. This lighthouse is owned and managed by the U.S. Coast Guard, and it is not open to the public.

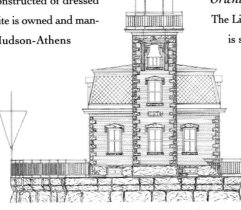

Above: **Hudson-Athens (Hudson City) Light**

Little Gull Island Light

Orient Point, Suffolk County

The Little Gull Island Light was first lit in 1869 and is still active today. An 81-foot, conical granite tower, it has a height of focal plane of 91 feet above sea level. The tower's original second-order Fresnel lens is on loan to the East End Seaport Museum & Marine Foundation in Greenport, NY. The keeper's house, a 2.5-story granite dwelling, was dismantled when the tower was automated in 1978. This light station is not open to the public.

Long Beach Bar Light (Replica)

Gardiners Bay, Greenport

Constructed in 1990, this lighthouse is a replica of the original Long Beach Bar Light, which was destroyed by fire in 1963. (The replica was actually built upon the foundation of the 1870 lighthouse.) Active as an aid to navigation, the structure consists of a square tower (with beveled edges) upon the roof of its keeper's dwelling. The lighthouse can be viewed (with binoculars) from NY Route 25, along the shoreline of Orient Harbor, and from Ram Island Road, on Shelter Island.

Montauk Point Light

Montauk, Suffolk County

Authorized to be built by George Washington, the Montauk Point Light has been operational since 1796. It was originally lit by 13 whale oil lamps. In 1860, the tower height was increased to accommodate a first-order lens. Today, the octagonal pyramidal tower stands at 110 feet and has a height of focal plane of 168 feet above sea level. It is constructed of sandstone and is painted white, with a brown band midway, and a black lantern. The tower was automated in 1987, when it was fitted with a DCB-224 optic. The 1838 keeper's house, a two-story colonial brick structure, was converted into a barn in 1860. Other structures include a sound signal building, an oil house, a storage building, and a radiobeacon. This light station is open to the public, and the keeper's house now serves as a museum.

Above: **Montauk Point Light**

Montauk Yacht Club Light

Star Island, Lake Montauk

Constructed circa 1930, this is one of the nation's oldest privately built and maintained lighthouses. It consists of a 60-foot, octagonal brick tower. The tower is painted white, with a shingled watch room and an octagonal lantern, and it is attached to a large yacht club complex.

New Dorp (Swash Channel Range Rear) Light

Staten Island, Richmond County

Operational from 1856 until 1964, this lighthouse consists of a white, square wooden tower that stands at 80 feet atop a 1.5-story keeper's dwelling. In 1891, the tower's original second-order Fresnel lens was replaced with a sixth-order range optic. The tower had a height of focal plane of 190 feet above sea level. Other structures on the site include a brick oil house and a garage. This lighthouse currently functions as a private residence, and it is not open to the public.

North Brother Island Light (Dwelling Only)

Bay of Brothers, New York City

Following years of abandon, the tower of this 1869 lighthouse is now gone, and the one-story wood-frame keeper's dwelling is in a state of disrepair. (The octagonal tower previously rose from the roof of the dwelling.) The original sixth-order Fresnel lens was replaced with a fourth-order Fresnel in 1900, and the light was discontinued in 1953. The structure can be viewed from the northeast shore of Randalls Island. It is not open to the public.

North Dumpling Light

Fishers Island, Suffolk County

The North Dumpling Light was active from 1871 until 1959, when it was replaced by a modern skeletal tower. Later, however, the light was returned to the old tower and the skeletal tower was removed. Standing at 31 feet (with a height of focal plane of 60 feet above sea level), the octagonal historic tower is a brick and wood shingle structure topped with a white lantern. It originally held a fifth-order Fresnel optic, which was later replaced with a 300 mm lens. Other features include a sound signal building, the keeper's quarters, a pier, and a boathouse. The lighthouse now functions as a private residence, and it is not open to the public.

Ogdensburg Harbor Light

Ogdensburg, St. Lawrence County

Now inactive, this lighthouse was first lit in 1834 and it was modified with an addition in 1900. The square stone tower stands at 65 feet and is painted white and gray, with a red lantern. Attached to the tower is the 1834 keeper's dwelling, a 1.5-story stone structure that was modified with wood in 1870. This former light station is now privately owned, and it is not open to the public.

Ogdensburg Harbor Light

Mouth of Oswegatchie River, Ogdensburg

Located at a spot called Lighthouse Point, this is a square stone tower, painted white and gray, with a red lantern. It stands at 65 feet and has a 1.5-story keeper's house. The structure, which was built circa 1870, now functions as a private residence.

Olcott Light

Olcott, Town of Newfane, Niagara County

A square, white, pyramidal tower with black lantern was established on Olcott pier in 1873. It was moved to the Olcott Yacht Club after its deactivation in *c.* 1930, and was demolished in 1963. A 27-foot replica was constructed by the Olcott Lighthouse Society in 2003.

Old Field Point Light

See page 62

Old Orchard Shoal Light

Oakwood Beach, Richmond County

Formerly part of the Waackaack Range, the Old Orchard Shoal Light dates from 1893, was automated in 1955, and is still operational today. The conical ("spark plug" style) tower is constructed of cast iron and stands at 35 feet. The lower portion of the tower is painted brown, while the upper portion is painted white. It originally held a fourth-order Fresnel lens. Today, the tower is fitted with a 250 mm optic, and it has a height of focal plane of 51 feet above sea level. The keeper's quarters are integral to the tower. This lighthouse is owned and managed by the U.S. Coast Guard and it is not open to the public.

Orient Point Light

See page 176

Oswego Harbor West Pierhead Light

Oswego, Oswego County

Still operational today, this light was first lit in 1934 and it was automated in 1968. The steel and cast-iron tower stands at 57 feet (the same height as its focal plane). It is painted white, with red trim. In 1995, its original fourth-order Fresnel lens was replaced with a VRB-25 optic. The fourth-order Fresnel is now on display at the H. Lee

White Maritime Museum in Oswego. The keeper's house, which is attached to the tower and dates from 1936, is a one-story structure made of reinforced concrete. Also on site is a radiobeacon, and another keeper's house (dating from 1822). This light station is owned and managed by the U.S. Coast Guard, and it is not open to the public.

Above: **Port of Genessee (Charlotte-Genessee) Light**

Plum Island (Plum Gut) Light

Orient, Suffolk County

This lighthouse tower was operational from 1870 until 1978. The octagonal wooden tower is painted white, with a black lantern, and rises at 55 feet above the two-story granite keeper's dwelling. The light originally held a fourth-order Fresnel lens, and it had a height of focal plane of 69 feet above sea level. In 1994, the Fresnel was given on loan to the East End Seaport and Marine Museum in Greenport, NY. Other structures on site include a brick oil house and a clapboard storage shed. In 1992, a modern, skeletal tower was constructed nearby. The historic tower is owned by the U.S. Department of Agriculture, and it currently serves as a U.S.D.A. animal disease center. East End Lighthouses are working toward the restoration of the lighthouse.

Point Aux Roches Light

Lake Champlain, near Plattsburgh

Constructed in 1858 using blue limestone block, this octagonal light tower was operational until 1989. It originally held a sixth-order Fresnel lens (later, a 250 mm optic), and it had a height of focal plane of 59 feet above sea level. The keeper's house, a 1.5-story wooden structure, was originally attached to the tower but has since been moved to an adjacent location. This site is not open to the public.

Port of Genessee (Charlotte-Genessee) Light

Rochester, Monroe County

First lit in 1822, this lighthouse was deactivated and its lamp was moved to a West Pier beacon in 1881. The Port of Genessee Light remained dark for several years, until it was finally relit in 1992. The octagonal rubble-stone tower stands at 40 feet and is topped with a black lantern that originally held 10 Argand lamps with reflectors. Today, the lighthouse uses a fourth-order Fresnel lens (focal plane 45 feet). The 1863 keeper's quarters is a 2.5-story brick structure, in the Victorian style. This light station is open to the public, and there is a museum in the keeper's quarters.

Princes Bay Light (Old)

Staten Island
(officially, New Jersey waters)

Operational from 1828 until 1922, this lighthouse was built during a time when Princes Bay had a large commercial oystering industry. The conical brownstone block tower originally held a third-and-one-half-order Fresnel optic, and it had a height of focal plane of 106 feet above sea level. The lantern has now been replaced by a statue. A walkway originally connected the tower to the 2.5-story keeper's house, a modified gothic structure made of brownstone. Other structures on site include an oil house and a bug light. In 1953, a black steel skeletal light tower was erected nearby. The historic lighthouse now functions as a private residence, and it is not open to the public.

Race Rock Light

See page 169

Robbins Reef Light

Staten Island, Richmond County

Lighting from the west side of the Maine Channel, on the upper New York Bay, the Robbins Reef Light was constructed in 1883. It was automated in 1966 and it is still operational today. The conical cast-iron tower stands at 45 feet and has a height of focal plane of 56 feet above sea level. It originally held a fourth-order Fresnel lens, and now uses a 300 mm optic. The lower portion of the tower is painted brown, and the upper portion is painted white. The keeper's quarters are integral to the "spark plug" style tower. This light is owned and managed by the U.S. Coast Guard, and it is not open to the public.

Rock Island Light

Orleans, Jefferson County

This lighthouse was constructed in 1882, and it was operational until the 1930s. The conical cast-iron and brick tower stands at 60 feet and is painted white, with a black lantern. It originally used a sixth-order Fresnel lens, and it had a height of focal plane of 40 feet above sea level. The keeper's house, also dating from 1882, is a 1.5-story Victorian dwelling constructed of wood. Other structures include a clapboard boathouse, a shop, a fieldstone smokehouse, a steel generator house, and a clapboard carpenter's shop. This light station now serves as a state park.

Rockland Lake Light

Hudson River, Scarborough

This red skeleton tower replaced an historic 1894 cast-iron ("spark plug" style) tower that was situated in the middle of the Hudson River. Eventually this earlier tower began to lean, earning it the nickname of "the leaning tower" of Rockland. It was demolished in 1923, the same year that the skeleton tower was constructed.

Romer Shoal Light

See New Jersey listings

Rondout Creek (Kingston) Light

Kingston, Ulster County

This light has been operational since 1915. It was automated in 1954, and its original sixth-order Fresnel lens has now been replaced with a 250 mm optic. The square brick tower stands at 48 feet, with a height of focal plane of 52 feet above sea level. It is painted yellow and topped with a black lantern. The keeper's house, which is attached to the tower, is a 2.5-story brick dwelling dating from 1915. A previous wooden tower, dating from 1837, and a stone tower and combination stone tower and keeper's house, dating from 1867, were both torn down, the latter in the 1950s. This lighthouse is owned by the City of Kingston. It is open to the public.

Sands Point Light (Old)

Port Washington, Nassau County

This historic 1809 lighthouse was replaced by a minor offshore light in 1922 (and then a modern steel skeletal tower in 1968), and it currently serves as a private residence. The 46-foot, octagonal brownstone tower is now topped with a faux lantern. The tower originally held 11 lamps, with 9-inch reflectors, which were replaced by a fourth-order Fresnel in 1856. The keeper's house is a 2.5-story colonial brick building, dating from 1868. This light is not open to the public.

Saugerties Light

Saugerties, Ulster County

Following 36 years of deactivation, this 1869 lighthouse was finally relit in 1990. (A modern tower, that had replaced the historic lighthouse, was removed in 1985.) The square brick tower stands at 46 feet and is topped with a black lantern. It originally held a sixth-order Fresnel lens (it now has a solar-powered optic), and it has a height of

Above: **Sands Point Light**

focal plane of 42 feet above sea level. The keeper's house, a 2.5-story Italianate brick building, was constructed in 1869. This lighthouse currently functions as a museum and a bed and breakfast.

Selkirk (Salmon River) Light

Pulaski, Oswego County

This lighthouse contains one of the few remaining old-style lanterns. First lit in 1838, it was deactivated in 1859. The site operated as a life-saving station from 1877 until the 1890s, and the tower was relit in 1999. Today, it functions as a private aid to navigation as well as a privately owned guest house (open to the public). The octagonal wooden tower rises at 32 feet above the 2.5-story fieldstone keeper's house. The tower is painted red, and the lantern is silver. It originally held eight lamps, with 14-inch reflectors. In 1989, it was installed with a 190 mm optic. It has a height of focal plane of 49 feet above sea level.

Shoal Point Light

Fourth Lake, Eagle Bay

This 1890s Adirondacks lighthouse was built to mark a hazard in the Fourth Lake. The octagonal tower holds a frame lantern at 30 feet above sea level. After years of neglect and abandon, the tower was fully restored in 2000–2001 (with the help of private donations and a state historical preservation grant of more than $19,000). Managed by the Fourth Lake Property Owners Association, the site is open to the public, but the tower is closed.

Sisters Island Light

Southwest of Chippewa Bay, St. Lawrence County

The Three Sisters Island Light was operational from 1870 until the 1950s. Standing at 60 feet, the square tower is constructed of dressed limestone brick (on a limestone block foundation). It is unpainted, except for its white trim. The keeper's quarters are integral to the tower. The only other structure on site is a shed. This lighthouse is now privately owned, and it is not open to the public.

Sodus Outer (Sodus Bay West Pier) Light

Sodus Bay entrance, Sodus Point

A 49-foot cast-iron tower mounted on a concrete and stone pier, the Sodus Outer Light was constructed in 1901 and is still active today (focal plane 51 feet). The tower is painted white, and its lantern has a red roof. Looking across the waters of Lake

Ontario, this lighthouse can be viewed from the grounds of the old Sodus Point Light, which was deactivated in 1901 and served as the keeper's quarters for the Sodus Outer Light. The site is open to the public, though the tower is closed.

Sodus Point Light

Sodus Point, Wayne County

Operational from 1871 until 1901, this lighthouse's dwelling was used as Coast Guard housing until 1984, and it now serves as a maritime museum. It consists of a 45-foot square limestone tower topped with a black lantern. It had a height of focal plane of 70 feet above sea level, and it originally held a sixth-order lens. In 1985, the tower was refitted with a third-and-a-half order optic. The keeper's house is a 2.5-story limestone dwelling. A modern cast-iron tower was constructed nearby in 1939.

South Buffalo North Side Light

Dunkirk, Chautauqua County
(relocated from the Buffalo Harbor's entrance)

Standing at 29 feet, the South Buffalo North Side Light was one of two "bottle-shaped" lighthouses established on the Buffalo Harbor, on Lake Erie, in 1903. It has since been moved to the grounds of the Dunkirk Historical Lighthouse and Veterans Park Museum, where it is open to the public.

Split Rock Point Light (Old)

Essex, Essex County (Lake Champlain)

Located on Whallon Bay, the old Split Rock Point Light was constructed in 1867 and was deactivated from 1928 until 2003 (during which time, it was replaced by a red steel skeletal tower). The octagonal limestone tower stands at 39 feet, and it is trimmed in red and white. The tower originally held a fourth-order Fresnel lens, and it had a height of focal plane of 100 feet above sea level. The 1.5-story wood and flagstone keeper's house was constructed in 1899 in the Greek Revival style. This historic tower is now privately owned (it serves as a summer home), and it is not open to the public.

Staten Island (Range Rear) Light

Richmondtown, Richmond County

This lighthouse is rear range to the West Bank Light. It was constructed in 1912 on Staten Island's Richmond Hill. The octagonal yellow-brick tower stands at 90 feet (with a height of focal

Above: **The Statue of Liberty**

plane of 231 feet above sea level) and retains its original second-order optic. It sits upon a foundation of gray limestone. The U.S. Coast Guard owns athis lighthouse, and the brick keeper's house is privately owned. This light station is not open to the public.

Statue of Liberty Light

Bedloe Island, New York Harbor

Also known as "Liberty Enlightening the World," this national monument functioned as a real working lighthouse from 1886 until 1902. A keeper operated and maintained the electric light, which could be seen for 24 miles at sea. The flame of her torch had glass inserts at its sides that helped it to shine more brightly. The power to generate the light came from an electric plant located on the island.

Stepping Stones Light

Kings Point, Nassau County

This operational lighthouse was first lit in 1877 and it was automated in 1967. It consists of a square brick tower, with granite trim and a black and white lantern, and it stands at 38 feet (with a height of focal plane of 46 feet above sea level) upon a granite and concrete pier. Its original fifth-order Fresnel lens has now been replaced with a 300 mm optic. The U.S. Coast Guard owns and manages this light station, which is not open to the public.

Stony Point (Henderson) Light (Old)

Henderson, Jefferson County

This historic lighthouse was operational from 1869 until 1945 (when it was replaced by a modern, skeletal steel tower). It consists of a square brick tower that is painted white, with a black lantern. The tower stands at 73 feet, and it originally held a fourth-order Fresnel lens. The keeper's house is a 1.5-story modified brick building constructed in 1869. Other structures include the foundation of an earlier (1830) tower. Privately owned, it is not open to the public.

Stony Point Light

Stony Point, Rockland County

Established in 1826 on the Hudson River, this light was inactive from 1925 (when a modern, pyramidal skeletal tower was constructed) until 1995, when it was relit as an exhibit. The historic octagonal fieldstone tower stands at 30 feet and is painted white and topped with a black lantern. It originally held eight patent lamps, with 12-inch reflectors. Today, the tower is equipped with a solar-powered, fourth-order Fresnel (on loan from the U.S. Coast Guard and the Hudson River Maritime Museum). It has a height of focal plane of 22 feet above sea level. The 1.5-story keeper's dwelling is a stone house (in the cape style), constructed in 1935. This light station is now a state historic site (open to the public).

Sunken Rock Light
Alexandria Bay, Jefferson County

Located on Bush Island, on the St. Lawrence River, this operational 1884 lighthouse was converted to solar power in 1988. The conical tower is now covered with white boards, and it is topped with a green lantern. It retains its original, sixth-order Fresnel lens. The light is now privately owned, and it is not open to the public.

Sylvan Beach Light
See Verona Beach Light, opposite page

Tarrytown Harbor (Kingsland Point) Light
See page 221

Thirty Mile Point Light (Old)
Barker, Niagara County

This lighthouse was constructed on Lake Ontario in 1876. It was inactive from 1959 until 1998, and today functions as a state park and a private aid to navigation. The square tower is made of limestone and it stands at 61 feet (with a height of focal plane of 71 feet above sea level). The white, black, and red lantern originally held a third-order Fresnel lens. The yellow-brick sound signal building was constructed in 1935, and the two-story limestone keeper's house dates from 1875. This light station is open to the public.

Throgs Neck Light
Bronx, New York

Marking the entrance to the East River, the current Throgs Neck Lighthouse—an automated skeleton tower, dating from 1934—is the fifth light tower built on this site. The original wooden lighthouse, constructed in 1827, was torn down because of construction at nearby Fort Schuyler. A temporary structure remained in

Above: **Thirty Mile Point Light**

service until 1890, when a new iron skeletal tower was built. This tower was replaced, in 1906, by a 35-foot redbrick tower, which remained active until the present structure was built. The site is now part of the SUNY Maritime College campus (which hosts a Maritime Industry Museum, with a lighthouse exhibit), and a faculty member now occupies the remaining keeper's house. Interestingly, the first keepers of the Throgs Neck Light are said to have operated a popular bar out of the keeper's house (unbeknownst to the U.S. Lighthouse Service), serving local anglers and hunters.

Tibbetts Point Light
Cape Vincent, Jefferson County

This 1854 lighthouse now has a youth hostel in the keeper's house. It was automated in 1981 and it still functions as an active aid to navigation as well as a museum. The conical brick and stucco tower stands at 58 feet and is painted white, with a black lantern. It retains its original fourth-order Fresnel lens, and it has a height of focal plane of 69 feet above sea level. The brick sound signal building dates from 1895, and the 2.5-story wooden keeper's house dates from 1880. Other structures on site include a duplex keeper's house (from 1907), a radiobeacon, an iron oil house, a garage, and a visitor center and museum (from 1994).

Titanic Memorial Light
South Street Seaport, Manhattan, New York

This 1913 light tower is a memorial to those who perished when the steamship Titanic sank in 1912. The structure has been relocated to the entrance to the South Street Seaport in lower Manhattan, from its original location above the East River on the roof of the old Seamen's Church Institute at the corner of South Street and Coenties Slip. From 1913 until 1967, the time ball at the top of the tower would drop each day to signal twelve noon to ships in the harbor.

Verona Beach (Sylvan Beach) Light
Erie Canal, at the eastern end of Oneida Lake, Verona Beach

Dating from 1917, the Verona Beach Light consists of an unpainted concrete tower, standing at 85 feet, with no lantern. The light is still active (though it is closed to the public), and the Verona Beach Lighthouse Association is working to restore it.

West Bank (Range Front) Light

Staten Island, Richmond County

Dating from 1901, the West Bank Light was automated in 1985 and it is still operational today. The conical ("spark plug" style) cast-iron tower is painted brown, on a black base, and it stands at 55 feet above sea level. It still has its original fourth-order Fresnel optic, and it has a height of focal plane of 59 feet above sea level. The keeper's quarters are integral to the tower. This lighthouse is owned and managed by the U.S. Coast Guard, and it is not open to the public.

Whitestone Point Light

Two miles west of Willets Point, Whitestone

This is a black, pyramidal skeleton tower, constructed circa 1908, with a continuous green light and a height of focal plane of 56 feet above sea level. The tower has a fog bell that strikes every 15 seconds. It replaced an ornate Victorian square pyramidal frame tower that was constructed in 1889.

New York City is now home to three lightships: *Ambrose* (South Street Seaport Museum, *see* pages 246–247); *Frying Pan* (Pier 63); and *Nantucket* (National Lighthouse Museum, Staten Island).

Pennsylvania

Erie North Pierhead Light

Erie Harbor, Presque Isle

Also known as Presque Isle North Pier Light, this 34-foot, tapering, black and white-banded beacon was constructed in 1858 to replace an earlier (1828) wooden tower that was toppled by a schooner in a gale in 1857. It is made of wrought iron, and encased in steel plates. The tower was moved 190 feet in 1882, and 509 feet in 1940 (when it was automated). In 1995, the original fourth-order Fresnel was removed from the black lantern and a solar-powered lens was installed in its place. The original keeper's quarters are located within a nearby lifesaving station.

Erie Land (Old Presque Isle) Light

Erie, Erie County

This lighthouse was operational from 1867 until 1899. It consists of a 49-foot conical tower of unpainted sandstone (with a brick lining). It originally held a third-order Fresnel lens, and it had a

height of focal plane of 128 feet above sea level. The Fresnel was sent to Marblehead, Ohio, in 1902. The tower is attached to a workroom and an oil room. The two-story wood-frame and brick keeper's house was constructed in 1867, in the salt box style, and was renovated in 1979. This site currently serves as a city park.

Erie Yacht Club Breakwater Light

Lake Erie, Erie

This is a 36-foot, cylindrical steel tower, painted white, with a black lantern. It is active April through October, as a private aid to navigation. The site is open to the public, though the tower is closed. The beacon is located at the entrance to the Erie Yacht Club basin.

Presque Isle Light

Erie, Erie County

First lit in 1873, this square brick tower stands at 68 feet and has a height of focal plane of 73 feet above sea level. It is painted white, and it sits upon a limestone foundation. The tower originally held a fourth-order Fresnel lens. Today, it uses a 300 mm optic. Attached to the tower is the keeper's house, a 1.5-story redbrick structure (in the gable style) built in 1872. Other structures include an oil house, a storage building, and a jetty. Now part of a state park, this lighthouse continues to serve as an active aid to navigation. The keeper's house now functions as a residence for park staff. The site is open to the public. Presque Isle is actually a sandspit peninsula. The first keeper here described it as the loneliest place on earth until a road was built in 1927 to connect it to the mainland.

Schuylkill River Range Lights

League Island, Philadelphia, Philadelphia County

Steel skeleton towers now hold the active lights on this site, which was originally established in 1875. A wood-framed keeper's dwelling is also on site, but it was badly damaged by fire in 1923.

Turtle Rock Light

Below the Girard Avenue Bridge, Philadelphia

Originally privately built by Frank Thurwanger to guide steamboat traffic, at a cost of $2,663, this 1887 light tower is generally inactive, though its beacon is displayed on special occasions. It consists of a cylindrical brick tower with a hexagonal lantern, mounted atop a one-story wing of a two-story brick clubhouse. The tower was restored in 1990. The Sedgeley Club may be rented for private functions, though the tower is closed.

THE SOUTH

Alabama

Mobile Middle Bay Light
Mobile, Mobile County

This hexagonal-shaped lighthouse was first lit in 1885, was automated in 1935 and remained in use until 1967. Built as a replica of the Hooper Straight Lighthouse in Talbot County, MD, the Mobile Middle Bay lighthouse stands at 54 feet (1.5 stories) and is constructed of wood. It was damaged by a hurricane in 1916 and was partially restored in 1984. In 1993, the lighthouse underwent stabilization, and the original lantern room was obtained and is currently undergoing renovation and restoration. Its focal plane is 54 feet above sea level, and it has a 155 mm optic (with a hazard warning). This lighthouse is white with red pilings. It is owned and managed by the Alabama Historical Commission and the Mobile Middle Bay Lighthouse Centennial Committee.

Mobile Point (Range Rear) Light
Fort Morgan State Park, Baldwin County

First lit in 1873, this skeleton lighthouse was originally located at the entrance to Mobile Bay. It was dismantled in 1979 and was later righted and restored at Fort Morgan State Park, where it is currently open to the public. A modern tower now stands in its place, at Mobile Bay, along with the original keeper's quarters (a two-story wooden bungalow) and a small brick building (possibly an oil house). Owned by the Alabama Historical Commission, the Mobile Point Light stands at 30 feet and is constructed of black iron pilings on a concrete foundation. Its fourth-order Fresnel optic was removed to Fort Morgan Museum when the light was deactivated in 1966. The lighthouse was taken into storage in 2004 and it is under restoration.

Sand Island Light
Gulf Shores, Baldwin County

Located off of Mobile Point near Gulf Shores, this 1873 brownstone lighthouse was automated in 1921 and remained in use until 1933. The 131-foot, conical, unpainted Gothic tower has a black lantern. It contained a second-order Fresnel lens (with a focal plane at a height of 132 feet), which is currently housed in the Fort Morgan Museum. The original keeper's quarters have been destroyed. Having withstood two hurricanes, this lighthouse is now seriously threatened by erosion, and studies are underway to assess its possible relocation.

Florida

Alligator Reef Light
Islamorada, Dade County

Countless vessels have sunk here, on the jagged coral reef. First lit in 1873, the Alligator Reef Light was automated in 1963 and it is still in use today. It is a 136-foot skeletal iron tower, painted white with a black lantern. The tower has a height of focal plane of 136 feet above sea level. It originally held a first-order Fresnel lens, and it is now equipped with a VRB-25 solar-powered optic. The keeper's quarters are integral to the tower. This light is owned and managed by the U.S. Coast Guard. It is not open to the public.

Amelia Island Light
See page 178

American Shoal Light
Summerland Key, Monroe County

This skeletal screwpile lighthouse has been operational since 1880. Standing at 109 feet (the same as its height of focal plane), it is constructed of iron, is octagonal and pyramidal in shape, and is painted brown, with a white center stairwell. The tower originally held a first-order drum Fresnel. It was automated in 1963 and, since then, has used a Vega VRB-25 solar-powered lens. The two-story keeper's house is an octagonal Victorian structure of wood and cast iron. This light is owned and managed by the U.S. Coast Guard, and it is not open to the public.

Anclote Key Light
Anclote, Pinellas County

First lit in 1887 and automated in 1952, this 102-foot, cast-iron skeletal light dominates the mouth of the Anclote River. Following an intensive restoration program, A TFB-220 optic was installed in the black lantern room, atop the brown central cylinder, and lit in September 2003. Now a private aid to navigation, its flashing white signal (focal plane 110 feet) can be seen for 19 miles. Other structures include the ruins of a brick oil house, the brick foundation of the keepers' dwellings, a concrete foundation for the cisterns, and a new park ranger's residence. This site is now part of a state park and wildlife refuge.

Boca Chita Light
Boca Chita Key, Miami-Dade County County

This 65-foot, conical limestone tower was permanently extinguished only hours after it was first lit as a private navigational aid in 1937, as it was deemed to constitute a hazard to navigation. Now it serves as an attraction in national park and is occasionally open for tours.

Cape Canaveral Light

Cocoa Beach, Brevard County

First lit in 1868, this light was automated in 1960 and is still in use today. It consists of a 145-foot, conical cast-iron plate tower (with a brick lining). It is painted with black and white bands, and is topped with a black lantern that originally held a first-order Fresnel lens (which is now on display at the Ponce de Leon Lighthouse). Today, it holds a DCB-224 optic, and the tower has a height of focal plane of 137 feet above sea level. The keeper's house and the oil house are now in ruins. The only other structure on site is a concrete block storage building. This site is owned by the U.S. Air Force, and it is not open to the public.

Cape Florida Light

Key Biscayne, Dade County

This 1846 lighthouse replaced an earlier tower, built in 1825, that was attacked and burned by Seminole Indians in 1836. (The keeper was badly wounded in this attack, and his companion was killed.) The second lighthouse is a conical, whitewashed redbrick tower, with a black top and steel stairs. It originally used a system of 17 Argand lamps with 21-inch reflectors. In 1855, the tower was equipped with a second-order Fresnel lens, and it was raised to its current height of 95 feet. The lighting apparatus was destroyed during the Civil War, in 1861, and it was not restored until 1867. In 1878, the light was deactivated and sold into private ownership. The lantern was relit in the 1960s or '70s, and then deactivated again in 1990. It was finally restored and relit in 1996 and, today, functions as a private aid to navigation, using a 300 mm optic. It has a height of focal plane of 100 feet above sea level. Now owned by the Florida Department of Natural Resources, this lighthouse is open to the public. The site contains replicas of some of the original outbuildings.

Cape San Blas Light

Apalachicola, Gulf County

The fourth tower to be built on this light station, this light was operational from 1885 until 1996. (The first three towers were destroyed by storms and high waves.) It consists of a cast-iron skeleton tower (with a central cylinder), standing at 90 feet and painted white, with a black lantern. The light originally held a third-order Fresnel lens, and it had a height of focal plane of 101 feet above sea level. In 1906, the lens was changed to a third-order bivalve. In 1918–19,

Above: **The skeletal Cape San Blas Light**

the tower was moved one-quarter mile north, to protect it from the encroaching sea. A two-story keeper's dwelling was constructed in 1919. Other structures include a radiobeacon (constructed in 1939), and a second keeper's dwelling. The light station is now owned by the U.S. Air Force. It is open to the public.

Cape St. George Light

Apalachicola, Franklin County

Located on Little St. George Island, on the Gulf of Mexico, this lighthouse was operational from 1852 until 1994. Due to beach erosion and hurricane damage it was nicknamed the "Leaning Tower of Florida," and was on the Lighthouse Digest Doomsday List of endangered lighthouses. In 2005, it was found in ruins after toppling into the sea. The conical, white brick tower once stood at 70 feet and was topped with a black lantern that was originally equipped with a third-order Fresnel lens. It had a height of focal plane of 72 feet above sea level. The keeper's house was gutted by fire in 1961, and the sound signal building is also in ruins. This lighthouse was owned by the U.S. Coast Guard, on lease to the Cape St. George Lighthouse Society.

Carysfort Reef Light

Key Largo, Monroe County

First lit in 1852, this light was automated in 1960 and it is still operational today. The red skeletal octagonal pyramidal tower, constructed of iron, stands at 120 feet. It is the first of the giant screwpile lighthouses on the Florida Keys. The tower originally used a revolving first-order Fresnel lens, and now uses a Vega VRB-25 optic. It has a height of focal plane of 100 feet above sea level. (The Fresnel is now on display at the Museum of South Florida History in Miami.) The keeper's quarters are integral to the tower. This lighthouse is now part of a marine sanctuary. It is not open to the public.

Cedar Keys (Seahorse Key) Light

Cedar Key, Levy County

Operational from 1854 until 1915, this hexagonal, white brick tower (with wood additions, put in after its decommissioning) rises at 23 feet above the one-story brick keeper's dwelling. The tower originally held a fourth-order Fresnel lens with a focal plane of 75 feet above sea level. Other structures include an oil house and a cistern. Owned by the U.S. Fish & Wildlife Service, this lighthouse now serves as a marine laboratory. It is not open to the public. In 1922, a modern skeletal tower was constructed nearby.

Cosgrove Shoal Light

South of the Marquesas Keys, Key West

This is a 54-foot, hexagonal pyramidal skeletal tower, with no lantern (though it may have originally had one). Constructed in 1935, the light is still in use, giving out a white flash every six seconds.

Crooked River (Carrabelle) Light

Carrabelle, Franklin County

Built to replace the Dog Island Light, in order to guide ships in the lumber trade, the Crooked River Light was operational from 1895 until 1995. The 100-foot square skeletal tower (with an internal cylinder) is constructed of iron. The lower part of the tower is painted white, the upper part is red, and it is topped with a black lantern. The lantern was originally fitted with a third-order Fresnel lens, and it had a height of focal plane of 115 feet above sea level. The light was automated in 1965. This tower is owned and managed by the City of Carrabelle and the Carrabelle Lighthouse Association, while the grounds are privately owned. This site is occasionally open to the public. The keeper's quarters has been relocated two miles west.

Dry Tortugas (Loggerhead Key) Light

See page 48

Egmont Key Light

St. Petersburg, Hillsborough County

First lit in 1858, this light was automated in 1989 and it is still in use today. The conical, white brick tower stands at 87 feet. The lantern, which was removed in the early 1960s to accommodate an aerobeacon, was originally fitted with a third-order Fresnel lens. It now uses a DCB-224, and it has a height of focal plane of 85 feet above sea level. The one-story keeper's house is built in the Florida Ranch style. This light station is now part of a wildlife preserve. The lighthouse is owned and managed by the U.S. Coast Guard and the Florida Department of Natural Resources. It is open to the public.

Fowey Rocks Light

See page 173

Gasparilla Island (Boca Grande) Lights

Boca Grande, Lee County

Both of these lights originally served as rear ranges for different light stations. The first historic tower on this site, dating from 1890, was automated in 1950, deactivated in 1966, and was finally relit in 1986. The octagonal ash wood tower rises at 44 feet atop the square keeper's dwelling, which is set on iron pilings. The light originally used a third-and-a-half-order Fresnel lens. Since 1986, it has used a 375 mm optic. It has a height of focal plane of 41 feet above sea level. The second tower was originally built in 1881, and it served as the Delaware Breakwater Rear Range Light until 1918. It was disassembled and moved in 1921, and was re-erected in Florida in 1927. It was first lit as a Gasparilla Island Light in 1932, and it is still operational today. It is a skeletal tower with a central column. It originally used a fourth-order Fresnel lens, and it has a height of focal plane of 105 feet above sea level. These lights are owned and managed by the Florida Park Service and by Barrier Island Park Society.

Hillsboro Inlet Light

See page 147

Jupiter Inlet Light

Jupiter, Palm Beach County

The Jupiter Inlet Light dates from 1860. It consists of a 105-foot, conical redbrick tower with a black base and a black lantern. The light retains its original first-order revolving Fresnel, and it has a height of focal plane of 146 feet above sea level. The keeper's house burned down in 1927. The site also features an oil house and a cemetery. This light is owned and managed by the U.S. Coast Guard and the Florida History Center & Museum and underwent a major restoration in 1999–2000, during which artifacts from a prehistoric burial mound were discovered at the site. Recently repaired after hurricane damage, it is open to the public, and the oil house now contains a museum.

Above: **Pensacola Light**

Key Largo Light

Key Largo, Monroe County

This 1959 structure is purely decorative. A square-pyramidal tower painted in a distinctive checkerboard pattern, its cast-iron lantern was salvaged from the original Rebecca Shoal Light in 1953, when that lighthouse was demolished. It is closed to the public.

Key West Light

Key West, Monroe County

Operational from 1848 until 1969, this is a conical brick tower. In 1894, the tower was raised up 20 feet, to its current height of 86 feet. It is painted white and topped with a black lantern. It originally used a system of 13 Argand lamps with 21-inch reflectors. In 1858, it was refitted with a third-order lens. The light was automated in 1915, and it is now equipped with a 175-watt, Hi-Tek M57 optic. Its height of focal plane is 91 feet above sea level. The 1887 keeper's house is a one-story wooden structure in the West Indian vernacular style. Other structures include a replica of the original oil house, two garages, a storage building, and an outhouse (from circa 1887). Owned and managed by Monroe County and the Key West Art and Historical Society, this lighthouse was restored in 1988 and now serves as a museum.

Molasses Reef Light

John Pennecamp Coral Reef State Park, Key Largo

A square pyramidal skeletal steel tower on a screwpile foundation, this tower was constructed in 1921 and is still in use today. It has a height of focal plane of 45 feet above sea level, and it gives out a red flash every 10 seconds. The lantern has now been replaced by a daymarker and a small navigation beacon, and the tower now has an automatic National Weather Service station.

Mount Dora Lighthouse

Mount Dora, Lake County

Also known as Lake Dora Light, this 35-foot, conical, brick and stucco lighthouse was built in 1988 as a private navigational aid. *See pages 202–203.*

Pacific Reef Light

*Biscayne National Park
(three miles southeast of Elliot Key)*

This is a 44-foot square pyramidal skeletal tower on a screwpile foundation. It was constructed in 1921 and is still in use, giving out a white flash every four seconds, at a height of focal plane of 44 feet above sea level. The site is open to the public. In 2000, the lantern room was relocated to Islamorada, where it is displayed on a square stone pedestal.

Pensacola Light

Pensacola, Escambia County

Situated at the entrance to Pensacola Bay, the Pensacola Light was first lit in 1859 and it suffered some damage in the Civil War. It consists of a 150-foot conical brick tower, painted black on top and white on bottom. The light was automated in 1965. It still uses its original first-order revolving lens, and it has a height of focal plane of 191 feet above sea level. The keeper's house, constructed in 1868, is a two-story brick duplex, in the federal/Italian eclectic style. Other structures include a workhouse (attached to the tower), a storage building, an oil house (with an attached shed), a three-bay garage, and a pump house. The U.S. Coast Guard owns the optic, and the Navy owns the buildings. This light station is open to the public.

Ponce de Leon (Mosquito) Inlet Light

See page 147

Pulaski Shoal Light

Key West, Gulf of Mexico

This 56-foot hexagonal pyramidal skeletal steel tower originally held an enclosed lantern. The light is managed by the U.S. Coast Guard, and it gives out a white flash every six seconds. It is located in the Gulf, west of Smith Shoal and about 30 miles northwest of Key West.

Sand Key Light
Key West, Monroe County

This 1853 lighthouse was automated in 1938. It was deactivated in 1989 and then relit in 1998. A 120-foot iron skeletal tower (with a central cylinder), it was the second screwpile lighthouse constructed on the Florida Keys. It is painted red, with black trim. The light originally used a first-order Fresnel lens. It now has a Vega VRB-25 solar-powered optic, and it has a height of focal plane of 109 feet above sea level. The lighthouse was severely damaged by a fire in 1989, and the keeper's house was demolished in 1996. This light station was previously served by an 1826 brick tower, which was destroyed in a hurricane, and then by a lightship (until 1853). It is now owned and managed by the U.S. Coast Guard, and it is not open to the public.

Sanibel Island Light
Sanibel, Lee County

First lit in 1884, the Sanibel Island Light was automated in 1949 and is still in use today. The brown, pyramidal skeletal tower (with a central column) is constructed of iron and stands at 102 feet. It was originally equipped with a third-order Fresnel lens. Since 1965, it has used a 300 mm optic. Its height of focal plane is 98 feet above sea level. The keeper's house is a one-story West Indian vernacular structure, set on iron piles. Other structures include a cistern, an oil house, and a second keeper's house. This light station is owned by the U.S. Coast Guard, on lease to the City of Sanibel. It is open to the public.

Smith Shoal Light
Key West, Gulf of Mexico

This is a modern (1933) hexagonal pyramidal skeletal tower, constructed of steel. Located 11 miles northwest of Key West, the tower is still in use as an active aid to navigation.

Sombrero Key Light
Marathon, Monroe County

The third screwpile lighthouse constructed on the Florida Keys, the Sombrero Key Light has been operational since 1858. The brown, skeletal octagonal pyramidal tower stands at 160 feet and is set on iron piles. It is constructed of cast iron and has a height of focal plane of 142 feet above sea level. The tower was automated in 1960. It originally held a first-order Fresnel lens and, since 1997, has used a VRB-25 solar-powered optic. The first-order lens is now on display at the Key West Lighthouse Museum. The keeper's quarters are integral to the tower. Owned and managed by the U.S. Coast Guard, this lighthouse is not open to the public.

Above: A 1902 view of St. Augustine Light

St. Augustine Light
St. Augustine, St. Johns County

Operational since 1874, the St. Augustine Light is located on Anastasia Island. The conical brick tower stands at 165 feet and is attached to a storage building. It is painted with black and white spiraling bands, and it is topped with a red lantern. It retains its original first-order Fresnel lens, and it has a height of focal plane of 161 feet above sea level. The light was automated in 1955, and the last keeper retired. The restored keeper's house is a two-story wood and brick Victorian duplex that now contains a museum, a theater, and a bookstore. Other structures include a wooden garage (from 1936) and a wooden Coast Guard Barracks (from 1941). Tours of the 219-stair lighthouse and grounds are available.

St. Johns Light
Mayport, Duval County

This light was erected in 1954, some 2 miles southeast of the decommissioned St. Johns River Light (*see* below). Built of concrete blocks, this 64-foot, octagonal light tower has an Art Deco concrete keeper's dwelling attached to it. Its Crouse-Hinds FB-61 optic emits four white flashes every 20 seconds at a focal-plane height of 83 feet above sea level. Part of the U.S. Naval Air Station Jacksonville, this lighthouse and the St. Johns River Light are not open to the public.

St. Johns River (Mayport) Light
Mayport, Duval County

Located at the entrance to the St. Johns River, this light was operational from 1859 until 1929. In 1887, the conical brick tower was raised 15 feet, to its current height of 81 feet. It is painted red, with a white lantern that originally held a third-order Fresnel lens. The light was automated in 1967. It had a height of focal plane of 77 feet above sea level. The keeper's house was dismantled, and there are no other structures on site.

St. Joseph Point Range Rear (Beacon Hill) Light

Mexico Beach, Gulf County (Relocated from St. Joseph Bay)

First lit in 1902, this lighthouse was moved to Simmons Bayou in 1979, and it now functions as a private residence. It consists of a square wooden tower that rises 41 feet atop a two-story, square wooden keeper's house. It is painted white, with a red roof and no lantern. The tower originally held a third-order lens, and it had a height of focal plane of 63 feet above sea level. This lighthouse is not open to the public. It was replaced by a skeletal tower in 1960.

St. Marks (Range Rear) Light

St. Marks, Wakulla County

This light station was first established in 1831. The current 73-foot, conical brick tower was first lit in 1842. It is painted white, with a black lantern, and it has a height of focal plane of 82 feet above sea level. The light was automated in 1960, and it was modified in 1967 to accommodate a new lantern. The tower originally held a fourth-order Fresnel lens, and today it holds a fifth-order Fresnel. The keeper's house is a one-story brick duplex, built in 1843. Ownership of the station was transferred from the Coast Guard to the U.S. Fish and Wildlife Service in 2006. The St. Marks Refuge Association is working to restore this light station, the grounds of which are open to the public.

Tennessee Reef Light

Islamorada (east of the middle Florida Keys, off Long Key)

Constructed in 1933, this octagonal pyramidal skeletal tower (with an enclosed lantern) is typical of a number of lighthouses constructed during the 1920s and '30s in the Florida Keys.

Tierra Verde Light

Cunningham Key, Tampa Bay

This 70-foot lighthouse was built in 2005 to resemble the two-story dwelling and lantern of the Boca Grande Light on Gasparilla Island. It serves as an active aid to navigation, as well as a marine center and educational facility that are open to the public.

Tortugas Harbor (Fort Jefferson) Light

Key West, Monroe County

This historic tower was constructed in 1876. It was automated in 1912, deactivated in 1921, and is operational today as a private aid to navigation. The hexagonal black iron tower stands at 82 feet, with a height of focal plane of 86 feet above sea level. From 1858, it held a fourth-order Fresnel lens. Today, the light is illuminated with 375-watt incandescent bulbs. Of the original keeper's house, only the foundation remains. This lighthouse is now part of the Fort Jefferson, Dry Tortugas National Park. It is open to the public.

Twenty-eight Foot Shoal Light

Key West, Gulf of Mexico
(west of Sand Key and south of the Tortugas)

This hexagonal pyramidal skeletal tower, constructed of steel, stands at 53 feet. It is operated by the U.S. Coast Guard.

Georgia

Cockspur Island Light

Tybee Island, Chatham County

Located on the Savannah River, north of Tybee Island, the Cockspur Island Light was operational from 1857 until 1909. During the Civil War, in April 1862, this lighthouse was caught in the line of fire between Union Forces, on Tybee Island, and Confederate forces, in Fort Pulaski. But, though more than 5,000 rounds of artillery were exchanged over the course of the 30-hour battle, the lighthouse was unscathed. The conical, white brick tower stands at 46 feet. It originally held a fourth-order optic. This light is now part of a national park, and it is open daily. Access is by boat, but the National Park Service does not provide boat access.

Above: **Cockspur Island Light, Georgia**

Little Cumberland Island Light

Brunswick, Camden County

Operational from 1838 until 1915, this conical brick lighthouse is painted white and topped with a black lantern. It stands at 60 feet tall. The lantern was originally lit using a system of 14 lamps, and it had a height of focal plane of 71 feet above sea level. Both the sound signal building and the keeper's house were demolished in 1968, and there are no other structures remaining on the site. This lighthouse was renovated in the 1990s. It is now privately owned, and it is not open to the public.

Sapelo Island Light
Darien, McIntosh County

First lit in 1820, the Sapelo Island Light was deactivated from 1899. After undergoing restoration in the 1990s, it was relit in 1998. The conical brick tower stands at 70 feet (with a height of focal plane of 79 feet above sea level), and it is painted with six red and white bands. It was originally equipped with a fourth-order Fresnel lens. The keeper's house was dismantled in 1902. Other structures include brick/mortar cisterns, and the remains of a brick oil house (dating from 1890). Owned by the Georgia Department of Natural Resources, this site currently serves as an estuarine sanctuary. It is open to the public. Nearby is the inactive Sapelo Island Range Front Light, a 25-foot, white iron skeletal tower (with a black lantern) that dates from 1877. The rear range beacon no longer exists.

Savannah Harbor Range Rear Light
Emmet Park, Savannah

Also known as the Old Harbor Light and the Beacon Range Light, this 1858 beacon is no longer active as an aid to navigation, and it now displays a decorative gas light. The structure—which is not really a lighthouse at all—consists of an ornate, 25-foot cast-iron tower. It is painted green, and it looks much like a large streetlight. It is located in Savannah's Emmet Park, off of East Bay Street.

St. Simons Island Light
Brunswick, Glynn County

This 1872 lighthouse was automated in 1954 and it is still operational today. It consists of a 104-foot cylindrical, white brick and iron tower. It retains its original third-order Fresnel lens, and it has a height of focal plane of 106 feet above sea level. The keeper's house is a two-story, brick, Victorian dwelling that is open to the public as a museum. This light is the only known light station in which a fatal shooting took place between lighthouse staff. On February 29, 1880, the assistant keeper argued with the head keeper, Fred Osborne. Osborne pulled a pistol and the assistant reached for his shotgun. At a range of almost 98 feet, the assistant fired his shotgun, loaded with buckshot, and hit Osborne in four places. Osborne later died. The assistant turned himself in to authorities after summoning medical assistance. He was acquitted of any wrongdoing. This lighthouse is open to the public. A previous structure on this site, a 75-foot, octagonal, brick-and-coquina, tabby-covered tower, constructed in 1810, was blown up by Confederate forces in 1861.

Tybee Island Light
Tybee Island, Chatham County

The first two towers built on this site, in 1736 and 1742, were both lost to erosion. A third tower, dating from 1773, was gutted by fire during the Civil War, in 1862. The "new" lighthouse, built in 1867 on the foundation of the previous one, consists of an octagonal brick tower attached to a workroom. It stands at 145 feet, and it is painted black with a white band. This lighthouse was automated in 1972 and it is still operational today. It was originally equipped with a system of oil lamps. Since 1867, the tower has held first-order Fresnel lens. It has a height of focal plane of 144 feet above sea level. An earthquake in 1886 extended some preexisting cracks in the tower. Also on site is the 1881 keeper's house, a two-story wooden ("stick" style) dwelling. Other structures include a first assistant keeper's house, a cistern, a brick fuel storage building, a brick summer kitchen, a garage, and a second assistant keeper's house (converted from a former Confederate barracks). This light station is owned and operated by the Tybee Island Historical Society. It is open to the public.

Louisiana

Barataria Bay Light
Barataria Bay, Gulf of Mexico

This is a wooden, square pyramidal skeletal tower, built in 1897, with a height of focal plane of 77 feet above sea level. It was automated circa 1945, and it now uses a 200 mm optic in place of its original fourth-order Fresnel lens. This light replaced an 1857 octagonal brick tower that was destroyed by a hurricane in 1893.

Chandeleur Island Light
New Orleans, St. Bernard County

The 100-foot, red-brown, iron skeleton lighthouse that stood at this site was the third to have been erected on Chandeleur Island. Built on pile foundations in 1896, it was originally installed with a third-order Fresnel lens (now on display at the Louisiana War Museum in Baton Rouge). An automated 300 mm optic (focal plane 99 feet) was installed in 1966, but this was deactivated when a new skeleton tower took over as the active aid to navigation in 2001. The surrounding land had been washed away by Hurricane George in 1998, and Hurricane Ivan left the old lighthouse about 300 yards offshore in 2001, but still this nineteenth-century tower survived all that the sea and sky could throw at it for more than a century until August 29, 2005, when Hurricane Katrina destroyed it altogether.

Above: A crew inspect the damage to the 1848 brick tower on Chandeleur Island after the 1893 storm that ultimately caused its demise

Hibernia Bank Building

Downtown New Orleans

Constructed in 1921, this 350-foot building is topped by an ornamental tower that originally held a navigational beacon. For many years, this was the tallest building in New Orleans—and the light had a height of focal plane of 349 feet above sea level. The building is located at 313 Carondelet Street.

New Canal Light

New Orleans, Orleans County

This light was relocated onshore, to its present site at the entrance to the Lake Pontchartrain Canal, in 1910, and was restored in 1976. Rising to a height of 32 feet, the square wooden tower (with an integral two-story platform bungalow-style keeper's house) has been operational since 1901. The structure is painted white, with a red roof. The tower originally held a fifth-order Fresnel lens but is currently installed with a 190 mm lens. It has a height of focal plane of 52 feet above sea level. There is also an administration building on site. The lighthouse suffered very heavy damage during Hurricane Katrina on August 29, 2005, but the Lake Pontchartrain Basin Foundation is working toward its restoration.

Pass a L'Outre Light

Head of Passes/Mississippi River Delta

The Pass a L'Outre Light was constructed in 1855, and it was deactivated in 1930. It consists of a cast-iron tower, with a brick lining, and is set upon a stone and timber pile foundation. The tower

is conical in shape, and it is painted with black and white spirals, and topped with a dark lantern. At the time of its construction, this lighthouse was fitted with a third-order Fresnel lens. The lighthouse is now abandoned.

Pass Manchac Light

Ponchatoula, Tangipahoa County

The Pass Manchac light station is situated on the west shore of Lake Pontchartrain. The first tower constructed on this site, in 1839, was eroded by water. The second tower, constructed in 1846, was a two-story Victorian dwelling, made from cypress, with a lantern mounted on the roof. In 1857, this structure was rebuilt as a 40-foot, cylindrical brick tower and dwelling. It had a height of focal plane of 45 feet above sea level. Originally fitted with a fourth-order Fresnel lens, the light was automated in 1941 and it remained in use until 1987. The lighthouse suffered damage during the Civil War, and its lantern was replaced in 1867. In 1868, it was relit with a fifth-order lens. Today, the white tower stands without its (formerly attached) keeper's quarters. The light is owned by the State of Louisiana and the Lake Maurepas Society. It is not open to the public.

Point au Fer Reef Light

Berwick, Terrebonne County

Located on Eugene Island, on Atchafalaya Bay, this 1916 lighthouse was replaced by a modern steel skeletal tower in 1975. The historic square, wooden tower is topped with an octagonal lantern. The one-story keeper's dwelling, a wooden platform bungalow structure, is integral to the tower. The dwelling is painted white, and the tower is black. The lantern originally held a fourth-order Fresnel lens, and it had a height of focal plane of 54 feet above sea level. This lighthouse is owned by the U.S. Coast Guard, and it is not open to the public.

Port Pontchartrain Light

Lake Pontchartrain, Milneburg

Operational from 1855 until 1929, this white, brick, hourglass-shaped lighthouse is topped with a red, octagonal lantern. It originally used a fifth-order Fresnel lens, and it had a height of focal plane of 42 feet above sea level. The Port Pontchartrain Light is now owned by the University of New Orleans. (The current light was preceded by two towers—the first built in 1832, and the second built in 1839. Both of these earlier towers were taken down.)

Sabine Pass East Jetty Light

offshore, Louisiana Point,
Sabine Pass, Cameron County

A modern cylindrical tower on pile foundations, its optic flashes white every 5 seconds. The original, 1924 structure was a skeletal tower atop the roof of a rectangular fog-signal building.

Sabine Pass Light

Sabine Pass, Cameron County

This lighthouse was operational from 1856 until 1952. The octagonal brick tower is supported by eight buttresses and stands at a height of 75 feet. Once painted white (now very faded), the black lantern originally held a third-order Fresnel lens—now on display at the Gulf Coast Maritime Museum in Port Arthur, Texas—with a height of focal plane of 85 feet above sea level. There is also a brick oil house on site. The keeper's house burned down in 1976. The Sabine Pass Light is currently under private ownership. There are plans to renovate it and turn it into a museum.

Above: **The offshore skeletal Ship Shoal Light**

Ship Shoal Light

Berwick, St. Mary County

Situated 10 miles south of Grand Isle, the Ship Shoal Light was in use from 1859 until 1972 (when it was replaced by a modern tower). It is a skeletal, cast-iron tower (with a central cylinder), is painted brown, and stands at 125 feet. The light originally used a second-order (and, later, a third-order) Fresnel lens, and it had a height of focal plane of 117 feet above sea level. It was automated in 1950. The platform bungalow-style keeper's dwelling is constructed of wood and cast iron. The light is currently owned by the U.S. Coast Guard, and it is not open to the public. There are plans to relocate the light to the Town of Berwick's lighthouse park.

South Pass Range Lights

Venice, Plaquemines County

This pair of lights is located at the entrance to the Mississippi River. The Rear Range Light has been operational since 1881. The 108-foot skeletal iron tower is painted white below the gallery, and black above. It was automated in 1971. It originally used a first-order Fresnel lens, and

currently uses a doublet. The tower's height of focal plane is 116 feet above sea level. The Front Range Light, a skeletal tower, dates from 1947. The U.S. Coast Guard owns these lights. They are not open to the public.

Southwest Pass Entrance Light

Southwest Pass entrance,
Plaquemines County

First lit in 1962, this lighthouse was automated in 1985 and it is still operational today. It consists of an 85-foot "Texas tower" style structure, made of concrete and steel and situated on top of a keeper's dwelling. The entire structure is situated on piles. The tower originally held a first-order Fresnel lens, and today it uses a DCB-224. Its height of focal plane is 95 feet above sea level. The two-story keeper's quarters are integral to the tower. Other structures on site include a radiobeacon and a helio pad. This light station is owned by the U.S. Coast Guard, and it is not open to the public.

Southwest Reef Light

Berwick, St. Mary County

Relocated from Atchafalaya Bay in 1987, this 1858 lighthouse was decommissioned in 1916, when the Point au Fer Reef Light was built. The square pyramidal skeletal tower stands at 40 feet and is constructed of iron plates. It originally held a fourth-order Fresnel lens, and it had a height of focal plane of 49 feet above sea level. The 1.5-story wood and cast-iron keeper's house was constructed in the Egyptian revival style in 1859. Owned by the Town of Berwick, this lighthouse is now part of a public park.

Two abandoned light towers still stand at the Southwest Pass entrance to the Mississippi River, one a conical tower (1839), and the other its skeletal replacement (1873). Both called the "Southwest Pass Light" in their day, the 1839 structure took over from an 1832 tower constructed by Winslow Lewis.

Tchefuncte River Range Rear Light

Madisonville, St. Tammany County

Located on the north side of Lake Pontchartrain, this 1868 lighthouse was automated in 1952 and is still operational today. The 43-foot conical brick tower, set on a stone foundation, is painted white, with a vertical black stripe. It was originally equipped with a fifth-order Fresnel lens (transferred from the Cat Island Light). Today, the light uses a 250 mm lens. It has a height of focal plane of 49 feet above sea level. The one-story wooden keeper's house, built in 1887, has been moved two miles upriver. All other structures have now been destroyed. The lighthouse is owned by the Town of Madisonville, and it is planned that it will become part of a museum/tourist attraction.

West Rigolets Light

Rigolets Chanel

The West Rigolets Light was operational from 1855 until 1945. It consisted of a round, wooden lantern mounted on top of a square house that was set upon pilings. One of the keepers of West Rigolets Lighthouse was found shot to death after his second night on the job—making this the only lighthouse whose keeper was killed during the Civil War. The square frame structure was built by Louisiana native Pierre G. T. Beauregard, who went on to become a top commander in the Confederate Army. Before its destruction by Hurricane Katrina in 2005, this was the only surviving lighthouse of its kind on the central Gulf Coast.

Mississippi

Biloxi Light

Biloxi, Harrison County

Located on the Mississippi Sound, this 1848 lighthouse is operational today as a private aid to navigation. It consists of a 61-foot, conical brick tower, encased by cast iron. The tower is painted white, with a black balustrade. Its original lens was a fifth-order Fresnel (now on display in the tower), and it has a height of focal plane of 48 feet above sea level. Today, the tower is equipped with another fifth-order Fresnel lens (installed in 1926). The keeper's dwelling was destroyed by a hurricane in 1969. Three women have served as the Biloxi Light's keeper: Mary

Above: **A 1901 view of Biloxi Light, with the keeper's dwelling**

J. Reynolds (1854–61); Maria Younghans (1867–1918); and her daughter, Miranda Younghans (1918–29). The lighthouse is now owned by the City of Biloxi. The tower's interior was restored in 1989–90, and it is occasionally open to the public.

Round Island Light (Under Reconstruction)

Mississippi Sound, East Pascagoula River

This 50-foot, conical brick light tower (which had been constructed in 1859 and deactivated in 1944) was overturned by Hurricane George in 1998. The Round Island Lighthouse Preservation Society is currently rebuilding the lighthouse, using as much of the original materials as possible. Round Island is a small island, located about three miles off Pascagoula Harbor. The site and the tower are closed to the public.

Ship Island Light (Replica)

Gulfport, Mississippi Sound

The original 1886 Ship Island Light was accidentally destroyed by fire in 1972 (after it had been replaced by a skeletal steel tower the year before). In 2000, the Friends of the Gulf Islands National Seashore constructed a replica of the historic tower: a 72-foot, square pyramidal wooden tower, painted white. The existing skeletal tower serves as an active aid to navigation, but the replica wooden tower was reported lost after Hurricane Katrina struck in 2005.

North Carolina

Bald Head ("Old Baldy") Light

Southport, Brunswick County

Located on Bald Head Island, on Cape Fear River, this light station was first established in 1794 and it is now an historic site with a museum. The current lighthouse was in use from 1817 until the 1930s, although it was deactivated from 1866 to 1880. The octagonal brick tower stands at 100 feet and is plastered with mottled stucco. It originally used a system of 15 lamps and reflectors, and it had a height of focal plane of 110 feet above sea level. Though the original keeper's quarters were destroyed, a replica was built in 2000, which houses the museum.

Bodie Island Light

Nags Head, Dare County

First lit in 1872, this is the third lighthouse ever built at this station, four miles north of the Oregon inlet. It was built with materials left over from the construction of a tower at Cape Hatteras. The Bodie Island Light consists of a 170-foot, conical tower constructed of brick, cast iron, and stone. It is painted with white and black horizontal bands, and it is topped by a black lantern. The light was automated in 1954 and it remains operational today, still using its original first-order Fresnel lens. It has a height of focal plane of 156 feet above sea level. The keeper's house is a two-story brick duplex, constructed in 1872. Other structures include a cistern, a storage building, and an oil house. This station is owned by the National Park Service, and it is currently under restoration.

Cape Hatteras Light

Buxton, Dare County

This 1870 lighthouse is located north of Cape Hatteras Point, on the Outer Banks. Standing at 207 feet, it is the tallest tower in the United States and, at the time of its building, was the tallest brick lighthouse in the world. The tower is painted with black and white spirals and has a redbrick base. It is considered an excellent example of the standard brick design used throughout the nation in the 1870s. The lantern originally held a first order Fresnel lens. Ever since the tower's completion, there had been a gradual encroachment of the sea upon the beach. Attempts at stopping the erosion were to no avail and, in 1935, the light was replaced by a steel skeleton tower (placed further back on a sand dune). The old tower was given over to the National Park Service, which erected a series

Above: **Bodie Island Light**

of wooden revetments that checked the erosion. In 1942, the Coast Guard resumed control over the tower (manning it as a lookout station until 1945) and, in 1950, the lighthouse was placed back in commission. Since 1972, it has used a DCB-24 lens. It has a height of focal plane of 198 feet above sea level. In the summer of 1999, it was moved even farther inland. The light is now part of a national park, with a visitor center and a museum.

Cape Lookout Light

Beaufort, Carteret County

First lit in 1859, this lighthouse was automated in 1950 and is still operational today. The conical brick tower stands at 169 feet. It is diagonally checkered in black and white, and it has a black lantern that originally held a first-order Fresnel lens. It has a height of focal plane of 156 feet above sea level and, today, uses a DCB-24 optic. In 1862, during the Civil War, the tower was damaged by Confederate troops and the lens and other parts were removed. By 1863, the lighthouse had been temporarily refitted with a third-order lens. The first-order lens was repaired and was finally restored in 1867. The keeper's house is a two-story brick structure, constructed in 1873 (and restored in 1988–90). Other structures on site include a brick oil house, a coal shed, two cisterns, a summer kitchen, and a stable. This light station is open to the public.

Currituck Beach Light

Corolla, Currituck County

Situated on Whale Head Bay, the Outer Banks, this 1875 lighthouse consists of a 162-foot conical redbrick tower, topped with a black lantern. The tower is attached to a "repair room." The light was automated in 1939. It is still in use today, and it includes a museum for visitors. It retains its original first-order Fresnel lens, and it has a height of focal plane of 158 feet above sea level. The 1876 keeper's house is a 2.5-story "stick" style duplex, constructed of wood. Other structures include a privy; the Currituck Lighthouse Depot (moved to the site in 1920 to be used as a second keeper's quarters), which now serves as a museum shop; two cisterns; and a storehouse/privy (now used as an office).

Ocracoke Island Light

Ocracoke, Hyde County

This light station was established in 1803, and the current tower dates from 1823. It was automated in 1955 and is still operational today. It consists of a conical, white brick tower (with a mortar surface) that stands at 65 feet (with a height of focal plane of 75 feet above sea level). In 1854, the original reflecting illuminating apparatus was replaced with a fourth-order Fresnel lens. By 1862, the light had been discontinued and its lens had been removed. It was relit in 1899, when it was supplied with a new model fourth-order Fresnel lens. This site is owned and managed by the U.S. Coast Guard and the National Park Service. The grounds (not the tower) are open to the public.

Price's Creek Range Front
West side of the Cape Fear River, north of Southport

Constructed in 1849, this long-forgotten 20-foot, conical brick tower was rediscovered in the 1980s. It is the last remainder of a series of range lights that were built to guide ships 25 miles up the Cape Fear River to Wilmington, NC. (Confederate ships also attempted to use this route to carry supplies past the Union blockade.) The lighthouse is located on private property and is not accessible, though it can be seen from the Bald Head Island ferry.

Roanoke River Light
Edenton, Washington County
(relocated from Abermarle Sound)

Originally located on Abermarle Sound atop iron screwpile foundations, the current Roanoke River Light was operational from 1903 until 1941. It was built to replace an 1866 screwpile structure that had itself replaced an 1835 lightship. It consists of a square, white, wooden tower rising from the roof of a two-story keeper's dwelling, and originally held a fourth-order Fresnel lens with a focal-plane height of 35 feet above sea level. In 1955, the lighthouse was relocated to Edenton as a private residence. It is not open to the public.

South Carolina

Bloody Point Bar Range Lights
Daufuskie Island

Constructed in 1883, at the southern tip of Daufuskie Island, the Bloody Point Front Range Lighthouse is perhaps one of the most forgotten and overlooked lighthouses along the Carolina and Georgia Coasts. It consists of a two-story residential structure that shone a fixed reflector lens out of its large upstairs dormer window. (The lighting apparatus is now gone.) The Rear Range Light was a steel skeletal tower with only three legs, tripod style, with a "wick house" underneath it (where the lantern was stored dur-

ing the day). This tower is now gone, but the oil house and the wick house are still there. Because of beach erosion, the Front Range Lighthouse was moved three quarters of a mile inland in 1899, to the spot where the Rear Range had stood. It is unknown whether or not the dwelling continued to be used as a lighthouse, following the move, or whether it then functioned as a keeper's house. The house is now privately owned, and it is not open to the public, nor is the site accessible.

Cape Romain Light (Old & New)
McLellanville, Charleston County

Located on Lighthouse Island, the newer, 150-foot, octagonal brick lighthouse was operational from 1858 until 1947. The upper two-thirds of the tower is painted black and white, and the lower one-third is painted white. The lantern originally held a first-order Fresnel lens, and the light had a height of focal plane of 161 feet above sea level. The brick keeper's dwelling was removed in the 1950s. Also on site is the bottom one-third (65 feet) of an older tower, dating from 1827. Both lighthouses are currently being stabilized. This site is part of a national wildlife refuge and is not open to the public.

Charleston Light (New)
Sullivans Island, Charleston County

First lit in 1962, this lighthouse was automated in 1975 and it is still operational today. The triangular tower stands at 140 feet (and it contains an elevator). It is constructed of steel and an aluminum alloy, and is set on a concrete foundation. The upper part of the tower is painted black, and the lower part is white. It retains its original DCB-24 optic, with a height of focal plane of 163 feet above sea level. This lighthouse is owned and managed by the U.S. Coast Guard. Its grounds are open to the public.

Georgetown Light
Georgetown, Georgetown County

The Georgetown Light is located on North Island, at the entrance to Winyah Bay. It has been in operation since 1812. It consists of an 87-foot, conical brick tower that is painted white, with a black lantern. It originally used a fourth-order Fresnel lens. The Fresnel is now on display at the USCG Station in Georgetown. The light was automated in 1986 and, since 1999, the lantern has been equipped with a VRB-25 solar-powered lens. It has a height of focal plane of 85 feet above sea level. The keeper's house has been demolished. This lighthouse is not open to the public.

Governor's Light

Little River, Horry County

This octagonal tower was erected in 1985 to honor past governors of South Carolina. Marked with black and white horizontal bands, it has a black lantern and serves as a private aid to navigation. It is not open to the public.

Haig Point (Range Rear) Light

Hilton Head, Beaufort County

Situated on Daufuskie Island, on Caliboque Sound, this 1872 lighthouse was deactivated in 1934, and then relit (as a private aid to navigation) in 1987. With a height of focal plane of 70 feet above sea level, the square wooden tower rises from atop the keeper's house. It is painted white, with a red roof, and is installed with a fifth-order Fresnel lens. The two-story wooden keeper's house was constructed in 1872, in the Victorian style, and was restored in 1986. This lighthouse now functions as a bed and breakfast and is open to the public.

Above: **Hunting Island Light**

Harbour Town Light

Hilton Head Island, Beaufort County

This red-and-white-banded beacon (1970) was built as a private aid to navigation marking the Inland Waterway and Calliboque Sound. The lantern room atop the 90-foot tower boasts a gift store as well as a flashing white optic.

Hilton Head Range Rear (Leamington) Light

Beaufort, Beaufort County

This lighthouse, located on Hilton Head Island, was in use from 1880 until 1932. The 94-foot skeletal pyramidal tower (with a central cylinder) is constructed of cast iron and painted white. In 1985, the lighthouse was restored and relit with a sodium vapor (decorative) optic. It has a height of focal plane of 136 feet above sea level. Other structures include an oil house and cisterns. (The keeper's house was relocated to the harbor.) This lighthouse is now privately owned, and it functions as a resort attraction. The Hilton Head Front Range Light was demolished.

Hunting Island Light

Beaufort, Beaufort County

A previous lighthouse on Hunting Island, built in 1859, was destroyed in 1863, during the Civil War. Operational from 1875 until 1933, the current Hunting Island Light is a conical cast-iron (brick-lined) tower that stands at 136 feet and has a height of focal plane of 140 feet above sea level. It originally used a second-order Fresnel lens. Other structures include two storage buildings, and oil house, and a cistern. The original keeper's house was destroyed. The tower was moved in 1889, because of erosion, which now represents a threat again. The tower's interior was renovated in 1991. The lighthouse is now part of Hunting Island State Park, and it is open to the public.

Morris Island (Old Charleston) Light

See page 178

Texas

Aransas Pass (Lydia Ann) Light

Lydia Ann Channel, north of Port Aransas

The lighthouse at Aransas Pass, a 55-foot octagonal brick tower, was completed in 1857. During the Civil War, control of the tower passed back and forth between Confederate and Union forces, and on Christmas Day 1862, Confederate general John B. Magruder ordered its destruction. Two kegs of powder were exploded inside the tower, damaging the upper 20 feet of brickwork and destroying most of the circular staircase. The tower was repaired after the war, and the station was electrified in 1928. But, by the middle of the twentieth century, the Aransas Pass had shifted over one mile south of the lighthouse. In 1952, the historic tower was deactivated and a new tower was built at a more suitable location for navigational aid. In 1973, the Aransas Pass Light was sold to a Mr. Charles Butt, who oversaw the restoration of the tower and its outbuildings, and hired live-in lightkeepers.

Half Moon Reef Light

Port Lavaca, Calhoun County

First lit in 1858, the Half Moon Reef Light was decommissioned after it was partially destroyed in a storm in 1942. Originally located offshore, in Matagorda Bay (where it was set upon an iron screw-pile foundation), the light was moved to a public park and restored by the Calgoun County Historical Commission in 1980. The hexagonal wood tower is painted white, with green trim. It originally held a fourth-order Fresnel lens. The one-story keeper's house is a wooden dwelling, built in the platform cottage style.

Kemah Light

Kemah, Galveston County

This 175-foot cylindrical blue-and-white-striped water tower with its octagonal red lantern was erected in 2006. A replica third-order Fresnel lens is being assembled from acrylic at the Ponce Inlet Lighthouse Museum, Florida. When installed, its flashing white signal will be visible for 23 miles. The light's grounds are open to the public.

Lake Conroe Lighthouse

Lake Conroe, Montgomery County

Also known as the Harbour Town Lighthouse, there has been a light on this lake, 40 miles north of Houston, since 1977, but the current 90-foot, stucco-covered octagonal tower (painted with red and white bands) with a copper top dates from 1999. After a tornado cut a swath through the lake, the Lake Conroe Lighthouse Association was forced to fund and supervise the repair of the tower. A private aid to navigation, this lighthouse is closed to the public.

Lydia Ann Light
(Formerly Aransas Pass)

Port Aransas, Aransas County

Located on Harbor Island, northwest of the Aransas Pass, the Lydia Ann Light was operational from 1857 until 1952, and it is in use today as a private aid to navigation. The octagonal, redbrick tower stands at 68-feet, on a timber piling foundation, and it is topped with a black lantern. The tower has a height of focal plane of 140 feet above sea level. It originally

Above: **Port (Point) Isabel Light in a 1934 photo**

used a fourth-order Fresnel lens, which is now on display at the Port Aransas Civic Center. The keeper's house, constructed in 1919, is a one-story wooden dwelling in the platform bungalow style. Other structures include five cisterns, an oil house, a storage building, and a radio shack. This light is not open to the public. A modern, skeletal steel tower was constructed nearby in 1990.

Matagorda Island Light

Port O'Connor, Calhoun County

This 1852 lighthouse was automated in 1959, was deactivated for some time in the 1990s, and is operational today as part of a state park. The conical, black cast-iron plate tower (with a brick lining) rises at 79 feet atop a stone, brick, and concrete foundation. It originally used a third-order optic, which is now on display at the Calhoun County Historical Museum in Port Lavaca. Since 1977, the tower has been fitted with a 250 mm solar-powered optic. Its height of focal plane is 90 feet above sea level. The tower has been moved once, in 1873. The keeper's house was dismantled, and no other structures survive. This light is owned by the U.S. Coast Guard, on lease to the Matagorda Island State Park. It is open to the public.

Point Bolivar Light

See page 47

See page 47

Port Isabel (Point Isabel) Light

Port Isabel, Cameron County

This light, located at the Brazos Santiago Pass, was operational from 1853 until 1905. The conical, white tower was originally lit by four lamps, 57 feet above the ground and 82 feet above sea level. By 1854, the light had been refitted with 15 lamps and 21 reflectors, and a third-order lens was installed in 1857. The top of the tower was destroyed during the Civil War. The light had to be overhauled, and the tower was refitted with a new lens, and relit in 1866. In the 1880s, the tower was raised about three feet to accommodate a third-order Fresnel lens. In 1995, a replica of the 1855 keeper's house was built. Complete restoration to the 1880s appearance of the lighthouse was completed in 2000. The light station is now an historic site, and it is open to the public.

Rockport's Texas Maritime Museum Lighthouse holds exhibits on the state's lighthouses and is an active aid to navigation. Constructed in 2003, this 48-foot, white, square-pyramidal tower is topped with a large, red-roofed observation room.

Sabine Bank Light
Sabine Pass, Jefferson County

Situated 15 miles off the Texas Coast, the Sabine Bank Light was operational from 1906 to 2002, when it was replaced by an automated signal on a skeleton tower. The conical, red cast-iron tower rises 72 feet from a cylindrical pier. The light was automated in 1945. It originally held a third-order Fresnel lens, replaced with a 190 mm lens. (The lantern, lenses, and clock mechanism are on display at the Gulf Coast Maritime Museum in Port Arthur, TX.) The tower's height of focal plane was 72 feet above sea level. The keeper's quarters are integral to the "spark plug" style tower. This lighthouse is owned and managed by the U.S. Coast Guard. It is not open to the public.

Virginia

Assateague Light
Assateague Island, Accomack County

Located at the south end of Assateague Island, this lighthouse has been in operation since 1867, weathering many major storms. The conical brick tower is painted white, with red bands, and stands at 142 feet. It originally held a first-order Fresnel lens and, later, a DCB-224. The Fresnel is now on display at the Oyster Museum in Chincoteague. The light was automated in 1965. Its height of focal plane was 154 feet above sea level. The keeper's house is a two-story concrete dwelling, built in 1910. There is also an oil house on site. This lighthouse is open to the public.

Cape Charles Light
Kiptopeke, Northampton County

First lit in 1867, this tower was built to replace a previous (unfinished) tower that was looted and destroyed by Confederate soldiers. It is situated on Smiths Island, at the entrance to the Chesapeake Bay. The octagonal skeletal tower (with a central column) is constructed of cast iron and stands at 191 feet. This is the tallest skeletal tower in the United States. It is painted white, with a black lantern. The tower originally held a first-order Fresnel lens, which was given

to the Mariners Museum when the light was automated in 1963. The lighthouse is still operational today, using a 190 mm solar-powered lens. It has a height of focal plane of 180 feet above sea level. The keeper's quarters were destroyed by a brush fire in 2000. Other structures on site include a brick coal house, a brick generator shed, and a brick cistern. This station is not open to the public.

Cape Henry Lights
See page 49

Jones Point Light
Alexandria, Alexandria County

This white skeleton tower, located on the Potomac River, was first lit in 1856. It consists of a conical lantern mounted on top of a 1.5-story square wooden keeper's house. The lantern is painted gray, and the house is white. The lantern was originally equipped with a fifth-order Fresnel lens. It was automated in 1919. In 1926, the light was moved about 100 feet away to a skeleton tower. The lantern was relit in 1995 and is still in use today, using a 155 mm lens. It has a height of focal plane of 60 feet above sea level. Open to the public, this light station is now part of a national park.

New Point Comfort Light
Bavon, Mathews County

The New Point Comfort Light is located at the entrance to Mobjack Bay. It was operational from 1806 until 1963 (when it was replaced by an offshore beacon). Constructed of ashlar sandstone, the 58-foot, octagonal tower is painted white, with a black lantern. It originally held a fourth-order Fresnel lens. The New Point Comfort Lighthouse Preservation Task Force is now working toward a complete restoration of the tower, the grounds of which are open to the public.

Newport News Middle Ground Light
Newport News, Newport News County

Located on Hampton Roads Harbor, this lighthouse dates from 1891. It was automated in 1954, and is still operational today. The conical ("spark plug" style), red cast-iron tower stands at 35 feet and

The lightship *Portsmouth* served as an active aid to navigation from 1916 until her retirement in 1964. Originally known as the lightship *Charles*, she was renamed several times before coming to rest at Portsmouth's waterfront where she is now a museum.

Above: **Newport News Middle Ground Light**

contains the keeper's quarters. It originally used a fourth-order Fresnel lens. Today, it is fitted with a 375 mm optic. It has a height of focal plane of 52 feet above sea level. This lighthouse is privately owned and is not open to the public.

Old Plantation Flats Light (Replica)

Cape Charles, Northampton County

This is a replica of an 1886 lighthouse that stood at the entrance to Old Plantation Creek. (The original was deactivated in 1962 and subsequently destroyed.) Built in 2004, it holds a modern reproduction of a fourth-order Fresnel lens and a 1942 bronze fog bell, originally used on a bell buoy. A rectangular, screwpile cottage-style keeper's house with a tower on its roof, it is open to the public as a museum.

Old Point Comfort Light

Hampton, Hampton County

The Old Point Comfort Light is situated at the entrance to Hampton Roads Harbor. It has been operational since 1802. The light consists of an octagonal conical tower, which is constructed of sandstone and stands at 54 feet. It is painted white, with a green lantern and a red roof. The lantern originally held 11 lamps, with 14-inch reflectors, but now holds a fourth-order Fresnel. Its height of focal plane is 54 feet above sea level. The 2.5-story keeper's house is in the Queen Anne Victorian style (wood-framed), and dates from 1900. Also on site is a garage. The U.S. Coast Guard owns the land and the tower, and the Army owns the dwelling. This light's grounds are open to the public.

A 2003 replica of the 1858 Stingray Point Light serves as a private aid to navigation and museum at Stingray Point Marina, Deltaville. The 34-foot, hexagonal, red-roofed, cottage-style structure has a tower and lantern on its roof. It holds a fifth-order Fresnel lens which emits a white flash every four seconds.

Smith Point Light

Sunnybank, Northumberland County

First lit in 1897, this light was automated in 1971 and is still operational today. It is located at the entrance to the Potomac River. The square brick tower rises 35 feet atop the two-story, octagonal keeper's dwelling (also constructed of brick). It is painted white, with a black lantern and a red base. The light originally used a fourth-order lens, though, it is now fitted with a DCB-24. It has a height of focal plane of 52 feet above sea level. This light station is privately owned, but the U.S. Coast Guard still maintains the optic. It is not open to the public.

Thimble Shoal Light

Hampton Roads, Hampton Roads County

Situated at the entrance to Hampton Roads, the Thimble Shoal Light has been operational since 1914. The conical ("spark plug" style), red cast-iron tower stands at 40 feet and contains the keeper's quarters. It originally held a fourth-order lens. Today, the lighthouse uses an RB 355 solar-powered optic, and it has a height of focal plane of 55 feet above sea level. The light was automated in 1964. This light is privately owned and is not open to the public. There were two previous towers: one constructed in 1872 (which burned down in 1880), and one constructed in 1891 (which burned down in 1909).

Wolf Trap Light

Mathews, Mathews County

The Wolf Trap Light, located on the lower Chesapeake Bay, was first lit in 1894. It was automated in 1971 and is still in use today. It consists of a square brick tower, rising 52 feet atop a two-story, octagonal brick keeper's dwelling, and topped with a black lantern. It originally used a fourth-order Fresnel lens. In 1996, the lantern was fitted with a Vega VRB-25, solar-powered optic. It has a height of focal plane of 52 feet above sea level. This light was sold to a private owner in 2005. It is not open to the public.

THE PACIFIC STATES

Alaska

Cape Decision Light
Petersburg, Wrangell Petersburg County

This square, white art deco lighthouse is located on southern Kuiu Island, in the Sumner Strait. It was first lit in 1932, was automated in 1974, and is still operational. Constructed of concrete on a rock foundation, the Cape Decision Light stands at 76 feet and uses a horn signal during times of fog. Its original third-order Fresnel lens was removed in 1996, and is now housed in the Clausen Museum in Petersburg. The tower is now fitted with a Vega VRB-25 optic, and has a focal plane at a height of 96 feet above sea level. Nearby structures include a fire-damaged tram, a dock, a boat house, a hoist house, a wooden paint shed with a tin roof, a small-span concrete bridge, and a wooden helipad.

Cape Hinchinbrook Light
Cordova, Valdez Cordova County

This operational lighthouse, with a focal plane of 235 feet above sea level, was first lit in 1934 and was automated in 1974. It consists of an octagonal, 67-foot, white art deco tower constructed from reinforced concrete, which is attached to a fog signal building. A previous tower, built in 1910, was destroyed after earthquakes weakened its foundation in the late 1920s. In 1998, the lighthouse's original third-order Fresnel lens was replaced with a Vega VRB-25 solar-powered lens. (The original lens is on display in the Valdez Heritage Center.) Other structures include a one-story concrete art deco keeper's house (1931), and a nearby radiobeacon. The Valdez museum plans to build a replica of the 1910 tower in downtown Valdez.

Cape Sarichef Light (Site)
Unimak Island

One of the most famous of the Alaskan lighthouses, and the westernmost light station in North America, the Cape Sarichef Light was one of two lighthouses that marked Unimak Pass, the primary passage through the Aleutian Islands into the Bering Sea. This was one of the most isolated light stations in Alaska. (For years, the only neighbor was a trapper, 10 miles away). The 1904 lighthouse, constructed of wood, was replaced by a concrete tower in 1950. This new, modern art–style tower was deactivated in 1979, and it was demolished in 1999. The site, which still contains a few outbuildings, now serves as a U.S. Fish & Wildlife station.

Cape Spencer Light
Glacier Bay National Park, near Juneau

A concrete, Art Deco-style light station (established 1925), this is a white, square tower above a rectangular, flat-roofed structure (once a combined fog signal building and keeper's quarters). Automated in 1974, its solar-powered Vega VRB-25 flashes white every 10 seconds (focal plane 105 feet).

Cape St. Elias Light
Cordova, Valdez Cordova County

Located at the south end of Kayak Island, the Cape St. Elias lighthouse was first lit in 1916, was automated in 1984, and is still operational. The square, white concrete art deco tower is located on the corner of the station's fog signal building. It stands at 55 feet tall and has a Vega VRB-25 solar-powered optic with a focal plane at a height of 85 feet above sea level. The tower's original third-order Fresnel lens is now housed within the Cordova Museum. There is also a three-story brick keeper's quarters, which is deteriorating, a radiobeacon, and a storage building. This lighthouse is owned by the U.S. Coast Guard and is on lease to the Cape St. Elias Lighthouse Keepers. It is open to the public.

Eldred Rock Light
Haines, Haines County

Situated on Alaska's Lynn Canal, this fully operational lighthouse was first lit in 1905 and was automated in 1973. The white octagonal tower is constructed of wood and is perched directly on top of the fog signal building. It stands at 56 feet high and has a 250 mm solar-powered optic with a focal plane of 91 feet above sea level. The original lens, a fourth-order Fresnel, was removed to a museum in Port Chilkoot in 1978. The keepers quarters are located within the fog signal building, below the tower. Other structures include a boathouse, helicopter pad, radio tower, cistern, oil house, and storage building. The lighthouse was renovated circa 1996. It is owned by the U.S. Coast Guard, on lease to the Sheldon Museum and Cultural Center, and is not open to the public.

Five Finger Islands Light
Frederick Sound, near Petersburg

This light station was first established in 1902 and was the site of the first Alaska Lighthouse built by the Lighthouse Service. The current tower was constructed in 1935, was automated in 1984, and is still operational. A 68-foot-high square, white concrete art deco tower, it is currently fitted with a Vega VRB-25 solar-powered optic (which replaced the original, 1902 fourth-order Fresnel lens in 1997). Its height of focal plane is 81 feet above sea level. The keeper's quarters are integral to the tower, and other structures include radiobeacons and cisterns. This station is owned by the U.S. Coast Guard, on lease to the Juneau Lighthouse Association, and is not open to the public.

Above: **Point Retreat Light**

Guard Islands Light

Tongass Narrows Entrance/Clarence Strait, near Ketchikan

First lit in 1924, the Guard Island Light is a 30-foot-high, square, white concrete tower situated on top of an oil house. This light was automated in 1969 and is still operational. In 1997, its fourth-order Fresnel optic was replaced with a Vega VRB-25 solar-powered lens. This lighthouse has a height of focal plane of 25 feet above sea level. The original sound signal building has been dismantled, but a radiobeacon is still present. The current tower replaced an earlier tower, built in 1904. The site is owned and operated by the U.S. Coast Guard, and is not open to the public.

Mary Island Light

Mary Island/Revillagigedo Channel, near Metlakatla

The Mary Island Light station was first established in 1903, and the current tower was constructed in 1937. Standing at 61 feet, this modern looking, square, white art deco tower is constructed of reinforced concrete on a concrete foundation. A sound signal building is attached on one side of the tower. It is fitted with a 250 mm optic, which replaced the original fourth-order Fresnel lens, and has a height of focal plane of 76 feet above sea level. This lighthouse was automated in 1969. It is owned and operated by the U.S. Coast Guard, and is not open to the public.

Odiak Pharos

Cordova, Orca Inlet

This 18-foot, white-painted octagonal light tower on a barge next to a bed-and-breakfast inn was privately built in the 1970s. It emits a fixed white light at a focal-plane height of 26 feet above sea level.

Point Retreat Light

Admiralty Island/Lynn Canal

This lighthouse was first lit in 1923, was automated in 1973, and is still operational today. It consists of a 25-foot-high, square, white concrete art deco tower situated on top of a fog signal

building. The original, first-order bivalve Fresnel lens was replaced with a 300 mm solar-powered lens. Its height of focal plane is 63 feet above sea level. The Cape Cod–style keeper's quarters stands at 1.5 stories high and is constructed of wood. Other structures include a cistern and a boathouse. This light is owned by the U.S. Coast Guard and is on lease to the Alaska Lighthouse Association. It is open to the public by private arangement.

Rockwell Lighthouse

Sitka, Baranof Island

A private aid to navigation with a fixed red light shining at a focal-plane height of 50 feet above sea level, this 42-foot, white-painted, octagonal wooden tower was constructed in 1977. The wood-frame structure that adjoins it is run as a bed-and-breakfast inn..

Sentinel Island Light

Juneau, Juneau Borough

Located at the entrance to Lynn Canal, on Auk Bay, the Sentinel Island Light station is an important guide for Alaskan transport and commerce. It is also an excellent example of art deco architecture. Standing at 51 feet, this 1935, square concrete tower (painted white, with a red lantern and roof) sits directly on top of its fog signal building. It has a Vega VRB-25 solar-powered optic, with a height of focal plane of 86 feet above sea level. In 2004, ownership of the light station was transferred to the Gastineau Channel Historical Society. They plan to establish a Southeast Alaska Maritime Interpretive Center here. Visitors can tour the light station by appointment only.

Tree Point Light

Revillagigedo Channel, near Metlakatla

The Tree Point Light was first lit in 1935 and was deactivated in 1969 (the same year it was automated). The square, concrete white art deco tower is attached to the oil house and stands at 66 feet. It was originally fitted with a fourth-order Fresnel lens, which was later replaced with a 300 mm optic. It had a height of focal plane of 86 feet above sea level. The current tower replaced an earlier tower, which dated from 1904. One of the lighthouse's old lenses and drive mechanisms is on display at the Ketchikan Historical Museum. This site is owned by the U.S. Coast Guard, and is not open to the public.

California

Alcatraz Island Light

Alcatraz Island, San Francisco Bay

This lighthouse shares an island with the famous federal penitentiary that once housed Al Capone and many other notorious criminals, and it has survived prison breakouts, riots, and burning. The light station was first established in 1854, and was the first on the West Coast. The Great San Francisco Earthquake of 1906 severely damaged the original lighthouse. The current tower was constructed in 1909, was automated in 1963, and is still operational. It consists of an unpainted, 84-foot-high octagonal/pyramidal concrete tower with a black lantern. It is fitted with a DCB-24 optic (which replaced the original third-order Fresnel lens). This light is owned and managed by the U.S. Coast Guard and the National Park Service. The grounds are open to the public.

Anacapa Island Light

Port Hueneme, Ventura County

Constructed in 1932, this cylindrical brick and concrete tower stands at 40 feet and has a height of focal plane of 277 feet. It is painted white, with black trim. This light was automated in 1968 and is still operational. In 1991, the original third-order Fresnel optic was replaced with a DCB-24 lens. (The original lens is now on display in the Island Visitor Center.) The concrete fog building, also dating from 1932, is in the Spanish revival style. Other structures include the original, one-story wooden keepers quarters (also in the Spanish revival style). The site is owned by the National Park Service. The grounds are open to the public and escorted tours are available.

Battery Point (Crescent City) Light

See pages 78 and 79

Cape Mendocino Light

Mendocino, Humboldt County

First lit in 1868, this white, 16-sided pyramidal tower is constructed of cast iron upon a concrete foundation. It stands at 43 feet, and has a height of focal plane of 422 feet above sea level. In 1950, the first-order lens was installed in a replica tower at the entrance to the Humboldt County Fairgrounds. A steel pole-style tower was constructed near the original site in 1951 and, in 1998, the original tower was relocated to Shelter Cove (where it is not accessible to the public).

Above: **Alcatraz Island early in the twentieth century**

Carquinez Strait Light

Vallejo, Solano County

This lighthouse was first placed in operation in 1910. The original building, a 28-room lighthouse weighing 150 tons, was constructed on a wooden pier. It had a fourth-order Fresnel lens and a height of focal plane of 56 feet above sea level. The Coast Guard abandoned the light in 1951. In 1955, the structure—minus its tower—was placed on a barge and towed two miles to its new location at Elliott Cove, where it was converted into a resort. Today, the building serves as a marina. (The original site is now an automated light station.)

East Brother Island Light

See page 188

Farallon Island Light

Southeast Farallon Island, San Francisco

This station, on the highest peak of southeast Farallon Island, was built in the days following the Gold Rush, in 1855–6, when ships were sailing to San Francisco in large numbers. The 41-foot conical tower is constructed of a brick lining surrounded by stone. The sharp, jagged slopes of the island rock made construction difficult and treacherous. The stone was quarried on the island and carried up the rock, on the backs of workers, in bundles of four and five. The light was automated in 1972 and is now equipped with a VEGA VRB optic (focal plane 358 feet). The original first-order lens is now on display at San Francisco's Maritime NHP Museum, at the visitor center across from the Hyde Street Pier. As the island is now a national wildlife refuge, the tower may only be seen from the water.

Fort Point Light

San Francisco Harbor Entrance

This light was first lit in 1864 and remained in use until 1934, when it was discontinued because of construction of the Golden Gate Bridge. It is a 27-foot iron tower, painted white with a black lantern, situated on top of a brick and granite fortress. It was equipped with a fourth-order Fresnel lens and had a height of focal plane of 110 feet above sea level. This site is owned and managed by the National Park Service and is not open to the public.

Lime Point Light

See page 189

Long Beach Light ("Robot Light")

San Pedro Middle Breakwater, Los Angeles

Labeled the "Robot Light" because of its unusual, machinelike appearance, this 1949 monolithic structure was the forerunner of a new kind of twentieth-century West Coast lighthouse. Designed to withstand earthquakes and seismic tidal waves, the 42-foot, white, rectangular concrete tower stands on a base of six columns. It features a 36-inch airway-type beacon that was initially controlled by remote from the Los Angeles Harbor Light.

Los Angeles Harbor Light

San Pedro, Los Angeles County

This uniquely designed 1913 lighthouse consists of a cylindrical steel tower standing at 69 feet. It is painted white, with vertical black stripes. The original, fourth-order Fresnel lens is now on display at the Los Angeles Maritime Museum, and the light is now equipped with a DCB-24 solar-powered optic. It has a height of focal plane of 73 feet above sea level. Originally known as the San Pedro Harbor Light, the tower was automated in 1972 and is still operational. Other structures include the original concrete oil house and a loading dock. The light is operated by the U.S. Coast Guard and is not open to the public.

Mile Rocks Light

offshore, San Francisco Bay

This beacon can be seen from Lincoln Park as it flashes white every 5 seconds at a height of focal plane of 49 feetv above sea level. Erected in 1906, the modern optic is mounted atop an orange-striped, white-painted, steel-and-concrete caisson near the Golden Gate. In 1966 the two upper sections of the steel, three-tired structure were removed and a helipad was instituted on the remaining tier.

Oakland Harbor Light

Oakland, Alameda County

First lit in 1903 and in use until 1966, this lighthouse has now been relocated from its original location at the Oakland Harbor entrance. The house has a square shape and is constructed of wood and set on concrete pilings. The two-story keeper's quarters are contained within the house (below the tower). After its deactivation, the lighthouse was sold to a private owner, and its lantern room was installed on the Mark Abbott Memorial Light in Santa Cruz. The Oakland Harbor Light is now known as Quinn's Lighthouse Restaurant.

Two private aids to navigation also operate at Long Beach. One is a 65-foot, white, conical steel tower in Rainbow Harbor named the Long Beach Lighthouse (2000), which also serves as the harbormaster's office. The second is known either as the Shoreline Marina Entrance Light or as Parkers' Lighthouse (1982). Its beacon shines from within a lantern mounted on the roof of a restaurant at the point of Shoreline Village.

Piedras Blancas Light

San Simeon, San Luis Obispo County

Located at the northern entrance to San Simeon Bay, this lighthouse was first lit in 1875, was automated in 1975, and is still operational. The 74-foot, white brick, conical tower stands separate from the brick fog signal building (of which only a shell remains). In 2002, the original first-order bivalve Fresnel optic was replaced with VRB-25 lens (focal plane 142 feet). The Fresnel is now on display at Pinederado Park in the city of Cambria, CA. This light is operated by the Bureau of Land Management and is not open to the public. The concrete, ranch-style keeper's quarters (built in 1960) has been moved to Cambria and now serves as a bed and breakfast.

Pigeon Point Light

Pescadero, San Mateo County

Pigeon Point Light is one of the most picturesque lighthouses on the Pacific Coast. Standing at 115 feet, this lighthouse was first lit in 1872. It was automated in 1974 and is still operational. The conical, white masonry tower is painted with black trim and is attached to a separate workroom. It has a DCB-24 optic (which replaced the original, first-order Fresnel) and has a height of focal plane of 148 feet above sea level. It is owned by the U.S. Coast Guard, on lease to the California Department of Parks & Recreation, and is open to the public. This headland took its name from the ship *Carrier Pigeon*, which wrecked here many years ago.

Above: **Pigeon Point Light, c. 1921**

Point Arena Light

Point Arena, Mendocino County

This light station was first established in 1870, but the lighthouse had to be reconstructed, in 1908, following the earthquake of 1906. The 115-foot white concrete tower (with a black gallery) is cylindrical in shape and is equipped with a DCB-224 optic. (It originally contained a first-order, rotating Fresnel.) Its height of focal plane is 155 feet above sea level. Other structures include an 1896 wood-framed Victorian sound building, four modern duplex keepers' quarters, two cisterns, an oil house and a modern well house. The site is operated by the Point Arena Lighthouse Keepers, Inc., and is open to the public. This station was used as the setting for the 1992 film *Forever Young.*

Point Blunt Light

Angel Island, San Francisco Bay

Established in 1915, Point Blunt Light Station is still in use today as an active aid to navigation and as housing for state personnel. In 1960, a new watch room was constructed, which allowed a view of the entire San Francisco Bay, and new quarters were completed in 1961 (four family units, each with three bedrooms). Personnel at Point Blunt also control the Southampton Shoals fog signal, as well as operating their own light and fog signals and the Raccoon Strait light and fog signals.

Point Bonita Light

See pages 104 and 105

Point Cabrillo Light

See page 93

Point Conception Light

See pages 98 and 99

Point Diablo Light

San Francisco, about 1 mile west of the Golden Gate Bridge

Not really a lighthouse, in the strictest sense, the Point Diablo Light consists of a navigation light mounted atop a square, white, one-story fog signal building (with a continuously operating fog signal that blasts every 15 seconds). Constructed in 1923, the structure is located on a headland, halfway between Point Bonita and Lime Point. (The keepers from the Lime Point Light originally maintained the beacon.) The site and tower are closed to the public.

Point Fermin Light

San Pedro Harbor, Los Angeles County

This 1874 wood-framed Italianate dwelling, with a 30-foot Italianate tower on top, was deactivated in 1942 and currently serves as part of a city park. It contained a fourth-order Fresnel lens and had a height of focal plane of 100 feet above sea level. Other structures include three cisterns, a concrete oil house, and a barn. This site is owned and operated by the City of Los Angeles and the Point Fermin Lighthouse Committee and is open to the public. (A new, pole-type light tower was built on the site in 1970. Its height of focal plane is 100 feet above sea level.)

Point Hueneme Light

Point Hueneme/Oxnard, Ventura County

This station was established in 1874, at the east entrance to the Santa Barbara Channel, and the current lighthouse was first lit in 1941. It was automated in 1972 and is still in operation today. This impressive white, art deco tower is constructed of concrete and stands at 48 feet. It retains its original, fourth-order Fresnel lens, and has a height of focal plane of 52 feet above sea level. This light is owned and operated by the U.S. Coast Guard and is not open to the public. Nearby, wreckage from the veteran passenger liner *La Janelle* can still be seen, where it was tossed up onto the beach during a storm in 1970.

Point Loma Light (New)

Southern end of Point Loma, San Diego

This operational light, first lit in 1891 and was automated in 1973, replaced the old Point Loma Light (which dates from 1855). The steel, skeletal tower (with an inner cylinder) stands at 70 feet high and retains its original, third-order Fresnel lens. The tower is painted white, with a black lantern. Its height of focal plane is 88 feet above sea level. The two-story wood-framed keepers quarters were constructed in 1891 in the Mission revival style. Other structures include a barn, a radiobeacon, and a cistern. The light station serves as U.S. Coast Guard housing, and is not open to the public.

Point Loma Light (Old)

Cabrillo National Monument, San Diego

First lit in 1855, this was the first lighthouse to be erected in Southern California The tower was abandoned in 1891 because it was situated at 462 feet above sea level—so high that the light was often obscured by high fogs. It is a white brick building with a conical tower (standing at 46 feet) and a green lantern. It used a third-order

Fresnel lens. In 1913, President Wilson proclaimed the tower as a national monument. It is currently cared for by the National Park Service. The site is open to the public, and the light is kept on at night for aesthetic effect.

Point Montara Light
Montara, San Mateo County

This 1928 lighthouse was automated in 1970 and is still operational today. This station was just a fog signal with a minor light until 1912, when a fourth-order lens was installed. Today, the conical, white steel tower stands at 30 feet high and has a height of focal plane of 70 feet above sea level. It uses a FA 251 optic. (The original, fourth-order Fresnel lens is now on display at the library at the College of Notre Dame in San Mateo.) Other structures include a two-story keeper's quarters (a Victorian Gothic duplex, constructed in 1875), a storage building, a tank house, and a 1960s dwelling. The site is owned by the U.S. Coast Guard, on lease to the California Department of Parks & Recreation, and is open to the public.

Point Piños Light
Pacific Grove, Monterey County

Dating from 1855, this is the oldest active lighthouse on the West Coast and it serves as an excellent example of lighthouses built during this era. For 25 years, it was run by women keepers. It was restored by the Pacific Grove Historical Society. The brick tower is conical and stands at 43 feet atop the white, Cape Cod–style, 1.5-story stone house (which serves as the keeper's quarters). It retains its original, third-order Fresnel lens, with a height of focal plane of 89 feet above sea level. Other structures include an oil house, a cistern, and a radiobeacon. This site is owned by the City of Pacific Grove and managed by their Museum of Natural History. It is open to the public Thursdays through Sundays.

Point Reyes Light
Gulf of the Farallones,
near Inverness, Marin County

Standing at 35 feet, this cylindrical, cast-iron lighthouse (with a brick lining) was first lit in 1870 and was deactivated in 1975, when an automated beacon was mounted

Above: **Point Loma Light (Old)**

on a cylindrical support on the nearby 1928 wooden fog signal building (built in the powerhouse architectural style). The old tower is painted white, with a red roof, and still holds its original, first-order rotating Fresnel optic (focal plane 294 feet above sea level). The station, currently under renovation, is owned by the National Park Service and the U.S. Coast Guard, and is open to the public Thursdays through Mondays. The 1975 beacon is still an active aid to navigation.

Point Sur Light
See pages 114 and 115

Point Vincente Light
Rancho Palos Verdes, Los Angeles County

This cylindrical, white concrete tower stands at a height of 67 feet, uses its original, third-order Fresnel lens, and has a height of focal plane of 185 feet above sea level. It was first lit in 1926 and it was automated in 1973. The two-story keeper's quarters, also built in 1926, is constructed of concrete and is in the Mission revival style. This site is an example of a complete twentieth century station constructed in the Spanish style. It is owned by the U.S. Coast Guard, and is open to the public during limited times.

Punta Gorda Light
Petrolia, Humboldt County

Located 13 miles south of Cape Mendocino, this lighthouse was operational from 1912 until 1951. The square tower (white, with a black lantern) is made of reinforced concrete and it stands at 27 feet high. It used a fourth-order bullseye lens and had a height of focal plane of 75 feet above sea level. This is a very difficult station to reach. In the late 1960s, it was occupied by squatters, who improved the property. Local authorities evicted these inhabitants, and the U.S. Bureau of Land Management (which owns the site) burned all of the buildings except for the lighthouse and the oil house. This is an historic site and it is open to the public.

Above: **Point Reyes Light**

Rubicon Point Light
Southwest shore of Lake Tahoe

The Rubicon Point Light bears the brunt of many jokes, as it looks much like a wooden outhouse. Built in 1916, this light was only active for a few years. It consists of a 12-foot frame tower, with no lantern. At about 63,000 feet, it has the highest elevation of any lighthouse in the United States. The Tahoe Heritage Foundation is working to restore the structure, which is believed to have been originally built by the U.S. Coast Guard (though accounts of its history vary).

San Luis Obispo (Port Harford Light)
Avila Beach, San Luis Obispo County

This is a white, Victorian masonry house (which serves as the keeper's quarters), attached to a square tower that stands at 40 feet. It has an octagonal lantern. The light was first lit in 1890 and it was deactivated in 1975. It used a fourth-order Fresnel lens (which is now on display at the County Museum) and had a height of focal plane of 116 feet above sea level. Other structures include an oil house, two cisterns, a radiobeacon, a privy, a shop, and two (circa 1960s) dwellings. The site is owned by the Port San Luis Harbor District and is open to the public.

Santa Cruz Light
Point Santa Cruz, Santa Cruz County

Following the death of a surfer here in 1965, his parents funded the erection of this lighthouse (1967), which is also known as the Mark Abbott Memorial Light. The white-painted, cast-iron lantern (which originally graced the now defunct Oakland Harbor Light, *see* page 315) sits atop a 39-foot, square, brick tower that adjoins a brick building that houses a surfing museum. Its light flashes white every five seconds at a focal-plane height of 60 feet above sea level.

Santa Cruz West Breakwater (Walton) Light
Santa Cruz, Santa Cruz County

A 42-foot, conical concrete tower, painted white with red and black trim, this lighthouse was erected in 2001 on the end of a jetty at the harbor entrance. It was funded by private donations and displays an occulting green signal.

Southampton Shoals Light
Relocated from San Francisco Harbor to San Joaquin Delta, Tinsley Island

First lit in 1905, this square lighthouse was constructed on wooden piles and contained a two-story keeper's quarters. It used a fifth-order Fresnel optic and had a height of focal plane of 52 feet. The Fresnel lens is now on display at the Angel Island Interpretive Center. After its deactivation in 1960, the light was relocated to Tinsley Island, where it is currently under private ownership and serves as a yacht club. It is open to the public by appointment.

St. George Reef Light
Crescent City, Del Norte County

Located six miles off of Point St. George, this light was operational from 1892 until 1975 and was relit in October 2002 after restoration. It was the country's most expensive lighthouse, costing $704,634, and it took 10 years to build. The square tower stands at 90 feet and is constructed of granite blocks on an elliptical concrete and granite foundation. It is painted white, with a black lantern. This lighthouse has a height of focal plane of 144 feet above sea level and originally used a first-order Fresnel lens, which was removed to the County Museum in 1975. The lantern room was destroyed during a helicopter accident in 2000, but a replica was installed in April 2002 with a solar-powered lens. The site is owned by Del Norte County, on lease to the St. George Reef Lighthouse Preservation Society, and is only occasionally open to the public.

Table Bluff Light
Relocated from Humboldt Harbor to Woodley Island

This 1892 lighthouse was automated in 1953 and remained in use until 1972. The white, square tower stands at 35 feet and is constructed of wood. It had a height of focal plane of 176 feet above sea level and originally used a rotating fourth-order lens (which was transferred to Point Loma Light in San Diego in 1953). The keeper's quarters and the sound signal building have been demolished. The light is now under private ownership and is not open to the public.

Trinidad Head Light
See page 114

Trinidad Memorial Light
Trinidad, Humboldt County

This inactive beacon is a replica of the Trinidad Head Light (see page 114), and it includes the original lantern, fourth-order Fresnel lens, and fog bell of that beacon. The Memorial Light was built in 1948 as a memorial to sailors lost at sea. It is located in a park at the foot of Trinity Street, just off U.S. 101 in Trinidad. The site is open to the public, though the tower is closed. (In 2003, Native

Visitors to Oakland may tour the lightship *Relief* which is docked there. She served from 1951 until 1975.

Americans of the Yurok tribe filed a suit against the city for removal or relocation of the structure, on grounds that the tribe owns the property on which it stands.)

Above: **Yerba Buena Island Light, c. 1910**

Yerba Buena Island (Goat Island) Light

Island in the San Francisco Bay

This octagonal, white masonry lighthouse was first lit in 1875. It was automated in 1958 and is still operational. The tower stands at 25 feet, is wood-framed, and contains an iron lantern. It retains its original, fifth-order Fresnel optic, and has a height of focal plane of 95 feet above sea level. The rectangular sound signal building (with a horn-type signal) is constructed of brick. Other structures include the keeper's quarters (a two-story wood-framed Gothic duplex dating from 1873) and an oil house. This light is owned and operated by the U.S. Coast Guard and is not open to the public.

Hawaii

Aloha Tower

At the foot of Fort Street, downtown Honolulu, Oahu

This 1926 beacon has been inactive since about 1970. It consists of a 184-foot square masonry tower, topped by a domed cupola. Though it was privately maintained, the light was an important navigational aid for ships arriving in Honolulu. The light here replaced the Honolulu Harbor Light that was established in a different location in 1869, but that light was later relit in its original location.

Barbers Point Light

Kalaeloa, Oahu Island, Honolulu County

Operational since 1933, the Barbers Point Light is a cylindrical, white concrete tower without a lantern. It stands at 71 feet above the ground and 85 feet above sea level, on a masonry foundation. The light originally used a fourth-order Fresnel lens. It was automated in 1964, when it was refitted with a DCB-224 lens. The lighthouse is owned by the U.S. Coast Guard, on lease to the Honolulu Department of Parks & Recreation. It is not open to the public.

Cape Kumukahi Light

Pahoa, Hawaii County

Located on the easternmost point of Hawaii Island, this 1934 lighthouse was automated in 1960 and is still operational today. It consists of a 125-foot skeletal pyramidal tower that is constructed of steel and set on a concrete foundation. Its original optic was a 375 mm lens. In 1934, the tower was fitted with its current optic, a DCB-24. It has a height of focal plane of 156 feet above sea level. The keeper's house and other structures were destroyed by a volcanic eruption. This lighthouse is owned and managed by the U.S. Coast Guard.

Diamond Head Light

Honolulu, Honolulu County

The Diamond Head Light is situated at Diamond Head, on Oahu Island. The 57-foot square concrete tower (painted white, with a red roof) has been operational since 1918. It was constructed using the watchroom from an earlier tower, built in 1899. The light was automated in 1924. It retains its original third-order Fresnel lens, with a height of focal plane of 147 feet above sea level. The one-story keeper's house, a wood-framed bungalow, dates from 1921. The lighthouse is owned and managed by the U.S. Coast Guard, and it is not open to the public.

Kauhola Point Light

Kauhola Point, Hawaii Island

Several ships have been wrecked off of Kauhola Point (which juts out into the Pacific Ocean and has reefs that extend out for roughly two miles), prompting the building of the first lighthouse here in 1897. The structure was wood framed, and by 1904 it was reported to be in a dilapidated condition. A temporary, pyramidal frame tower was constructed in 1917. Several years after, in the 1930s, the new permanent light was finally erected. It is an 86-foot conical structure built of reinforced concrete. The welded metal lantern originally housed two 36-inch airway beacons (one for backup) that flashed red and green as they revolved. Remaining on the site today is the tower, minus its lantern room, and some of the original outbuildings.

Kaunakakai Range Front Light

Kaunakakai Harbor, Molokai

This active 1912 lighthouse gives off a continuous red light at a height of focal plane of 41 feet above sea level. It is a 26-foot, square pyramidal skeletal frame tower mounted on a small workroom. The rear range tower, which is a similar, 38-foot structure (without a workroom), is about 500 feet inland. The site is open to the public, though the tower is closed.

Kilauea Point Light
Amalu, Kauai County

Situated north of Kilauea, on Kauai Island, this historic lighthouse was operational from 1913 until 1976 (when it was replaced by a nearby pole tower). It was an important landfall light, marking the way for ships bound to Honolulu from Asia. The tower stands at 52 feet, is conical in shape, and is made of reinforced concrete. It used a second-order Fresnel lens, and it had a height of focal plane of 216 feet above sea level. The one-story keeper's house is built from local stone. Other structures include two assistant keeper's houses, three garages, three cisterns, an oil storage building, and a radiobeacon electronics building. The lighthouse suffered damage from a hurricane in 1992. Now part of a national wildlife refuge, the light is open to the public.

Makapu'u Point Light
Waimanalo, Honolulu County

This 1909 lighthouse still contains its original hyper-radiant lens—the largest lens of any lighthouse in the United States, with a diameter of 8 feet, 2 inches. All commerce coming from the west coast of North America to Honolulu passes the Makapu'u Point Light. The 46-foot, cylindrical brick tower is painted white and topped with a black lantern. It has a height of focal plane of 420 feet above sea level. The light was automated in 1974. The keeper's house was demolished. There is currently a radiobeacon on the site. Owned and managed by the U.S. Coast Guard, this light station is not open to the public.

Molokai (Kalaupapa) Light
Kaluapap, Maui County

First lit in 1909, this lighthouse was automated in 1970 and is still operational today. It consists of a 138-foot, octagonal concrete tower, painted white and topped with a black lantern. The tower has a height of focal plane of 213 feet above sea level. It originally used a second-order bivalve Fresnel. Today, it uses a DCB-24 optic. The keeper's house is a 1.5-story bungalow, constructed of volcanic rock. Other structures include a storage building, and a second concrete keeper's house (dating from

1951). This station is owned and managed by the U.S. Coast Guard and the National Park Service. It is open to the public, and tours are available by appointment. For information, call 808-567-6802, ext. 22 or 26, or e-mail kala_interpretation@nps.gov.

Nawiliwili Harbor Light
Nawiliwili, Kauai County

The Nawiliwili Harbor Light is located at Ninini Point, on Kauai Island. Operational since 1933, the cylindrical, buff-colored concrete tower stands at 86 feet on a masonry foundation, uses a DCB-24 lens (installed in 1985), and has a height of focal plane of 118 feet above sea level. The tower originally held a first-order bivalve Fresnel. Automated in 1953, this lighthouse is owned and managed by the U.S. Coast Guard. It is open to the public on selected days.

Pyramid Rock Light
Mokapu Peninsula, Kaneohe, Oahu

The Pyramid Rock Light is a 15-foot, square concrete workhouse with a beacon mounted on the roof. Located at the summit of a pyramidal rock, the beacon flashes a white light every four seconds, at a height of focal plane of 101 feet above sea level.

The above list of Hawaii lighthouses does not include a series of concrete pyramidal towers, with equipment rooms in the base, built circa 1915 (and as late as 1929). These include: **Coconut Point Light**, *Hilo Harbor, Hawaii Island*; **Kailua Point Light**, *Kukailimoku Point, at the western entrance to the harbor at Kailua-Kona, Hawaii Island*; **Ka'uiki Head Light**, *south side of Hana Bay, Maui*; **Kawaihae Light**, *Kawaihae Harbor in Kawaihae, Hawaii Island*; **Keahole Point Light**, *southwest of Keahole-Kona International Airport, Hawaii Island*; **Kuki'i Point Light**, *north side of Nawiliwili Harbor, Kauai*; **Kukuihaele Light**, *Kukuihaele, Hawaii Island*; **Mahukona Light**, *Mahukona Harbor, about five miles south of the northernmost point of Hawaii Island*; **Lahaina Light**, *Auau Channel, Maui*; **McGregor Point Light**, *one mile southwest of Maalaea, Maui*; **Napo'opo'o Light**, *Cook Point, on the north side of Kealakekua Bay, Hawaii Island*; and **Pauka'a Point Light**, *Pauka'a, about two miles north of downtown Hilo, Hawaii Island*.

Above: Nawiliwili Harbor Light

There are also a number of modern, skeletal towers and post-mounted optics in Hawaii. These include:

Hanamanioa Point Light, *Cape Hanamanioa, Maui;* **Ka'ena Point Passing Light**, *westernmost point of Oahu;* **Ka Lae Light**, *Na'alehu, Hawaii Island;* **La'au Point Light**, *southwest point of Moloka'i;* **Laupahoehoe Point Light**, *Laupahoehoe, Hawaii Island;* **Makahu'ena Point Light**, *near Po'ipu, Kauai;* **Miloli'i Point Light**, *Miloli'i, Hawaii Island;* **Nakalele Point Light**, *northwest point of Maui;* **Palaoa Point Light**, *Kaunolu Village, Lanai;* **Pa'uwela Point Light**, *Pa'uwela, Maui;* and **Pepeekeo Point Light**, *Pepeekeo, Hawaii Island.*

Oregon

Cape Arago (Cape Gregory) Light
See page 105

Cape Blanco Light
See page 101

Cape Meares Light
Oceanside, Tillamock County

This historic light was operational from 1890 until 1963 (when it was replaced with a modern tower). The 40-foot, octagonal tower is constructed of brick, sheathed in iron, and is attached to a workroom. It is painted white, with black trim. The tower held a first-order Fresnel lens, and it had a height of focal plane of 217 feet above sea level. The keeper's house was demolished in 1968, and no other structures remain on site. The Cape Meares Light is now part of a state park and national wildlife refuge. It is open to the public.

Cleft of the Rock Light
Near Yachats, Lincoln County

Built in 1976, 10 miles north of Heceta Head, by a former lighthouse keeper, this light exhibits an alternating white–red signal (focal plane 110 feet). A 31-foot, white, square-pyramidal wooden tower with red trim, it was formally recognized as a private aid to navigation in 1979. It was modeled on Vancouver's Fiddle Reef Lighthouse. Also a private residence, this beacon is not open to the public.

Coquille River (Bandon) Light
See page 212

Heceta Head Light
See page 114

Pelican Bay Lighthouse
Brookings Harbor, Curry County

The house that Bill and Jo Ann Cady built in 1990 is unusual in that it has a white-painted, 35-foot, octagonal light tower attached to it. The optic within the black lantern acts as a private aid to navigation with a flashing white signal (focal plane 141 feet). Although closed to the public, it can be seen from nearby.

Tillamook Rock Light
Seaside, Clatsop County

Tillamook Rock is one of the most exposed light stations on the Pacific coast, and this 1881 lighthouse has received many batterings from heavy storms. The square white tower (constructed of basalt masonry, brick, and iron) stands at 62 feet, and it originally used a first-order Fresnel lens. More than once, the protective glass of the lantern (which is 133 feet above sea level) has been shattered by giant waves. The light was discontinued in 1957. The keeper's quarters are integral to the tower. There is also a cistern and a storage building. Owned by Eternity at Sea Marketing, this lighthouse now functions as a columbarium. It is not open to the public.

Umpqua River Light
Reedsport, Douglas County

Operational since 1894, the Umpqua River Light is a conical, white, stuccoed brick tower. It stands at 61 feet and is topped with a green lantern and a red dome. The light was automated in 1966, and it retains its original first-order Fresnel lens. The light's height of focal plane is 165 feet above sea level. The tower is attached to a workroom, and there are also two oil houses on site. The keeper's dwelling was razed in the 1950s. This lighthouse is owned by the U.S. Coast Guard, on lease to Douglas County Parks & Recreation. It is open to the public.

Warrior Rock Light
Northern tip of Sauvie Island, St. Helens

The original lighthouse, built in 1889, was a wooden square pyramidal structure. In 1930, this lighthouse was replaced with a white, octagonal concrete tower (with no lantern), which was mounted on the original square sandstone foundation. The structure was repaired in 1969, after it was seriously damaged when a passing barge collided into it. The ruins (basement and chimney) of the original keeper's quarters are nearby, hidden by forest. The original fog bell is on display at the Columbia County Historical Courthouse in St. Helens. The beacon is active, and it is managed by the U.S. Coast Guard. The tower is not open to the public.

Yaquina Bay Light (Old)
Newport, Lincoln County

Now serving as a museum within Yaquina Bay State Park, this 1871 lighthouse was in use for only three years before being deactivated, in 1874. More than 120 years later, in 1996, the light was relit. It consists of a white, square wooden tower that rises 51 feet above the two-story clapboard keeper's house. With a height of focal plane of 161 feet above sea level, the tower originally used a fifth-order Fresnel lens. Today, it is fitted with a 250 mm optic. The light is owned by the State of Oregon, on lease to the Lincoln County Historical Society, and it is open to the public.

Yaquina Head Light
Newport, Lincoln County

Located three miles north of the entrance to Yaquina Bay, this light has been operational since 1873. The conical brick tower stands at 93 feet (162 feet above sea level) and is attached to a workroom. It is painted white, with a green lantern and a red dome. The light was automated in 1966, and it still uses its original first-order fixed Fresnel lens. The keeper's house and a number of other structures have been demolished. Remaining structures include a cistern (dating from 1873) an oil house (from 1889), both of which were rehabilitated in 1992, and a whip antenna (from 1993). This light station is owned by the Salem District Bureau of Land Management. It is open to the public.

The lightship *Columbia* was established in 1892 to mark the mouth of the Columbia River and was the first to serve on the Pacific coast. In 1979, after several ships had served here, a navigational buoy finally took over and the west coast's last lightship was retired. The last *Columbia* is now at Astoria's Columbia River Maritime Museum. *See also* page 248.

Above: **Yaquina Head Light**

Washington

Admiralty Head Light
See page 118

Alki Point Light
Seattle, King County

Located on Elliott Bay, on Puget Sound, this station was first established in 1887, when the only light was a brass kerosene lantern hung on a post on the side of a barn. The current light tower was built in 1913, and it was automated in 1984. The octagonal masonry tower stands at 37 feet and is attached to its sound signal building. The tower is painted white, with red and black trim. It originally held a fourth-order Fresnel lens, but, since 1998, has held a VRB-25. It has a height of focal plane of 39 feet above sea level. The keeper's house is a 1.5-story wood-frame structure. Other structures include a garage and a store room/coal building. This light station currently serves as a museum, as an active aid to navigation, and as housing for the U.S. Coast Guard.

Browns Point Light
Tacoma, Pierce County

This 1933 lighthouse is situated at the east entrance to Commencement Bay. It consists of a 34-foot, square, white concrete tower, without a lantern, and it has a height of focal plane of 38 feet above sea level. The light was automated in 1963. Since 1997, it has used a VRB 25 optic. The tower originally used a 375 mm optic. The keeper's house, built in 1903, is a 1.5-story wooden structure, in the neoclassical style. There is also an oil house, a garage, and a boathouse. This light station is owned by the U.S. Coast Guard, on lease to the Metropolitan Park District of Tacoma. It is open to the public.

Burrows Island Light
Anacortes, Skagit County

First lit in 1906, this light was automated in 1972 and is still operational today. The white, square wood tower stands at 34 feet atop its fog signal building. It has a height of focal plane of 57 feet above sea level, and it originally used a fourth-order Fresnel lens. In 1994, the tower was fitted with a 300 mm optic. The keeper's house is a two-story duplex, constructed of wood. There is also a storage building on site. This lighthouse is owned and managed by the U.S. Coast Guard, and it is not open to the public.

Bush Point Light

South Whidbey Island, Bush Point

Dating from 1933, the Bush Point Light consists of a 20-foot pyramidal concrete tower, painted white, and with no lantern. It is active, with a focal plane of 25 feet above sea level and a white flash every 2.5 seconds. The site is open to the public, though the tower is closed.

Cape Disappointment Light

Ilwaco, Pacific County

Situated on North Point Island, on the Columbia River, the Cape Disappointment Light has been operational since 1856. The conical, dressed stone tower stands at 53 feet and is attached to its oil house. It is painted white, with a black band, and is topped by a black lantern room. When built, the tower was equipped with a first-order Fresnel lens. In 1898, however, the lantern was refitted with a fourth-order Barbier & Bernard lens. The light, which was automated in 1962, has a height of focal plane of 220 feet above sea level. The keeper's house is no longer present, and the only remaining structure is an oil house. Although situated in a state park, the light tower is closed to the public.

Cape Flattery Light

Neah Bay, Clallam County

This 1857 light is located on Tatoosh Island, at the entrance to the Strait of Juan de Fuca. Native Americans used the island as a fishing and whaling station, and there were skirmishes between them and the lighthouse construction crew. The conical sandstone and brick tower stands at 65 feet, with a height of focal plane of 165 feet above sea level. It originally used a first-order Fresnel lens. The light was automated in 1977 and, since 1996, has used a VRB-25 lens. Its light can be seen for 19 miles. The Cape Flattery Light was renovated by the U.S. Coast Guard in 1994. It is not open to the public.

Cattle Point Light

San Juan Island, South San Juan Channel

This light station was established in 1888 and the current lighthouse was built in 1935. Still active today, it is a white, octagonal cylindrical concrete tower mounted atop a square fog signal building. The tower has a focal plane of 94 feet above sea level. It gives off a white flash every four seconds, and the fog horn blasts every 15 seconds. The grounds are open to the public (though the tower is closed), and a trail leads to the lighthouse from a picnic shelter located inside the powerhouse for the island's former radio station.

Destruction Island Light

Kalaloch, Jefferson County

First lit in 1891, this light consists of a 94-foot, conical dressed stone tower, attached to a storage building. It is painted white, with a black gallery. At 147 feet above sea level, the tower originally held a first-order Fresnel lens. The light was automated in 1968 and, in 1995, it was fitted with a VRB-25 solar-powered optic. (The original Fresnel is on loan to the Westport Maritime Museum.) The keeper's house is a 1.5-story wood-frame dwelling. Other structures include a concrete sound signal building, two oil houses, a marine railway, and a cart storage house. This station is owned and managed by the U.S. Coast Guard, and it is not open to the public.

Dofflemyer Point Light

Boston Harbor (north of Olympia), at the entrance to Budd Inlet

The Dofflemyer Point Light is an octagonal cinderblock tower, painted white. When it was built in 1934, the tower had a small, square lantern that has now been removed. The beacon is still active, with a height of focal plane of 30 feet above sea level. It flashes a white light (three seconds on, and three seconds off). Managed by the U.S. Coast Guard, the site and tower are closed to the public.

Ediz Hook Lights

Relocated to Fourth and Albert streets, Port Angeles

In 1865, the first lighthouse was constructed on Ediz Hook. Resembling a country schoolhouse, it consisted of a two-story dwelling with a pitched roof and a small tower at one end. Its lantern room housed a fixed, fifth-order Fresnel lens. A pyramid-shaped fog bell structure was added in 1885. By the turn of the century, the lighthouse was in disrepair and mariners had complained that the fog bell was not loud enough. To correct both problems, a new fog signal building with an attached octagonal light tower was constructed nearby in 1908. The lantern room and lens were removed from the old lighthouse and installed in the new one, though the light source was changed from a coal oil lamp to an incandescent oil vapor lamp. In 1936, this second Ediz Hook Lighthouse was replaced by a modern beacon installed on a nearby Coast Guard control tower. The 1908 lighthouse was sold and relocated across the harbor to Port Angeles, where it now functions as a private residence.

Gig Harbor Light

Gig Harbor, near Tacoma, Pierce County

This privately-maintained lighthouse is a 15-foot, white, hexagonal concrete structure from the late 1980s, displaying a flashing red light.

Grays Harbor (Westport) Light

Westport, Grays Harbor County

Operational since 1898, the Grays Harbor Light is a 107-foot, octagonal pyramidal tower constructed of brick. It is painted white, with a green roof. With a height of focal plane of 123 feet above sea level, the tower originally used a third-order Fresnel lens (which is still in the tower, but which is no longer operational). Today, the light uses an FA-251 optic. The sound signal building burned down in 1916, and the keeper's house was removed. There are two oil houses remaining on the site. This station is owned by the U.S. Coast Guard, on lease to the Westport Maritime Museum. It is open to the public.

Lime Kiln Light

Friday Harbor, San Juan County

Situated on Dead Mans Bay, at San Juan Island, the Lime Kiln Light was built in 1919. It consists of an octagonal concrete tower that rises 38 feet atop its sound signal building. The structure is painted white, with a red roof. The original optic was a 375 mm lens. The light was automated in 1962 and, in 1998, was refitted with a VRB-25 lens. Its height of focal plane is 55 feet above sea level. The keeper's house is a 1.5-story wood dwelling, dating from 1914. Other structures include a second keeper's house, a cistern, and three storage buildings. This station is on lease to the State of Washington Department of Parks & Recreation, and it is open to the public. The tower now functions as a whale research laboratory.

Marrowstone Point Light

Port Townsend, Jefferson County

This light station was established at Admiralty Inlet in 1882. The current lighthouse, dating from 1912, is a short, squat concrete structure that stands at 28 feet (the same as its height of focal plane) atop a square fog signal building. The light was automated in 1962, and presently uses a 250 mm lens. The keeper's house is a 1.5-story Victorian wood-frame dwelling, constructed in 1895. This station now functions as an active aid to navigation, and as a research site for the U.S. Geological Survey. It is open to the public. Other structures include a boathouse (from 1895), a pump house and laboratory buildings (from 1993), wet labs (from 1976 and 1993), an effluent settling/water treatment pond (1976), and a seawall (from 1922).

Mukilteo Light

See page 151

New Dungeness Light

Sequim, Clallam County

This 1857 lighthouse was automated in 1976 and is still in use today. The 63-foot, conical tower is constructed of sandstone, brick, and stucco. It is painted white, with a white lantern and a red roof, and it was originally equipped with a third-order Fresnel lens. The tower was remodeled in 1906. In 1927, the upper portion of the tower was removed, and a fourth-order lens was installed. The light has used a VRB-25 optic since 1998. The tower has a height of focal plane of 67 feet above sea level. The 1.5-story frame keeper's house, in the Georgian style, dates from 1905. There is also a brick sound signal building (from 1927), a frame barn/garage (1877), an oil house/paint shed (1894), a coal and oil house (from 1907). This station is licensed to the New Dungeness Chapter of the U.S. Lighthouse Society. It is open to the public.

North Head Light

Ilwaco, Pacific County

This lighthouse, constructed in 1898, is located north of the mouth to the Columbia River. The conical, dressed stone tower (with a brick lining) rises to 65 feet above the land and 194 feet above sea level. The light was automated in 1961, and it is painted white, with a red roof. The tower was originally equipped with a first-order Fresnel lens. It later used a fourth-order lens and, in 1999, it was fitted with a VRB-25. The keeper's house is a two-story brick structure. Other structures include an assistant keeper's house, two garages, a cistern, two oil houses, a storage building, and a chicken coop. The operational lighthouse is now part of a state park, and the two keeper's houses are now used as vacation rentals.

Patos Island Light

Eastsound, San Juan County

First lit in 1908, this operational lighthouse was automated in 1974. Its square, wood tower—painted white, with green trim and a red roof—rises 35 feet atop its fog signal building (which dates from 1898). The tower's original fourth-order Fresnel lens is

Above: North Head Light

now installed at the Admiralty Head Light. Today, the Patos Island Light uses a 300 mm solar-powered lens. It has a height of focal plane of 52 feet above sea level. The original keeper's house was dismantled in 1983, but there remains a modern keeper's house on site. Owned and managed by the U.S. Coast Guard, the grounds of this light station are open to the public.

Point No Point Light
Hansville, Kitsap County

Lighting from the Kitsap Peninsula, on Puget Sound, the Point No Point Light was constructed in 1879. The square, brick and stucco tower stands at 30 feet between the office and the sound signal building (which was added in 1900). It is painted white, with a red roof. The light was automated in 1977. Other structures include the keeper's house, a two-story wood-frame structure, and a metal oil house. In 2006, the original fourth-order Fresnel lens was deactivated and the navigational light was transferred to a modern optic mounted outside the lantern. The light is owned by the U.S. Coast Guard, on lease to Kitsap County Parks & Recreation. It is open to the public.

Point Roberts Light
Point Roberts, Whatcom County

A 25-foot, skeletal tower with a flashing white signal was erected here after the original structure was destroyed by a storm in the 1930s. There has been discussion about building a replica of the old lighthouse, whose grounds are open to the public.

Point Robinson Light
Vashon Island, King County

The Point Robinson Light is located on the east end of Maury Island, on Puget Sound. Operational since 1915, it consists of a 40-foot, square masonry and concrete tower, which is attached to a fog signal building. The tower is painted white, with a red roof and green trim. The light was automated in 1978. It uses a fifth-order Fresnel lens, and it has a height of focal plane of 40 feet above sea level. Other structures include the keeper's house (a 1.5-story wood-frame structure), an assistant keeper's house, a coal shed/oil house, an equipment house, a garage (c. 1930s), the pad of a boathouse, and a marine railway. This light is on lease to the Vashon Island Park District. It is open to the public.

Above: Point Wilson Light

Point Wilson Light
Port Townsend, Jefferson County

Established in 1879, the Point Wilson Light station is located at the entrance to Admiralty Inlet, on Puget Sound. The current tower was first lit in 1914, and it was automated in 1977. The octagonal masonry and concrete tower rises at 46 feet atop its fog signal building. It is painted white, with a red roof. The tower retains its original fourth-order Fresnel lens, and it has a height of focal plane of 51 feet above sea level. An earlier tower (equipped with the same Fresnel) rose from the two-story keeper's house, which is still present on site. Other structures include a second keeper's house, a radiobeacon, and two oil houses. This operational lighthouse is open to the public by prior arrangement.

Skunk Bay Lighthouse
Hansville, Kitsap County

This octagonal, white-painted, wooden light tower supports a red lantern which was salvaged from Smith Island after its Cape Cod-style home collapsed in the 1950s. Its fixed red signal is privately maintained and it is inaccessible to the public.

Turn Point Light
Roche Harbor, San Juan County

Operational since 1936, this light consists of a 44-foot, square, white concrete tower, situated on a concrete foundation. The light was automated in 1974. It retains its original 300 mm optic, and it has a height of focal plane of 44 feet above sea level. The keeper's house is a two-story wooden dwelling, dating from 1893. There is also a sound signal building. The Turn Point Light is owned and managed by the U.S. Coast Guard and the Bureau of Land Management. It is not open to the public.

West Point Light
See page 59

The lightship that today bears the *Swiftsure* name was actually a relief vessel for when its namesake was brought in for maintenance. Decommissioned in 1960, she is now located at the Northwest Seaport Maritime Heritage Center, Seattle.

THE GREAT LAKES

Illinois

68th Street Crib (Dunne Crib) Light

South Chicago

This lighthouse was built in 1909, upon the crib that (for many years) was the water intake for South Chicago. The metal tower stands at 50 feet, and it is hexagonal in shape, with a silver-gray lantern. While it was under construction, it was the scene of a large fire that claimed the lives of 60 workmen. The active lighthouse is maintained by the Chicago Department of Water, and the site and tower are closed to the public.

Chicago Harbor Light

Chicago, Cook County

First lit in 1893, the Chicago Harbor Light played an important role in the development of Chicago's port. The white (originally, red), conical cast-iron tower (with a brick lining) stands at 48 feet upon a rubble-stone and concrete pier. The beacon was originally equipped with a third-order Fresnel lens (which is now at the Cabrillo National Monument in California), and its focal plane is 82 feet above sea level. In 1919, the tower was moved to a breakwater. It was automated in 1979. The keeper's quarters are integral to the tower, and a sound signal building and a boathouse are attached. This lighthouse was restored in 1997. It is owned and managed by the U.S. Coast Guard, and it is not open to the public.

Chicago Harbor Southeast Guidewall Light

Chicago Harbor, Lake Michigan

This 1938 light tower marks a breakwall near the city's Navy Pier. It is a 30-foot, white, square pyramidal steel tower, with the upper half closed and the lower half open (skeletal). Still active today, the light can best be seen by boat.

Four Mile Crib Light

Chicago

This red skeletal light tower gives off a white flash every 15 seconds, with a height of focal plane of 66 feet above sea level. Managed by the Chicago Department of Water, the site and tower are closed to the public.

Above: Little Fort Light, the 1849 predecessor to Waukegan Harbor Light

Grosse Point Light

See page 205

Waukegan Harbor (Little Fort) Light

Waukegan, Lake Michigan

This 35-foot, circular cast-iron tower was first lit in 1899, outfitted with a fourth-order Fresnel lens. The lighthouse was relocated 1,400 feet in 1905, when the pier it stood on was extended. The structure caught fire in 1967, and the fog signal building and lantern were virtually destroyed (and they were later demolished). In lieu of a new lantern, the tower was capped with a flat steel lid and topped with a green acrylic lens. Today, the white tower is painted with a bright green band. The site is open to the public.

William E. Dever Crib Light

Chicago Harbor, Lake Michigan

A square skeletal tower constructed upon a large, cylindrical water intake structure, the Dever Crib Light has a height of focal plane of 72 feet above sea level and can be viewed from the Chicago waterfront. The NOAA Great Lakes Environmental Research Laboratory also maintains a weather station at this crib. Also known as the Harrison–Dever Crib, the signal here is a flashing white light.

Wilson Avenue Crib Light

North Chicago waterfront, Lake Michigan

A flashing white light mounted on a 47-foot, cylindrical tower atop a water intake structure (focal plane 68 feet).

Indiana

Buffington Harbor Breakwater Light

Buffington Harbor, East Chicago

Still active, this 1926 light consists of a steel tower mounted atop an oval-shaped fog signal building, with a height of focal plane of 48 feet. The entire structure is painted red, though the paint has faded to a red orange. It is located on the end of the breakwater on the east side of Buffington Harbor. The site and tower are privately maintained and are closed to the public.

 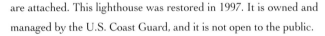

There are three lights actively serving the harbor at Calumet, Lake Michigan, Indiana, all constructed *c.* 1995. Calumet Harbor Breakwater South End Light is a square, white skeleton tower with a red band and an alternating signal of red and white flashes. Calumet Harbor Entrance South Side Light is a 27-foot, white cylindrical tower with a green band and flashing green signal. Calumet Harbor Light is a white, cylindrical tower with a red band and flashing red signal.

Gary (West Breakwater) Light
Gary Harbor, Gary

This round, faded red steel tower stands at 40 feet upon a concrete pier at the end of the Gary Harbor breakwater. The tower is tapered near the top, where there is a walkway and a lantern room (with cross-hatched metal bars). Constructed in 1911, the beacon still guides vessels into the U.S. Steel Gary Works complex. Today, it uses a modern plastic lens, though it retains its original sixth-order lens as a backup.

Indiana Harbor East Breakwater Light
Indiana Harbor, East Chicago

Located at the end of the breakwater in East Chicago, this 1935 structure consists of a 75-foot, square cylindrical steel tower mounted atop a raised steel platform. It is still active today, flashing a green light at a height of focal plane of 78 feet above sea level. The beacon is managed by the U.S. Coast Guard, and the site and tower are closed to the public. The structure is a copy of a more well-known pierhead lighthouse at Port Washington, WI.

Michigan City Breakwater Light
Michigan City Harbor, Lake Michigan

Giving out a red flash every four seconds, at a focal-plane height of 36 feet above sea level, this beacon can be seen from the Michigan City East Pierhead Light. Built in 1911, it is a white square pyramidal tower with a horizontal red band. It is not open to the public.

Michigan City East Pier Light
See page 218

Michigan City Light (Old)
Michigan City, LaPorte County

Built in 1858 (deactivated 1904), this keeper's dwelling with a white, wooden tower is now a maritime museum in Washington Park.

Michigan

Alpena Light
Alpena, Lake Huron

Because of this unique light tower's resemblance to the Russian space satellite, the bright red, cast-iron skeletal structure has been nicknamed "Sputnik" by the local residents. First lit in 1914, at the entrance to the Thunder Bay River, it is believed to be the third lighthouse built in this area. The tower is 80 feet tall, and the upper part of the structure is enclosed.

Au Sable Light
Grand Marais, Alger County

This 1874 Lake Superior lighthouse was known as the Big Sable Light until 1910. The conical, white tower stands at 87 feet and is topped with a black lantern, with a height of focal plane of 107 feet above the sea. The lantern originally held a third-order Fresnel lens. The light was automated in 1958, and now the beacon uses a 300 mm solar-powered lens. The two-story redbrick keeper's dwelling, and matching, redbrick fog signal building are still standing, as are several other structures, including a steel oil house, a second brick keeper's house, two brick privies, and a brick cistern. The National Park Service is in the process of restoring the lighthouse to its 1909–10 appearance, and the grounds are open to the public.

Au Sable North Pierhead Light
Au Sable, Iosco County

Originally established in 1873 with a brown skeleton tower linked to the shore by an elevated walkway, the current, 25-foot north pierhead light is a white skeleton tower displaying a fixed red light.

Bayfield Rock Range Lights
Sugar Island, St. Mary's River

This station was established in 1892 with the erection of two post-mounted lanterns. These were replaced in 1913 with octagonal-pyramidal structures. The current lights are both skeleton towers displaying a fixed white signal.

Beaver Head (Beaver Island) Light
South of St. James, Charlevoix

Operational from 1858 until 1962, the Beaver Head Light is a cylindrical, yellow-brick tower that stands at 46 feet and had a height of focal plane of 103 feet above sea level. The light used a fourth-order Fresnel lens, which is now housed in the yellow-brick keeper's dwelling.

Other structures include a redbrick sound signal building, an oil house, a garage, and a storage building. A radiobeacon tower was constructed on the site in 1962. This light station is now owned by the Charlevoix Public School District, and its buildings are used as classrooms.

Big Bay Point Light
Big Bay, Marquette County

This square redbrick tower is topped with a white lantern that the U.S. Coast Guard relit in 1990, after 29 years of deactivation. The 65-foot tower was built in 1896, and it originally used a third-order Fresnel lens, with a height of focal plane of 60 feet above sea level. The two-story redbrick keeper's dwelling (a duplex) now functions as a bed and breakfast. A third keeper's house was added in the 1920s. Also on site is a redbrick sound building, an oil house, two brick outhouses, a dock, and a well house.

Big Sable Point Light (Grand Point Au Sable Light)
Ludington, Mason County

This beacon, located on the east shore of Lake Michigan, has been operational since 1867. The 112-foot, conical brick tower was encased in iron plate in 1900. It is painted black and white. The tower originally used a third-order Fresnel lens, which was transferred to the Rose Hawley Museum in Ludington. It presently uses a 300 mm optic, with a height of focal plane of 106 feet above sea level. The two-story brick keeper's house, which is attached to the tower, was modified in 1909 and in 1948. Owned by the State of Michigan, this light station now doubles as a museum.

Bois Blanc Island Light (Old)
Mackinac Island, Cheboygan County

The Bois Blanc Island Light was in use from 1867 until 1924 (a new tower was constructed nearby in 1941). The historic, square yellow-brick tower stands at 38 feet and is topped with a white lantern. The beacon originally used a fourth-order Fresnel lens, and it had a height of focal plane of 53 feet above the sea. The 1.5-story yellow-brick keeper's dwelling is attached to the tower. Other structures include a brick oil shed, a brick outhouse, and a cement boathouse on the south side of the island. This lighthouse is now privately owned, and it is not open to the public.

Above: **Charlevoix South Pierhead Light**

Charity Island Light
Standish, Huron County

This 1857 lighthouse was operational until 1939. The conical, white brick tower is topped with a black lantern and the Arenac County Historical Society is working to restore it. The light was originally lit by a kerosene lamp and, later, with an acetylene lamp. The privately-owned keeper's dwelling was razed in 2003 and a replica has been built on the old foundations. It is not open to the public.

Charlevoix South Pierhead Light
Charlevoix, Lake Michigan

This 1948 skeletal steel tower is located on the south breakwater at the entrance to Round and Charlevoix Lakes. The tower is open at the bottom, and its 10-sided lantern holds a fifth-order Fresnel lens. It replaced an earlier frame tower that had been constructed on the north pier in 1885 and moved to the south pier in 1914.

Cheboygan Crib Light
See page 212

Cheboygan River Range Front Light
Cheboygan, Cheboygan County

This 1880 lighthouse consists of a square, white wooden tower that originally used a sixth-order Fresnel lens. It currently displays a locomotive-type lamp from the gallery. The integral two-story wood-frame keeper's house also dates from 1880. The Cheboygan River Range Front Light is owned by the Great Lakes Lightkeepers Association, and it is not open to the public. The rear range light was replaced with a skeletal tower.

Copper Harbor Light
See page 210

Copper Harbor Range Lights
Copper Harbor, Lake Superior

The original pair of Copper Harbor Range Lights were built in 1865, and they guided ships through the passage into Copper Harbor. At that time, the keeper of the lights lived at nearby Fort Wilkins. The existing historic lighthouse, built in 1869, is located inside Copper Harbor State Park. It is a brown and yellow keeper's dwelling, from which the rear range light was shown from an upper window. This house is now used as a residence for state park rangers. The rear range light was replaced by a skeletal steel tower, built in 1964, and the current front steel tower was built in 1927.

Crisp Point Light
Paradise, Luce County

Located 13 miles west of Whitefish Point, on Lake Superior, the Crisp Point Light was operational from 1904 until 1947. The 58-foot, conical brick tower is painted white, with a black lantern, and it is attached to an entrance room. The lantern was originally equipped with a fourth-order Fresnel lens, and it had a height of focal plane of 58 feet above sea level. The sound signal building was destroyed during a storm in 1963, and the keeper's house and all other original structures have also been demolished. This historic site is now owned by Luce County and the Crisp Point Lighthouse Historical Society. Although the tower itself is under restoration, its grounds are open to the public.

Detour Reef Light
Detour, Chippewa County

First lit in 1931, this lighthouse was automated in 1974 and is still operational today. It is located at the mouth of the St. Mary's River, on Lake Huron. At 63 feet tall, the square reinforced concrete and steel tower is painted white, with a red roof. It has a height of focal plane of 74 feet above sea level, and it uses a VRB-25 lens. The tower was originally equipped with a third-and-a-half-order Fresnel optic, which is now on display at the Detour Passage Historical Museum. The keeper's quarters are integral to the tower. This light is owned by the U.S. Coast Guard and on lease to the Detour Reef Light Preservation Society. It is open to the public.

Detroit River (Bar Point Shoal) Light
South Rockwood, Wayne County

This station was first established in 1875, when a lightship station was placed near the shoal. Over the years, the light has been an important player in the development of shipping and transportation between Lake Huron and Lake Erie. The historic tower was first lit in 1885. It is constructed of cast-iron plate (with a brick lining), stands at 49 feet, and is conical in shape. The tower is painted white, with a black upper. It uses a fourth-order lens, and it has a height of focal plane of 55 feet above sea level. The keeper's quarters are integral to the tower, and the sound signal building is attached. Also on site is a storage building and a radiobeacon. Owned by the U.S. Coast Guard, this light station is not open to the public.

Eagle Harbor Light
Eagle Harbor, Keweenaw County

Dating from 1871, this beacon was automated in 1980 and is still in use today. The octagonal, white brick tower rises at 44 feet atop its 1.5-story redbrick keeper's dwelling. The tower originally held a fourth-order Fresnel lens, but, since 1968, it has used a DCB-224 optic. Its height of focal plane is 60 feet above sea level. There is also a rectangular steel-frame sound signal building, as well as a brick oil house, four cement garages, two assistant keeper's dwellings (relocated from a lifesaving station across the harbor), and a radiobeacon. This light is open to the public.

Eagle Harbor Rear Range Light
Lake Superior, Keweenaw Peninsula (original site)

Also known as the Cedar Creek Range Rear Light, this lighthouse was constructed in 1877 at the entrance to Eagle Harbor, at the Keweenaw Peninsula, on Lake Superior. It consisted of a light that shone through the window of a cupola, on the roof of the keeper's dwelling. This light was decommissioned in 1911, and its light was transferred to new metal towers. The lighthouse was relocated in the 1930s, and it now serves as a private residence (and is not open to the public). The front range companion to this light was destroyed.

Eagle River Light
Eagle River, Keweenaw County

This square, stone light tower was operational from 1874 until 1908. Its beacon was important to the prosperity of the copper industry on Lake Superior. The tower, which replaced a previous lighthouse constructed in 1854, is painted white, topped with a conical lantern, and sits upon a stone foundation. The keeper's quarters occupy 1.5 stories within the tower. This lighthouse now functions as a private residence, and it is not open to the public.

Fort Gratiot (Port Huron) Light
Port Huron, St. Clair County

First lit in 1829, this is the oldest surviving lighthouse in Michigan. The conical brick tower originally stood at 74 feet and was equipped with a fifth-order Fresnel lens. In 1861 the tower's height was increased to 86 feet, and in 1874 a brick duplex keeper's dwelling was added. Today the tower uses a DCB-24 optic, and it has a height of focal plane of 86 feet above sea level. A brick sound signal building, dating from 1901, remains (though it has been gutted). This station is owned by the city of Port Huron and it is open to the public.

Forty Mile Point Light

Rogers City, Presque Isle County

The Forty Mile Point Light has been operational on Lake Huron since 1897. It consists of a square, white brick tower, set upon wood pilings and topped with a black lantern. The tower uses a fourth-order lens and stands at 52 feet, with a height of focal plane of 66 feet above the sea. The light was automated in 1969. The 2.5-story redbrick keeper's house is attached to the tower. Other structures include a brick sound signal building, an oil house, two privies, a barn, and a bath house. This light station is now part of a county park, and its grounds are open to the public.

Fourteen Foot Shoal Light

Cheboygan, Cheboygan County

Still in use today, this 1930 beacon is situated at the entrance to Cheboygan Harbor. The conical, reinforced concrete and steel tower is painted white with red trim. It is situated upon its rectangular keeper's house, with a height of focal plane of 55 feet above sea level. The tower originally held a fourth-order Fresnel lens, but today it uses a 250 mm optic. The sound signal building is integral to the tower. This lighthouse is owned and managed by the U.S. Coast Guard, and it is not open to the public.

Fourteen Mile Point Light

Ontonanagon, Keweenaw Peninsula, Lake Superior

Operational from 1894 until 1934, this square brick light tower was gutted by a fire in 1984. In the early 1990s the structure was sold to private owners, who have restored the fog signal building and are working to restore the lighthouse.

Frankfort North Breakwater Light

Frankfort, Benzie County

The wave-swept North Breakwater is the site of this pyramidal 67-foot steel tower. The present light was built in 1932 on a station established in 1873. Now automated, it is still in service.

Above: **Frankfort North Breakwater Light**

Above: **Grand Haven South Pierhead Lights**

Frying Pan Island Light

Relocated to Sault Sainte Marie

Formerly located in the De Tour Passage at Frying Pan Island, this 1887 lighthouse was relocated to the Coast Guard base in Sault Sainte Marie (where it is currently on display) after it was replaced by a modern automated light. It is a white, conical cast-iron tower, standing at approximately 20 feet tall.

Grand Haven South Pierhead Lights

Grand Haven, Ottawa County

Located on the Grand River, this pair of beacons dates from 1905 and is still in use today. The Inner Light is a 51-foot, conical, red cast-iron tower, situated upon a pier. It originally used a sixth-order Fresnel, and today uses a 250 mm optic. The outer light, a 36-foot, square red cast-iron tower (with a wood frame), is also set upon a pier. It uses a 190 mm optic (originally, a sixth-order Fresnel) and it has a height of focal plane of 42 feet above sea level. The outer light tower was moved once, in 1905. The sound signal building is integral to the outer light tower, which was sheathed in iron in 1922. Owned and managed by the U.S. Coast Guard, these lights are open to the public.

Grand Island East Channel Light

Munising, Alger County

This Lake Superior beacon was in operation from 1870 until 1913. (It was replaced by a pair of range lights installed at Munising in 1908.) The Grand Isle East Channel Light is a square, wood-frame tower on a brick foundation. It is attached to the keeper's dwelling, a 1.5-story wood-frame house. This historic light house is now privately owned, and it is not open to the public.

Grand Island Harbor Range Rear Light

Christmas, Alger County

In use from 1914 until 1969, the conical, black steel tower stands at 62 feet and is topped with a white lantern. The structure, also known as Christmas Light, sits upon a concrete pier, and it has a height of focal plane of 70 feet above sea level. This light station is now owned and managed by the U.S. Forest Service and the U.S. Department of Agriculture. It is open to the public. The front range companion to this light was torn down in 1969 to make room for the Bay Furnace Directional Light, a 20-foot conical tower, painted white with a dark base and lantern, and a flashing white signal.

Grand Island North (Old North) Light
Munising, Alger County

First lit in 1867 with a fourth-order Fresnel lens, the Grand Island North Light was operational until 1961 (when it was replaced by a pole tower). The 40-foot, square brick tower is still standing today. It is attached to the two-story brick keeper's dwelling. Other structures include an oil house, a storage building, an outhouse, and a well. The lighthouse has been restored, but not modernized. It now serves as a private summer home, and it is not open to the public.

Grand Marais Harbor Range Lights
Grand Marais, Alger County

These Lake Superior towers, also known as the Grand Marais Harbor of Refuge Inner and Outer Lights, date from 1895 and 1898, and both are still in use. The front, or outer range light is a white, skeletal steel tower, standing at 34 feet upon a concrete pier. The rear, or inner range light is also a white, skeletal tower, though it is constructed of concrete (not steel). This tower stands at 55 feet, and uses a fifth-order lens. Other structures include a sound signal building, and a two-story brick (over frame) keeper's dwelling. This light station is open to the public, and the Grand Marais Historical Society operates a museum within the keeper's dwelling.

Grand Traverse Light
Northport, Leelanau County

This lighthouse, situated on the Leelanau Peninsula on Lake Michigan, now serves as a museum (located within a state park). The beacon, which was in use from 1858 until 1972 (when it was replaced by a skeletal tower), consists of a nine-sided tower, constructed of brick, wood, and iron, that rises 47 feet above the roof of the 2.5-story keeper's dwelling (in the Midwest Victorian style). The structure is painted red, with black trim. The light had a height of focal plane of 50 feet above sea level. It originally used a fifth-order Fresnel lens and, later, a fourth-order Fresnel (which is on display in the museum). There is also a brick sound building (in the Flemish revival style), as well as a brick and metal oil house.

Granite Island Light
Marquette, Marquette County

First lit in 1869, the Granite Island Light is one of the oldest surviving lighthouses on Lake Superior. The light became less important to navigation in the 1920s, when ships ran less frequently between the island and the shore. It was succeeded by two steel towers—the first constructed in 1939, and the second in 1995. The historic light is a 40-foot, square granite tower, topped with a black lantern. The beacon originally used a fourth-order Fresnel lens, and it had a height of focal plane of 96 feet. A two-story granite and limestone keeper's house is attached to the tower. There is also a bell tower–style sound building, and a brick oil house. This lighthouse is now privately owned, and not open to the public.

Gravelly Shoal Light
Off Point Lookout, near Charity Island

This 65-foot, square art deco style, white concrete tower is a sibling of the Conneaut Harbor and Huron Harbor lights in Ohio. It is surmounted by a black steel skeletal radiobeacon tower, and mounted on a circular concrete crib. The tower was constructed in 1939. It has a fog horn, uses a 375 mm lens, and has a height of focal plane of 75 feet above sea level. This light was designed to be controlled by remote from Tawas Point, and there are no keeper's quarters. Managed by the U.S. Coast Guard, the site and tower are closed to the public.

Grays Reef Light
St. Ignace, Emmet County

The historic Grays Reef Light was constructed in 1936 and is still operational today. It consists of a 65-foot, octagonal, reinforced concrete and steel tower that rises above the square keeper's dwelling. The tower is white, with a black lantern. It uses a 190 mm optic and it has a height of focal plane of 82 feet above sea level. The original third-and-a-half-order Fresnel lens is now on display at the Harsha House Museum in Charlevoix, Michigan. The light was automated in 1976, and there is now a radiobeacon on site. The Grays Reef Light station is owned and managed by the U.S. Coast Guard, and it is not open to the public.

Grosse Ile North Channel Range Front Light
Grosse Ile, Wayne County

Located on the Detroit River, this light was in use from 1906 until 1963. The octagonal, white wooden tower stands at 50 feet upon a concrete pier. The rear range companion to this light was lost before 1940. This light station now functions as a museum, owned by the

Grosse Isle Historical Society, and it is open to the public during limited times. The keeper's house, a 2.5-story Victorian dwelling, is located off site and is privately owned. The Historical Society also owns the Detroit River Livingstone Channel original light towers, numbers 25 and 26, which can be viewed on the museum grounds.

Gull Rock Light
Copper Harbor, Keweenaw County

Gull Rock Light is a 46-foot, square yellow-brick tower that has been operational since 1867. The tower, which is attached to the two-story brick keeper's house, has a height of focal plane of 50 feet, and it currently uses a 250 mm optic. (The beacon's original fourth-order Fresnel lens is now on display at the Great Lakes Shipwreck Museum in Whitefish Point, MI.) This light is owned by the Gull Rock Lightkeepers and the Michigan Lighthouse Conservancy who are restoring it. It is not open to the public.

Harbor Beach Light
Harbor Beach, Huron County

This active lighthouse was first lit in 1885. The white tower is conical in shape and constructed of cast-iron (with a brick lining). It stands at 45 feet tall (54 feet above sea level), and uses a 190 mm lens. Originally, the tower used a fourth-order Fresnel. The keeper's quarters are integral to the tower. This light was automated in 1968. It is owned by the U.S. Coast Guard, and it is not open to the public.

Harsen's Island Range Lights
Harsen's Island, St. Clair River, near Lake St. Clair

Established in 1934, these lights are still managed by the U.S. Coast Guard although they were sold at auction in 2002. The private owner plans to restore them. and they are not open to the public. Both display a fixed green signal: the front range light is a 26-foot, cylindrical, steel tower; the rear range light is a 30-foot, cylindrical, steel, skeletal tower with a flared top, the bottom quarter of which is enclosed by steel plates.

Holland Harbor (South Pierhead) Light
See page 206

Huron Island Light
Skanee, Marquette County

This Lake Superior light station was originally established, in 1868, as a lifeboat station. The lighthouse was constructed in 1877. It is a square, granite and brick tower, which stands at 39 feet (197 feet

above sea level), is topped with a white lantern and is attached to a 1.5-story keeper's house. The lantern originally held a third-and-a-half-order Fresnel lens. Today, however, it uses an electric oscillator light. This light station is owned by the U.S. Fish & Wildlife Service, and it is open to the public.

Isle Royale Light
Houghton, Keweenaw County

This octagonal, red sandstone tower was constructed in 1875. It stands at 61 feet above the land and 72 feet above the water, and it originally used a fourth-order Fresnel lens. The light was automated in 1913 and it is still in use today. A two-story red sandstone keeper's house is attached to the tower. This light station is now part of the Isle Royale National Park, and the grounds are open to the public.

Keweenaw Waterway Lower Entrance Light
Jacobsville, Houghton County

Also known as the Portage Lake Lower Entrance Light, this 1920 light tower was automated in 1973 and is still operational. The octagonal, white brick and reinforced concrete tower stands at 31 feet, with a height of focal plane of 68 feet, and uses a fourth-order optic. The sound signal apparatus is integral to the tower, and there is also a radiobeacon on site. This lighthouse is owned and managed by the U.S. Coast Guard, and it is not open to the public.

Keweenaw Waterway Upper Entrance Light
Keweenaw Peninsula, Hancock

This 1950 cylindrical steel tower mounted atop a one-story concrete fog signal building has a height of focal plane of 82 feet, and it emits a white flash every 15 seconds. This light station was first established in 1874. The site and tower are closed to the public, but the light can be viewed from the adjacent F. J. McClain State Park.

Lake St. Clair Light
Lake St. Clair, Detroit

The Lake St. Clair Light marks a bend in a hidden channel that runs from the St. Clair River down to the Detroit River. The 53-foot tower, constructed in 1941, is a cylindrical steel structure on an octagonal concrete base.

Lansing Shoal Light
Naubinway, Mackinac County

This light was first lit in 1928. (Previous to its building, the station was served by lightships.) It is a 59-foot, square tower of reinforced concrete and steel. The tower was automated in 1976. Today, it is equipped with a 190 mm, solar-powered optic, and the third-order lens is on display at the Michigan State Historical Society in Lansing. The keeper's quarters are integral to the tower. This light station, which is owned by the U.S. Coast Guard, is not open to the public.

Little Rapids Cut Range Rear Light (Dwelling Only)

Mission Point, St. Mary's River, Sault Sainte Marie

The two-story keeper's house is all that remains of this 1895 lighthouse. The house was renovated in 2002. Also on site is a modern, 40-foot skeletal tower, which serves as the Bayfield Rock Range Rear Light. Managed by the U.S. Corps of Engineers, the site and the tower are closed to the public (but parking is available nearby).

Little Sable Point Light

See page 45

Little Traverse (Harbor Point) Light

Harbor Springs, Emmet County

Operational from 1884 until 1963 (when it was replaced by a skeletal tower), the Little Traverse Light is a square, 40-foot redbrick tower topped with a black lantern. The light used a fourth-order Fresnel lens. The two-story redbrick keeper's quarters are attached to the tower. Other structures include a wooden sound building and a summer kitchen (attached to the lighthouse by a covered portico). This lighthouse is now privately owned, and it is not open to the public.

Lower Nicolet West Range Front Light

Relocated to the north end of Neebish Island

Originally constructed at Windmill Point, Detroit, in 1907, this lighthouse was relocated to Neebish Island in 1931. It is a 55-foot, slender cylindrical steel tower, painted red. Next to it is the modern skeletal tower that replaced it in 1993.

Ludington North Breakwater Light

See page 225

Mackinac Point Light

Mackinaw City, Emmet and Cheboygan counties

Built of Cream City Brick in 1892, this handsome cylindrical tower, topped with a red-and-white lantern, adjoins the brick keeper's dwelling, which resembles a small castle. Deactivated in 1957, the light is now a museum, and visitors may climb the tower.

Manistee (North Pierhead) Light

See page 201

Manistique (East Breakwater) Light

See page 199

Manitou Island Light

Copper Harbor, Keweenaw County

This is an 80-foot, white iron skeletal tower (with a central column). Along with the light at Whitefish Point, this is the oldest skeletal tower on the Great Lakes. It played an important role in the growth of Michigan's copper industry. The beacon originally used a third-order Fresnel lens (today, a 190 mm optic). It was automated in 1978, and it has a height of focal plane of 81 feet above the sea. The keeper's dwelling is a two-story, rectangular wood-framed structure that is attached to the tower via an enclosed passageway. There is also a boathouse on site. This light station is currently owned by the Keweenaw Land Trust. Its grounds are open to the public.

Marquette Harbor Light

Marquette, Marquette County

This historic light tower was first lit in 1866. The square, redbrick tower stands at 40 feet tall, with a height of focal plane of 77 feet above sea level. It originally used a fourth-order Fresnel lens (now on display at the Marquette Maritime Museum), and today uses a DCB-24 optic. The two-story brick keeper's quarters are integral to the tower. This U.S. Coast Guard light station is leased by the Marquette Maritime Museum, which offers tours to the public.

Martin Reef Light

Cedarville, Mackinac County

Situated east of the straits of Mackinac, this 1927 beacon shines its fourth-order lens across Lake Huron at a height of focal plane of 65 feet above sea level. The square, 52-foot tower is constructed of reinforced concrete and steel and is painted white, with a red roof. It originally used a third-order Fresnel lens. The keeper's quarters are integral to the tower. This lighthouse is owned and managed by the U.S. Coast Guard, and it is not open to the public.

McGulpins Point Light

Mackinaw City, Emmet County

This beacon was operational from 1869 until 1906, when it was replaced by the Old Mackinac Point Light. Located at the south point of Michilmackinac Harbor, it is an octagonal, yellow-brick tower with no lantern. Attached to the tower is the original keeper's house, a two-story yellow-brick dwelling. This lighthouse now serves as a private residence, and it is not open to the public.

Mendota (Bete Grise) Light

See page 210

Menominee (North Pier) Light

Menominee, Menominee County

This Lake Michigan lighthouse was first lit in 1927. The octagonal, red cast-iron tower stands at 34 feet (focal plane 46 feet). It is set upon a white base and is topped with a black lantern that originally held a fourth-order lens. The light was automated in 1972. Today, it uses a 300 mm optic. The sound signal building was dismantled. The light is owned and managed by the U.S. Coast Guard.

Middle Island Light

Alpena, Alpena County

Located between Thunder Bay Island and Presque Isle, on Lake Huron, this restored 1905 lighthouse consists of a 71-foot, conical brick and stucco tower, which is attached to a service room. The tower is painted white, with an orange band in the middle. It originally used a fourth-order Fresnel lens, and it has a height of focal plane of 78 feet above sea level. The keeper's house is a 2.5-story brick duplex. There is also a brick sound building, an oil house, two brick privies, a woodshed/garage, and the ruins of a former lifesaving station. Owned by the U.S. Coast Guard and the Middle Island Lighthouse Keepers Association, this light station is open to the public by appointment.

Minneapolis Shoal Light

Escanaba, Delta County

First lit in 1935, the Minneapolis Shoal Light was automated in 1979 and is still operational today. The octagonal, steel and reinforced concrete tower stands at 70 feet and has a height of focal plane of 82 feet above sea level. The tower is cream-colored, and it is set upon a concrete pier, on a concrete crib. It is lit with a fourth-order Fresnel. The keeper's quarters are integral to the tower, which is owned and managed by the U.S. Coast Guard and is not open to the public.

Mission Point Light (Old)

Traverse City, Grand Traverse County

Operational from 1870 until 1933, this square wooden tower rises at 30 feet upon the 1.5-story wooden keeper's dwelling. It is painted white, with black trim. Other structures include a brick pump

house, a brick storage shed, a log house (dating from 1856), and a wood-frame garage. This lighthouse now functions as a private residence for the town parks caretaker. It is open to the public. The new light is a 20-foot, white, cylindrical, concrete tower on a square equipment room atop a circular crib.

Munising Range Lights

Munising, Alger County

First lit in 1908, both of these beacons are white, conical steel plate towers. The front range light stands at 58 feet, with a height of focal plane of 79 feet above sea level. It originally used a set of Adam & Westlake reflectors. Today, the front range light is lit by locomotive-style headlamps. The rear range stands at 33 feet, with a height of focal plane of 107 feet above sea level. This tower was originally equipped with locomotive headlamps. The keeper's house is a two-story brick and frame structure. Also on site is a square brick oil house with a stamped tin roof. This light station is owned by the National Park Service, and it is not open to the public.

Muskegon South Pierhead and Breakwater Lights

Muskegon, Muskegon County

The South Pierhead light is a 48-foot, red, conical cast-iron tower with a fourth-order Fresnel lens in its red lantern. The South Breakwater light is a conical, red cast-iron tower. It stands at 53 feet, with a height of focal plane of 70 feet above sea level, and it uses a 300 mm optic. Originally, the tower held a fourth-order Fresnel lens. There is no public access to these lights, but they may be viewed from Pere Maquette Park.

North Manitou Shoal Light

Glen Arbor, Leelanau County

This light tower replaced a lightship on Lake Michigan in 1935. The white, square steel tower stands at 63 feet atop the square keeper's house. Originally equipped with a fourth-order lens, the light now uses a DCB-24 lens and has a height of focal plane of 79 feet above sea level. The keeper's quarters are integral to the tower, and there is also a wooden boathouse and a radiobeacon on site. This lighthouse is owned and managed by the U.S. Coast Guard, and it is not open to the public. The light was automated in 1980.

Old Mackinac Point Light

Mackinaw City, Cheboygan County

This 1892 lighthouse grew out of a foghorn station, built in 1890. It was in use until 1957, when it was decommissioned with the construction of the Mackinac Bridge. Originally fitted with a fourth-order optic, the cylindrical, redbrick tower stands at 40 feet. The tower is attached to a two-story, "castle" type brick keeper's house. There is also a brick sound building on site. The Old Mackinac Point Light is now a museum, owned and managed by the Mackinac Island State Park Commission.

Ontonagon West Pierhead Light

Ontonagon (western side of the mouth of the Ontonagon River)

This light station was first established in 1875, and the current lighthouse dates from *c.* 1900. (The first light constructed at this station was relocated three times before being swept out to sea.) The active, square pyramidal skeletal tower (with an enclosed workroom beneath the lantern) has a height of focal plane of 31 feet above sea level, and it now uses a 300 mm lens. It was originally maintained by the keepers from the Ontonagon Light. Managed by the U.S. Army Corps of Engineers, this site and tower are closed to the public. The light can be viewed at a distance from the shore.

Ontonagon Light

Ontonagon, Ontonagon County

Located at the mouth of the Ontonagon River, on Lake Superior, this square, yellow-brick tower stands at 34 feet and is topped with a black lantern. The beacon was first lit in 1866, when it used a fifth-order Fresnel lens (which is now on display at the Ontonagon County Historical Society). Attached to the tower is a 1.5-story yellow-brick keeper's house, which was modified with a kitchen in 1890. Other structures include an oil house and a privy. The light was deactivated in 1964, and it is now used for Coast Guard auxiliary meetings and is a destination for historical tours.

Passage Island Light

Houghton, Keweenaw County

The Passage Island Light was important to the silver mining industry and the Canadian Grain Trade. Constructed in 1882, the octagonal fieldstone tower stands at 44 feet and has a white and red lantern. The light was automated in 1978. Originally equipped with a fourth-order Fresnel lens, it now uses a 190 mm lens, with a height of focal plane of 78 feet above the sea. The 1.5-story keeper's house is made of fieldstone, in the

Above: **Northwest elevation, Passage Island Light**

Norman Gothic style. There is also a fog signal building, constructed of corrugated metal, as well as a steel tramway and a tram winch house, a steel radio tower, a wooden helicopter landing pad, a boathouse, and docks. Owned by the U.S. Coast Guard, this light station is now part of a national park. The grounds are open to the public.

Peche (Peach) Island Range Rear Light

Relocated to Marine City

This lighthouse was active from 1908 until 1983. It is a 66-foot cast-iron tower, painted white. Originally located on a crib off of Peche Island (at the entrance to the Detroit River), the light was relocated in 1983 to Lighthouse Park, on the St. Clair River in Marine City. The site is open to the public, though the tower is closed.

Peninsula Point Light

Stonington Peninsula, Delta County

This square, unpainted, brick tower (1866) stands 40 feet high and has a black lantern. Deactivated in 1936, it is open to the public.

Petoskey Pierhead Light

Petoskey, Emmet County

A white, steel cylinder with square, red base on the west pierhead.

Pipe Island Light

Detour Village, St. Mary's River, Lake Superior

Originally constructed in 1888, this octagonal brick tower has had its lantern removed and replaced (in 1937) with a steel skeletal tower. The beacon is still in use today. It is not open to the public.

Poe Reef Light

Cheboygan, Mackinac County

Operational since 1929, the Poe Reef Light consists of a 60-foot, square concrete tower, painted with white and black bands and a red roof. It was originally fitted with a third-order optic, and now uses a 375 mm optic. The light's height of focal plane is 71 feet above the sea. A three-story keeper's dwelling is integral to the tower. This lighthouse is owned and managed by the U.S. Coast Guard, and it is not open to the public.

Point Betsie Light

See page 202

Point Iroquois Light

Bay Mills, Chippewa County

Situated on Lake Superior, this former guide to the St. Mary's River now functions as a museum. The 65-foot, conical brick tower is painted white, with a black lantern. First lit in 1871, the lantern originally held a fourth-order Fresnel lens, which was sent to the Smithsonian Institution in 1963. Another fourth-order lens, from the St. Martin's Reef Light, is now on display in the two-story brick (Cape Cod–style) keeper's dwelling. The tower was deactivated in 1971. Other structures include an assistant keeper's dwelling, and a boathouse.

Pointe Aux Barques Light

Port Hope, Huron County

Operational since 1857, this lighthouse now features a museum for the Thumb Area Bottom Preserve (located within the 1.5-story brick keeper's house, which is attached to the light tower), and the Pointe Aux Barques Reef is a popular spot for divers to view shipwrecks. The 89-foot, conical brick tower is painted white, with black and red trim. It originally used a third-order Fresnel lens and, today, uses a DCB-224 optic (focal plane 93 feet). Other structures include a red iron oil house, a garage, and a redbrick assistant keeper's dwelling (added in 1933). This light station is open to the public.

Port Austin Reef Light

Port Austin, Huron County

First lit in 1878, this light is a 60-foot, square buff tower, constructed of yellow brick. Originally fitted with a fourth-order Fresnel lens, the tower now uses a 200 mm glass optic (focal plane 76 feet). The brick sound signal building, built in 1899, is attached to the tower. This light is owned by the U.S. Coast Guard, on lease to Port Austin Reef Light Association. It is not open to the public.

Port Sanilac Light

See page 218

Portage River (Jacobsville) Light

Jacobsville, Houghton County

This lighthouse was in use from 1870 until 1900. The 45-foot, conical, brick tower is topped with a red lantern. It was originally equipped with a fifth-order Fresnel lens. There is a one-story brick keeper's dwelling. This lighthouse is now a bed-and-breakfast inn.

Poverty Island Light

Fairport, Delta County

Poverty Island is located on Lake Michigan. The 1874 lighthouse was deactivated in 1976 (when it was replaced by a nearby skeletal tower), and then relit in 1982. It is a white, conical brick tower, standing at 60 feet above land and 80 feet above the sea, and with no lantern. The tower was originally equipped with a fourth-order lens. Today, it uses a 300 mm optic. The 1.5-story keeper's dwelling is also constructed of brick (with a wood frame). There are a number of other minor buildings, and a pier. Now located within a national wildlife refuge, this lighthouse is not open to the public.

Presque Isle Harbor Breakwater Light

Marquette Harbor, Lake Superior

The Presque Isle Harbor Breakwater Light, a cylindrical steel and concrete tower, stands at the end of a 2,600-foot breakwater at the end of Presque Isle Park. It was constructed in 1941 and is still active today. The grounds of the light tower are open to the public.

Presque Isle Lights

Presque Isle, Presque Isle County

This light station is now a museum, and one of the towers still functions as an active aid to navigation. The first Presque Isle Light, which was operational from 1840 until 1871, is a 38-foot, white conical tower. The lower two-thirds of the tower is constructed of stone, and the upper third is brick. This light used a fourth-order lens. The second tower was first lit in 1871, and it is still in use. It is a conical, white brick tower, standing at 109 feet, with a height of focal plane of 113 feet above sea level. This tower retains the use of its original third-order Fresnel lens. A two-story (Cape Cod–style) brick keeper's dwelling was rebuilt in 1939, and this now houses a historical museum and gift shop, open from mid-May to mid-September.

Rock Harbor Light

Houghton, Keweenaw County

The Rock Harbor is located on Middle Island Passage, on Lake Superior. The cylindrical, brick and stone tower was operational from 1855 until 1879, and it was important to the development of the copper industry. The tower stands at 50 feet, with a height of focal plane of 70 feet above sea level. It was originally equipped with a fourth-order Fresnel lens. Attached to the tower is a 1.5-story rubble-stone keeper's house. The light was abandoned from 1859 until 1875. It is currently part of a national park.

Rock of Ages Light

Houghton, Keweenaw County

Situated off of Isle Royale, on Lake Superior, the building of the Rock of Ages Light was a major engineering feat because of its isolated location. Now part of a national park, the 1908 lighthouse is a 117-foot, cylindrical ("bottle-shaped") tower of steel, masonry, and concrete. It is painted white, with a black base and lantern. It originally used a second-order revolving Fresnel lens (now on exhibit within the park). The light was automated in 1978. It has a height of focal plane of 130 feet above the sea, and today it uses a 190 mm optic. The keeper's quarters are integral to the tower.

Above: Rock of Ages Light

Round Island Light

See page 206

Round Island Light (St. Mary's River Light)

Raber, Chippewa County

This 35-foot, square wooden tower was first lit in 1892. The structure is covered in brown shingles, with white trim, and is topped by a black lantern (that is 40 feet above sea level). The two-story wooden keeper's quarters are integral to the tower. This light station now serves as a private summer home, and it is not open to the public. A modern, pole tower has been constructed nearby.

Round Island Passage Light

Mackinac Island, Mackinac County

The Round Island Passage Light was first lit in 1948, was automated in 1973, and is still operational. The white skeletal tower, of reinforced concrete, rises 60 feet atop a red keeper's house. The tower originally used a sealed beam optic. Today it uses a 190 mm optic, and it has a height of focal plane of 71 feet above sea level. There is also a radiobeacon on site. The historic lighthouse is owned and managed by the U.S. Coast Guard, and it is not open to the public.

Saginaw River (Range Rear) Light

Bay City, Bay County

Located at the entrance to the Saginaw River, this square brick tower (operational 1876–1960) stands at 61 feet and is painted white, with black trim. It had a height of focal plane of 77 feet above sea level. This lighthouse is now owned by Dow Chemical Company and is currently undergoing restoration. It is not open to the public.

Sand Hills Light

Eagle River, Keweenaw County

First lit in 1919, this lighthouse was used as a barracks during World War II. The square, 91-foot tower is constructed of yellow brick and is attached to a two-story yellow-brick keeper's house. Other structures include a masonry/stucco sound building, an oil house, a garage, a barracks building, and a concrete breakwater. The light was discontinued in 1954, and its original lens, a fourth-order Fresnel, is now on display at the Dossin Great Lakes Museum in Detroit. The lighthouse now operates as a bed-and-breakfast inn.

Sand Point (Baraga) Light

Baraga, Baraga County

The Sand Point (Baraga) Light is a square, unpainted brick tower, topped with a white lantern. It was constructed in 1878. The tower is attached to its keeper's house, a two-story brick structure. This historic lighthouse is now owned by the Keweenaw Bay Indian Community, and it is not open to the public. There is now a modern, skeletal tower nearby.

Sand Point (Escanaba) Light

Escanaba, Delta County

This beacon was first operational from 1867 until 1939 (when it was replaced by an offshore crib). The tower's lantern was removed at the time of its deactivation, and the structure was used as Coast Guard housing until 1985. In 1989, the lantern was replaced and relit with a fourth-order lens. Standing at 41 feet (with a height of focal plane of 44 feet above sea level), it is a square, white brick tower with a black, octagonal lantern. A 1.5-story brick keeper's house is attached to the tower. Owned by the U.S. Coast Guard, on lease to the Delta County Historical Society, this light now functions as a museum.

Seul Choix Pointe Light

Gulliver, Schoolcraft County

Seul Choix Pointe is the only harbor of refuge in this part of Lake Michigan. The historic lighthouse, which dates from 1895, is a conical, white brick tower, standing at 78 feet with a height of focal plane of 80 feet above sea level. The light originally used a third-order Fresnel lens. It was automated in 1972, and now uses a DCB-24 optic. The two-story brick keeper's house (in the gable style) was modified with an assistant keeper's dwelling in 1925. There is also a redbrick sound building, two redbrick oil houses, a barn, a workshop, a garage (formerly, a boathouse), a second assistant keeper's house, two outhouses, and a dock. This light station now functions as an active aid to navigation, as a museum, and as part of a public park. This lighthouse was replaced by an offshore steel crib beacon.

Six Mile Point Range Rear Light

Relocated to the Les Cheneaux Historical Maritime Museum, Cedarville

This sleek, white, tapered cylindrical tower was originally built on the St. Mary's River, south of Mission Point. It probably dates from around 1930, when several range lights of this design were built along the St. Mary's River. The structure is now on display at the Les Cheneaux Historical Maritime Museum, in Cedarville.

Skillagalee (Ile Aux Galets) Light

Cross Village, Emmet County

This Lake Michigan beacon has been operational since 1888. It is a 58-foot, octagonal brick tower, painted white and topped with a black lantern. Originally installed with a fourth-order Fresnel lens, the light now uses a 300 mm optic. All other structures on the site have been razed (including the sound building and the keeper's house). The lighthouse is owned and managed by the U.S. Coast Guard. It is not open to the public.

South Fox Island Light

Traverse City, Leelanau County

South Fox Island is located on the approach to the Straits of Mackinac, on Lake Michigan. Originally built in 1905 at Sapelo Island, Georgia, this 60-foot, skeletal steel tower with black lantern was moved in 1934 to replace the old lighthouse of 1868 which still stands nearby. Badly deteriorating, the former tower is a 30-foot, square, brick tower, painted white with red trim. It is owned by the Michigan Department of Natural Resources and is not open to the public.

South Haven South Pierhead Light

See page 209

South Manitou Island Light

Leeland, Leelanau County

This hexagonal, wooden tower stands at 54 feet upon a screw-pile foundation, and it is attached to a 2.5-story yellow-brick keeper's house via a covered passageway. The dwelling is painted white, and the piles are red. The tower was first lit in 1885, and it was deactivated in 1967. Other structures on site include a sound building and a whistle shed. This lighthouse is now owned and managed by the National Park Service, and it currently functions as a park exhibit.

Spectacle Reef Light

Bois Blanc Island, Cheboygan County

First lit in 1874, the Spectacle Reef Light is considered the best specimen of monolithic stone masonry in the United States. It stands on a submerged limestone reef, off the eastern end of the Straits of Mackinaw. The conical limestone tower stands at 93 feet, or 86 feet above sea level. It is naturally colored, and trimmed in red. The light's original second-order Fresnel is now on display at the Great Lakes Historical Society Museum in Vermillion, OH. The light was automated in 1972, and it now uses a solar-powered optic. The keeper's quarters are integral to the tower, and a brick sound signal building is attached. There is also an oil house, and a storage building. The light is owned by the U.S. Coast Guard, and it is not open to the public.

Squaw Island Light

Gladstone, Emmet County

Squaw Island is located north of Beaver Island, on Lake Michigan. The Squaw Island Light dates from 1892. It is an octagonal redbrick tower, unpainted, and topped with a black lantern. The tower is attached to the two-story redbrick keeper's dwelling. The lighthouse is now privately owned, and it is not open to the public.

St. Clair Flats S. Channel Range Lights (Old)

Algonac, St. Clair County

These lighthouses are situated off of Harsens Island, on Lake St. Clair. The rear range tower was in use from 1859 until 1907. It is a 40-foot, conical, brick/block structure, with a height of focal plane of 30 feet above sea level. It originally used a fourth-order lens. The tower was automated in 1970. The front range tower also dates from 1859, and it is still operational today. This light consists of a 17-foot, conical redbrick tower, with a height of focal plane of 20 feet above sea level. It uses a sixth-order Fresnel lens. The keeper's house, which was formerly attached to the rear range tower, was destroyed in the early 1930s. Ownership of this pair of lights transferred from the U.S. Coast Guard to the Save Our South Channel Lights Association in 2004. They are not open to the public.

St. Helena Island Light
St. Ignace, Mackinac County

The St. Helena Island Light was first lit in 1873. It consists of a 71-foot, conical, white brick tower, topped with a red lantern. It originally used a third-and-a-half-order Fresnel lens. The light was automated in 1922, and it is still operational today, with a 250 mm optic. The keeper's house is a 1.5-story brick cottage. Other structures include an oil house and a privy. An assistant keeper's house and a boathouse were both demolished. In addition to being an active guide to navigation, this light station is also a maritime heritage education center. It is open to the public.

St. James (Beaver Harbor) Light
St. James, Charlevoix County

This 41-foot, cylindrical, white brick tower (which was originally painted yellow) has a height of focal plane of 38 feet above sea level, and uses a fourth-order Fresnel lens. This light was first lit in 1870, and it was automated in 1927. The keeper's dwelling was dismantled during World War II. The lighthouse is owned by the U.S. Coast Guard, on lease to the Town of St. James. It is not open to the public.

St. Joseph North Pierhead Lights
See page 230

St. Martin Island Light
Fairport, Delta County

This 1905 lighthouse is no longer in use. Located on St. Martin Island, on Lake Michigan, it consists of a 75-foot, hexagonal exoskeletal tower, constructed of reinforced concrete and painted white, with a black lantern. It originally used a fourth-order Fresnel lens (now on display at the Point Iriquois Light station's keeper's dwelling) and, later, a 190 mm lens. There is also a brick sound building, as well as a 2.5-story brick keeper's house, and an oil house. The light station is not open to the public.

St. Marys River Upper Range Rear Light
Brimley, Chippewa County

Formerly host to a pair of lights (of the second, or front range tower, only the foundation survives), this light station now consists of a pyramidal, white wooden tower, standing at 30 feet upon piling and grillage piers, and its Victorian keeper's house, a two-story wood-frame dwelling. This 1887 lighthouse is now abandoned. It is privately owned, and it is not open to the public.

Stannard Rock Light
Manitou Island, Marquette County

Because of the difficulty in constructing this light (which sits upon a protective, concrete- and stone-filled crib), the Stannard Rock Light is considered one of the top ten engineering feats in the United States. First lit in 1882, this is a 110-foot, conical, dressed stone tower. It is topped with a black lantern that originally held a second-order Fresnel lens. (The Fresnel is now on display at the Marquette Maritime Museum.) The tower was later fitted with a 300 mm lens, and it had a height of focal plane of 102 feet above sea level. The keeper's quarters are integral to the tower. The lighthouse is owned by the U.S. Coast Guard, and it is not open to the public.

Sturgeon Point Light
Harrisville, Alcona County

The Sturgeon Point Light, on Lake Huron, has been in use since 1869. It is a conical, brick tower, painted white, with red trim, and standing at 71 feet. It has a height of focal plane of 69 feet above sea level. The tower originally used a sixth-order Fresnel, and it now retains the third-and-a-half-order lens that it has used since 1889. It was automated in 1939. The two-story keeper's house is constructed of limestone and brick, in the Cape Cod style. There is also an original brick privy on site. In addition to operating as an active aid to navigation, this light station now functions as a museum (operated by the Alcona Historical Society).

Tawas Point (Ottawa Point) Light
See page 226

Thunder Bay Island Light
Alpena, Alpena County

First lit in 1832, this operational lighthouse consists of a conical, white brick tower, topped with a red lantern. In 1857, the tower was heightened to its current 50 feet. It originally used a fourth-order Fresnel lens. The light was automated in

1980, and it is now equipped with a 190 mm optic. Attached to the tower is the rectangular keeper's house, a two-story yellow-brick structure. There is also a brick sound building, an oil house, a storage building, a boathouse, and a dock (on the west side of the island). The light is now part of a national wildlife refuge that provides nesting for colonial migratory birds. It is not open to the public.

Waugoshance Light

Waugoshance Island, Emmet County

Waugoshance Island is located on Lake Michigan. Its timber crib foundation (filled with stone) was the first major crib structure built for a lighthouse on the Great Lakes. The 76-foot, conical tower was constructed of brick, and encased in iron in 1883. It originally used a birdcage lantern that held a fourth-order Fresnel lens. The keeper's quarters, which are integral to the tower, are now a burned out shell. The light was operational from 1851 until 1912 (when it was replaced by the White Shoal and Grays Reef lights). Owned by the U.S. Coast Guard, the abandoned station is not open to the public.

Wawatam Lighthouse

St. Ignace, Mackinac County

Also known as St. Ignace Lighthouse, this 52-foot, white, hexagonal tower was a decoration at a highway rest stop until it was dismantled in 2004. It was gifted to the city and reassembled at the Wawatam Dock in 2006 to serve as a guide for the city marina.

White River Light

Fruitland, Muskegon County

Owned by the Fruitland Township, this light station now functions as a museum. The 38-foot, limestone tower was in use from 1875 until 1960. It is octagonal in shape, and topped with a black lantern. The beacon's original fourth-order Fresnel lens is on display in the museum—within the 1.5-story limestone keeper's dwelling. Other structures include an oil house, a garage, and a workshop/storage building. A lifesaving station was established, across the channel from the light, in 1875.

White Shoal Light

Mackinaw City, Emmet County

Situated northwest of Waugoshance Island, on Lake Michigan, this light station was established in 1891 with a lightship. (It was one of the first three lightship stations on the Great Lakes.) The tower, which dates from 1910 and is still in use, is unique, as it is the only red-and-white striped (barber pole–style) tower in the United States. It is conical in shape, stands at 121 feet, and is constructed of terra cotta and steel (with a brick lining). The light was automated in 1976. It uses a 190 mm optic, with a height of focal plane of 125 feet above the sea. The beacon's original second-order Fresnel lens is on display at the Whitefish Point Light. The keeper's quarters are integral to the tower. This lighthouse is owned and managed by the U.S. Coast Guard, and it is not open to the public.

Whitefish Point Light

Whitefish, Chippewa County

This 1861 lighthouse consists of a 76-foot, skeletal cast-iron tower, painted white, with a red roof, and a two-story keeper's dwelling which was modified in 1894 and 1911. It originally used a third-order Fresnel, and now uses a DCB-24 optic (automated 1970).

William Livingstone Memorial

Belle Isle, Detroit

This ornate white marble beacon was constructed in 1929, to honor the late William Livingstone, president of the Lake Carriers' Association from 1902 until 1925 (the year of his death). The memorial has a white flashing light that is visible, to the east, for 16 miles.

Windmill Point Light

Detroit (at the entrance to the Detroit River from Lake St. Clair)

This beacon marks the north side of the Detroit River entrance. The first light was built at this location in 1838, and it was rebuilt in 1866, 1875, and 1891. The present structure, a white, conical tower encased in steel plates, was constructed in 1933. It radiates a white flashing light over Lake St. Clair, at a height of focal plane of 42 feet. The light is located in Detroit Mariners Park.

Commissioned in 1921, the *Huron* served as a relief vessel for other Great Lakes lightships. After 1940 this was the only lightship on the Great Lakes and the only lightship to keep its post during World War II. Retired from service in 1970, she now stands in Pine Grove Park in Port Huron. *See* pages 248–249.

Minnesota

Duluth Harbor North Breakwater Light
Duluth, St. Louis County

This beacon has been lighting the way for ships on Lake Superior since 1910. It is a cylindrical, steel and cast-iron tower, 37 feet tall, on a concrete breakwater foundation. The tower is painted white, with a black tower and base. It uses a fifth-order Fresnel lens, with a height of focal plane of 46 feet above the sea. The light is owned and managed by the U.S. Coast Guard, and it is not open to the public.

Duluth South Breakwater Lights
Duluth, St. Louis County

Dating from 1901, this pair of towers was very important to the development of Duluth as a port. The inner light is one of the oldest skeletal towers on Lake Superior. Standing at 67 feet, it is steel framed, with a central black stairwell, and it is topped with a white, iron lantern. The tower uses a fifth-order Fresnel lens, with a height of focal plane of 68 feet above sea level. The outer light consists of a cylindrical brick tower that rises 35 feet atop its keeper's house. It is painted white, with a red roof. The light was automated in 1976. It uses a fourth-order lens and has a height of focal plane of 44 feet above sea level. These lights are owned and managed by the U.S. Coast Guard, and they are not open to the public.

Grand Marais Light
Grand Marais, Cook County

The historic Grand Marais Light has been operational since 1922. It is a 34-foot white, skeletal tower, constructed of steel and set upon a concrete pier. The tower is equipped with a fifth-order optic, and it has a height of focal plane of 48 feet above sea level. There is also a radiobeacon on site. This light station is owned and managed by the U.S. Coast Guard and the Cook County Historical Society. Its grounds are open to the public.

Minnesota Point Light (Ruins)
Duluth, west side of Superior Entry

Inactive since 1885, all that now remains of this 1858 lighthouse is a ruined redbrick tower that is truncated about halfway up. The keeper's cottage-style dwelling was attached to the tower. The structure is located on the west side of Superior Entry, at the entrance to the harbor of Superior. The site is open to the public.

Above: **Minnesota Point Light, 1934**

Split Rock Light
See pages 93 and 245

Two Harbors East Breakwater Light
Two Harbors

First lit in 1897, this is an active, 25-foot, square pyramidal steel skeleton tower with a workroom below the lantern. The structure is painted white, and the lantern roof is painted red. It is located at the end of the breakwater near the Two Harbors light station. Managed by the U.S. Coast Guard, the site and tower are closed to the public.

Two Harbors Light
Two Harbors, Lake County

First lit in 1892, the Two Harbors Light is situated between the Agate and Burlington bays, and it played an important role in the development of the Mesabi Range iron industry. The beacon is a 49-foot, square brick tower, on a stone foundation. It is painted red, with white trim. The light originally used a fourth-order Fresnel lens, which is now on display at the Inland Seas Museum in Vermillion, OH. Since 1970, the light has been equipped with a DCB-224 optic (focal plane 78 feet). The tower was automated in 1982. Attached to the tower is the keeper's house, a two-story red-brick dwelling. This light station is also serves as a museum and a bed-and-breakfast inn.

Ohio

Ashtabula Harbor Light

Ashtabula, Ashtabula County

This light station was established at the entrance to Ashtabula Harbor, on Lake Erie, in 1836. The current tower dates from 1905. During a winter storm in 1928, the 40-foot beacon was completely covered by ice, and the two keepers had to thaw the door and tunnel their way out through ice that was five feet thick in places. The light is still operational, and it also serves as a museum. The tower was enlarged and moved to its present location in 1916. It is a cylindrical, white steel structure (with iron plating and black trim), that rises atop a square house. It originally used a fourth-order Fresnel lens, which was removed in 1995 and placed in the museum.

Cleveland Harbor Pierhead Lights

Cleveland, Cuyahoga County

These 1911 Lake Erie lighthouses are still in use. The west tower consists of a 67-foot, conical tower of cast iron, brick, and wood. The structure is painted white, and is topped with a black lantern. The beacon's original optic was a fourth-order Fresnel lens, and it has a height of focal plane of 63 feet above sea level. This light was automated in 1965. The east light, a conical, white iron tower with a black lantern, stands at 25 feet (with a height of focal plane of 31 feet above sea level). It originally used a fourth-order Fresnel lens, and now uses a 300 mm solar-powered optic. The keeper's quarters are integral to the west tower, and a steel sound building is attached. A tall white cylinder supports a modern optic as Cleveland East Entrance Light. These lights are owned by the U.S. Coast Guard and are not open to the public.

Conneaut Harbor West Breakwater Light

Conneaut, Ashtabula County

Located at the entrance to the Conneaut River, on Lake Erie, this 1936 light consists of a 60-foot, steel pyramid, painted white with a black middle band, and without a lantern. The light was automated in the early 1970s. It has a height of focal plane of 80 feet above sea level, and uses a 375 mm optic. The 1.5-story keeper's house is a T-shaped structure that was modified to a duplex in 1905. The light is based on a prototype "Remote Control Pierhead Station for the Great Lakes" that was designed in 1934, and there is a one-story yellow-brick control building that housed an auxiliary generator and was used to monitor the light. The U.S. Coast Guard owns the tower, and the keeper's house and the control building are privately owned. This station is not open to the public.

Fairport Harbor West Breakwater Light

Fairport Harbor, Lake County

Built in 1925, this square, brick and steel tower stands at 42 feet, with a height of focal plane of 56 feet above the sea. The tower is painted white, with a red roof, and it is attached to the two-story keeper's dwelling. The beacon originally used a fourth-order Fresnel. Today, however, it uses a 300 mm optic. There is also a radiobeacon on site. Owned and managed by the U.S. Coast Guard, this light station is not open to the public.

Grand River (Fairport Harbor) Light

Fairport Harbor, Lake County

Operational from 1871 until 1925, this Lake Erie lighthouse has served as a museum since 1945. The conical, sandstone and brick tower stands at 69 feet. The tower retains its original, third-order Fresnel lens, and it has a height of focal plane of 102 feet above sea level. A two-story brick and stone keeper's house is in the federal style. The light station/museum is owned and operated by the Village of Fairport Harbor and the Fairport Harbor Historical Society.

Huron Harbor Light

Huron, Erie County

First lit in 1936, this Lake Erie light was automated in 1972 and is still operational. It consists of a 72-foot, white, pyramidal steel tower without a lantern. The beacon is fitted with a 375 mm optic, and it has a height of focal plane of 80 feet above sea level. There is no keeper's house, as the keeper (when there was one) operated the light by remote control from a small, brick-faced station on the shore. There is a radiobeacon on site. This light station is owned and managed by the U.S. Coast Guard. It is not open to the public.

Lorain Light

Lorain, Lorain County

Situated on the West Harbor Breakwater of Lake Erie, the Lorain Light was in use from 1917 until 1966, when it was replaced by a light on the new outer breakwater wall. The historic tower is square in shape and stands at 51 feet. It is constructed of concrete and steel, and is painted white, with red trim. The tower was originally equipped with a fourth-order Fresnel lens, and it had a height of focal plane of 60 feet above the sea. The keeper's quarters are integral to the tower. This light is now a community landmark, owned by the Port of Lorain Foundation, Inc. The tower is not open to the public.

Marblehead Light
(Formerly Sandusky Bay Light)
Marblehead, Ottawa County

This 1821 beacon is located at the entrance to Sandusky Bay, on Lake Erie. The lighthouse is a 65-foot, conical limestone tower, painted white, with red trim. It originally used a system of 13 lamps and reflectors. A subsequent third-order lens is now at the Marblehead Coast Guard station. The light was automated in 1958 and it was equipped with a plastic beacon in 1969. A two-story Victorian keeper's house dates from 1880. Other structures include a barn and an outhouse (on the adjacent property). Owned by the Ohio Department of Natural Resources, this light is open to the public. The Ottawa County Historical Society owns the original 1823 keeper's house, a one-story fieldstone structure, located three miles from the light.

South Bass Island Light
Put-In-Bay, Ottawa County

The South Bass Island Light was in use from 1897 until 1962. The square, redbrick tower stands at 60 feet and is topped with a white, 10-sided lantern. It originally used a fourth-order lens (focal plane 74 feet; now on display at the Lake Erie Historical Society Museum, on South Bass Island). The 2.5-story brick keeper's dwelling is in the Queen Anne style. Other structures include a wood-frame barn/chicken house and an iron storage house (both from 1899). The historic tower is now part of a biological research facility, owned by the Ohio State University. It is not open to the public. A modern, white skeletal tower was erected nearby (and is still in use).

Toledo Harbor Light
Harbor View, Lucas County

First lit in 1904, the Toledo Harbor Light was automated in 1965 and is still operational. It is a conical, 69-foot tower, constructed of brick and steel. The tower is dark in color, and it rises from a buff, three-story Romanesque keeper's dwelling. A brick and steel sound building is attached to the structure. The light is owned and managed by the U.S. Coast Guard, and it is not open to the public. It retains its original third-and-one-half-order lens.

The 352-foot Perry Memorial (1915) on South Bass Island commemorates the Battle of Lake Erie in the War of 1812. Its pink granite column is topped with a bronze urn, from which shines an alternating signal.

Vermillion Light was raised in 1991 at the Inland Seas Maritime Museum as a replica of the 1877 lighthouse that once stood in the harbor. It is a 16-foot, white-and-red, octagonal, steel tower.

West Sister Island Light
West Sister Island, Lucas County

West Sister Island is located at the entrance to Maumee Bay, at the western end of Lake Erie. The 1848 tower, which is still operational, is among the oldest lighthouses still standing on the Great Lakes, and it played an important role in the growth of shipping in this region. At 55 feet tall (focal plane 57 feet), the white limestone and brick tower is conical in shape, with a black balcony. It has no lantern. It originally used a fourth-order lens, and now uses a 300 mm optic. The tower was renovated in 1868, and it was automated in 1937. The keeper's dwelling was removed in 1945. Owned and managed by the U.S. Coast Guard, this lighthouse is not open to the public.

Wisconsin

Algoma North Pierhead Light
See pages 208–209

Ashland (Harbor) Breakwater Light
Ashland, Ashland & Bayfield Counties

Built in 1915, this light is located at the end of a detached breakwater that extends from near Ashland far out into Chequamegon Bay. The structure is made of reinforced concrete and steel; it is white with a black lantern and stands 58 feet high. The upper part of the tower is cylindrical, the main section, hexagonal. A keeper's dwelling and a boathouse were built onshore in 1916. It is an active aid to navigation but not open to the public.

Asylum Point Light
Asylum Point County Park, Oshkosh, Lake Winnebago

A 31-foot conical stone tower dating from 1940. The grounds are open to the public.

Bailey's Harbor Light
Bailey's Harbor, Door Peninsula, Lake Michigan

Operational from the early 1850s until 1869, this lighthouse consists of a keeper's house attached to a 52-foot rubble-stone tower with a rare birdcage-style lantern. It was replaced by the Bailey's Harbor Range Lights (no longer operational), and it is now a private residence.

Boyer Bluff Light
Washington Island, off the tip of Door Peninsula

Located on the northwest corner of the island, this 80-foot, square-pyramidal steel skeletal tower has a focal-plane height of 220 feet and is an active aid to navigation (white flash every 6 seconds).

Bray's Point (Rockwell) Light
Bray's Point, near downtown Oshkosh

A privately maintained lighthouse, the Bray's Point Light was constructed in 1909. It consists of a 42-foot, octagonal cylindrical brick tower (naturally cream-colored) with an ornate (open) iron lantern.

Calumet Harbor Light
Columbia Park, near Pipe

This 70-foot, square-pyramidal, steel skeletal tower was originally used as a water tower at the Fond du Lac table factory. It was moved to its present location in 1936 and is now a private navigational aid and observation tower. A smaller, hourglass-shaped tower once stood nearby, but was removed in 2003. The park is open to the public.

Cana Island Light
Cana Island, eastern Door Peninsula

Built of Cream City brick c. 1870, this 81-foot, white conical tower was encased in steel in 1902. The light is still active, and the attached brick keeper's quarters and oil house serve as a museum. A rock causeway (sometimes flooded) for pedestrians connects the island to the mainland.

Chamber's Island Light
Chamber's Island

This lighthouse (1868) is an octagonal Cream City brick tower (lantern removed) integrated with the brick keeper's house. Deactivated in 1961, it is occasionally open for public tours in the summer and fall.

Chequamegon Point Light
Bayfield, Bayfield County

Built in 1896, this light was moved away from the shore by 150 feet in 1987 and replaced by a cylindrical tower nearby. Standing 42 feet tall, this tower is made of iron, is white, square-pyramidal

in shape, and has an enclosed workroom on the lower level. It is not operational and now abandoned. The light is within park boundaries and the grounds are accessible to the public.

Devils Island Light
Bayfield, Bayfield County

This square-pyramidal cast-iron tower, standing 71 feet tall, was built in 1898. There is an 1891 Queen Anne–style keeper's house nearby. An active aid to navigation, and an attraction in a national park, the tower is open to the public in summer.

Dunlap Reef Range Rear Light
Relocated to Sturgeon Bay, Door Peninsula

This lighthouse was originally built in 1881, on a limestone and timber crib, north of the Michigan Street Bridge in Sturgeon Bay. It consisted of a two-story frame keeper's house, with a square cylindrical frame tower mounted on the roof. The beacon was deactivated in 1925. The following year, the house (with the tower removed) was relocated to 400 South Fourth Avenue, where it is now a private residence.

Eagle Bluff Light
See page 230

Fond du Lac (Lakeside Park) Light
Lakeside Park, downtown Fond du Lac

Dating from 1933, this Lake Winnebago lighthouse (still active today) is open to the public in the summer for self-guided tours from 8 A.M. until dusk. The white, octagonal wooden tower stands at 56 feet and displays a flashing red light.

Grassy Island Range Lights
Relocated to the east side of the Fox River mouth, Green Bay

By the 1870s, Green Bay was booming as the world's largest shingle market. To guide ships through the newly dredged channel, this pair of range lights was constructed on a wooden pier in 1872. Both were built of wood and painted white, each with an octagonal cast-iron lantern and a fixed white light. The front range light stood at 25 feet, and the rear at approximately 35 feet. There was also a detached keeper's dwelling, an oil storage building, a boathouse, and a dock. Over the years, the channel was widened and new technological developments made the lights obsolete. In 1966, when the lights were scheduled for destruction, members of the Green Bay Yacht Club arranged for the lights to be relocated to the Yacht Club property, on the east side of the river, where they still stand today.

Green Bay Harbor Entrance Light

Green Bay (north of the entrance to Green Bay), Lake Michigan

This is a cylindrical steel art deco tower, standing on a concrete caisson. Built in 1935, the beacon is still active, with a height of focal plane of 72 feet above sea level. Managed by the U.S. Coast Guard, this light is not open to the public.

Gull Island Light

Off Michigan Island, Lake Superior

In 1928, this skeletal iron structure was constructed as an unmanned light tower on Gull Island. It stands at 50 feet (with a height of focal plane of 55 feet above sea level) and is painted black (to increase its effectiveness as a daymarker). The tower was originally fitted with a 375 mm acetylene powered light and was equipped with an automatic sun valve so that it could operate untended. The light was electrified in the 1950s, and today uses a 250 mm solar-powered optic.

Kenosha (Southport) Light

Simmons Island, Kenosha, Kenosha County

First lit in 1866, this 55-foot conical tower made of Milwaukee's Cream City brick was deactivated in 1906 but relit in 1996 as a private aid to navigation. The grounds are open to the public.

Kenosha Pierhead/North Breakwater Lights

Kenosha, Kenosha County

A 1906 red, conical cast-iron tower replaced Kenosha Light and is still active (focal plane 50 feet). A white cylinder with green band stands on the opposite pier.

Kevich Light

Port Ulao, Grafton, Ozaukee County

A 40-foot white stucco-clad tower with black lantern and attached residence, this light was built by the Bennett family in 1981 atop a 120-foot bluff and is a certified navigational aid. Its alternating white light has a focal-plane height of 160 feet above sea level. The light is privately maintained and is not open to the public.

Kewaunee Pierhead Light

Kewaunee, Kewaunee County

This white, steel, rectangular fog-signal building was built in 1909 beside a front range light (1891) at the end of a breakwater on the north side of the Kewaunee River entrance. In 1931, the range light was removed and its red-roofed lantern and fifth-order Fresnel lens were moved onto a 43-foot, white, square steel tower that had been newly constructed on the roof of the fog-signal building. Today, the original lens still shines its fixed white light (focal plane 45 feet). It is closed to the public. The Breakwater light, also at Kewaunee River entrance, is a 37-foot, white, cylindrical tower with red band.

LaPointe (Long Island) Light

Bayfield, Bayfield County

This light was built in 1896 to replace a wooden tower of 1858. The ruins of the old light and its keeper's dwelling still remain near the new tower. The present light is a 65-foot, white skeletal tower with central column. This is one of the oldest skeletal lights on the Great Lakes. The grounds are open to the public.

Long Tail Point Light (Ruins)

Green Bay, Lake Michigan

Operational from 1849 until 1859, this now ruined, 65-foot stone tower is located near the end of Long Tail Point, three miles north of the city of Green Bay. Two later lighthouses constructed on the point have completely disappeared. Accessible only by boat, this abandoned light station is not open to the public.

Manitowoc Breakwater Light

Manitowoc, Lake Michigan

Also known as Manitowoc Pierhead Light, this 40-foot, white, cylindrical steel tower (black lantern) and integral square steel keeper's dwelling is located at the end of the northern breakwater in the harbor. Constructed in 1918 and automated in 1971, its fifth-order Fresnel lens has an alternating white signal (focal plane 52 feet). Visitors may walk the breakwater or view the light from the south breakwater, but cannot gain access to the tower.

Michigan Island New Light

Bayfield, Bayfield County

This tower was moved from its original location in Pennsylvania in 1919 and was reassembled ten years later on Michigan Island to replace the earlier light. The white steel skeletal tower stands 118 feet high and its grounds are open to the public.

Michigan Island Old Light

Bayfield, Bayfield County

This 1857 light is a 64-foot, whitewashed, conical masonry tower with black lantern, connected to a keeper's house. Originally built in the wrong location, this tower was not used until *c.* 1869. Deactivated in 1929, the light is open to the public in summer.

Milwaukee Breakwater Light

Milwaukee, Lake Michigan

Built in 1926, at the end of Milwaukee's outer breakwater, this light tower rises from the square, white, Art Deco two-story keeper's quarters. An active aid to navigation, its black lantern houses a modern optic (focal plane 61 feet above sea level, red flash every 10 seconds). It can be viewed from a pier near Festival Park in Milwaukee.

Milwaukee Pierhead Light

Milwaukee, Lake Michigan

Built in 1906 to replace an 1857 light, this conical, red steel tower with black lantern stands 41 feet tall (focal plane 45 feet). Its fifth-order Fresnel lens emits a red flash every 4 seconds with a range of 12 miles. It is located at the end of a pier in Milwaukee Harbor to mark the Milwaukee and Kinnickinnic river entrances. The light can be viewed from Milwaukee's Festival Park.

Neenah (Kimberly Point) Light

Kimberly Point Park, Neenah

This active lighthouse, on the shore of Lake Winnebago in Neenah, was first lit in 1945. It is constructed of brick and block, and it rises at 40 feet above the water. The tower is painted white, and the lantern room is black. The site is open to the public.

North Point Light

Milwaukee, Lake Michigan

This octagonal-pyramidal tower was built in 1888 and later raised 35 feet (in 1913) to a height of 74 feet. The white lighthouse, with red lantern (focal plane 154 feet), was deactivated in 1994 but is now a major tourist attraction in Lake Park.

Outer Island Light

Bayfield, Bayfield County

This 90-foot, white, conical brick tower (1874), with black trim and lantern (focal plane 129 feet), is attached to a wood-frame keeper's house via a covered passageway. The lighthouse and its outbuildings are endangered by the erosion of the bluff on which they stand. It is an active navigational aid, and its grounds are open to visitors.

Pilot Island Light

Pilot Island, off the tip of Door Peninsula

Previously known as Port des Morts Light, this square tower with black lantern rises to 41 feet above the red roof of the Cream City brick keeper's dwelling (1873). An active navigational aid

(modern optic, focal plane 48 feet), it is not open to the public, but can be seen from the Northport–Washington Island ferry.

Peshtigo Reef Light

Peshtigo Point, Green Bay

This 1936 beacon, still active today, consists of a 72-foot steel tower situated upon a concrete crib. The tower is painted white, with a broad red band, and the lantern is black. It also has a fog horn. Before it was automated, keepers from the Sherwood Point Light also maintained the Peshtigo Reef Light. Managed by the U.S. Coast Guard, the site and tower are closed to the public.

Plum Island Range Lights

Plum Island, off the tip of Door Peninsula

The front range light is a white, square-pyramidal steel skeletal tower with a red-and-white daymark. Constructed in 1964, it is an active aid to navigation (alternating red signal, focal plane 41 feet). The rear light is a 65-foot, white, square-pyramidal, iron skeletal tower with a red-roofed lantern. Built in 1897, its original fourth-order Fresnel lens (focal plane 80 feet) is still in use. The lights can be seen from the Northport–Washington Island ferry.

Port Washington Breakwater

Port Washington, southeastern Wisconsin

Located at the end of a breakwater, this 58-foot, square, white Art Deco steel tower curves into a wider base. Built in 1935, its open-arched concrete foundation allows visitors to pass beneath it, though walking on the breakwater can be dangerous. Its lantern room has been removed and a modern beacon now emits the signal (focal plane 78 feet). This light originally utilized the brick keeper's house from the Old Port Washington Light (located on shore), which was built in 1860 and deactivated in 1903. Currently a museum, this light station is open to the public in summer.

Pottawatomie Light

Rock Island, off the tip of Door Peninsula

This was Wisconsin's first federal lighthouse station on Lake Michigan. Situated in Rock Island State Park, its square limestone tower with black lantern rises to 41 feet atop a red-roofed limestone keeper's dwelling. Built in 1858 and deactivated in 1988, the light station is currently under restoration and open for public tours. Rock Island is accessible via passenger ferry from Washington Island.

Racine North Breakwater Light
See page 199

Raspberry Island Light
Bayfield, Bayfield County

Located in The Apostle Islands National Lakeshore, Raspberry Island Light (1863) is under restoration and endangered due to bluff erosion. Made of wood, with a square, white tower and black lantern, the tower rises to 35 feet above the integral two-story, red-roofed keeper's house. It is open to the public.

Rawley Point Light
Two Rivers, Manitowoc County

Situated within Point Beach State Forest, this 111-foot, skeletal, white, octagonal-pyramidal cast-iron tower with a two-story watch room and red lantern has been active since 1894 (automated 1979, modern optic, focal plane 113 feet, range 25 miles). Also referred to as Two Rivers Point Light, this tower replaced an earlier brick tower (c. 18__, the bottom part of which is still standing nearby, attached to its two-story, red-roofed, white-painted brick keeper's quarters. Though not open to the public, vacation accommodations in the keeper's dwelling are available to U.S. Coast Guard personnel. Visitors can view the light station from the beach in the state park. Rawley Point Light was originally erected in Chicago and displayed at the 1893 Columbian Exposition before being moved to its present site in 1894.

Sand Island Light
Bayfield, Bayfield County

A Gothic, octagonal, 40-foot tower of red-brown sandstone, this light was built in 1881. The attached keeper's quarters are Norman Gothic in style. This is an active aid to navigation that also serves as a national park attraction. Volunteer keepers offer guided tours in the summer.

Sheboygan Breakwater Light
Sheboygan, Lake Michigan

The lantern has been removed from this red, conical cast-iron tower, which was built in 1915. The beacon is still operational, however, with a modern optic. Visitors can walk along the breakwater from Deland Park, but the tower is closed to the public.

Sherwood Point Light
Green Bay, Lake Michigan

Automated in 1983, Sherwood Point was the last staffed lighthouse on the Great Lakes. Its 37-foot, white, square, brick tower is attached to the 1.5-story keeper's dwelling, built in 1883. Still operational today, its original fifth-order Fresnel lens was replaced in 1892 with a fourth-order Fresnel lens, and this, too, was replaced in 2002 with a modern optic. This lighthouse is sometimes open to the public during the Door County Lighthouse Walk in May.

Sturgeon Bay Ship Canal Lights
See pages 221–222

Two Rivers Light
Relocated to Twin Rivers, Manitowoc County

This 36-foot square pyramidal frame tower (with the upper portion closed) has been inactive since 1969. The lighthouse was first constructed in 1886, and it was rebuilt in 1928. There was never a keeper's dwelling, because the beacon was tended by the Rawley Point keepers. The structure is painted red, with a white lantern. It is the only example of a frame pierhead light left on the upper Great Lakes. Originally located at the end of the harbor breakwater, the tower was relocated in 1975 and is now situated on Jackson Street (as part of the Rogers Street Fishing Village). The tower is open to the public from May through October, though there is a small admission fee.

Wind Point Light
See pages 226 & 227

Wisconsin Point/Superior Harbor Entry Light
Superior, Douglas County

Also known as Superior South Light, this is a white, concrete, cylindrical tower, with a red-roofed lantern, attached to a cylindrical fog-signal building. Built in 1913, the 56-foot tower is an active aid to navigation and is located at the end of a breakwater that marks the entrance to Superior Bay. It is closed to visitors.

Milwaukee was named Cream City for the hue of its buildings. This was due to high levels of lime and sulphur in local clay. Milwaukee's Cream City brick was the primary local building block for over seventy years from the 1830s.

BIBLIOGRAPHY

Adams, W.H. Davenport. *Lighthouses and Lightships: A Descriptive and Historical Account of Their Mode of Construction and Organization*. N.Y.: C. Scribner and Co., 1870.

Baird, David M. "Lighthouses of Canada," *Canadian Geographic*, 1982, 102(3): 44–53.

Baldwin, Leland B. *The Keelboat Age on Western Waters*. Univ. of Pittsburgh Press, 1941.

Banta, R.E. *The Ohio*. N.Y.: Rinehart & Co., 1949.

Bathurst, Bella. *The Lighthouse Stevensons*. N.Y.: HarperCollins, 1999.

Beaver, Patrick. *A History of Lighthouses*. Seacaucus, N.J.: Citadel Press, 1973.

Bush, Edward F. "The Canadian Lighthouse," *Canadian Historic Sites*, 1975, (9): 5–107.

Caravan, Jill. *American Lighthouses: A Pictorial History*. Phila.: Courage Books, 1996.

Chase, Mary Ellen. *The Story of Lighthouses*. N.Y.: W.W. Norton & Co., 1965.

Clifford, Mary Louise, and J. Candace Clifford. *Women Who Kept the Lights: An Illustrated History of Female Lighthouse Keepers*. Williamsburg, Va.: Cypress Communications, 1993.

Corbin, Thomas. *The Romance of Lighthouses & Lifeboats*. Phila.: J.B. Lippincott, 1926.

Crump, Harry T. "Canadian Lighthouse Lens and Fog Systems on the Great Lakes Before Automation," *Inland Seas*, 1993, 49(2): 84–87.

Curtis, Muriel M. "From Santa Marta to Key Biscayne," *Update* (Hist. Assn. of Southern Florida), 1988, 15(2): 12–14.

Davis, Richard A., Jr. *The Evolving Coast*. N.Y.: Scientific American Library, 1997.

Dean, Love. "The Kalaupapa Lighthouse," *Hawaiian Jnl. of History*, 1989, 23: 137–169.

De Wire, Elinor. *Guardians of the Lights*. Sarasota, Fla.: Pineapple, 1995.

Dillon, Rodney E., Jr. "'A Gang of Pirates'": The Confederate Lighthouse Raids in Southeast Florida, 1861," *Florida Historical Quarterly*, 1989, 67(4): 441–457.

Farraday, Michael. *A Course of Six Lectures on the Various Forces of Matter and Their Relations to Each Other*. London: R. Griffin, 1861.

Fazio, Michael W. "Benjamin Latrobe's Designs for a Lighthouse at the Mouth of the Mississippi River," *Jnl. of the Soc. of Architectural Historians*, 1989, 48(3): 232–247.

Gleason, Sarah C. *Kindly Lights: A History of Lighthouses of Southern New England*. Boston: Beacon Press, 1991.

Graham, Donald. *Keepers of the Light: A History of British Columbia's Lighthouses and Their Keepers*. Madeira Park, B.C.: Harbour Publishing Ltd., 1987.

———. *Lights of the Inside Passage: A History of British Columbia's Lighthouses and Their Keepers*. Madeira Park, B.C.: Harbour Publishing Ltd., 1993.

Grant, John, and Ray Jones. *Legendary Lighthouses*. Old Saybrook, Conn.: Globe Pequot Press, 1998.

Gray, Doug. "Putting Out the Lightkeepers," *Freshwater* [Canada], 1994, 9(1): 3–7.

Hamilton, Harlan. *Lights & Legends: A Historical Guide to Lighthouses of Long Island Sound, Fishers Island Sound and Block Island Sound*. Stamford, Conn.: Wescott Cove Publishing, 1987.

Hardy, W.J. F.S.A. *Lighthouses: Their History and Romance*. N.Y.: Fleming H. Revell, 1895.

Hart, Cheryl. "The Queen's Wharf Lighthouse," *Freshwater*, 1987, 2(1): 40–43.

Hart, Frederick C. "Keepers of the Matinicus Light: Isaac H. and Abbie E. (Burgess) Grant and Their Families," *New England Hist. and Genealogical Register*, 1994, 150 (October): 391–416.

Hatcher, Harlan. *Lake Erie*. Indianapolis: Bobbs-Merrill Co., 1945.

Hawkins, Bruce. "A Miserable Piece of Workmanship: Michigan's First Lighthouse," *Michigan History*, 1989, 73(4): 40–42.

Heap, D.P. *Ancient and Modern Lighthouses*. Boston: Ticknor & Co., 1889.

Havighurst, Walter. *The Long Ships Passing: The Story of the Great Lakes*. N.Y.: Macmillan, 1961.

———. *Voices on the River: The Story of the Mississippi Waterways*. N.Y.: Macmillan, 1964.

Hefner, Robert J. "Montauk Point Lighthouse: A History of New York's First Seamark," *Long Island Hist. Jnl.* 1991, 3(2): 205–216.

Holland, F. Ross, Jr. *America's Lighthouses: An Illustrated History*. N.Y.: Dover Publications, 1988.

———. *Great American Lighthouses* Wash., D.C.: Preservation Press, 1989.

———. *Lighthouses*. New York: Barnes & Noble, 1997.

International Association of Marine Aids to Navigation and Lighthouse Authorities. *Lighthouses of the World*. Old Saybrook, Conn.: Globe Pequot Press, 1999.

Johnson, Arnold Burges. *The Modern Light-House Service*. Wash., D.C.: Government Printing Office, 1889.

Larabee, Benjamin W., *et al. America and the Sea: A Maritime History*. Mystic, Conn.: Mystic Seaport Museum, 1998.

Majdalany, Fred. *The Eddystone Light*. Boston: Houghton Mifflin, 1960.

Nash, John. *Seamarks: Their History and Development*. London: Stanford Maritime Press, 1985.

Noble, Dennis L. *Lighthouses & Keepers: The U.S. Lighthouse Service and Its Legacy*. Annapolis, Md.: Naval Institute Press, 1997.

O'Connor, William D. *Heroes of the Storm*. Boston: Houghton Mifflin, 1904.

Patey, Stan. *The Coast of New England: A Pictorial Tour from Connecticut to Maine*. Camden, Me.: International Marine, 1996.

Putnam, George R. *Lighthouses and Lightships of the United States*. Boston: Houghton Mifflin, 1917.

Putnam, George R. *Sentinel of the Coasts: The Log of a Lighthouse Engineer*. N.Y.: W.W. Norton & Co., 1937.

Reynaud, Leonce. *Memoir Upon the Illumination and Beaconage of the Coasts of France*, trans Peter C. Hains. Wash., D.C.: Government Printing Office, 1876.

Roberts, Bruce, and Ray Jones. *American Lighthouses: A Comprehensive Guide*. Old Saybrook, Conn.: Globe Pequot Press, 1998.

———. *Eastern Great Lakes Lighthouses*. Old Saybrook, Conn.: Globe Pequot, 1996.

———. *Western Great Lakes Lighthouses*. Old Saybrook, Conn.: Globe Pequot, 1996.

Rogue, Jean. *Ships and Fleets of the Ancient Mediterranean*, trans. Susan Frazer. Middletown, Conn.: Wesleyan Univ. Press, 1981.

Schmitt, Paul J. "The Last Lightship on the Great Lakes," *Michigan Historical Magazine*, 1996, 80(4): 38–42.

Shaw, Barbara. "There's No Life Like It: Reminiscences of Lightkeeping on Sambro Island," *Nova Scotia Hist. Review*, 1983, 3(1): 64–70.

Smith, Chadwick Foster. *Seafaring in Colonial Massachusetts*. Boston: Colonial Society of Massachusetts, 1980.

Snow, Edward Rowe. *Famous New England Lighthouses*. Boston: Yankee Publishing Co., 1945.

———. *Great Sea Rescues and Tales of Survival*. N.Y.: Dodd, Mead & Co., 1958.

———. *Great Storms and Famous Shipwrecks of the New England Coast*. Boston: Yankee Publishing Co., 1943.

———. *The Lighthouses of New England, 1716–1935*. N.Y.: Dodd, Mead & Co., 1945.

Spencer, Herbert R. "The First Federal Lighthouse on the Great Lakes," *Inland Seas*, 1966, 22(2): 127–128.

Sterling, Robert Thayer. *Lighthouses of the Maine Coast and The Men Who Keep Them*. Brattleboro, Vt.: Stephen Daye Press, 1935.

Stevens, M. James, "Biloxi's Lady Lighthouse Keeper," *Jnl. of Mississippi History*, 1974, 36(1): 39–41.

Stevenson, Alan. *A Rudimentary Treatise on the History, Construction, and Illumination of Lighthouses*. London: J. Weale, 1850.

Stevenson, D. Alan. *The World's Lighthouses Before 1820*. London: Oxford U. P., 1959.

Stick, David. *Graveyard of the Atlantic: Shipwrecks of the North Carolina Coast*. Chapel Hill: Univ. of North Carolina Press, 1952.

Storer, W. Scott, "The Guiding Light of Boston Harbor," *New England Galaxy*, 1977, 18(4): 36–42.

Sutherland, Donald. "The Guardian of Saint George Reef: America's Costliest Lighthouse," *Sea History*, 1992 (63): 20–23.

Talbot, Frederick A. *Lightships and Lighthouses*. Phila: J.B. Lippincott, 1913.

Terras, Donald J. *The Grosse Point Lighthouse, Evanston, Illinois: Landmark to Maritime History and Culture*. Evanston, Ill.: Windy City and Grosse Point Lighthouse Preservation Fund, 1995.

Twain, Mark. *Life on the Mississippi (1874)*. N.Y.: Viking Penguin, 1985.

U.S. Coast Guard. *Historically Famous Lighthouses*. Wash., D.C.: Government Printing Office, 1957.

Van Hoey, Mike. "Preserving the Lights of the Straits," *Michigan History*, 1986, 70(5).

Vogel, Mike. "Buffalo: Beacon to the Heartland," *Anchor News*, 1988, 19(5): 84–89.

Weaver, Helene. "John Brown's Imperial Towers: End of an Era," *Inland Seas*, 1992, 48(3): 161–163.

White, Richard D., Jr. "Saga of the Side-wheel Steamer *Shubrick*: Pioneer Lighthouse Tender of the Pacific Coast," *American Neptune*, 1976, 36(1): 45–53.

Wiley, Peter B. *Yankees in the Land of the Gods: Commodore Perry and The Opening of Japan*. N.Y.: Penguin Books, 1990.

Willoughby, Malcolm F. *Lighthouses of New England*. Boston: T.O. Metcalf Co., 1929.

Wilmerding, John. *American Marine Painting*. N.Y.: Harry N. Abrams, 1987.

SOURCES FOR THE GAZETTEER INCLUDE:

The National Maritime Initiative
The University of North Carolina at Chapel Hill, http://www.unc.edu/~rowlett/lighthouse/index.htm
The Lighthouse Depot, www.lhdepot.com
U.S. Coast Guard, www.uscg.mil/history/collect.html
Lighthouses of the Great Lakes, http://lighthouse.boatnerd.com/default.htm
The Lighthouses of the Western Great Lakes, http://www.terrypepper.com/lights/index.htm
Midwest Connection, http://www.midwestconnection.com

Neenah Heritage, http://www.ci.neenah.wi.us/CH_Heritage.htm
Great Lakes Lighthouses, www.GreatLakesLighthouses.com
History In The Making, http://www.cnyric.org/history/intro/schools.htm
The Lightkeeper, http://hometown.aol.com/thelightkeeper/HudsonRiverLightkeepers.html
The National Lighthouse Museum, www.lighthousemuseum.org
The New Jersey Lighthouse Society, http://njlhs.burlco.org
Rod's Photo Gallery, http://home.neo.rr.com/rodsphotogallery/IndexLarge.html
South Street Seaport Museum, www.southstreetseaport.org
Lighthouse Friends, www.lighthousefriends.com
North Carolina's Outer Banks, http://www.outer-banks.com

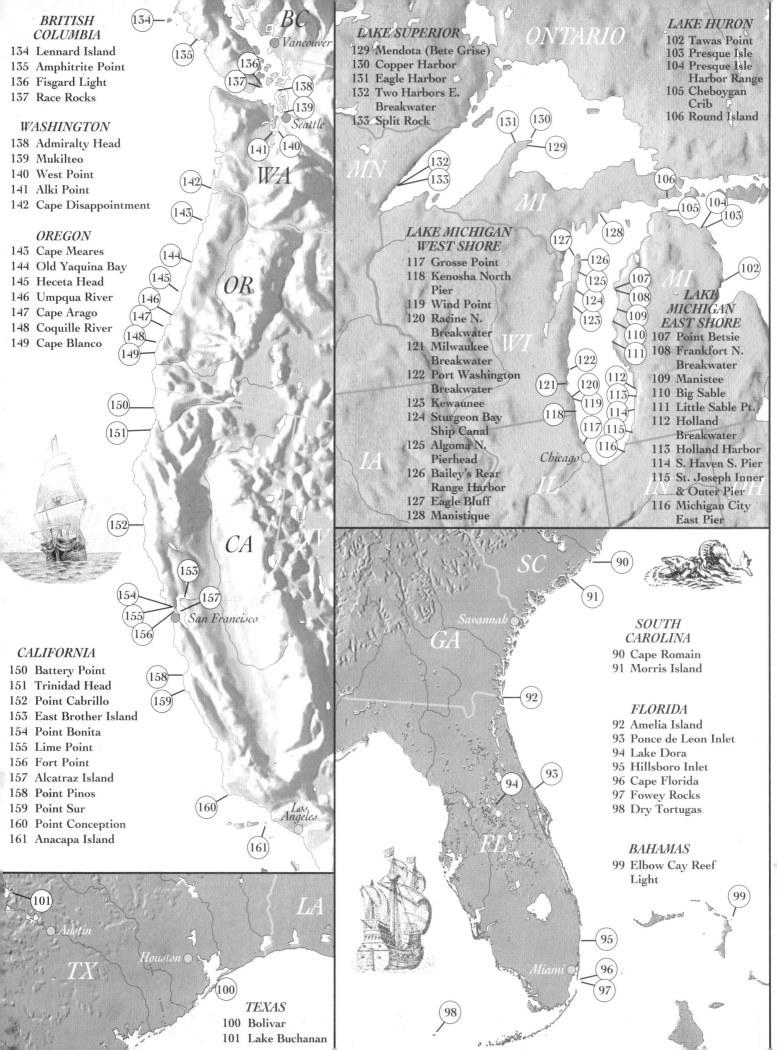

BRITISH COLUMBIA
134 Lennard Island
135 Amphitrite Point
136 Fisgard Light
137 Race Rocks

WASHINGTON
138 Admiralty Head
139 Mukilteo
140 West Point
141 Alki Point
142 Cape Disappointment

OREGON
143 Cape Meares
144 Old Yaquina Bay
145 Heceta Head
146 Umpqua River
147 Cape Arago
148 Coquille River
149 Cape Blanco

CALIFORNIA
150 Battery Point
151 Trinidad Head
152 Point Cabrillo
153 East Brother Island
154 Point Bonita
155 Lime Point
156 Fort Point
157 Alcatraz Island
158 Point Pinos
159 Point Sur
160 Point Conception
161 Anacapa Island

TEXAS
100 Bolivar
101 Lake Buchanan

LAKE SUPERIOR
129 Mendota (Bete Grise)
130 Copper Harbor
131 Eagle Harbor
132 Two Harbors E. Breakwater
133 Split Rock

LAKE MICHIGAN WEST SHORE
117 Grosse Point
118 Kenosha North Pier
119 Wind Point
120 Racine N. Breakwater
121 Milwaukee Breakwater
122 Port Washington Breakwater
123 Kewaunee
124 Sturgeon Bay Ship Canal
125 Algoma N. Pierhead
126 Bailey's Rear Range Harbor
127 Eagle Bluff
128 Manistique

LAKE HURON
102 Tawas Point
103 Presque Isle
104 Presque Isle Harbor Range
105 Cheboygan Crib
106 Round Island

LAKE MICHIGAN EAST SHORE
107 Point Betsie
108 Frankfort N. Breakwater
109 Manistee
110 Big Sable
111 Little Sable Pt.
112 Holland Breakwater
113 Holland Harbor
114 S. Haven S. Pier
115 St. Joseph Inner & Outer Pier
116 Michigan City East Pier

SOUTH CAROLINA
90 Cape Romain
91 Morris Island

FLORIDA
92 Amelia Island
93 Ponce de Leon Inlet
94 Lake Dora
95 Hillsboro Inlet
96 Cape Florida
97 Fowey Rocks
98 Dry Tortugas

BAHAMAS
99 Elbow Cay Reef Light